Story and Art by
Rumiko Takahashi

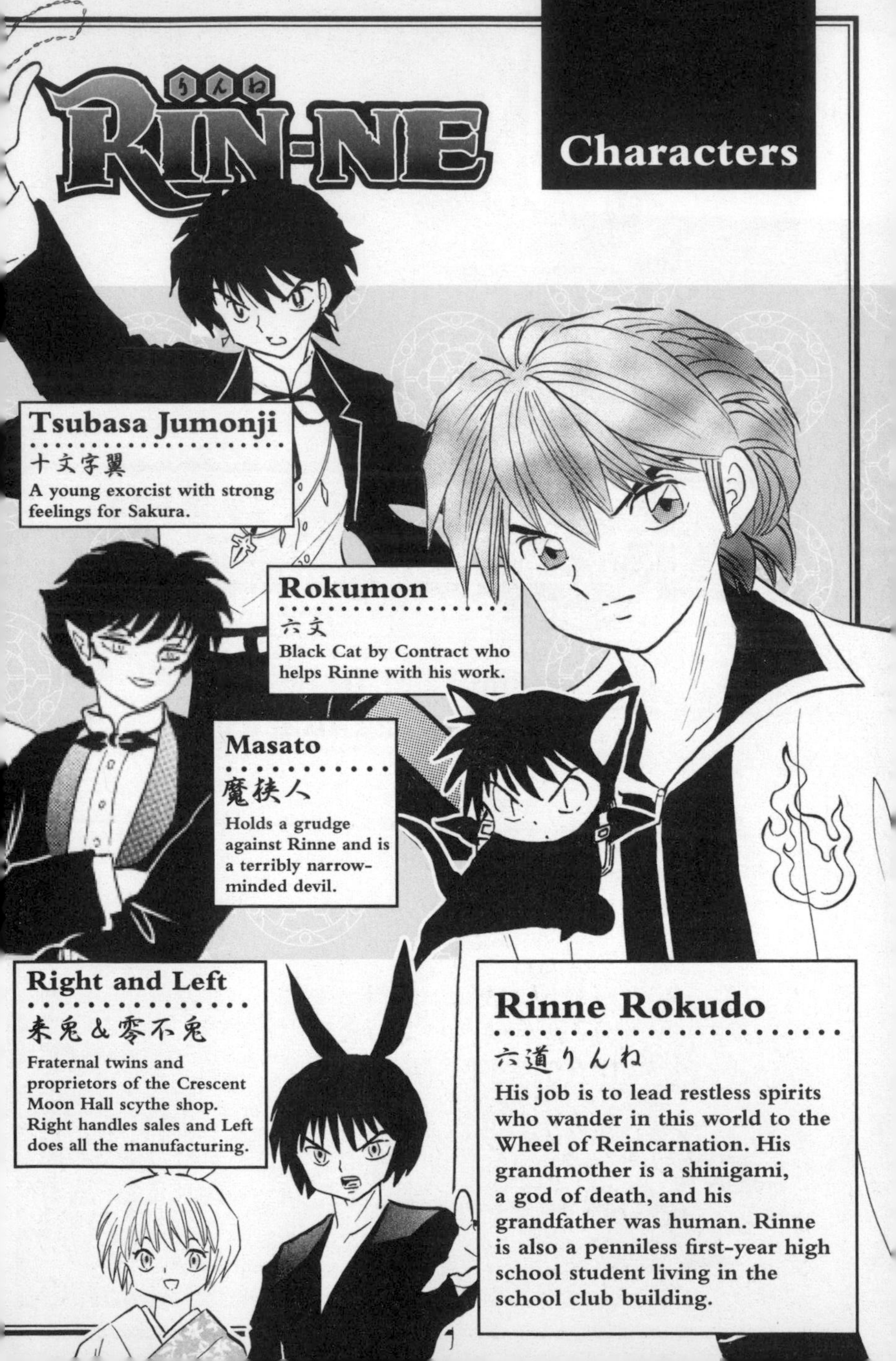

RIN-NE

Characters

Tsubasa Jumonji

十文字翼

A young exorcist with strong feelings for Sakura.

Rokumon

六文

Black Cat by Contract who helps Rinne with his work.

Masato

魔狭人

Holds a grudge against Rinne and is a terribly narrow-minded devil.

Right and Left

来兎&零不兎

Fraternal twins and proprietors of the Crescent Moon Hall scythe shop. Right handles sales and Left does all the manufacturing.

Rinne Rokudo

六道りんね

His job is to lead restless spirits who wander in this world to the Wheel of Reincarnation. His grandmother is a shinigami, a god of death, and his grandfather was human. Rinne is also a penniless first-year high school student living in the school club building.

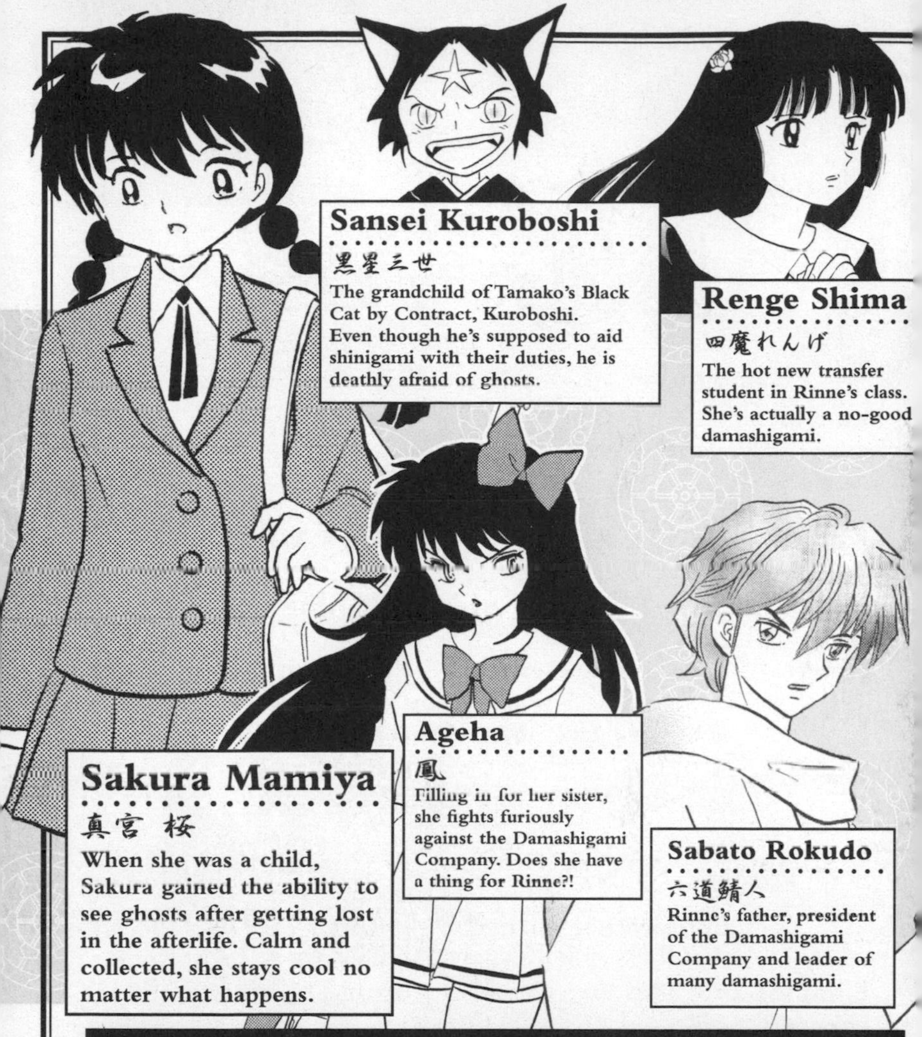
Sansei Kuroboshi
黒星三世
The grandchild of Tamako's Black Cat by Contract, Kuroboshi. Even though he's supposed to aid shinigami with their duties, he is deathly afraid of ghosts.
Renge Shima
四魔れんげ
The hot new transfer student in Rinne's class. She's actually a no-good damashigami.
Ageha
鳳
Filling in for her sister, she fights furiously against the Damashigami Company. Does she have a thing for Rinne?!
Sakura Mamiya
真宮 桜
When she was a child, Sakura gained the ability to see ghosts after getting lost in the afterlife. Calm and collected, she stays cool no matter what happens.
Sabato Rokudo
六道鯖人
Rinne's father, president of the Damashigami Company and leader of many damashigami.

The Story So Far

Together, Sakura, the girl who can see ghosts, and Rinne, the shinigami (sort of), spend their days helping spirits that can't pass on to reach the afterlife, and deal with all kinds of strange phenomena at their school.

When Sakura and Rinne get roped into helping his grandmother, Tamako, do some much-needed deep cleaning in her home, they rescue her Black Cat by Contract, Kuroboshi, who had been trapped in a closet and forgotten. As a result, Rinne is asked to help train Kuroboshi's grandchild, Sansei Kuroboshi, even though he's deathly afraid of ghosts! Poor Rinne never gets a break... What catastrophe awaits him next?!

RIN-NE

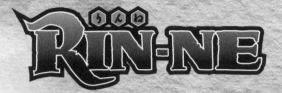

Contents

CHAPTER 179: BLACK CAT CHILDREN'S MEET

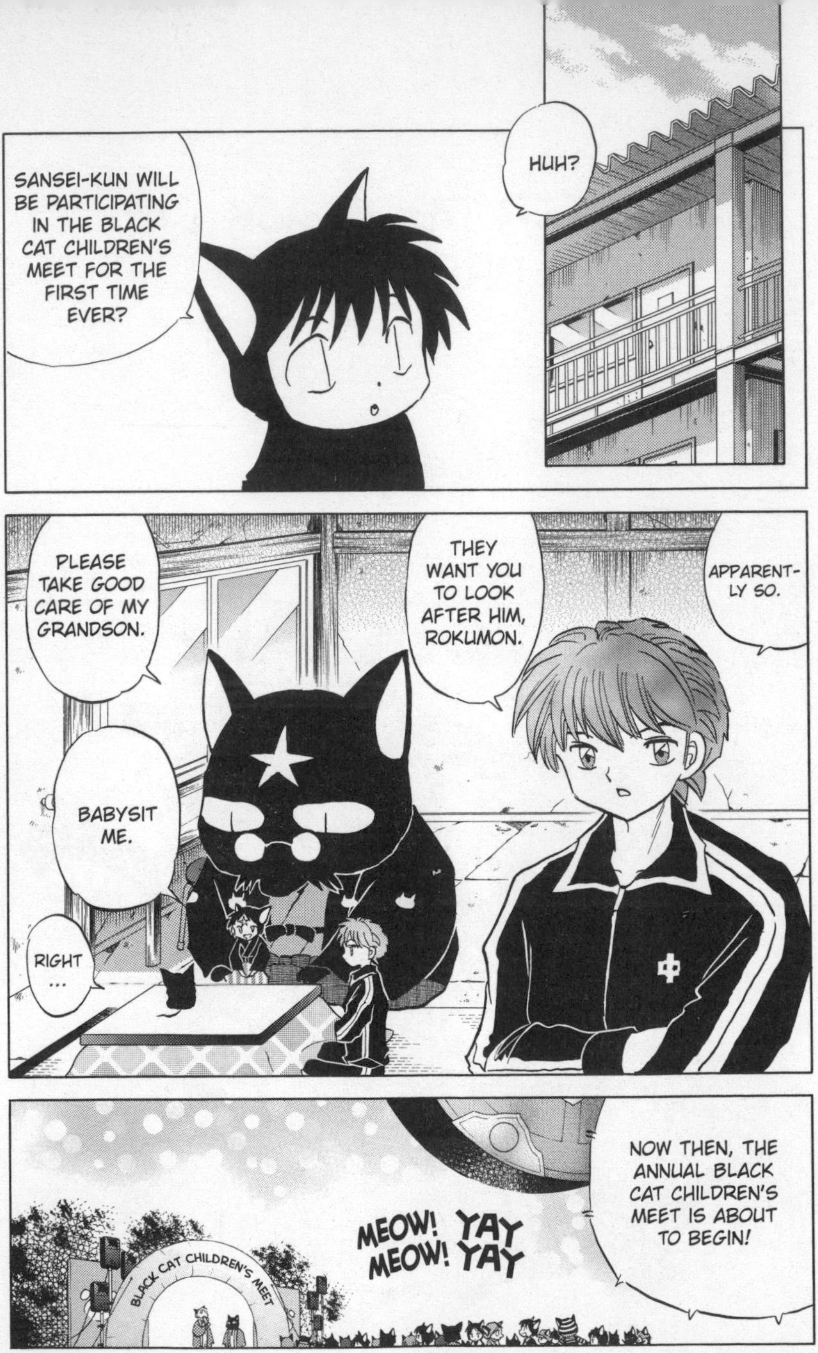
HUH?
SANSEI-KUN WILL BE PARTICIPATING IN THE BLACK CAT CHILDREN'S MEET FOR THE FIRST TIME EVER?
APPARENT-LY SO.
THEY WANT YOU TO LOOK AFTER HIM, ROKUMON.
PLEASE TAKE GOOD CARE OF MY GRANDSON.
BABYSIT ME.
RIGHT ...
NOW THEN, THE ANNUAL BLACK CAT CHILDREN'S MEET IS ABOUT TO BEGIN!
YAY YAY
MEOW! MEOW!
BLACK CAT CHILDREN'S MEET

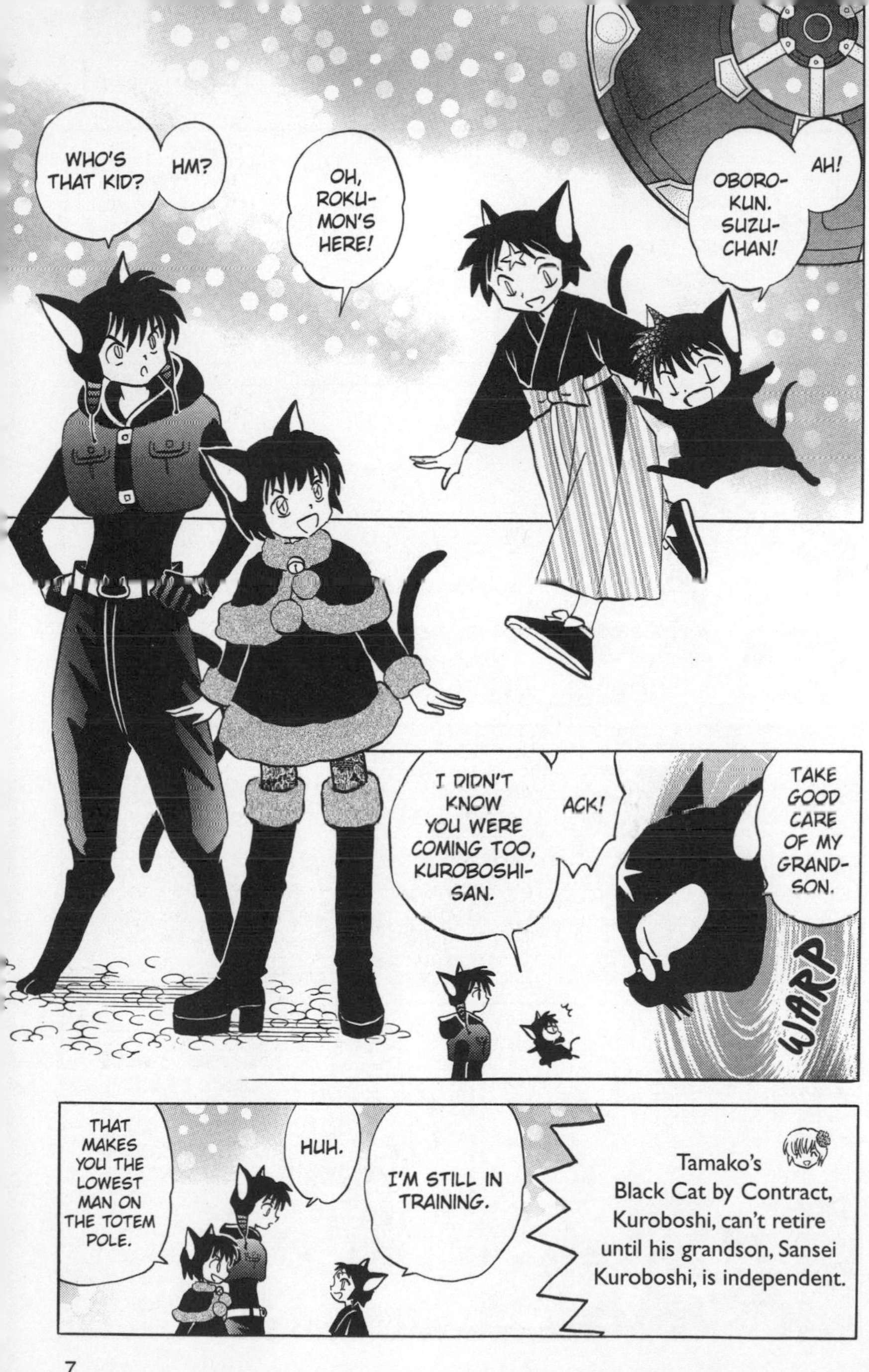
AH!
OBORO-KUN. SUZU-CHAN!
OH, ROKUMON'S HERE!
HM?
WHO'S THAT KID?
TAKE GOOD CARE OF MY GRANDSON.
WARP
ACK!
I DIDN'T KNOW YOU WERE COMING TOO, KUROBOSHI-SAN.
Tamako's Black Cat by Contract, Kuroboshi, can't retire until his grandson, Sansei Kuroboshi, is independent.
I'M STILL IN TRAINING.
HUH.
THAT MAKES YOU THE LOWEST MAN ON THE TOTEM POLE.

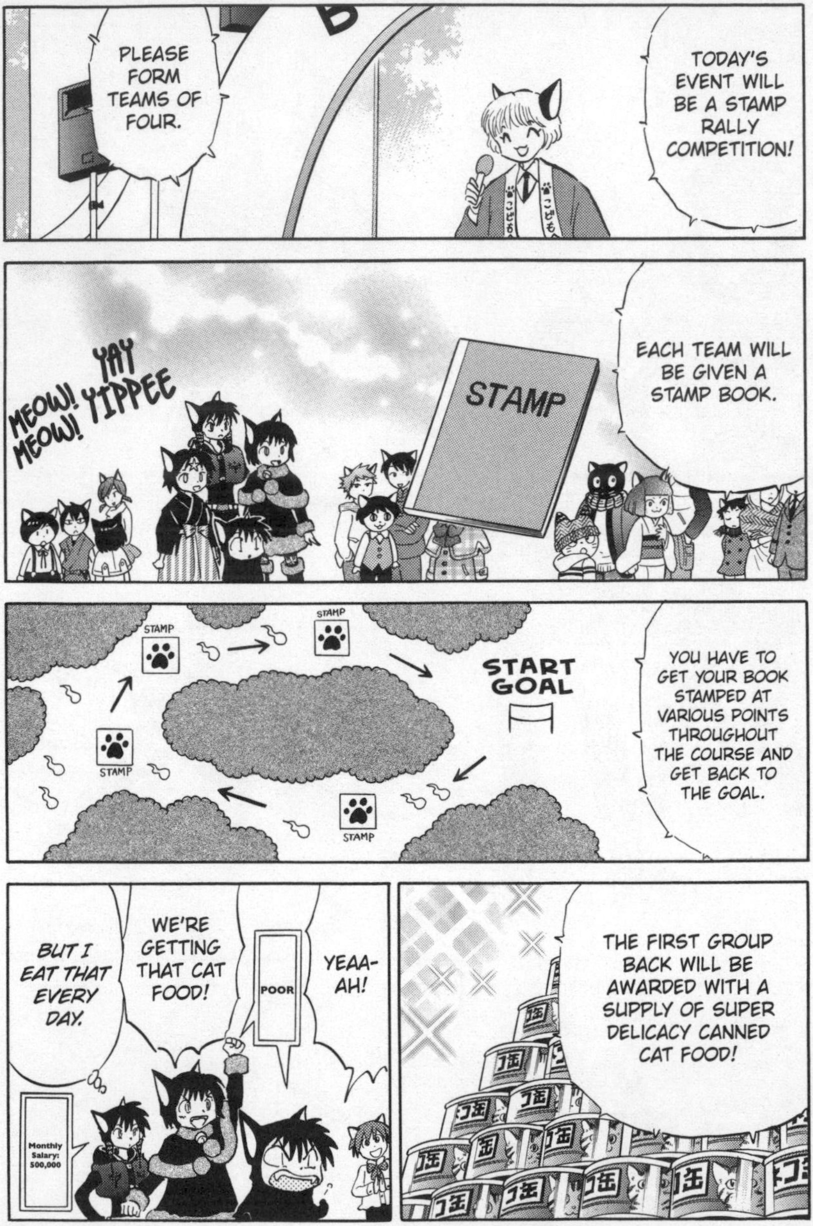
TODAY'S EVENT WILL BE A STAMP RALLY COMPETITION!
PLEASE FORM TEAMS OF FOUR.
EACH TEAM WILL BE GIVEN A STAMP BOOK.
STAMP
YAY
YIPPEE
MEOW! MEOW!
YOU HAVE TO GET YOUR BOOK STAMPED AT VARIOUS POINTS THROUGHOUT THE COURSE AND GET BACK TO THE GOAL.
START
GOAL
STAMP
STAMP
STAMP
STAMP
THE FIRST GROUP BACK WILL BE AWARDED WITH A SUPPLY OF SUPER DELICACY CANNED CAT FOOD!
YEAA-AH!
POOR
WE'RE GETTING THAT CAT FOOD!
BUT I EAT THAT EVERY DAY.
Monthly Salary: 500,000

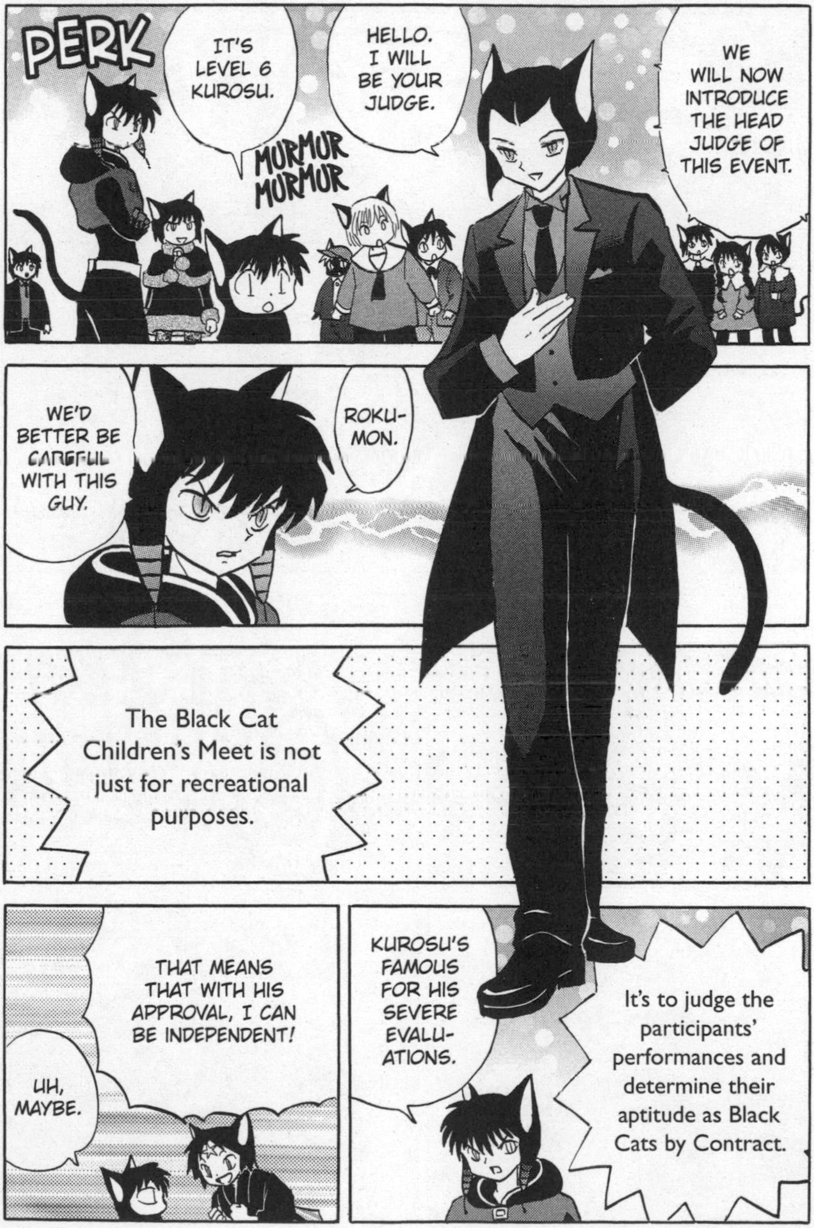
WE WILL NOW INTRODUCE THE HEAD JUDGE OF THIS EVENT.
HELLO. I WILL BE YOUR JUDGE.
IT'S LEVEL 6 KUROSU.
MURMUR MURMUR
PERK
ROKU-MON.
WE'D BETTER BE CAREFUL WITH THIS GUY.
The Black Cat Children's Meet is not just for recreational purposes.
It's to judge the participants' performances and determine their aptitude as Black Cats by Contract.
KUROSU'S FAMOUS FOR HIS SEVERE EVALU-ATIONS.
THAT MEANS THAT WITH HIS APPROVAL, I CAN BE INDEPENDENT!
UH, MAYBE.

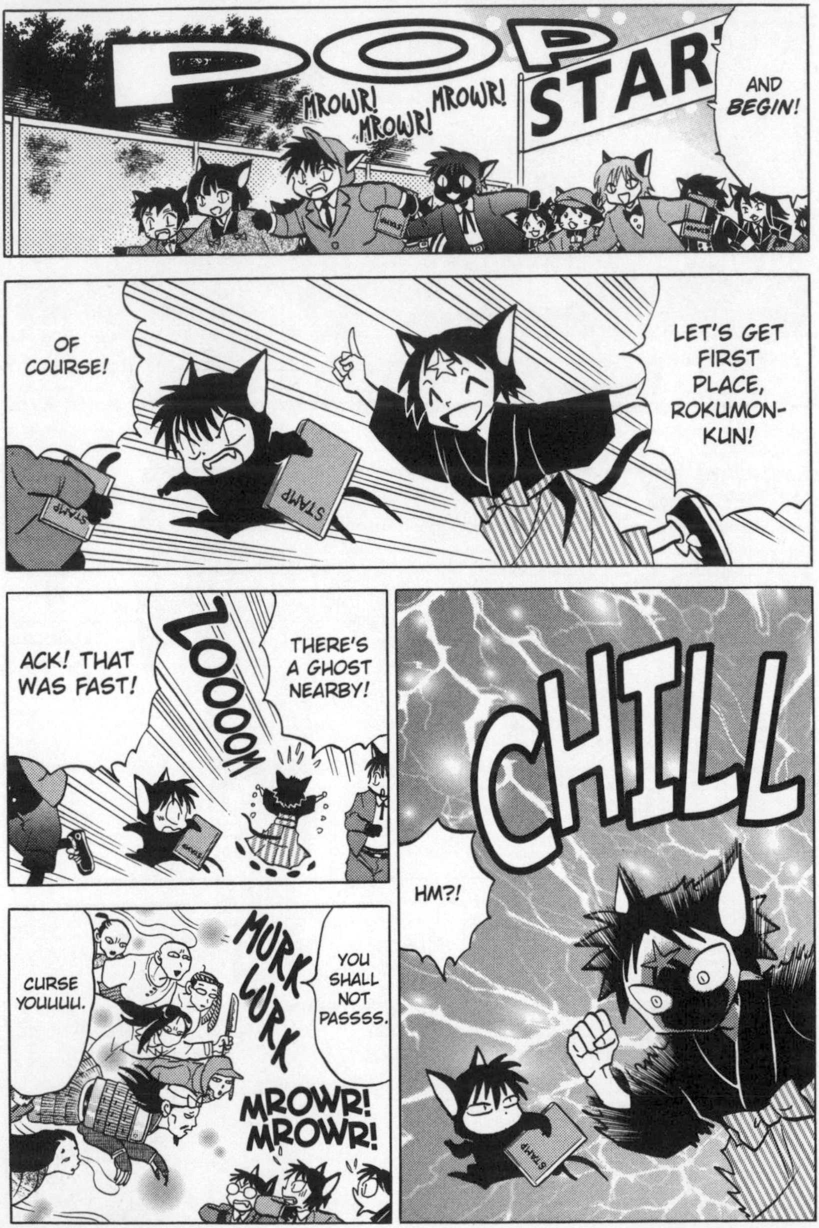
AND BEGIN!
POP
STAR
MROWR!
MROWR!
MROWR!
LET'S GET FIRST PLACE, ROKUMON-KUN!
OF COURSE!
STAMP
STAMP
CHILL
HM?!
THERE'S A GHOST NEARBY!
ZOOOOOM
ACK! THAT WAS FAST!
YOU SHALL NOT PASSSS.
MURK WURK
CURSE YOUUUU.
MROWR! MROWR!

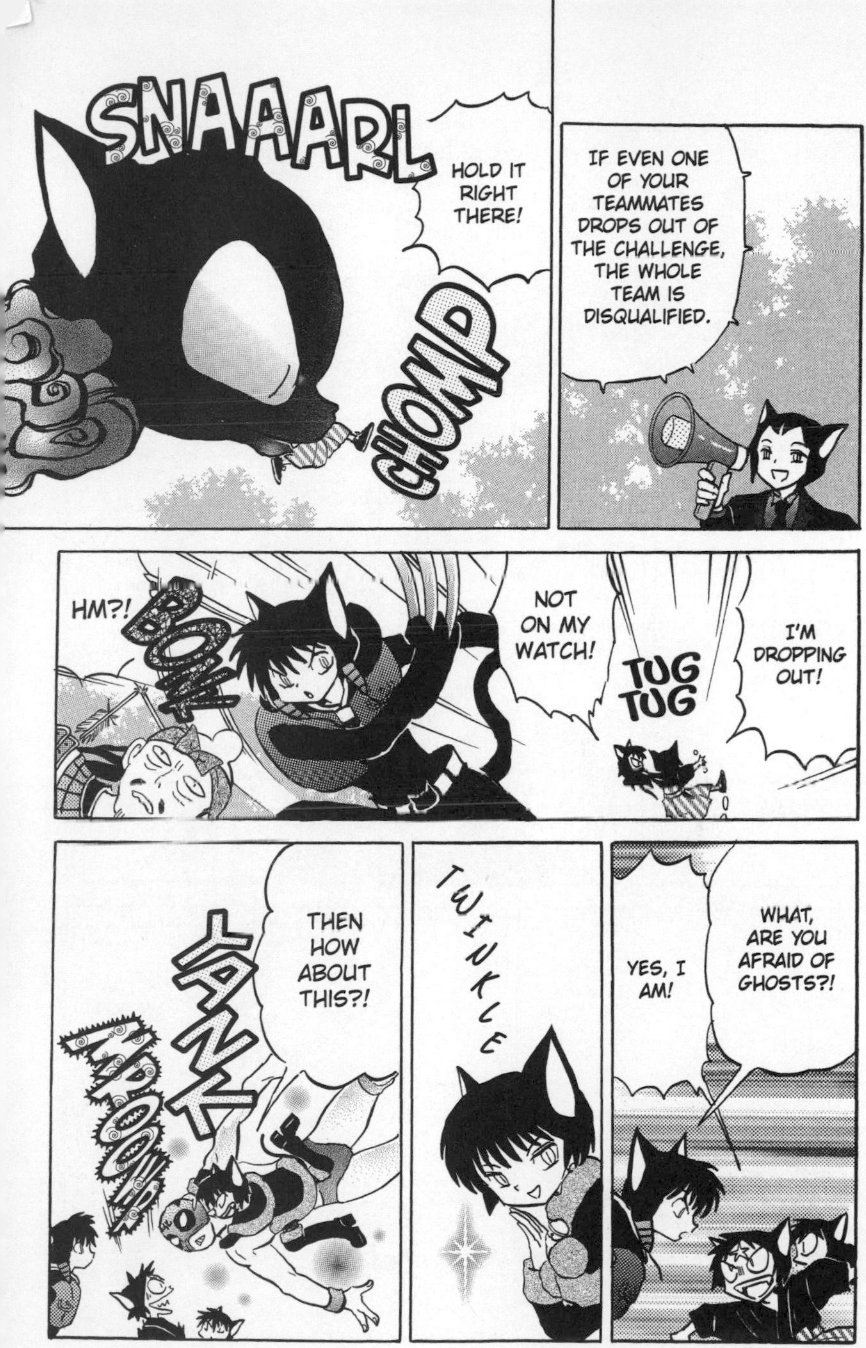
IF EVEN ONE OF YOUR TEAMMATES DROPS OUT OF THE CHALLENGE, THE WHOLE TEAM IS DISQUALIFIED.
HOLD IT RIGHT THERE!
SNAAARL
CHOMP
I'M DROPPING OUT!
TUG TUG
NOT ON MY WATCH!
BONK
HM?!
WHAT, ARE YOU AFRAID OF GHOSTS?!
YES, I AM!
TWINKLE
THEN HOW ABOUT THIS?!
YANK
WPOOM!!

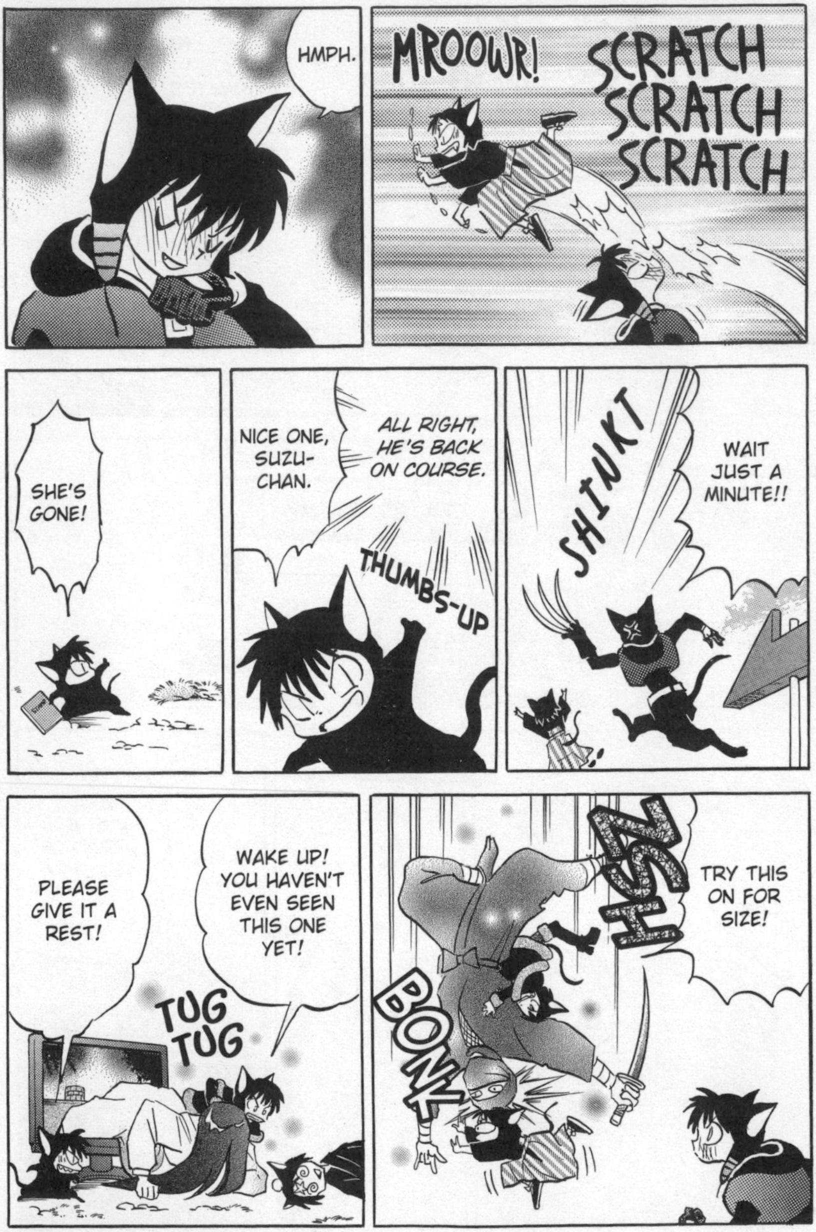
MROOWR!
SCRATCH SCRATCH SCRATCH
HMPH.
WAIT JUST A MINUTE!!
SHINKT
ALL RIGHT, HE'S BACK ON COURSE.
NICE ONE, SUZU-CHAN.
THUMBS-UP
SHE'S GONE!
TRY THIS ON FOR SIZE!
ZSHH
BONK
WAKE UP! YOU HAVEN'T EVEN SEEN THIS ONE YET!
PLEASE GIVE IT A REST!
TUG TUG

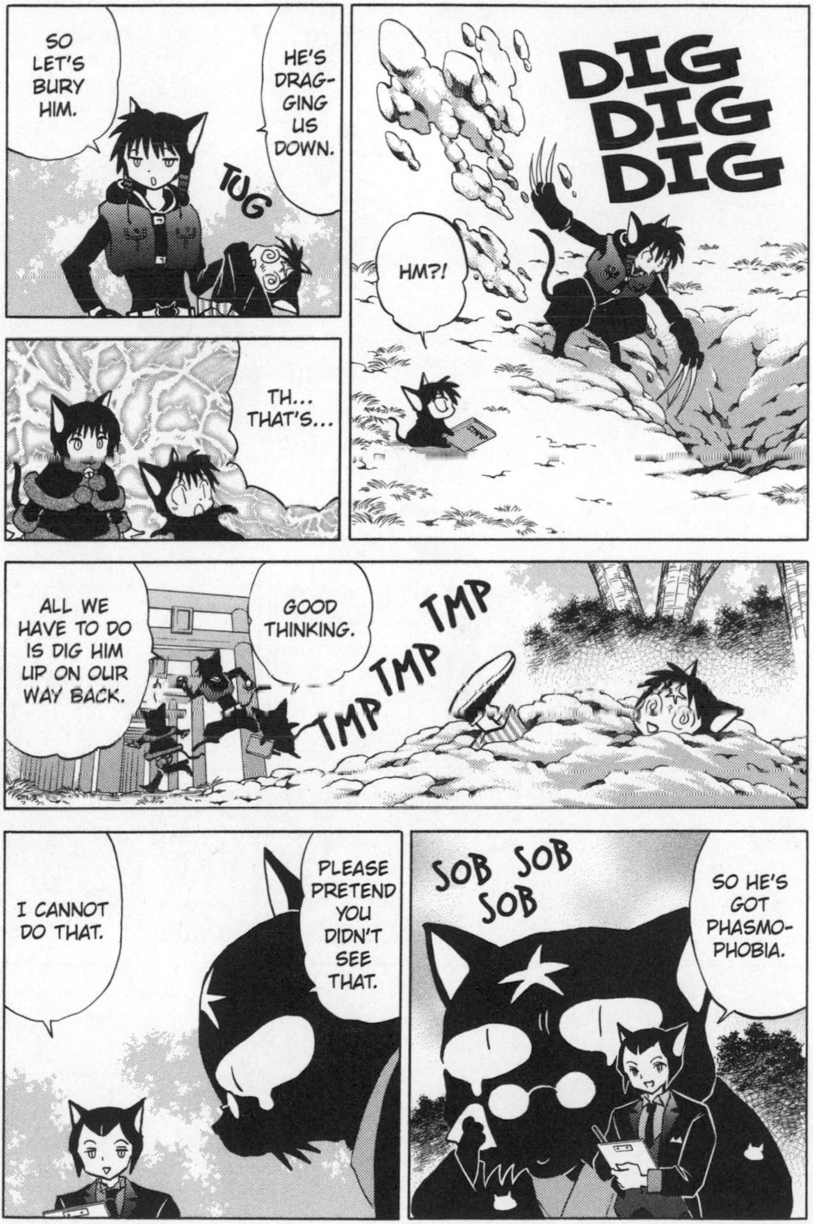
DIG DIG DIG
HM?!
HE'S DRAGGING US DOWN.
SO LET'S BURY HIM.
TUG
TH... THAT'S...
TMP TMP TMP
GOOD THINKING.
ALL WE HAVE TO DO IS DIG HIM UP ON OUR WAY BACK.
SO HE'S GOT PHASMOPHOBIA.
SOB SOB SOB
PLEASE PRETEND YOU DIDN'T SEE THAT.
I CANNOT DO THAT.

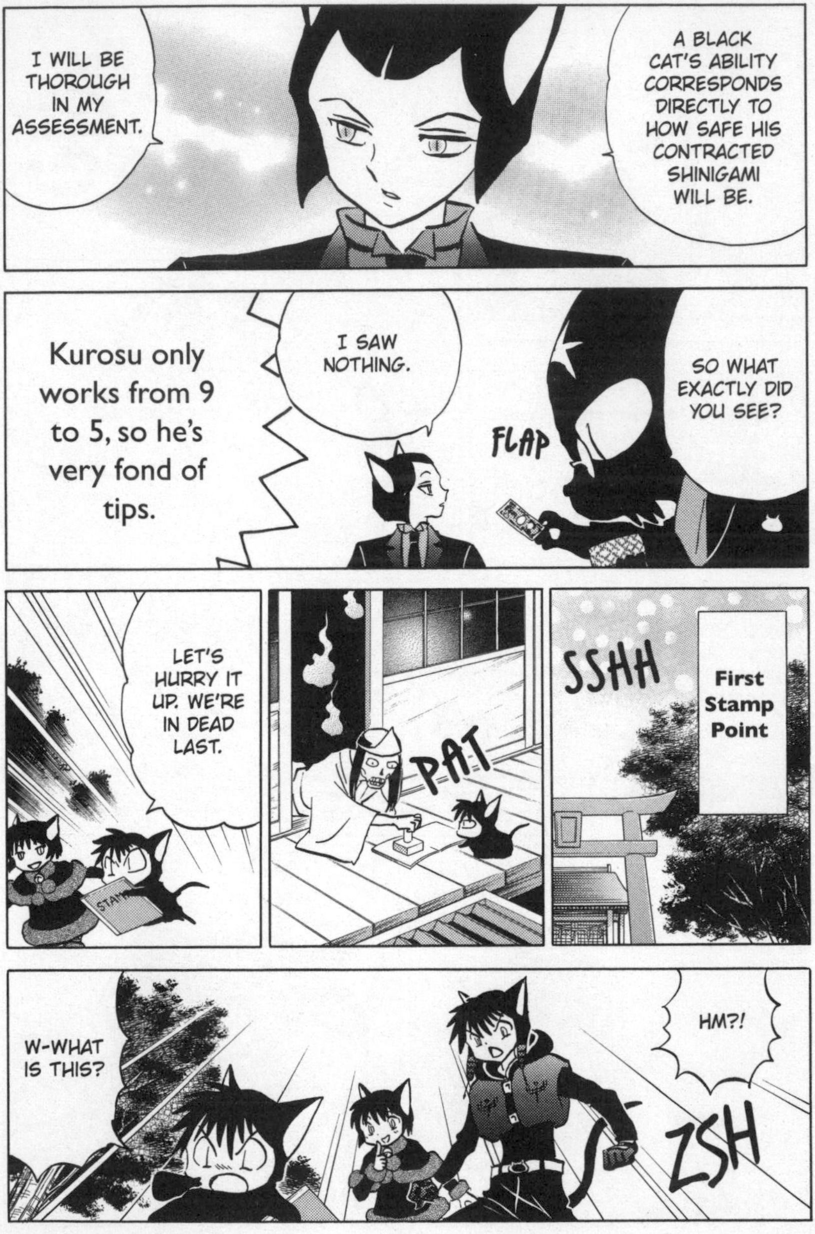
A BLACK CAT'S ABILITY CORRESPONDS DIRECTLY TO HOW SAFE HIS CONTRACTED SHINIGAMI WILL BE.
I WILL BE THOROUGH IN MY ASSESSMENT.
SO WHAT EXACTLY DID YOU SEE?
FLAP
I SAW NOTHING.
Kurosu only works from 9 to 5, so he's very fond of tips.
First Stamp Point
SSHH
PAT
LET'S HURRY IT UP. WE'RE IN DEAD LAST.
HM?!
ZSH
W-WHAT IS THIS?

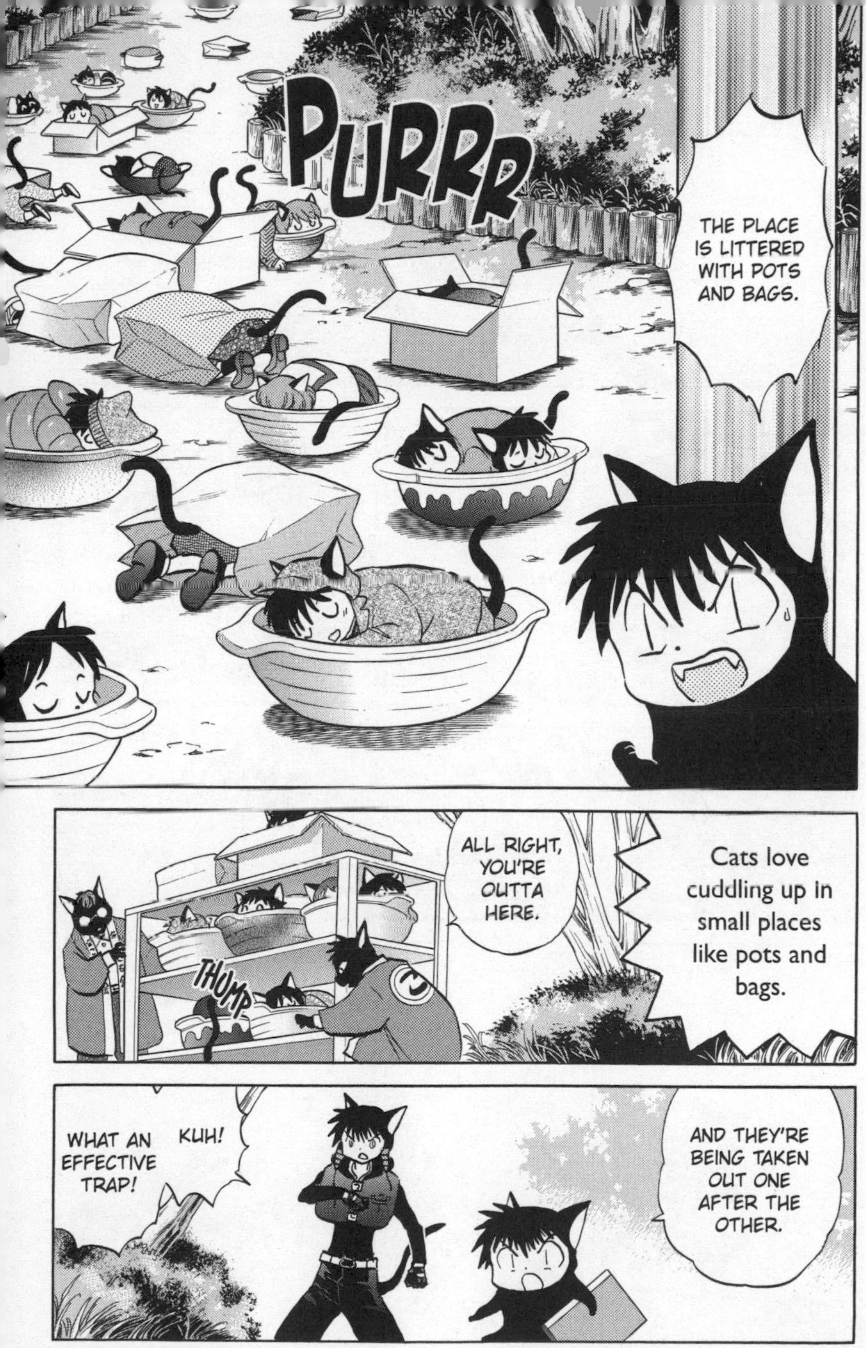
THE PLACE IS LITTERED WITH POTS AND BAGS.
PURRR
Cats love cuddling up in small places like pots and bags.
ALL RIGHT, YOU'RE OUTTA HERE.
THUMP
AND THEY'RE BEING TAKEN OUT ONE AFTER THE OTHER.
KUH!
WHAT AN EFFECTIVE TRAP!

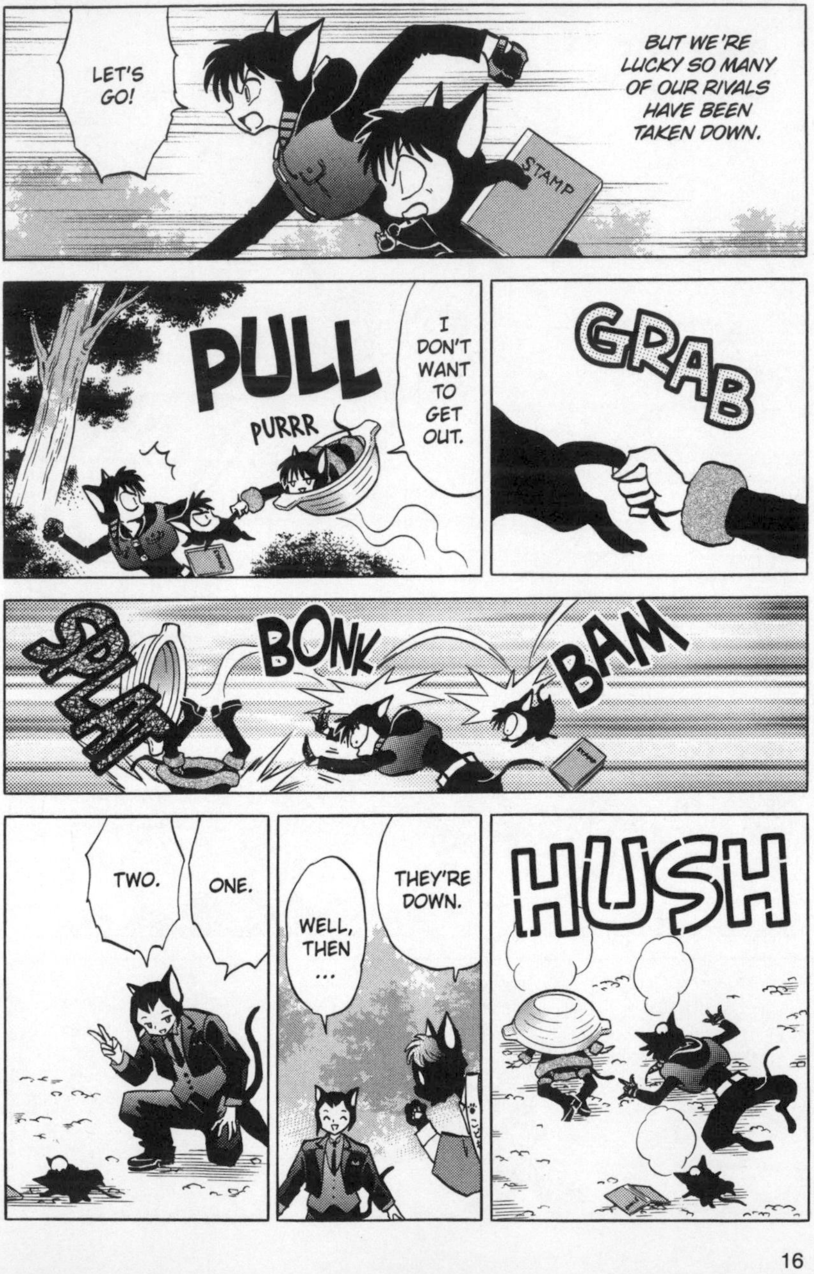
BUT WE'RE LUCKY SO MANY OF OUR RIVALS HAVE BEEN TAKEN DOWN.
LET'S GO!
STAMP
GRAB
I DON'T WANT TO GET OUT.
PULL
PURRR
BAM
BONK
SPLAT
HUSH
THEY'RE DOWN.
WELL, THEN ...
ONE.
TWO.

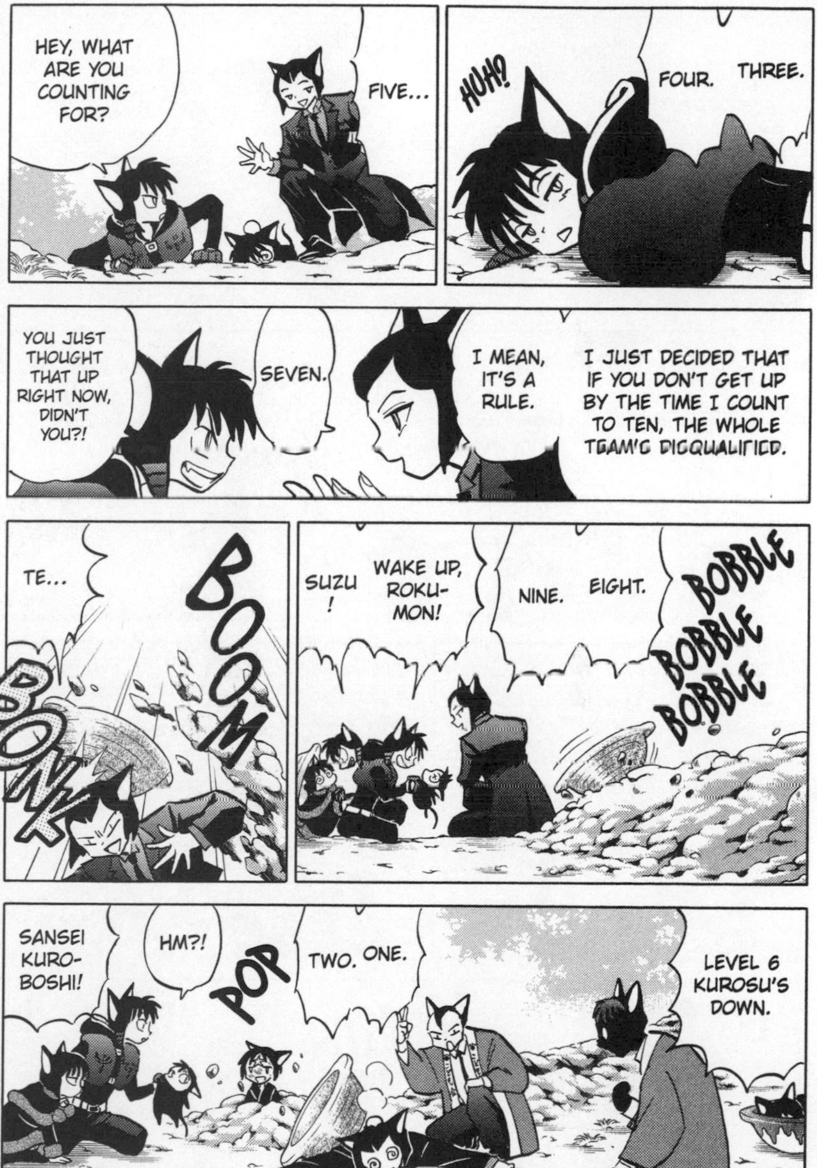
THREE.
FOUR.
HUH?
FIVE...
HEY, WHAT ARE YOU COUNTING FOR?
I JUST DECIDED THAT IF YOU DON'T GET UP BY THE TIME I COUNT TO TEN, THE WHOLE TEAM'S DISQUALIFIED.
I MEAN, IT'S A RULE.
SEVEN.
YOU JUST THOUGHT THAT UP RIGHT NOW, DIDN'T YOU?!
BOBBLE BOBBLE BOBBLE
EIGHT.
NINE.
WAKE UP, ROKU-MON!
SUZU!
BOOM
TE...
BONK
LEVEL 6 KUROSU'S DOWN.
ONE.
TWO.
POP
HM?!
SANSEI KURO-BOSHI!

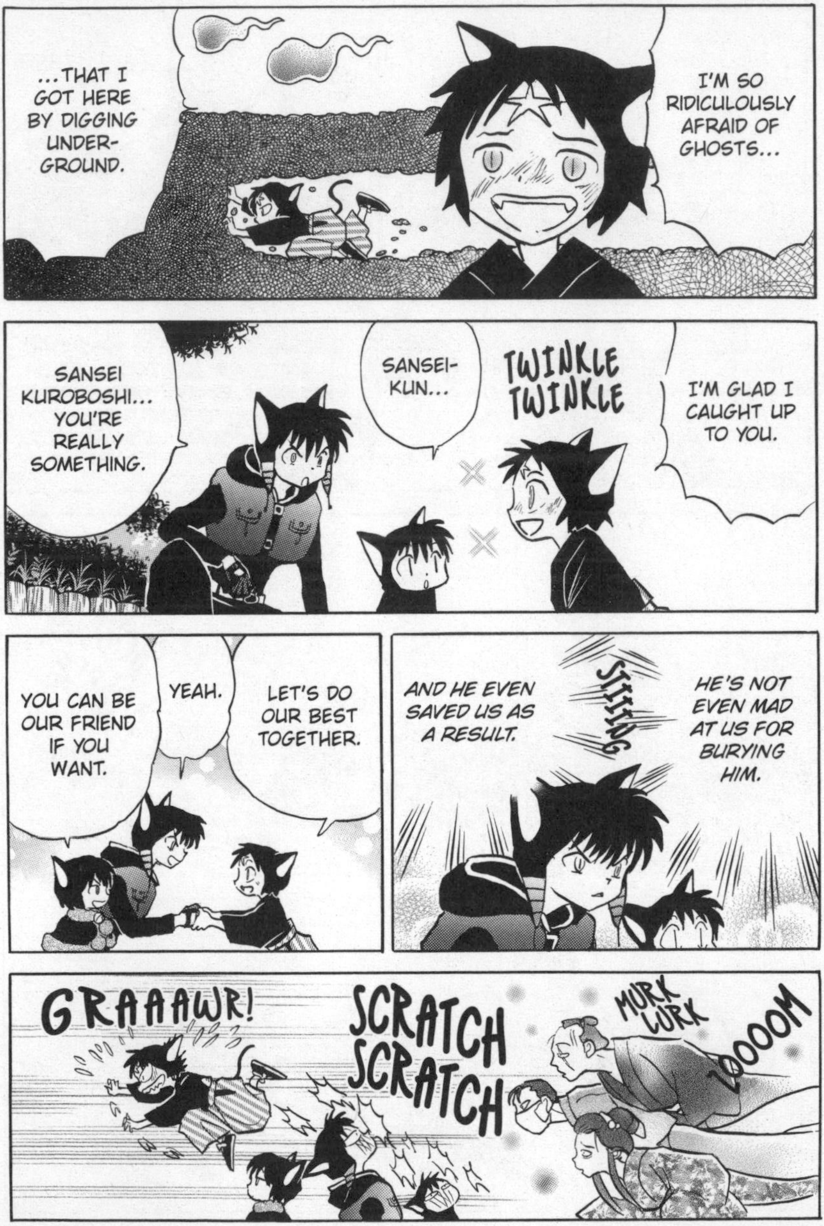
I'M SO RIDICULOUSLY AFRAID OF GHOSTS...
...THAT I GOT HERE BY DIGGING UNDER-GROUND.
I'M GLAD I CAUGHT UP TO YOU.
TWINKLE TWINKLE
SANSEI-KUN...
SANSEI KUROBOSHI... YOU'RE REALLY SOMETHING.
HE'S NOT EVEN MAD AT US FOR BURYING HIM.
STIIING
AND HE EVEN SAVED US AS A RESULT.
LET'S DO OUR BEST TOGETHER.
YEAH.
YOU CAN BE OUR FRIEND IF YOU WANT.
ZOOOOM
MURK LURK
SCRATCH SCRATCH
GRAAAWR!

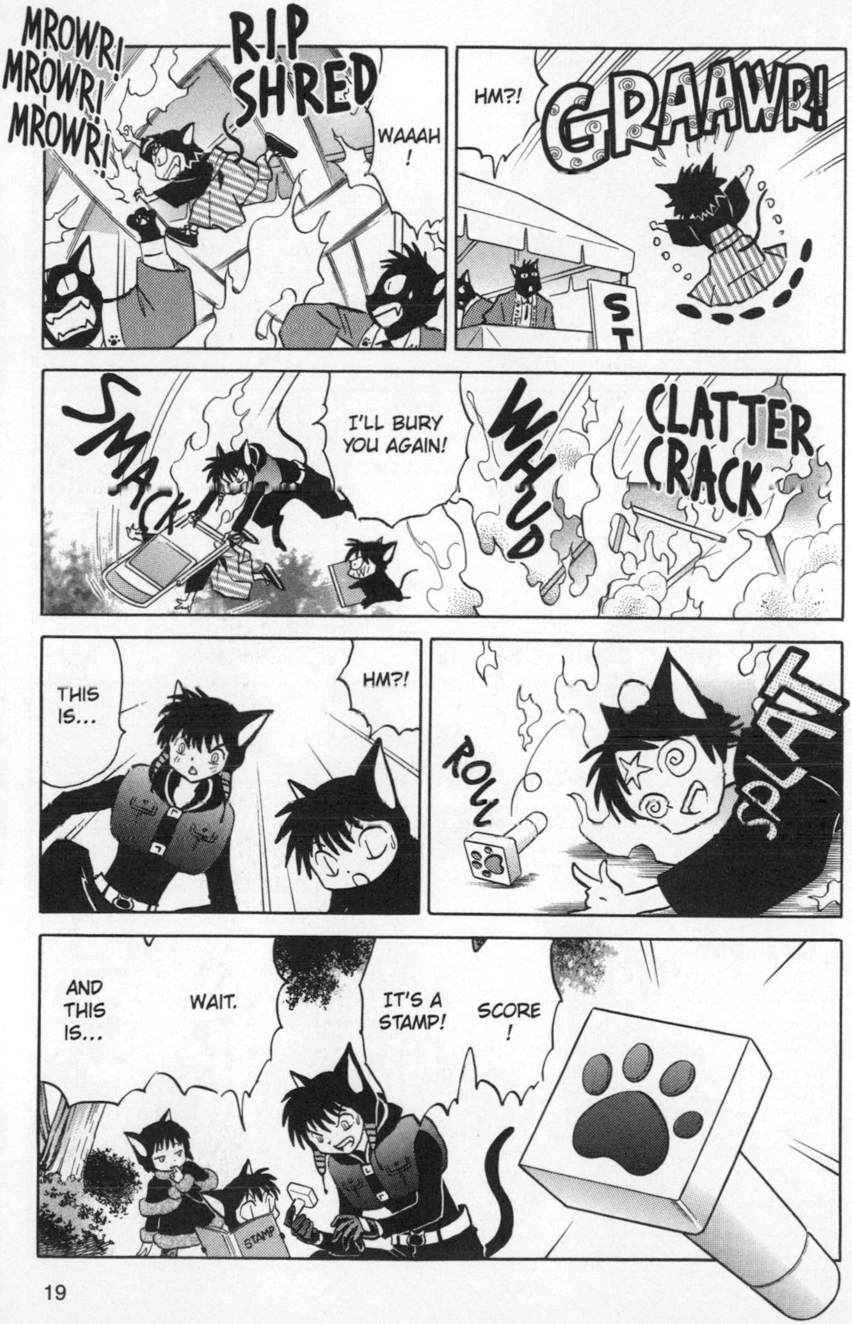
HM?!
GRAAWR!
ST
MROWR! MROWR! MROWR!
RIP SHRED
WAAAH!
CLATTER CRACK
WHUD
I'LL BURY YOU AGAIN!
SMACK
SPLAT
ROLL
HM?!
THIS IS...
SCORE!
IT'S A STAMP!
WAIT.
AND THIS IS...
STAMP

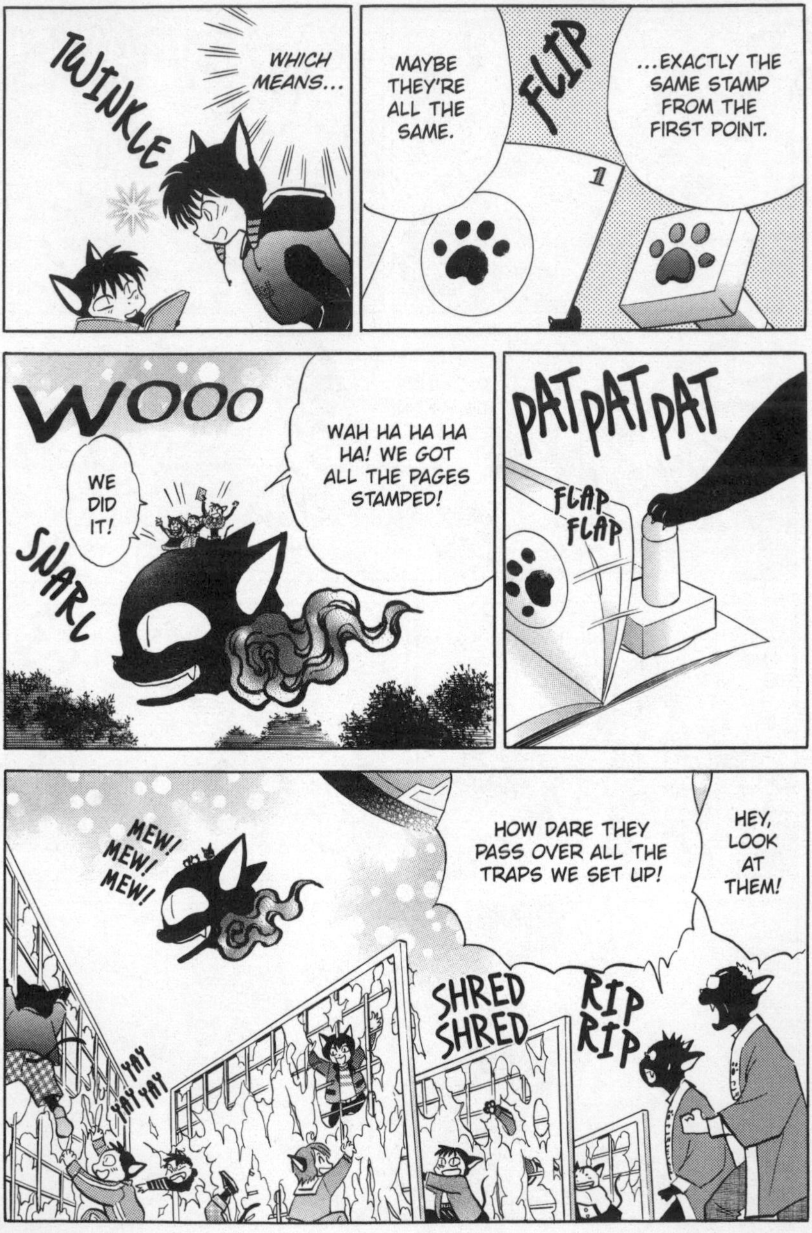
...EXACTLY THE SAME STAMP FROM THE FIRST POINT.
FLIP
MAYBE THEY'RE ALL THE SAME.
WHICH MEANS...
TWINKLE
PATPATPAT
FLAP FLAP
WAH HA HA HA HA! WE GOT ALL THE PAGES STAMPED!
WOOO
WE DID IT!
SNARL
HEY, LOOK AT THEM!
HOW DARE THEY PASS OVER ALL THE TRAPS WE SET UP!
RIP RIP
SHRED SHRED
MEW! MEW! MEW!
YAY YAY YAY

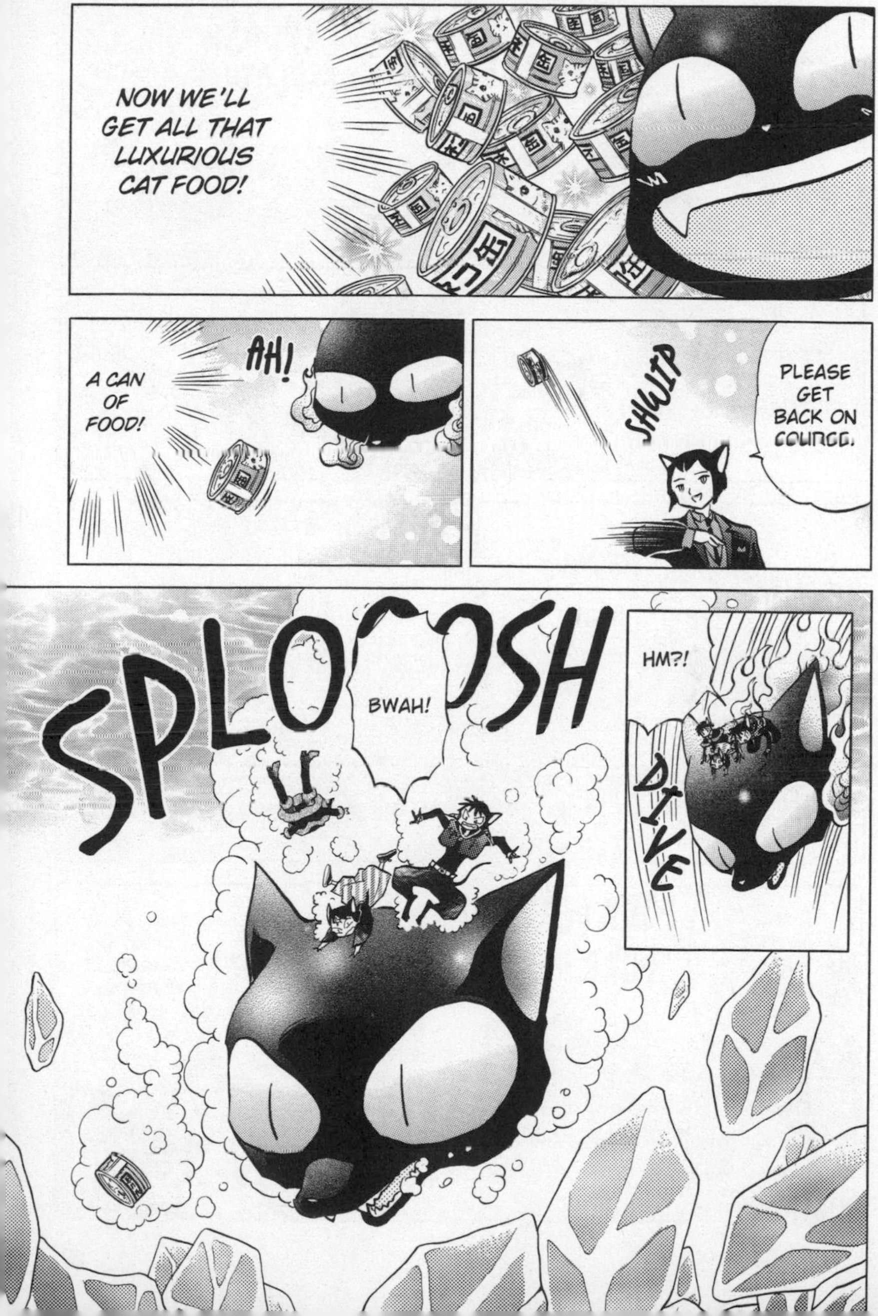
NOW WE'LL GET ALL THAT LUXURIOUS CAT FOOD!
PLEASE GET BACK ON COURSE.
SHWIP
AH!
A CAN OF FOOD!
HM?!
DIVE
SPLOOOSH
BWAH!

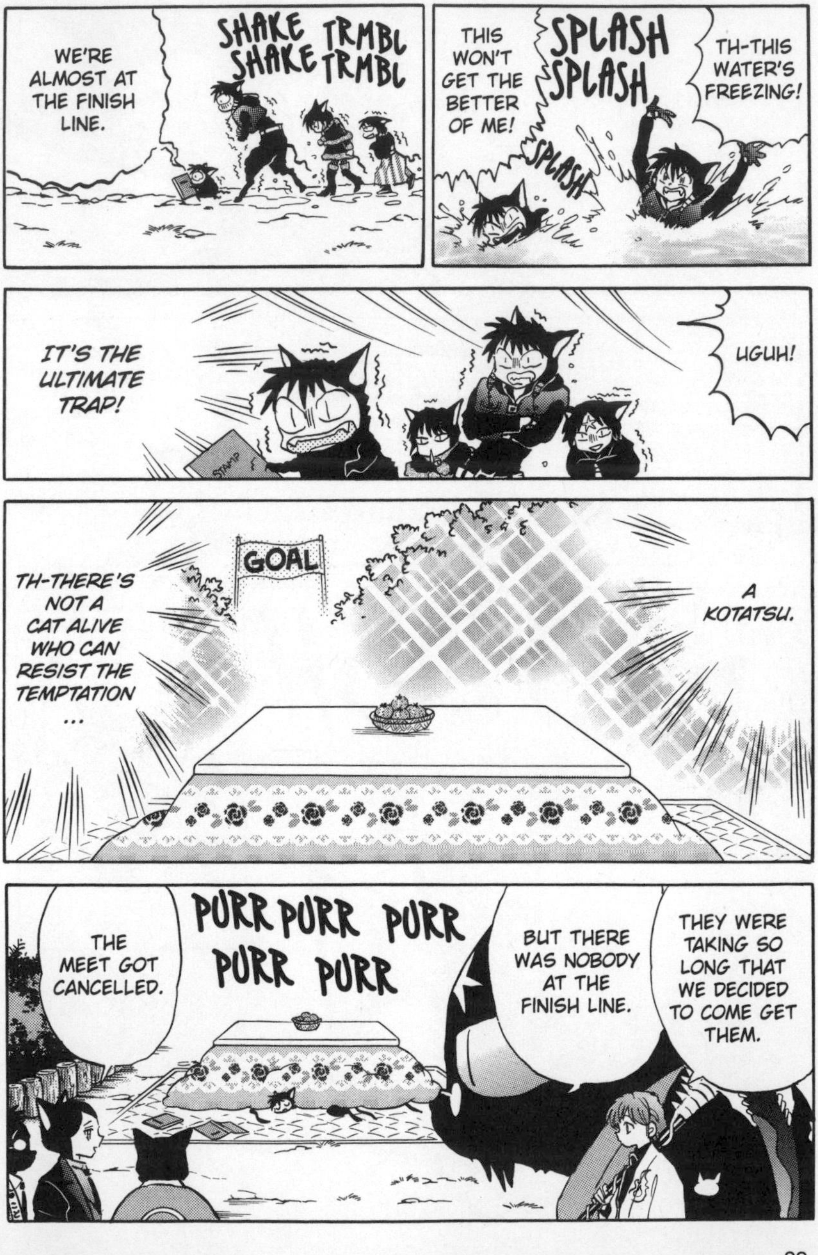
TH-THIS WATER'S FREEZING!
SPLASH SPLASH
THIS WON'T GET THE BETTER OF ME!
SPLASH
TRMBL TRMBL
SHAKE SHAKE
WE'RE ALMOST AT THE FINISH LINE.
UGUH!
IT'S THE ULTIMATE TRAP!
STAMP
A KOTATSU.
GOAL
TH-THERE'S NOT A CAT ALIVE WHO CAN RESIST THE TEMPTATION ...
THEY WERE TAKING SO LONG THAT WE DECIDED TO COME GET THEM.
BUT THERE WAS NOBODY AT THE FINISH LINE.
PURR PURR PURR
PURR PURR
THE MEET GOT CANCELLED.

CHAPTER 180: THE CURSED VALENTINE

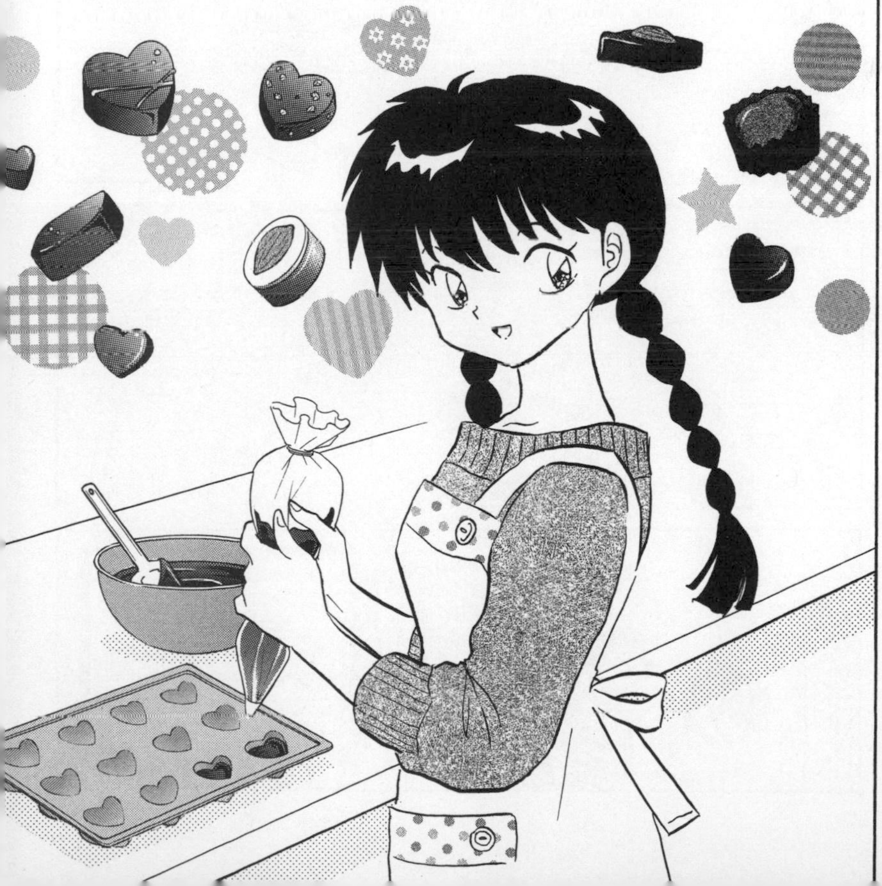

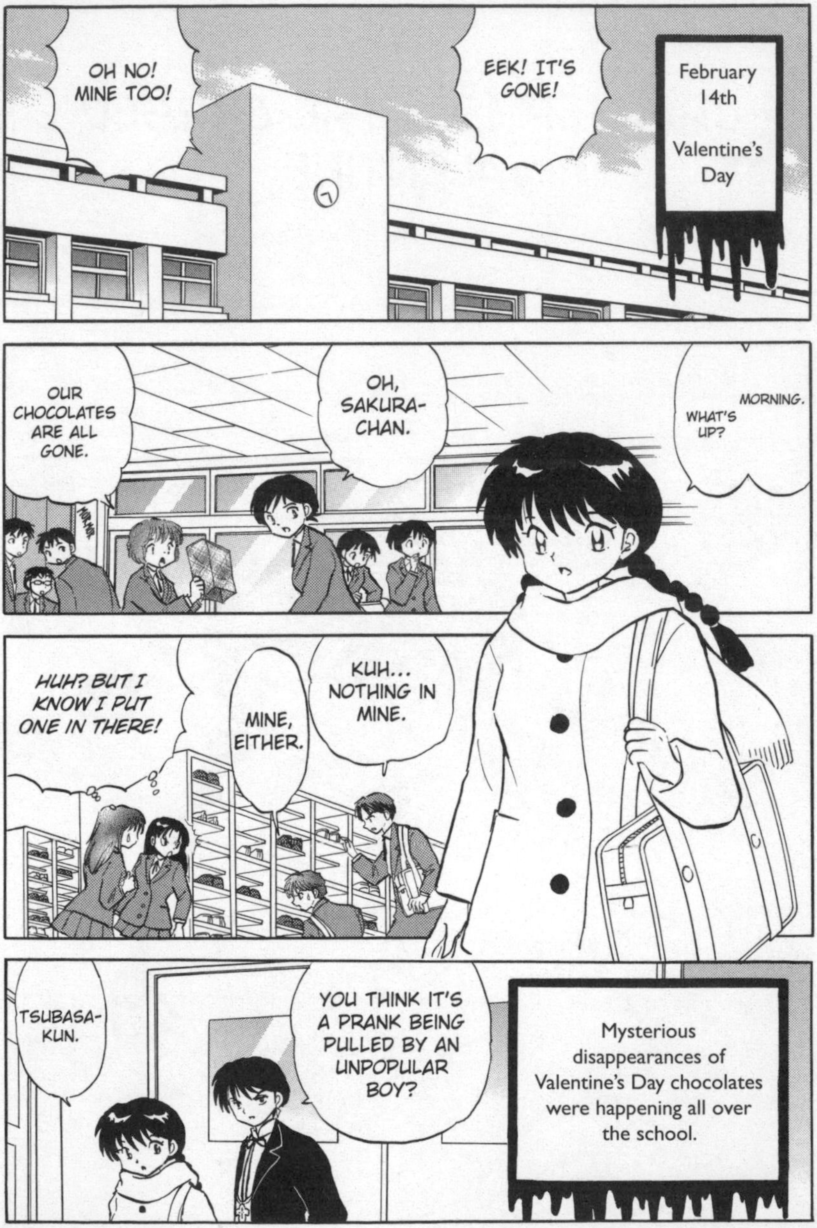
February 14th Valentine's Day
EEK! IT'S GONE!
OH NO! MINE TOO!
MORNING.
WHAT'S UP?
OH, SAKURA-CHAN.
OUR CHOCOLATES ARE ALL GONE.
KUH... NOTHING IN MINE.
MINE, EITHER.
HUH? BUT I KNOW I PUT ONE IN THERE!
Mysterious disappearances of Valentine's Day chocolates were happening all over the school.
YOU THINK IT'S A PRANK BEING PULLED BY AN UNPOPULAR BOY?
TSUBASA-KUN.

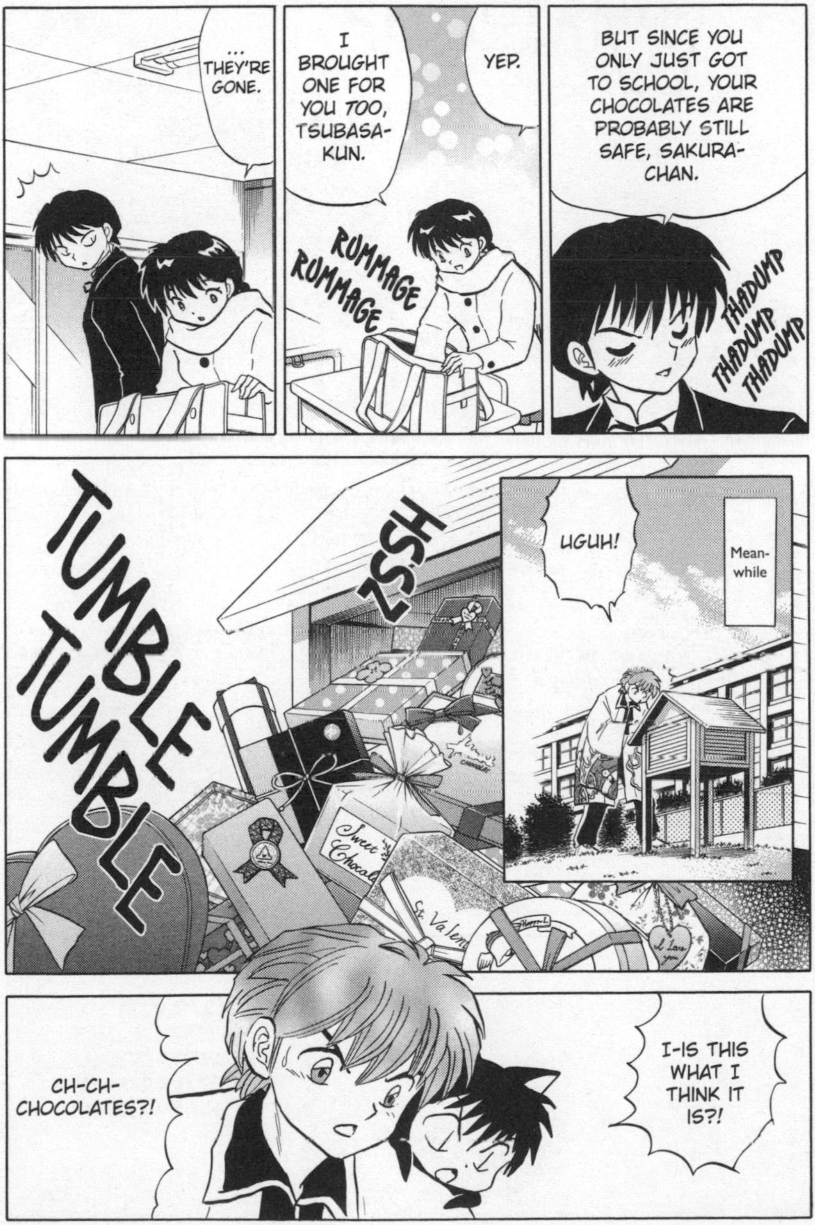
BUT SINCE YOU ONLY JUST GOT TO SCHOOL, YOUR CHOCOLATES ARE PROBABLY STILL SAFE, SAKURA-CHAN.
THADUMP THADUMP THADUMP
YEP.
I BROUGHT ONE FOR YOU TOO, TSUBASA-KUN.
RUMMAGE RUMMAGE
... THEY'RE GONE.
Mean-while
UGUH!
ZSSH
TUMBLE TUMBLE
I-IS THIS WHAT I THINK IT IS?!
CH-CH-CHOCOLATES?!

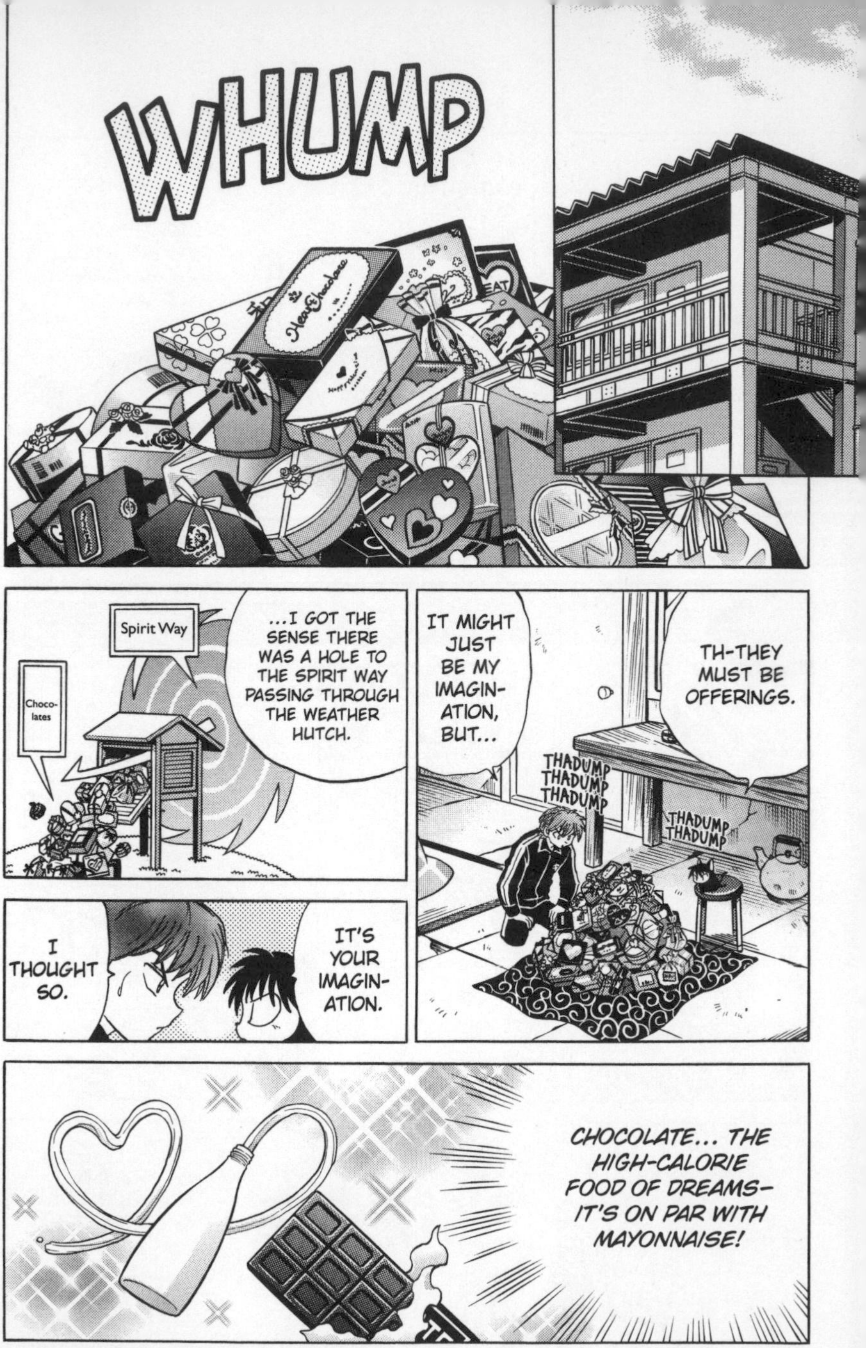
WHUMP
TH-THEY MUST BE OFFERINGS.
IT MIGHT JUST BE MY IMAGINATION, BUT...
THADUMP THADUMP THADUMP
THADUMP THADUMP
...I GOT THE SENSE THERE WAS A HOLE TO THE SPIRIT WAY PASSING THROUGH THE WEATHER HUTCH.
Spirit Way
Chocolates
IT'S YOUR IMAGINATION.
I THOUGHT SO.
CHOCOLATE... THE HIGH-CALORIE FOOD OF DREAMS— IT'S ON PAR WITH MAYONNAISE!

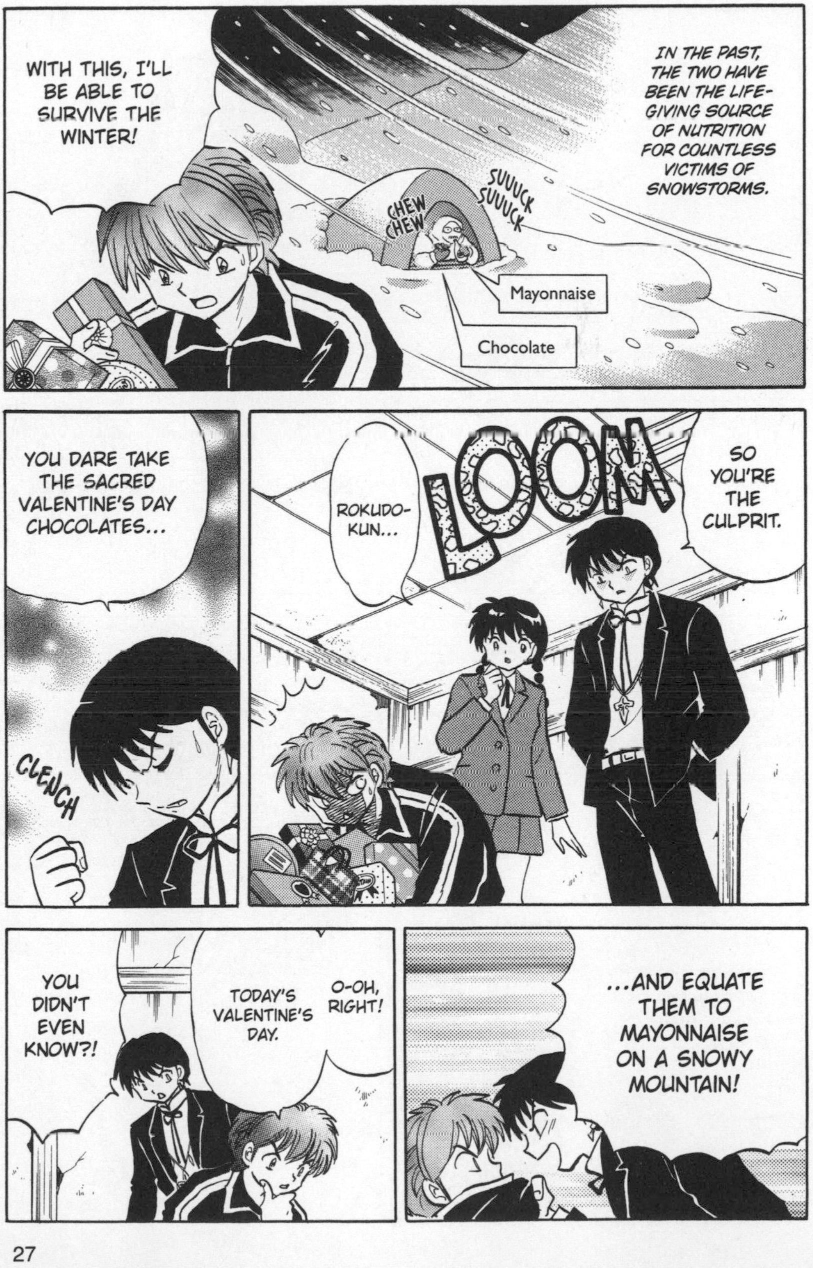
IN THE PAST, THE TWO HAVE BEEN THE LIFE-GIVING SOURCE OF NUTRITION FOR COUNTLESS VICTIMS OF SNOWSTORMS.
WITH THIS, I'LL BE ABLE TO SURVIVE THE WINTER!
SUUUCK SUUUCK
CHEW CHEW
Mayonnaise
Chocolate
SO YOU'RE THE CULPRIT.
LOOM
ROKUDO-KUN...
YOU DARE TAKE THE SACRED VALENTINE'S DAY CHOCOLATES...
CLENCH
...AND EQUATE THEM TO MAYONNAISE ON A SNOWY MOUNTAIN!
O-OH, RIGHT!
TODAY'S VALENTINE'S DAY.
YOU DIDN'T EVEN KNOW?!

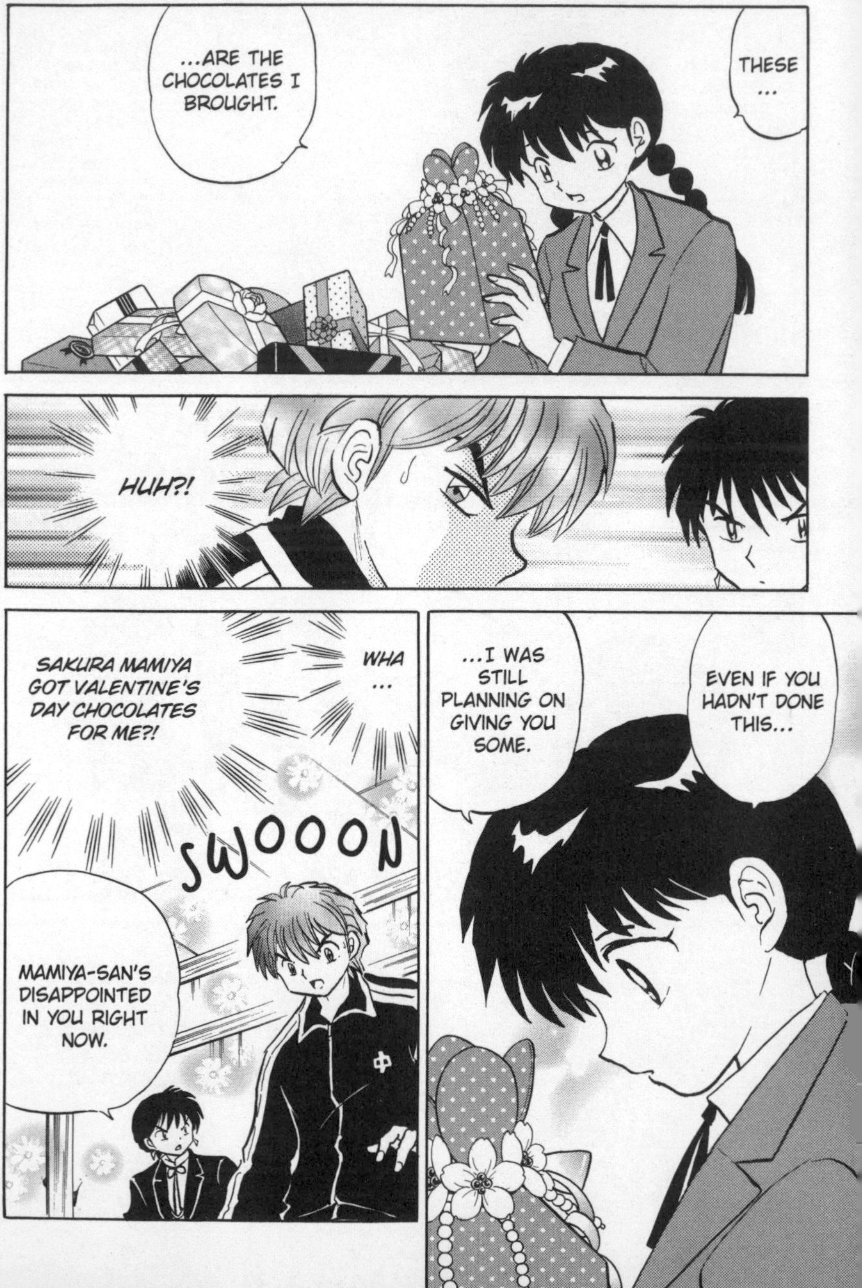
THESE...
...ARE THE CHOCOLATES I BROUGHT.
HUH?!
EVEN IF YOU HADN'T DONE THIS...
...I WAS STILL PLANNING ON GIVING YOU SOME.
WHA...
SAKURA MAMIYA GOT VALENTINE'S DAY CHOCOLATES FOR ME?!
SWOOON
MAMIYA-SAN'S DISAPPOINTED IN YOU RIGHT NOW.

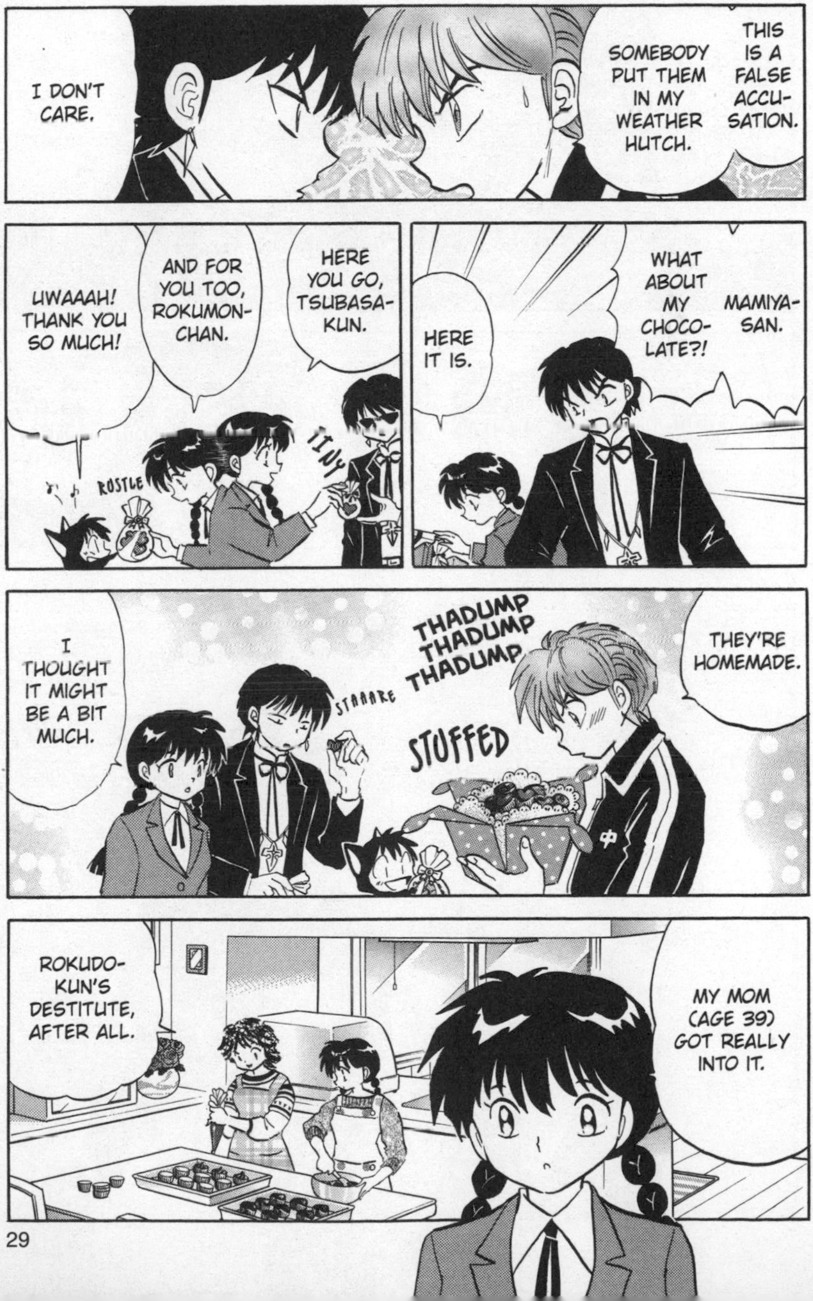

THIS IS A FALSE ACCUSATION.
SOMEBODY PUT THEM IN MY WEATHER HUTCH.
I DON'T CARE.
MAMIYA-SAN.
WHAT ABOUT MY CHOCOLATE?!
HERE IT IS.
HERE YOU GO, TSUBASA-KUN.
TINY
AND FOR YOU TOO, ROKUMON-CHAN.
RUSTLE
UWAAAH! THANK YOU SO MUCH!
THEY'RE HOMEMADE.
THADUMP THADUMP THADUMP
STUFFED
STAAARE
I THOUGHT IT MIGHT BE A BIT MUCH.
MY MOM (AGE 39) GOT REALLY INTO IT.
ROKUDO-KUN'S DESTITUTE, AFTER ALL.

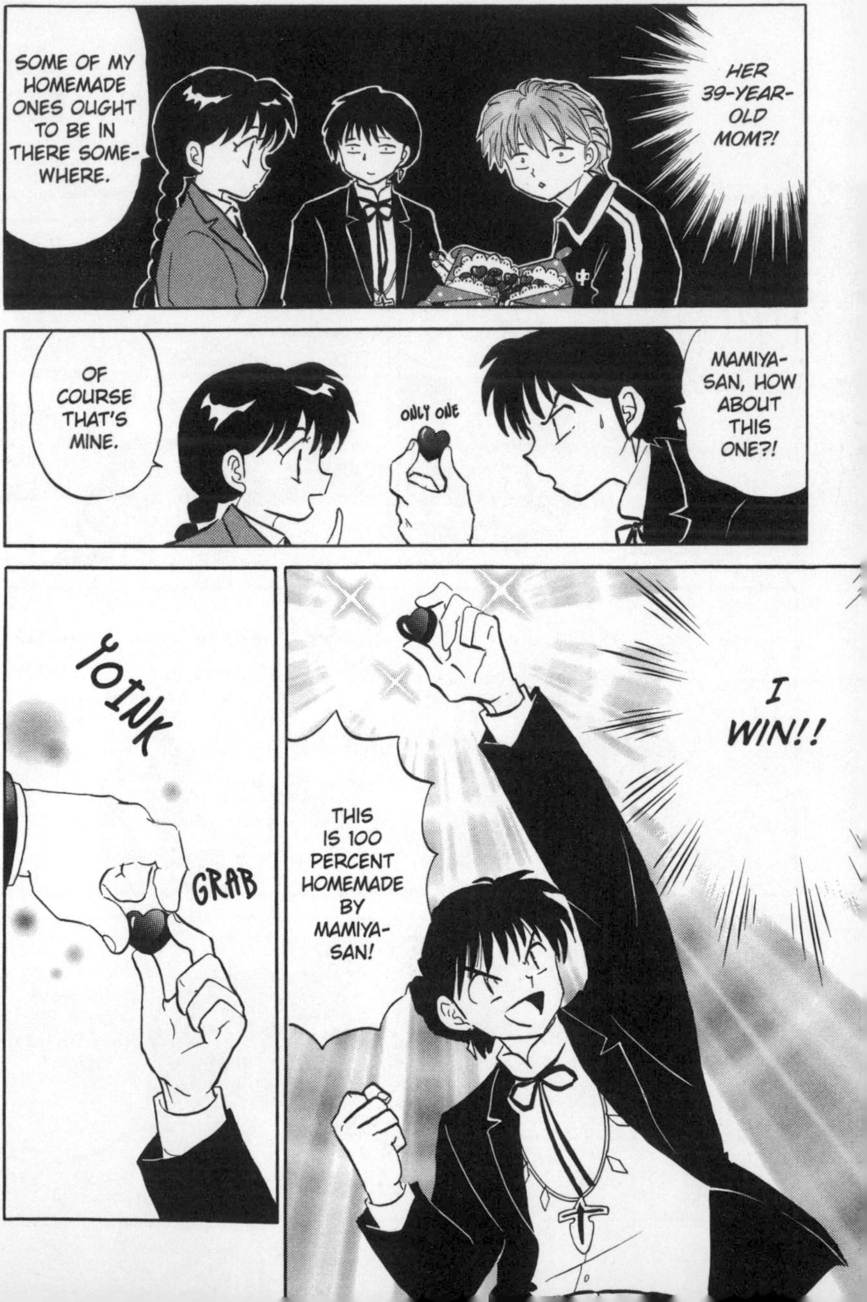
HER 39-YEAR-OLD MOM?!
SOME OF MY HOMEMADE ONES OUGHT TO BE IN THERE SOME-WHERE.
MAMIYA-SAN, HOW ABOUT THIS ONE?!
ONLY ONE
OF COURSE THAT'S MINE.
I WIN!!
THIS IS 100 PERCENT HOMEMADE BY MAMIYA-SAN!
YOINK
GRAB

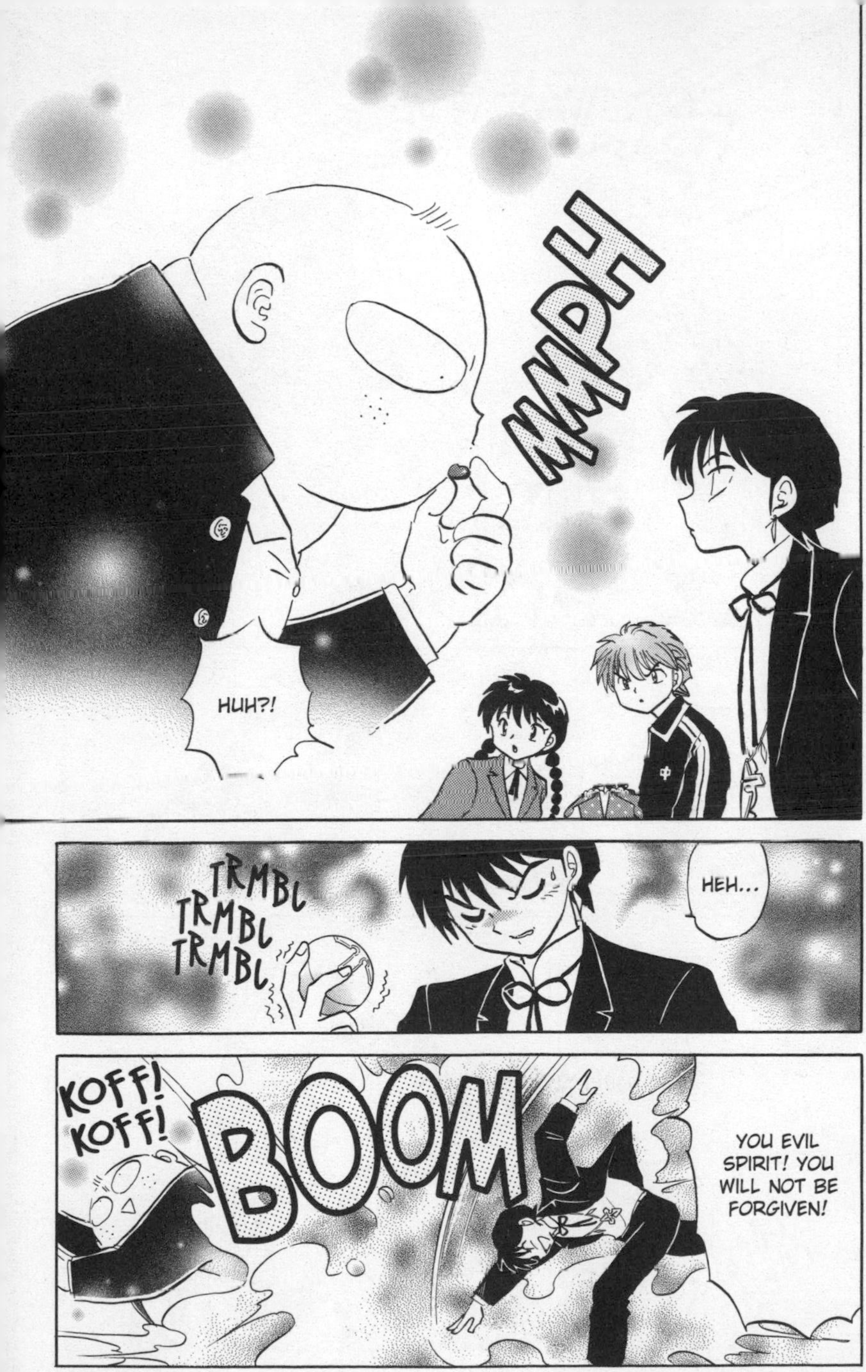
MMPH
HUH?!
HEH...
TRMBL
TRMBL
TRMBL
YOU EVIL SPIRIT! YOU WILL NOT BE FORGIVEN!
BOOM
KOFF! KOFF!

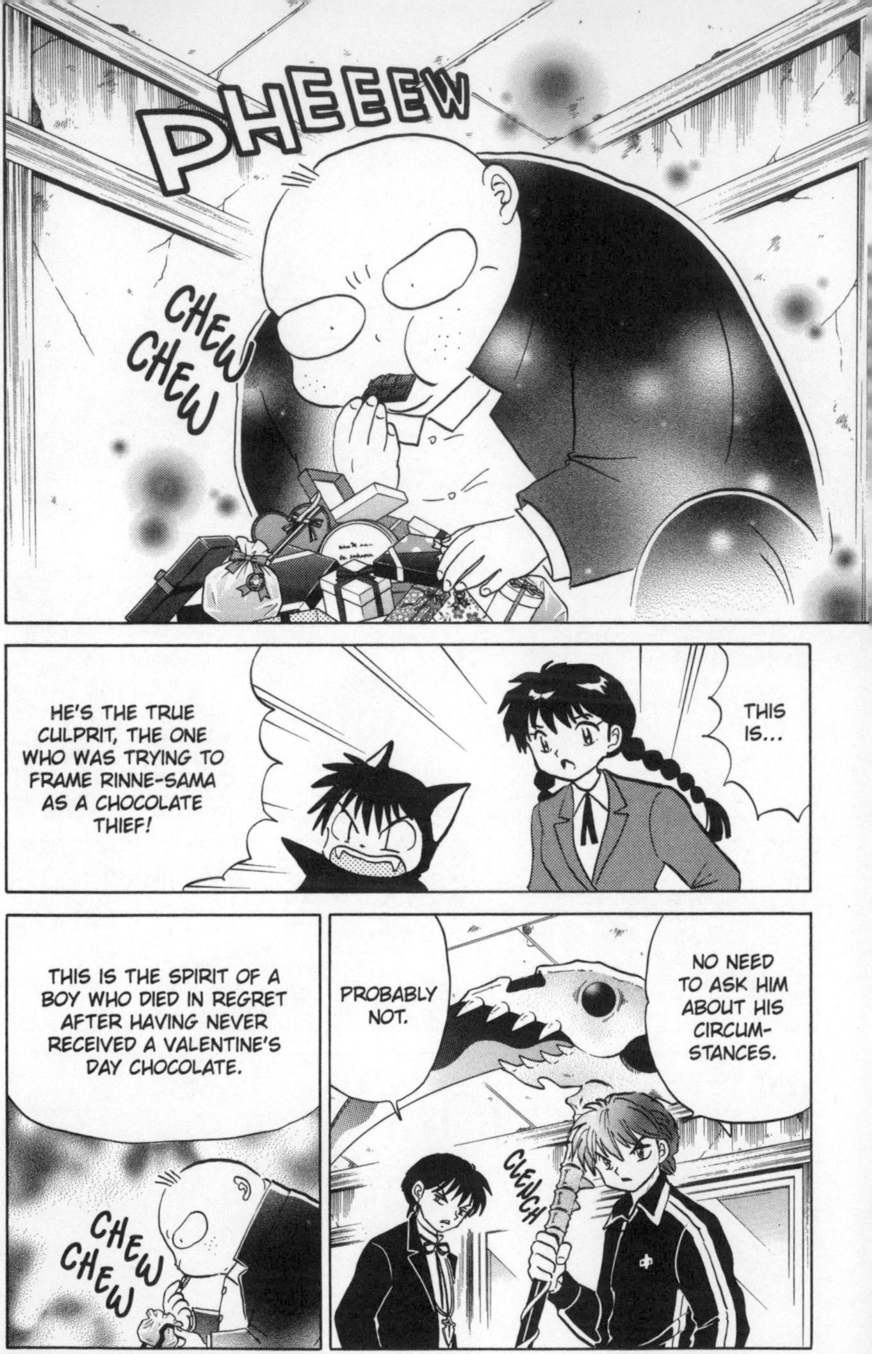
PHEEEW
CHEW CHEW
THIS IS...
HE'S THE TRUE CULPRIT, THE ONE WHO WAS TRYING TO FRAME RINNE-SAMA AS A CHOCOLATE THIEF!
NO NEED TO ASK HIM ABOUT HIS CIRCUM-STANCES.
PROBABLY NOT.
CLENCH
THIS IS THE SPIRIT OF A BOY WHO DIED IN REGRET AFTER HAVING NEVER RECEIVED A VALENTINE'S DAY CHOCOLATE.
CHEW CHEW

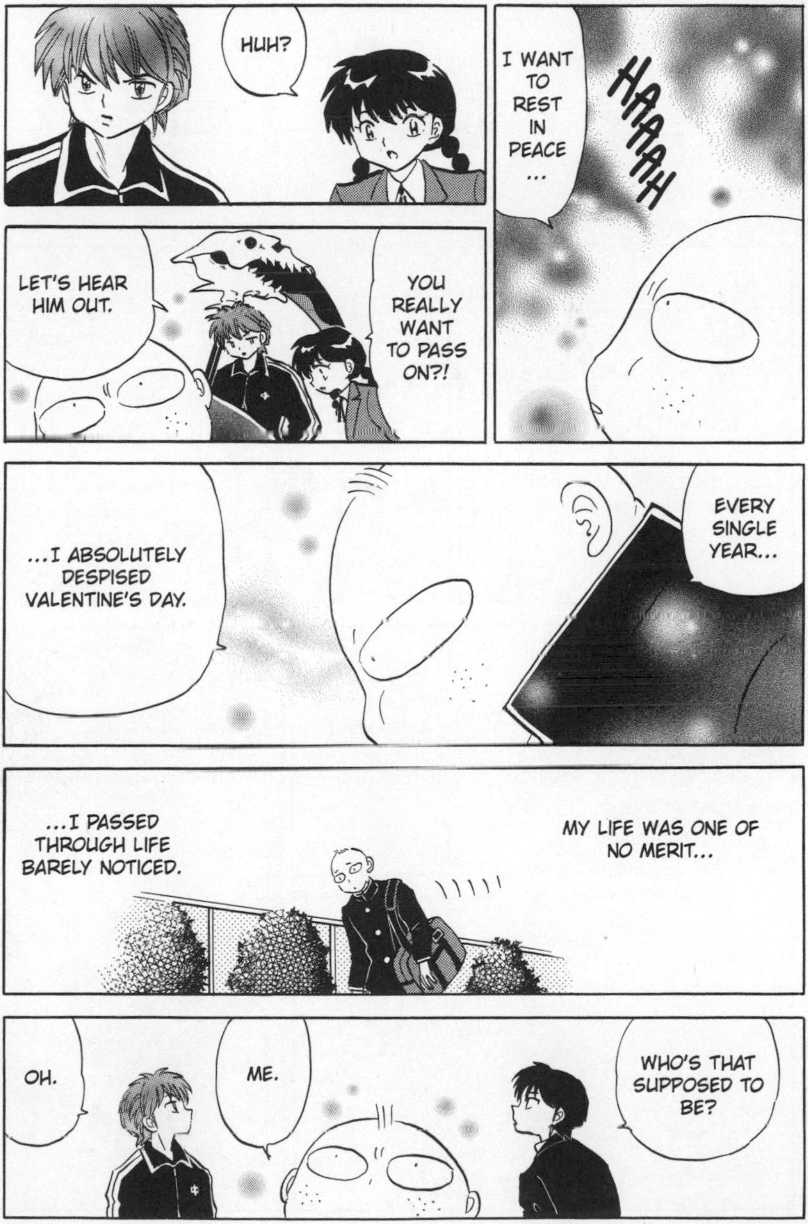
I WANT TO REST IN PEACE...
HAAAAH
HUH?
YOU REALLY WANT TO PASS ON?!
LET'S HEAR HIM OUT.
EVERY SINGLE YEAR...
...I ABSOLUTELY DESPISED VALENTINE'S DAY.
MY LIFE WAS ONE OF NO MERIT...
...I PASSED THROUGH LIFE BARELY NOTICED.
WHO'S THAT SUPPOSED TO BE?
ME.
OH.

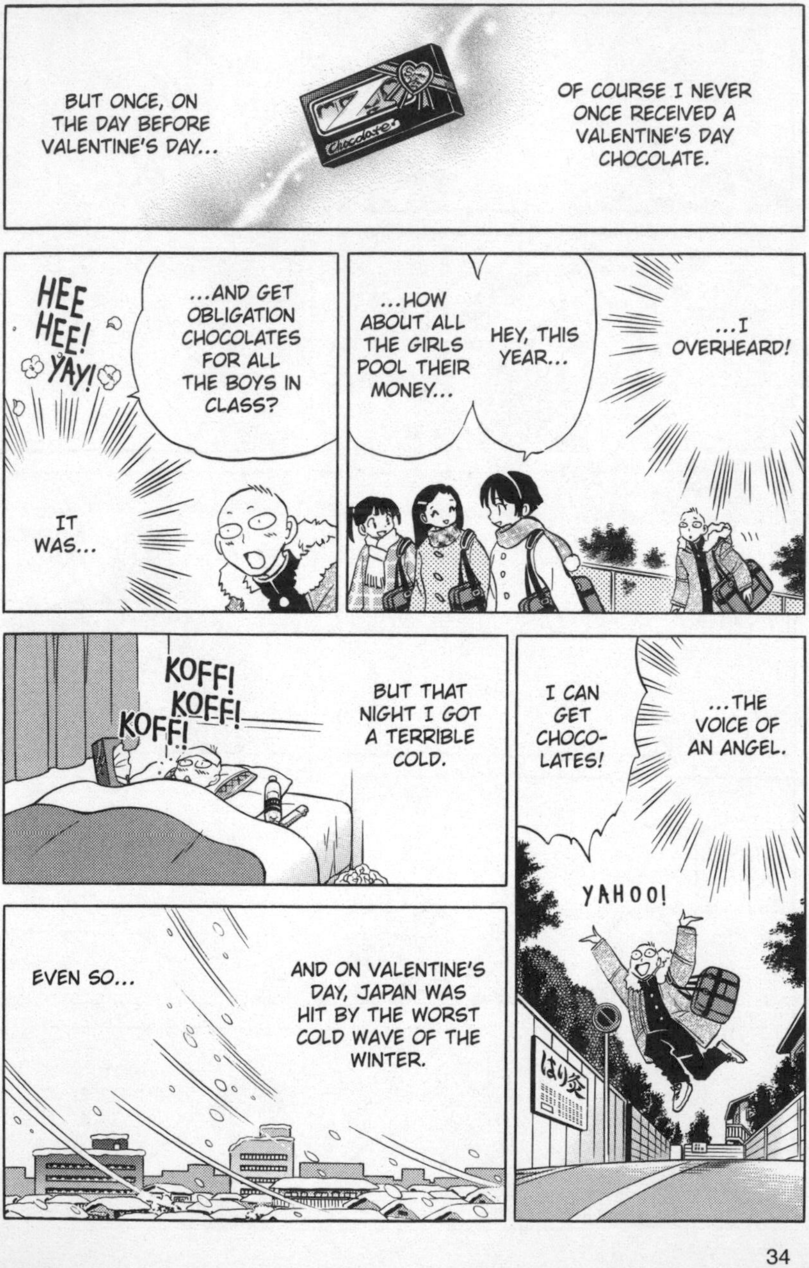
OF COURSE I NEVER ONCE RECEIVED A VALENTINE'S DAY CHOCOLATE.
Chocolate
BUT ONCE, ON THE DAY BEFORE VALENTINE'S DAY...
...I OVERHEARD!
HEY, THIS YEAR...
...HOW ABOUT ALL THE GIRLS POOL THEIR MONEY...
...AND GET OBLIGATION CHOCOLATES FOR ALL THE BOYS IN CLASS?
HEE HEE! YAY!
IT WAS...
...THE VOICE OF AN ANGEL.
I CAN GET CHOCO-LATES!
YAHOO!
はり灸
BUT THAT NIGHT I GOT A TERRIBLE COLD.
KOFF! KOFF! KOFF!
AND ON VALENTINE'S DAY, JAPAN WAS HIT BY THE WORST COLD WAVE OF THE WINTER.
EVEN SO...

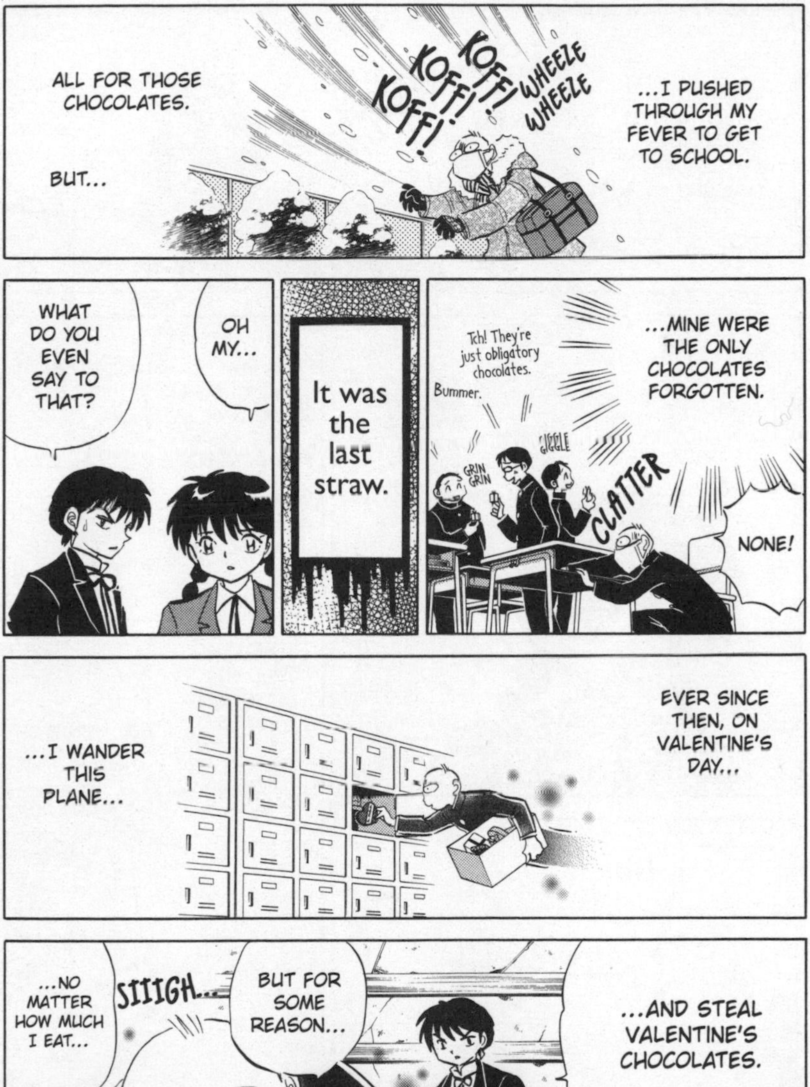
...I PUSHED THROUGH MY FEVER TO GET TO SCHOOL.
WHEEZE WHEEZE
KOFF! KOFF! KOFF!
ALL FOR THOSE CHOCOLATES.
BUT...
...MINE WERE THE ONLY CHOCOLATES FORGOTTEN.
Tch! They're just obligatory chocolates.
Bummer.
GIGGLE
GRIN GRIN
CLATTER
NONE!
It was the last straw.
OH MY...
WHAT DO YOU EVEN SAY TO THAT?
EVER SINCE THEN, ON VALENTINE'S DAY...
...I WANDER THIS PLANE...
...AND STEAL VALENTINE'S CHOCOLATES.
BUT FOR SOME REASON...
SIIIGH...
...NO MATTER HOW MUCH I EAT...

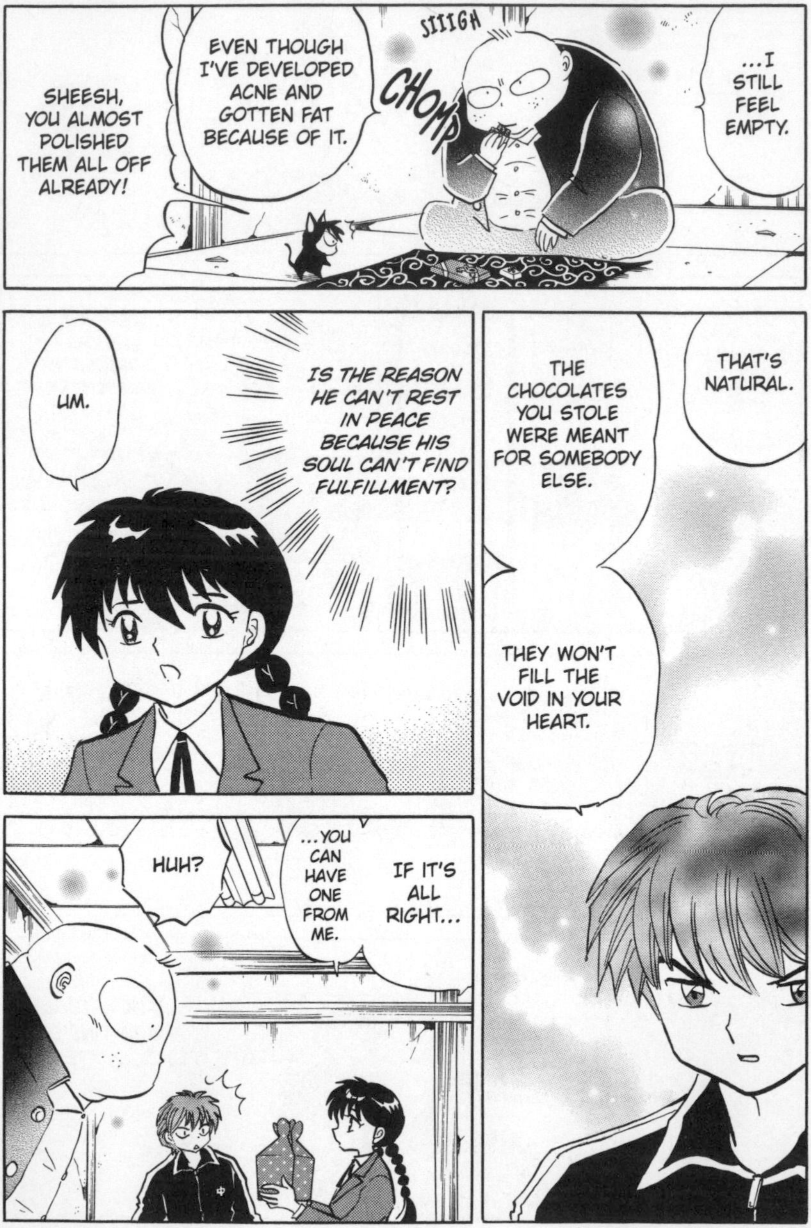
...I STILL FEEL EMPTY.
SIIIGH
CHOMP
EVEN THOUGH I'VE DEVELOPED ACNE AND GOTTEN FAT BECAUSE OF IT.
SHEESH, YOU ALMOST POLISHED THEM ALL OFF ALREADY!
THAT'S NATURAL.
THE CHOCOLATES YOU STOLE WERE MEANT FOR SOMEBODY ELSE.
THEY WON'T FILL THE VOID IN YOUR HEART.
IS THE REASON HE CAN'T REST IN PEACE BECAUSE HIS SOUL CAN'T FIND FULFILLMENT?
UM.
IF IT'S ALL RIGHT...
...YOU CAN HAVE ONE FROM ME.
HUH?

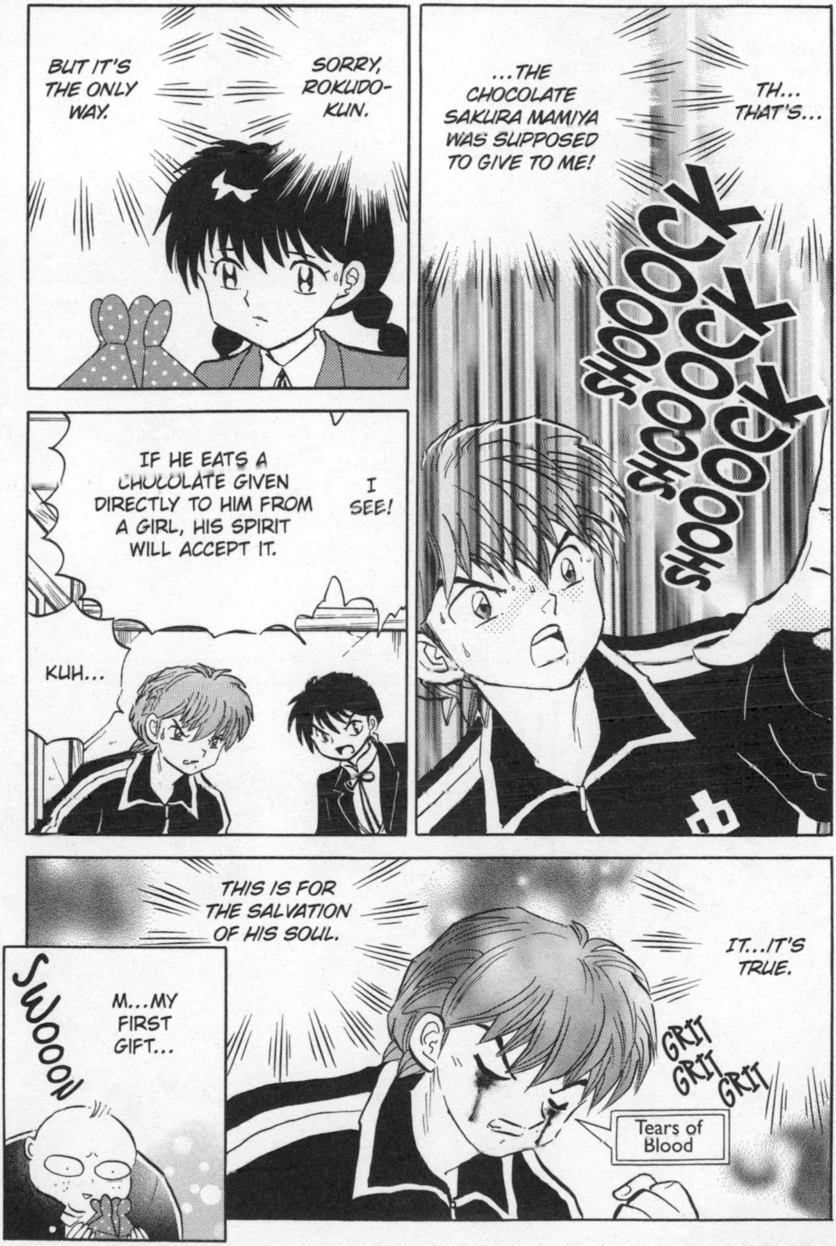
TH... THAT'S...
...THE CHOCOLATE SAKURA MAMIYA WAS SUPPOSED TO GIVE TO ME!
SHOOOCK
SHOOOCK
SHOOOCK
SORRY, ROKUDO-KUN.
BUT IT'S THE ONLY WAY.
I SEE!
IF HE EATS A CHOCOLATE GIVEN DIRECTLY TO HIM FROM A GIRL, HIS SPIRIT WILL ACCEPT IT.
KUH...
THIS IS FOR THE SALVATION OF HIS SOUL.
IT...IT'S TRUE.
GRIT GRIT GRIT
Tears of Blood
SWOOOON
M...MY FIRST GIFT...

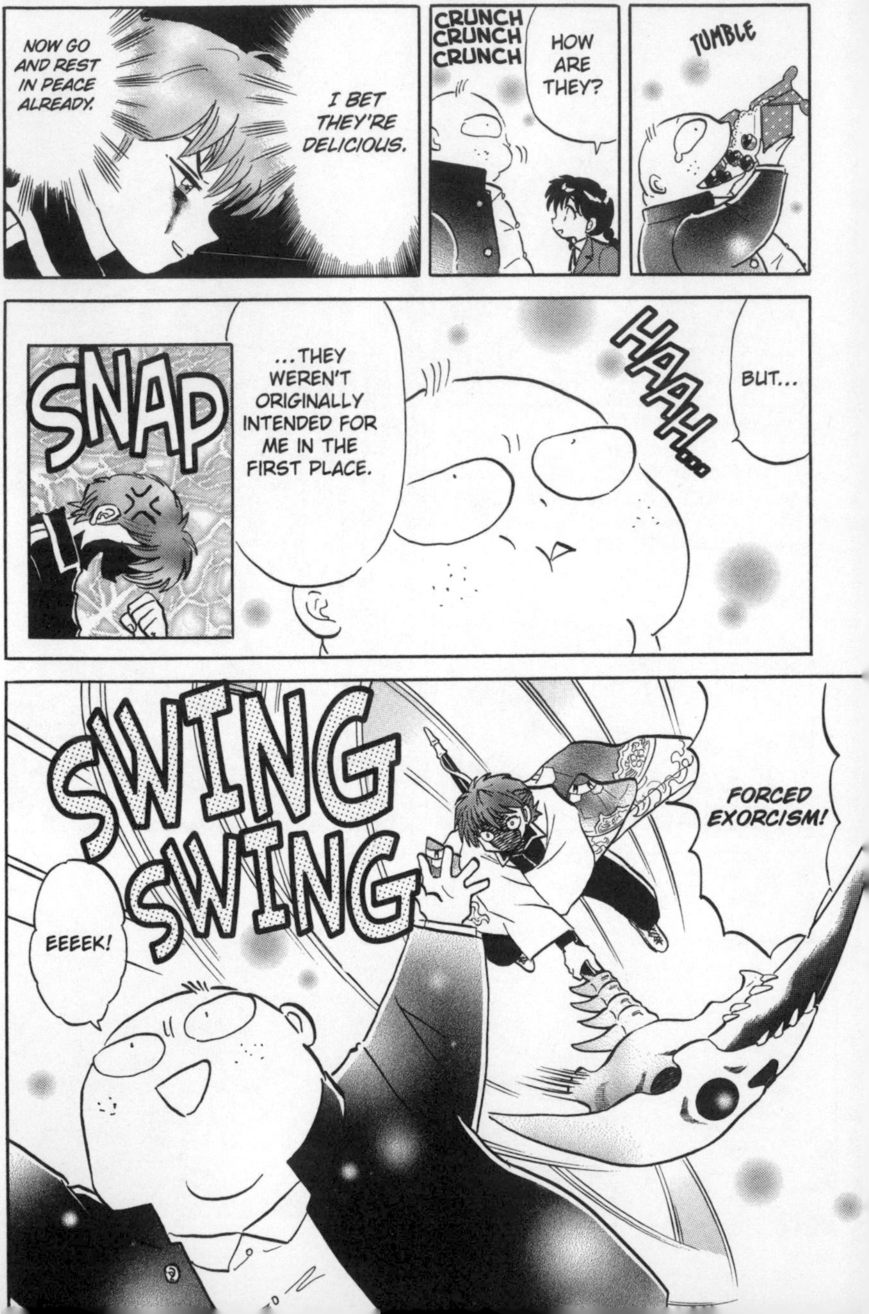
TUMBLE
CRUNCH CRUNCH CRUNCH
HOW ARE THEY?
I BET THEY'RE DELICIOUS.
NOW GO AND REST IN PEACE ALREADY.
BUT...
HAAAH...
...THEY WEREN'T ORIGINALLY INTENDED FOR ME IN THE FIRST PLACE.
SNAP
FORCED EXORCISM!
SWING SWING
EEEEK!

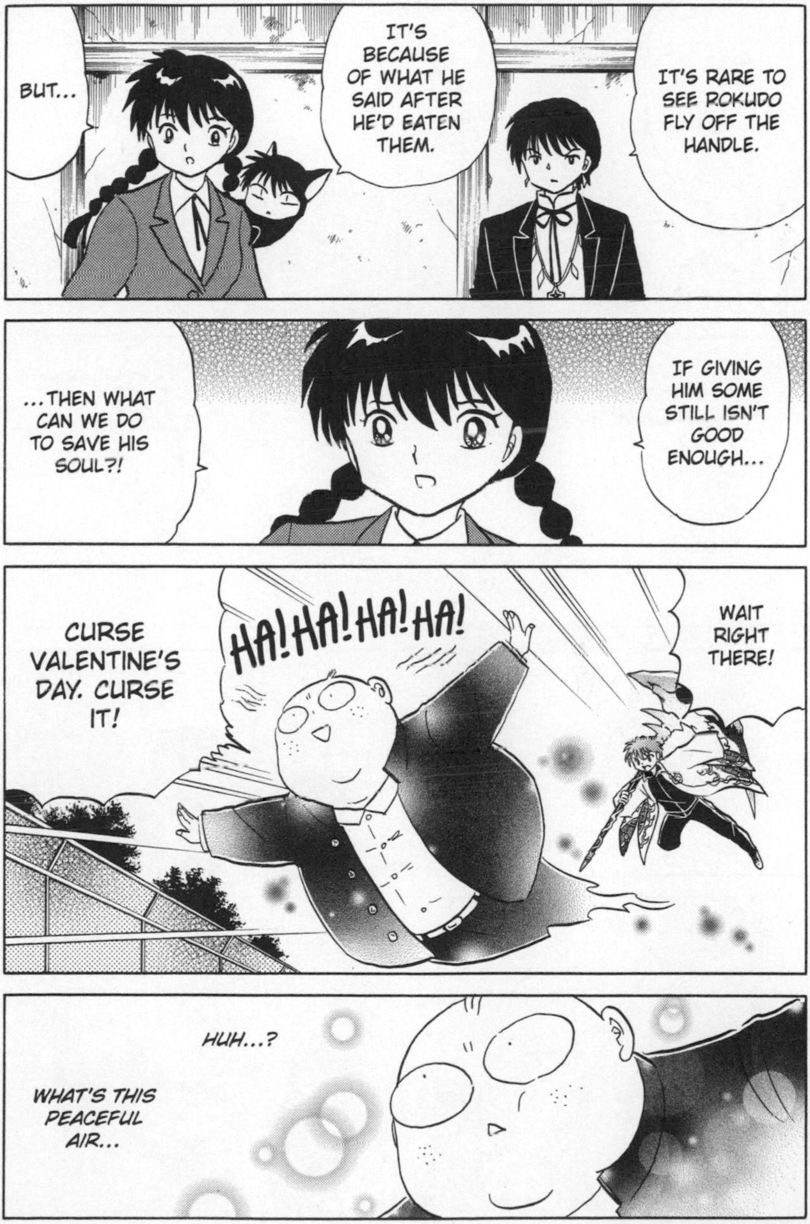
IT'S RARE TO SEE ROKUDO FLY OFF THE HANDLE.
IT'S BECAUSE OF WHAT HE SAID AFTER HE'D EATEN THEM.
BUT...
IF GIVING HIM SOME STILL ISN'T GOOD ENOUGH...
...THEN WHAT CAN WE DO TO SAVE HIS SOUL?!
WAIT RIGHT THERE!
HA! HA! HA! HA!
CURSE VALENTINE'S DAY. CURSE IT!
HUH...?
WHAT'S THIS PEACEFUL AIR...

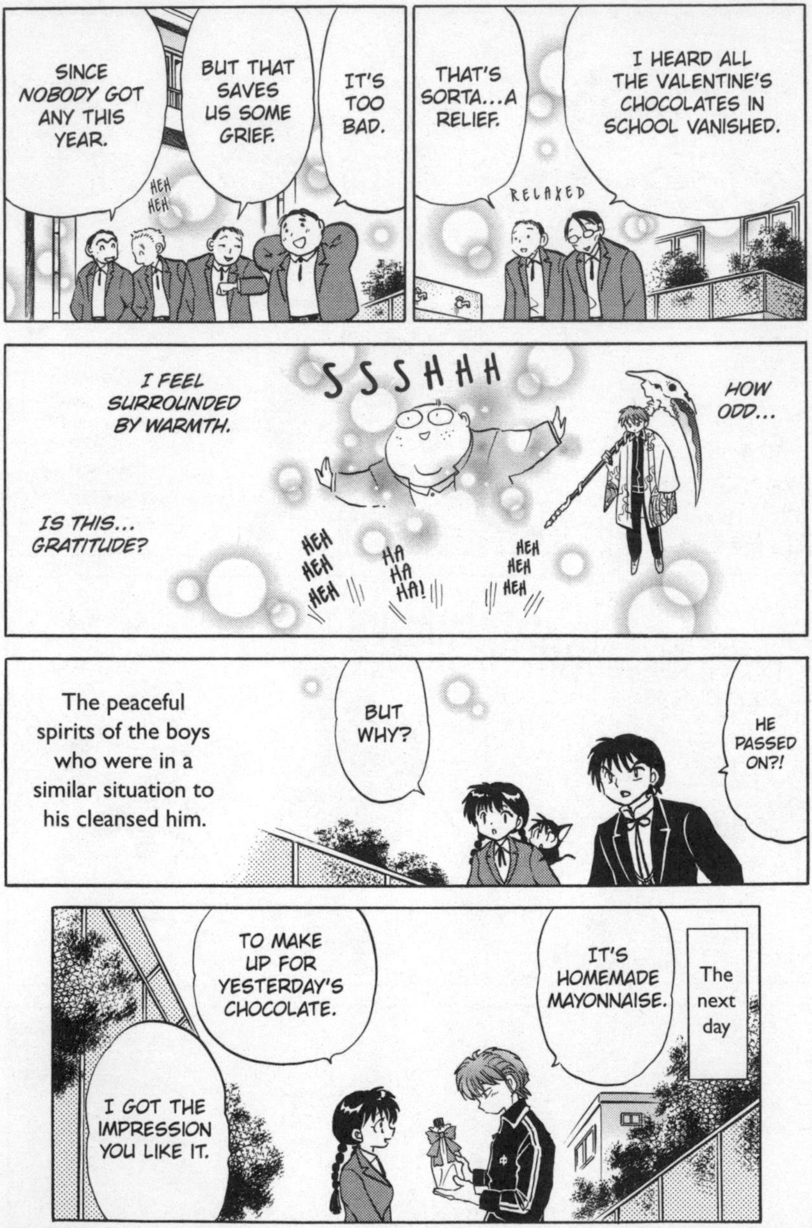
I HEARD ALL THE VALENTINE'S CHOCOLATES IN SCHOOL VANISHED.
THAT'S SORTA...A RELIEF.
RELAXED
IT'S TOO BAD.
BUT THAT SAVES US SOME GRIEF.
SINCE NOBODY GOT ANY THIS YEAR.
HEH HEH
HOW ODD...
SSSHHH
I FEEL SURROUNDED BY WARMTH.
IS THIS... GRATITUDE?
HEH HEH HEH
HA HA HA!
HEH HEH HEH
HE PASSED ON?!
BUT WHY?
The peaceful spirits of the boys who were in a similar situation to his cleansed him.
The next day
IT'S HOMEMADE MAYONNAISE.
TO MAKE UP FOR YESTERDAY'S CHOCOLATE.
I GOT THE IMPRESSION YOU LIKE IT.

CHAPTER 181: TYPE-A DEMON, TYPE-B SHINIGAMI

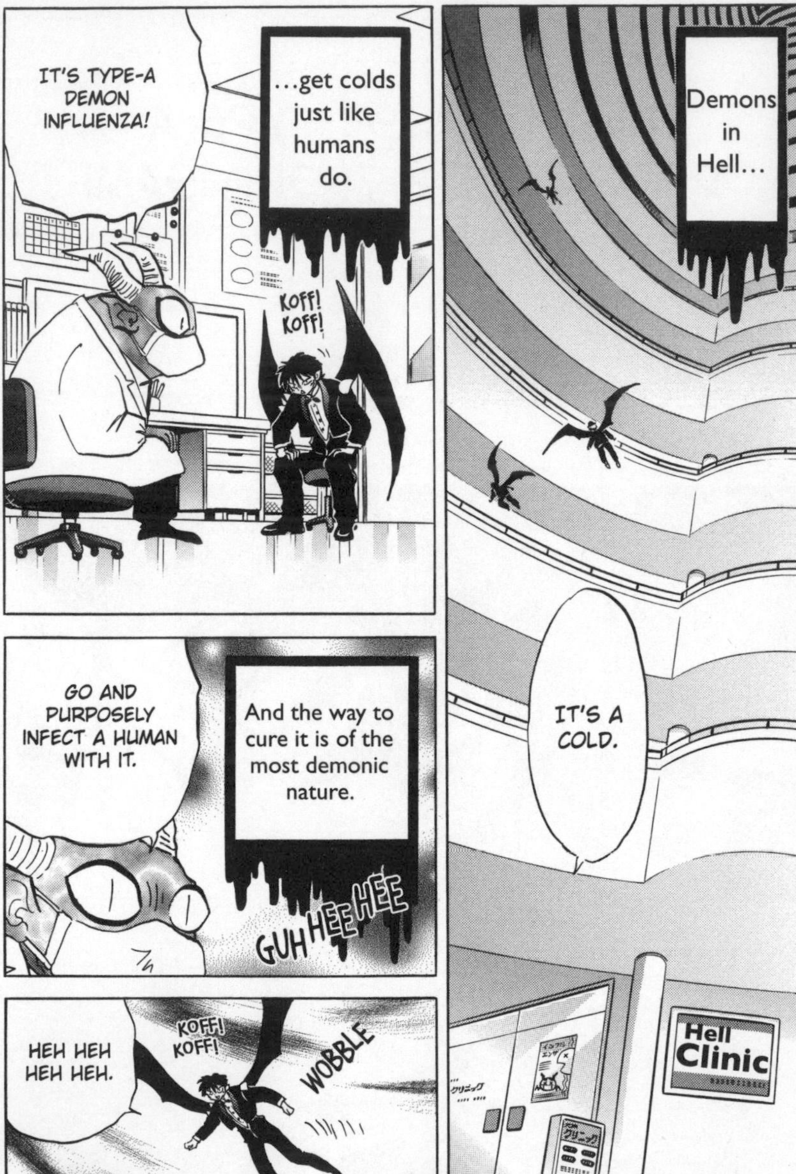
Demons in Hell…
IT'S A COLD.
Hell Clinic
…get colds just like humans do.
IT'S TYPE-A DEMON INFLUENZA!
KOFF! KOFF!
And the way to cure it is of the most demonic nature.
GO AND PURPOSELY INFECT A HUMAN WITH IT.
GUH HEE HEE
HEH HEH HEH HEH.
KOFF! KOFF!
WOBBLE

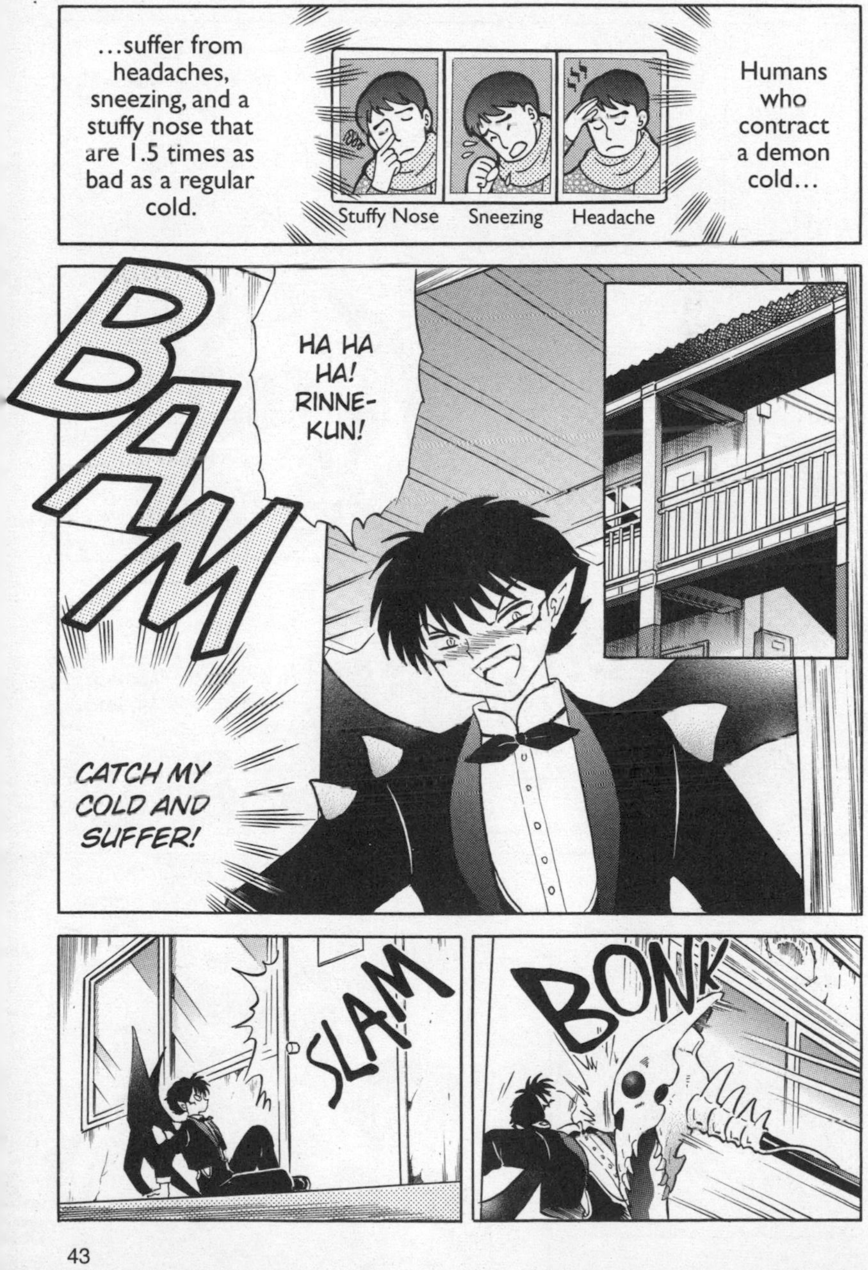
Humans who contract a demon cold…
…suffer from headaches, sneezing, and a stuffy nose that are 1.5 times as bad as a regular cold.
Stuffy Nose
Sneezing
Headache
HA HA HA! RINNE-KUN!
BAM
CATCH MY COLD AND SUFFER!
BONK
SLAM

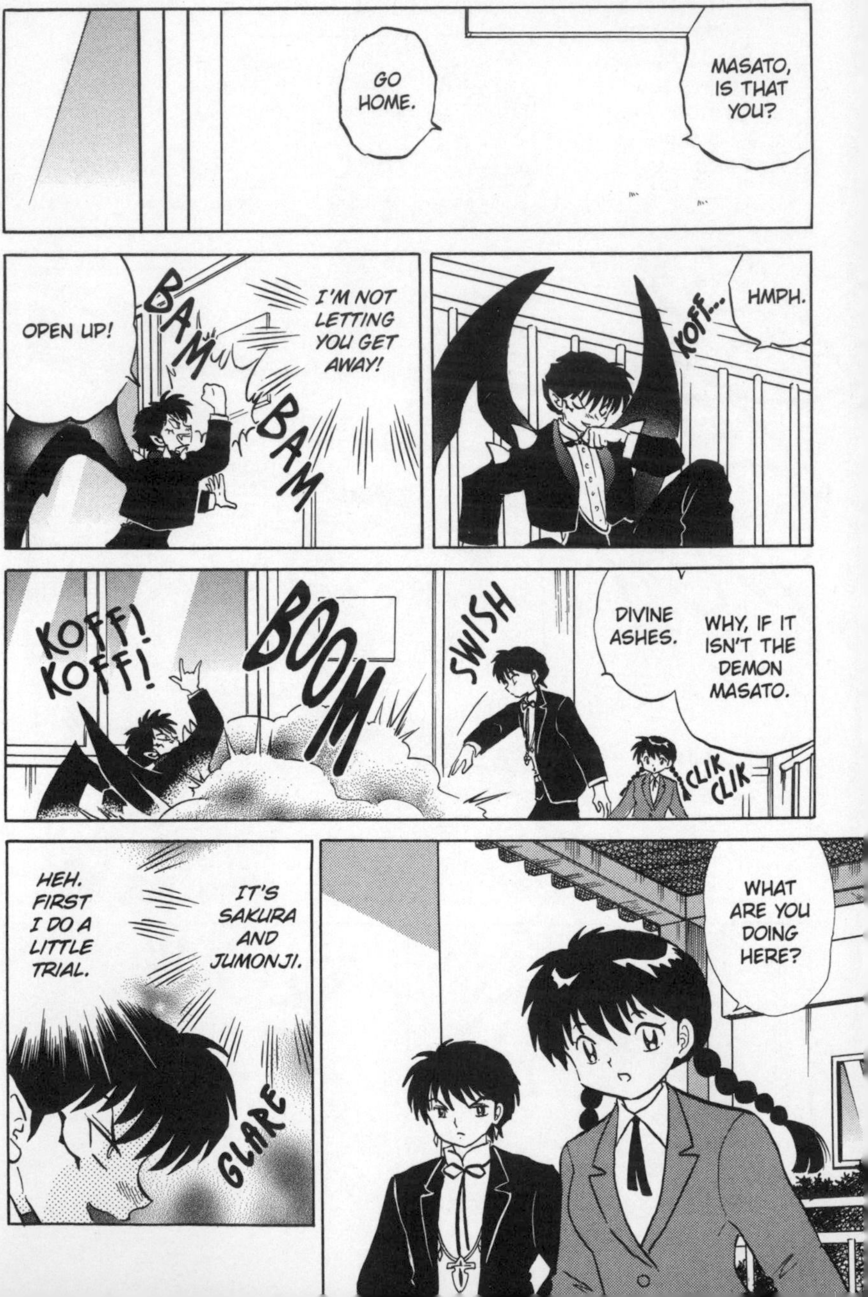
MASATO, IS THAT YOU?
GO HOME.
HMPH.
KOFF...
I'M NOT LETTING YOU GET AWAY!
BAM BAM BAM
OPEN UP!
WHY, IF IT ISN'T THE DEMON MASATO.
DIVINE ASHES.
SWISH
CLIK CLIK
BOOM
KOFF! KOFF!
WHAT ARE YOU DOING HERE?
IT'S SAKURA AND JUMONJI.
HEH. FIRST I DO A LITTLE TRIAL.
GLARE

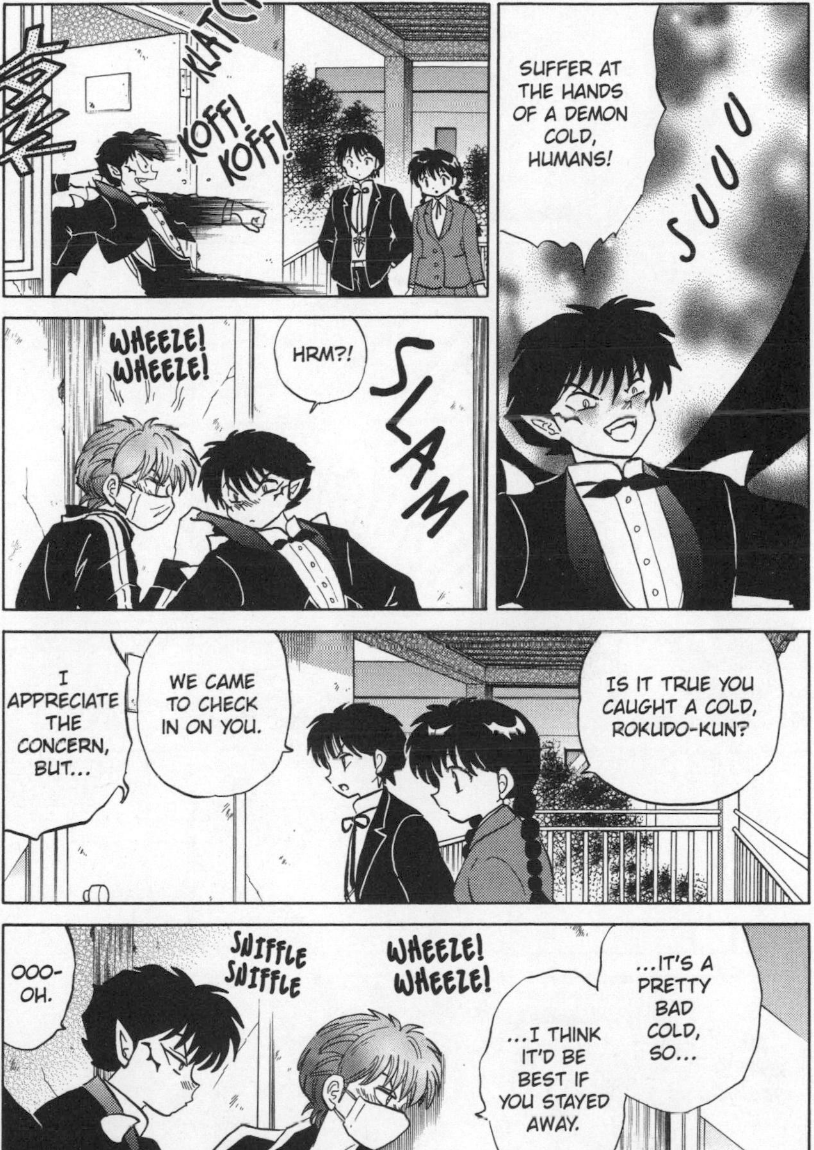
SUFFER AT THE HANDS OF A DEMON COLD, HUMANS!
SUUU
KLATCH
YANK
KOFF! KOFF!
SLAM
HRM?!
WHEEZE! WHEEZE!
IS IT TRUE YOU CAUGHT A COLD, ROKUDO-KUN?
WE CAME TO CHECK IN ON YOU.
I APPRECIATE THE CONCERN, BUT...
...IT'S A PRETTY BAD COLD, SO...
...I THINK IT'D BE BEST IF YOU STAYED AWAY.
WHEEZE! WHEEZE!
SNIFFLE SNIFFLE
OOO-OH.

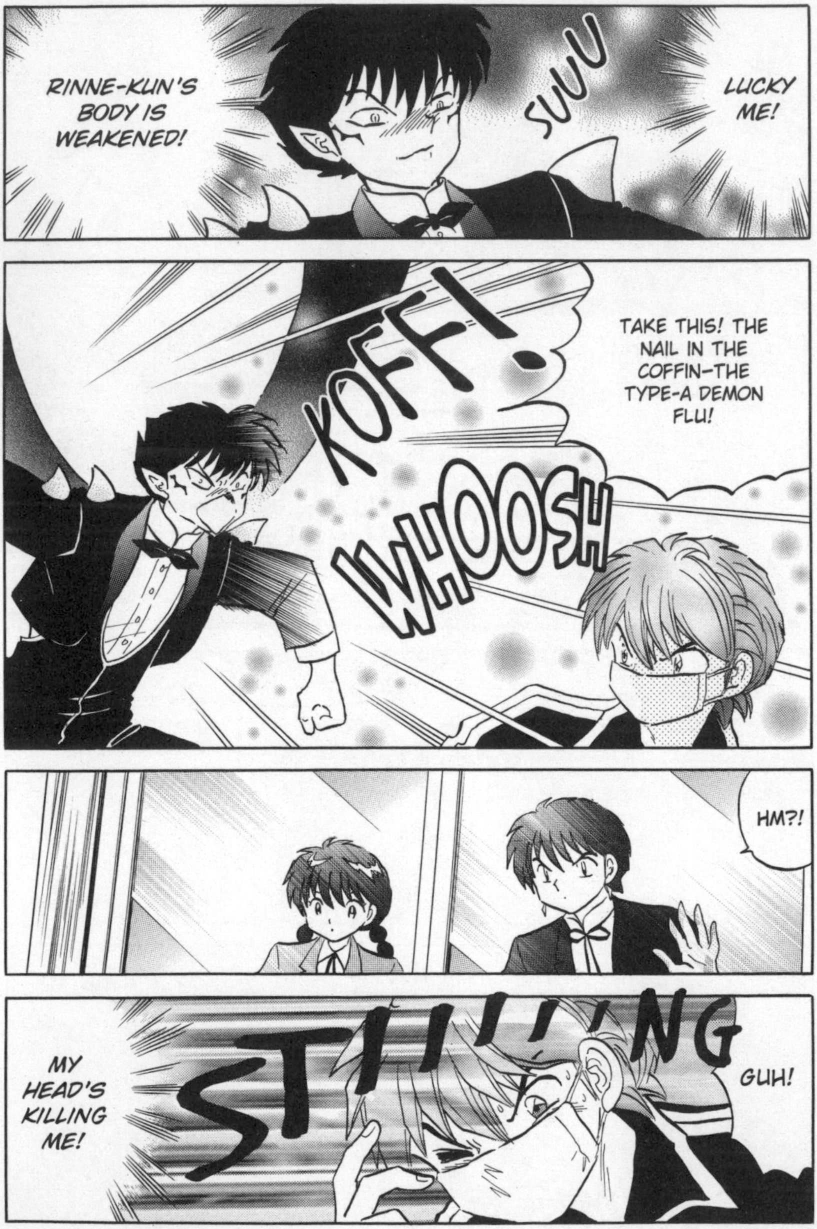
LUCKY ME!
SUUU
RINNE-KUN'S BODY IS WEAKENED!
TAKE THIS! THE NAIL IN THE COFFIN—THE TYPE-A DEMON FLU!
KOFF!
WHOOSH
HM?!
GUH!
STIIIING
MY HEAD'S KILLING ME!

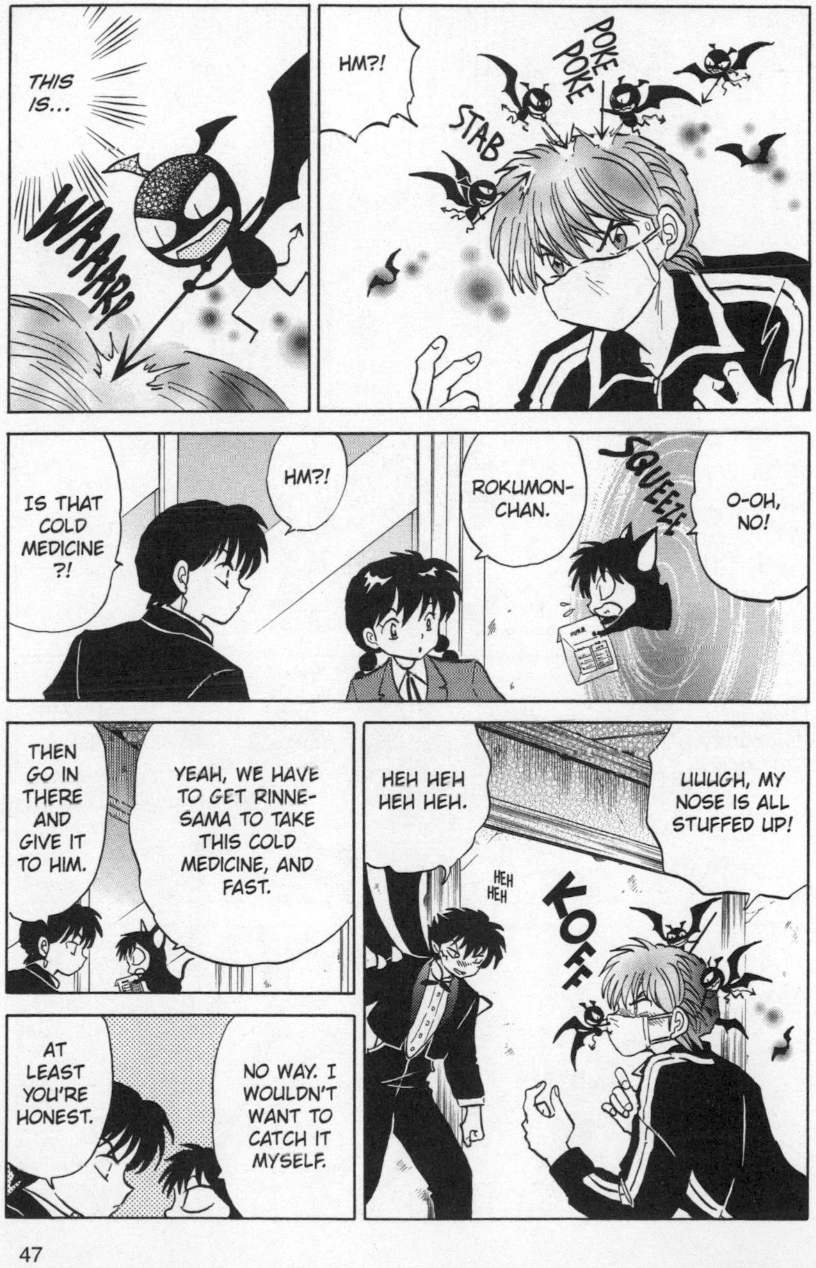
HM?!
POKE POKE
STAB
THIS IS...
WAAARR
O-OH, NO!
SQUEEZE
ROKUMON-CHAN.
HM?!
IS THAT COLD MEDICINE?!
UUUGH, MY NOSE IS ALL STUFFED UP!
HEH HEH HEH HEH.
HEH HEH
KOFF
YEAH, WE HAVE TO GET RINNE-SAMA TO TAKE THIS COLD MEDICINE, AND FAST.
THEN GO IN THERE AND GIVE IT TO HIM.
NO WAY. I WOULDN'T WANT TO CATCH IT MYSELF.
AT LEAST YOU'RE HONEST.

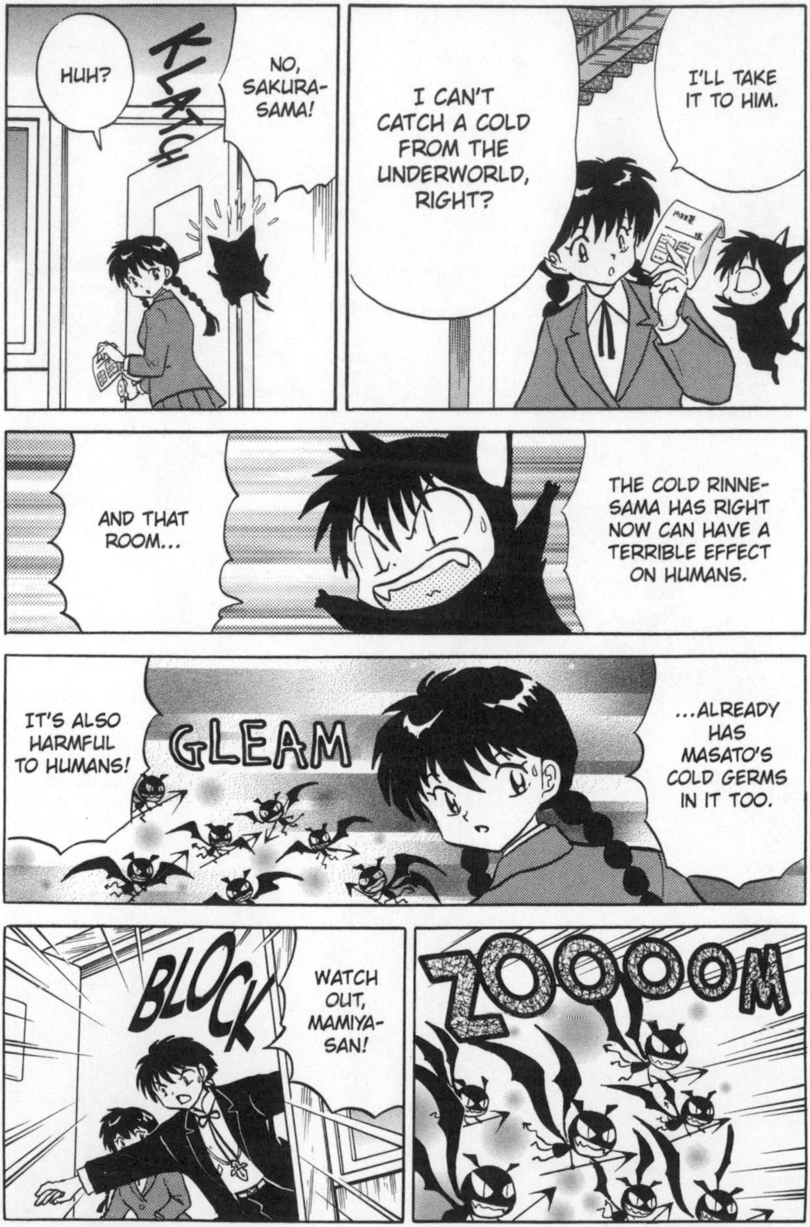
I'LL TAKE IT TO HIM.
I CAN'T CATCH A COLD FROM THE UNDERWORLD, RIGHT?
NO, SAKURA-SAMA!
KLATCH
HUH?
THE COLD RINNE-SAMA HAS RIGHT NOW CAN HAVE A TERRIBLE EFFECT ON HUMANS.
AND THAT ROOM...
...ALREADY HAS MASATO'S COLD GERMS IN IT TOO.
GLEAM
IT'S ALSO HARMFUL TO HUMANS!
ZOOOOOM
WATCH OUT, MAMIYA-SAN!
BLOCK

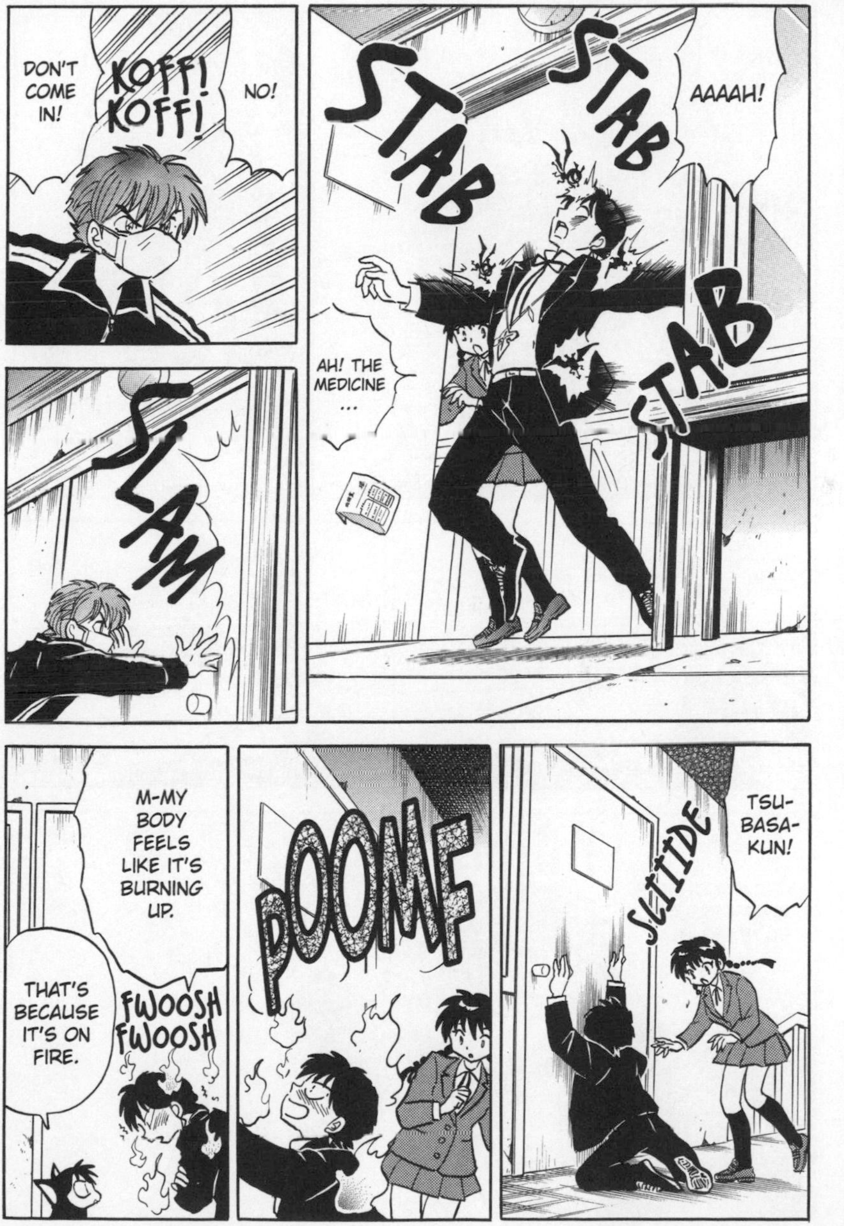
STAB
STAB
AAAAH!
STAB
AH! THE MEDICINE ...
DON'T COME IN!
KOFF! KOFF!
NO!
SLAM
TSU-BASA-KUN!
SLIIIDE
POOMF
M-MY BODY FEELS LIKE IT'S BURNING UP.
FWOOSH FWOOSH
THAT'S BECAUSE IT'S ON FIRE.

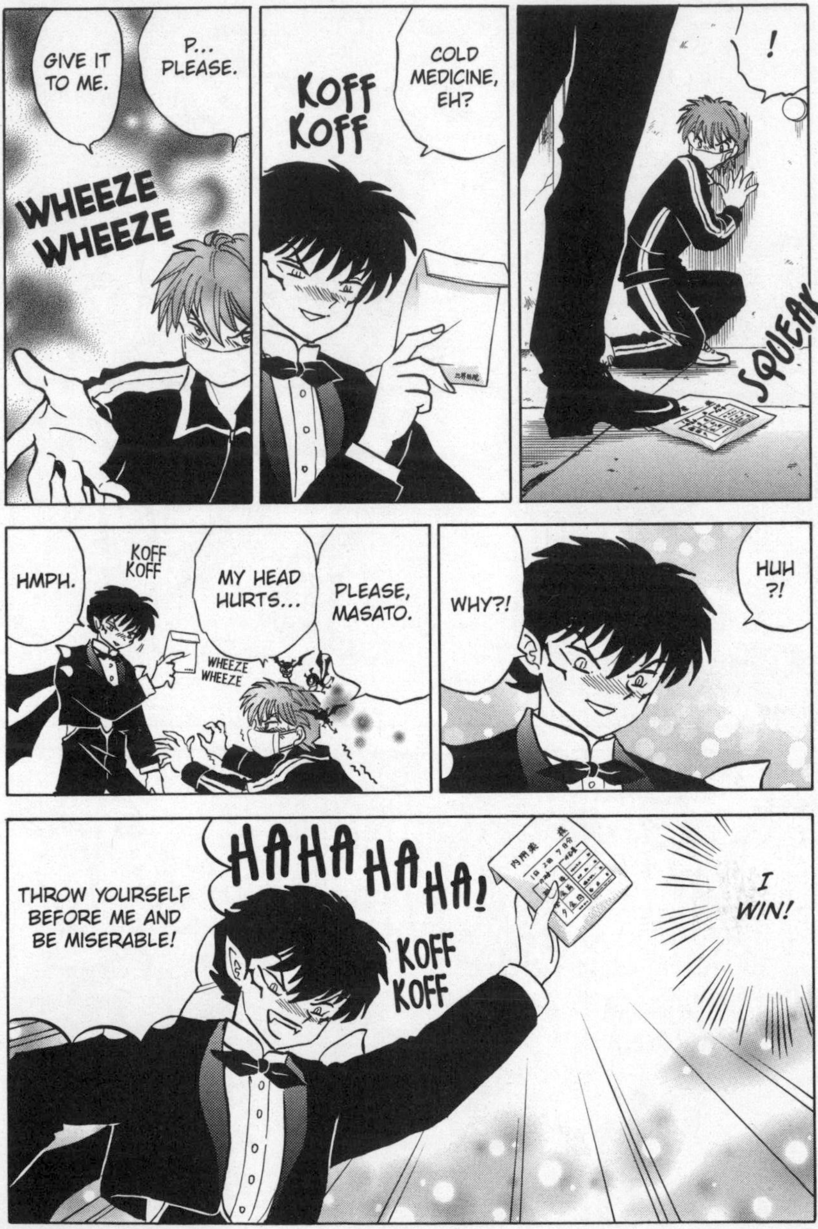
!
SQUEAK
COLD MEDICINE, EH?
KOFF KOFF
P... PLEASE.
GIVE IT TO ME.
WHEEZE WHEEZE
HUH ?!
WHY?!
PLEASE, MASATO.
MY HEAD HURTS...
WHEEZE WHEEZE
KOFF KOFF
HMPH.
I WIN!
HAHAHAHA!
KOFF KOFF
THROW YOURSELF BEFORE ME AND BE MISERABLE!

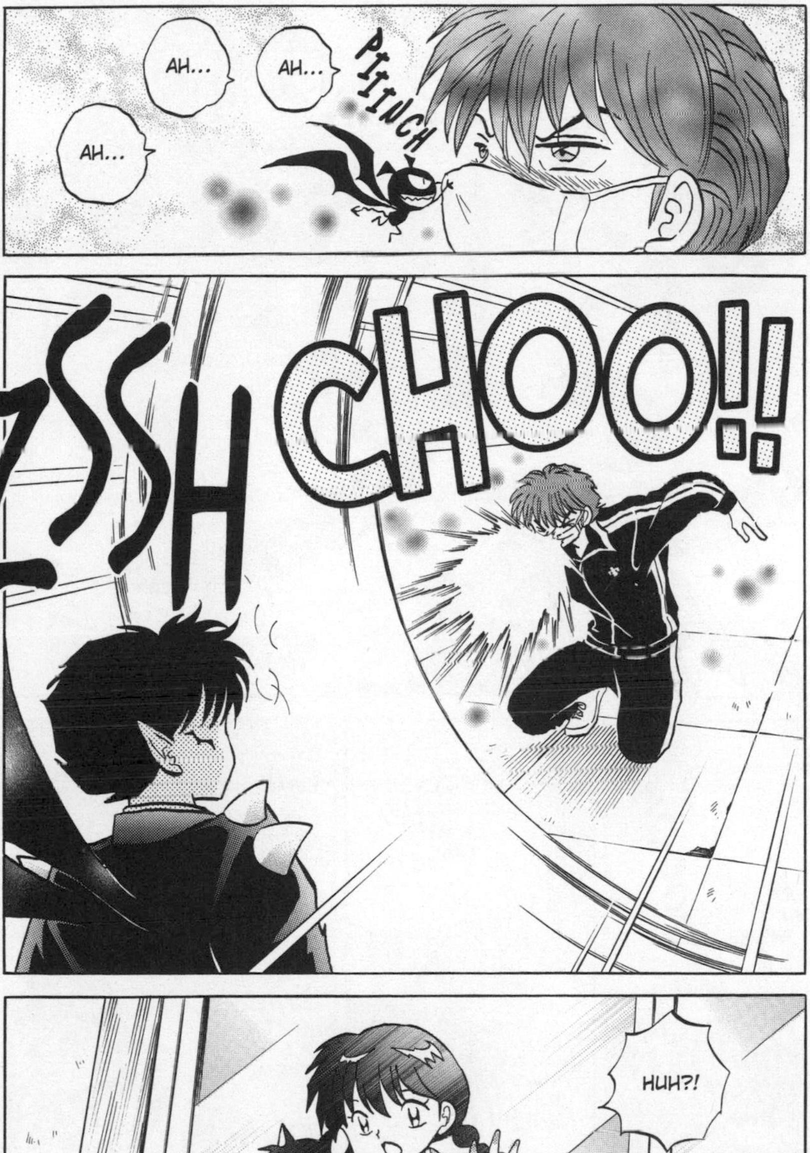
PIIINCH
AH...
AH...
AH...
ZSSH CHOO!!
HUH?!

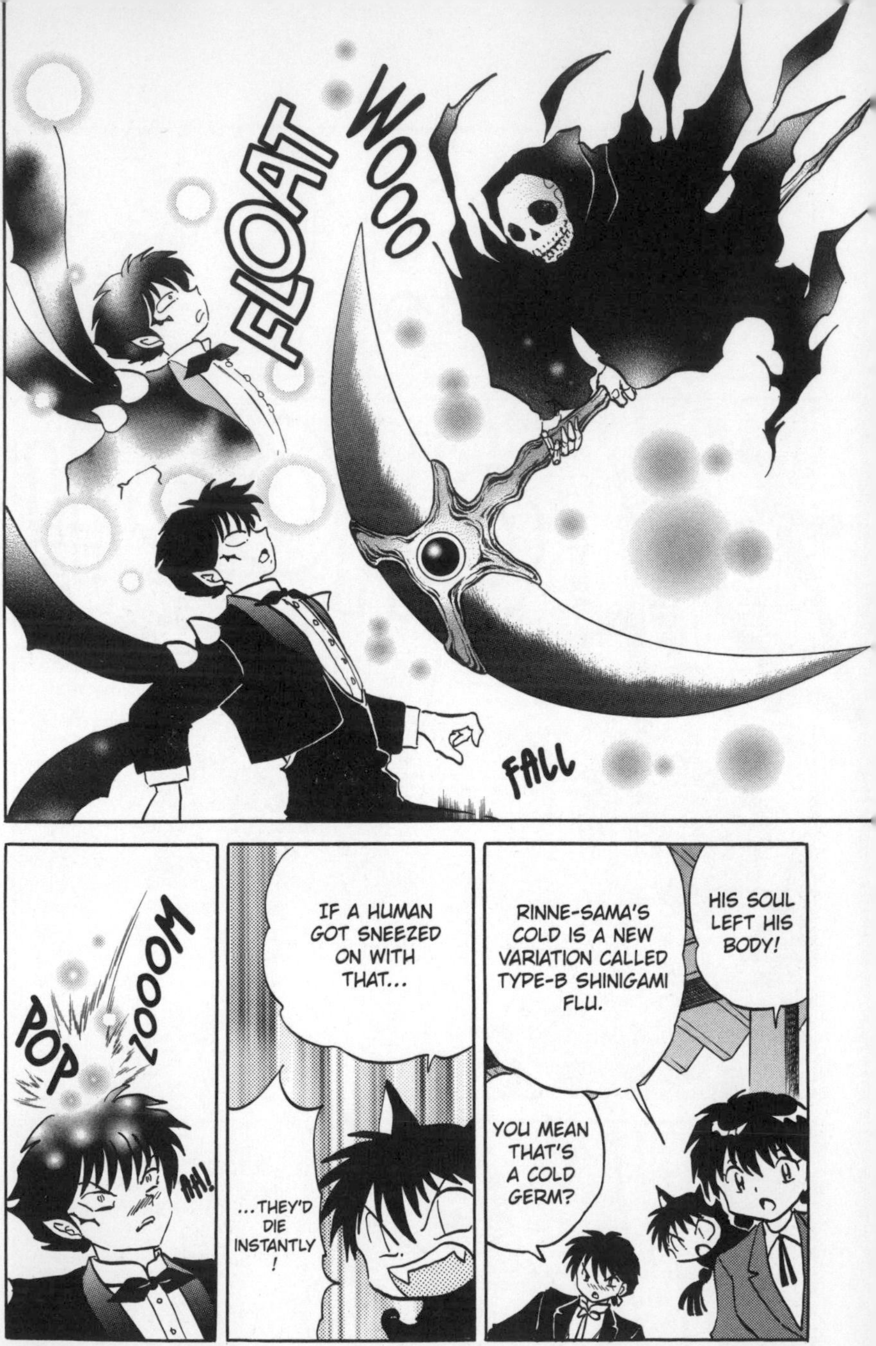
WOOO
FLOAT
FALL
HIS SOUL LEFT HIS BODY!
RINNE-SAMA'S COLD IS A NEW VARIATION CALLED TYPE-B SHINIGAMI FLU.
YOU MEAN THAT'S A COLD GERM?
IF A HUMAN GOT SNEEZED ON WITH THAT...
...THEY'D DIE INSTANTLY!
ZOOOOM
POP
AH!

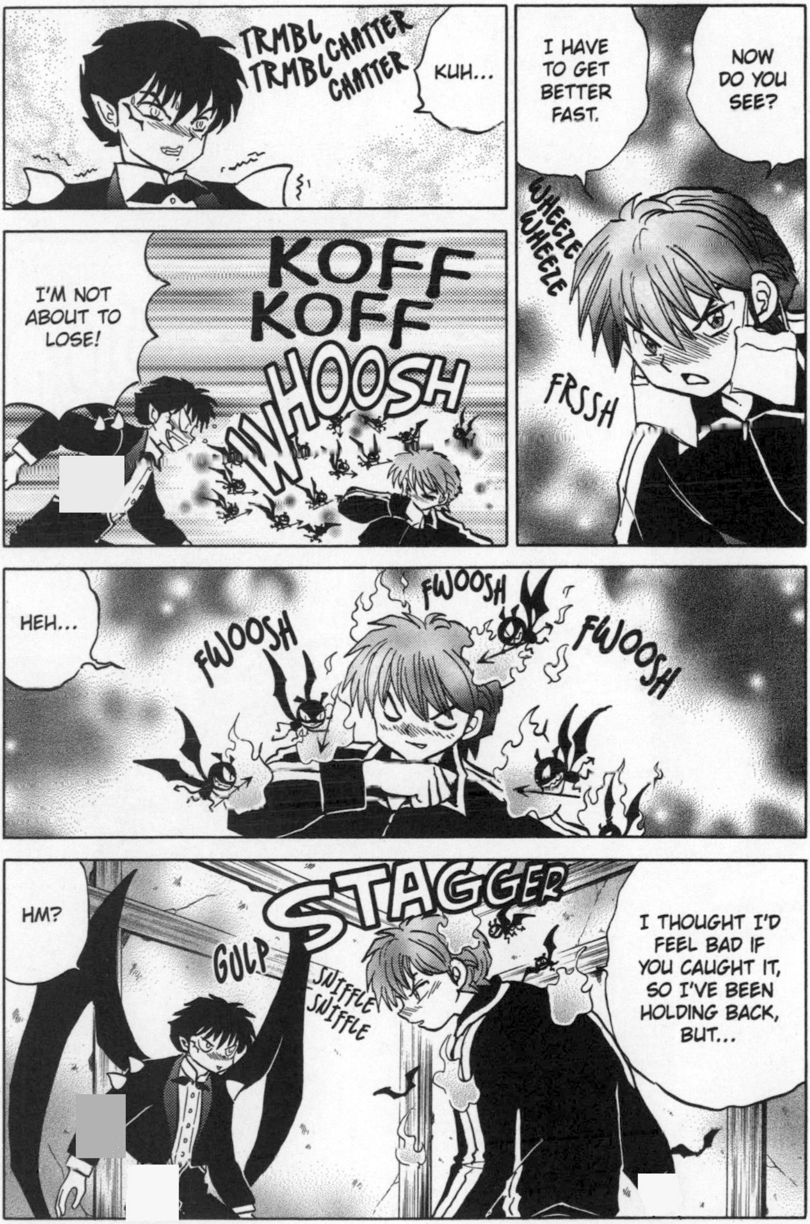
NOW DO YOU SEE?
I HAVE TO GET BETTER FAST.
WHEEZE WHEEZE
FRSSH
KUH...
CHATTER CHATTER
TRMBL TRMBL
KOFF KOFF
I'M NOT ABOUT TO LOSE!
WHOOSH
FWOOSH
FWOOSH
FWOOSH
HEH...
I THOUGHT I'D FEEL BAD IF YOU CAUGHT IT, SO I'VE BEEN HOLDING BACK, BUT...
STAGGER
SNIFFLE SNIFFLE
GULP
HM?

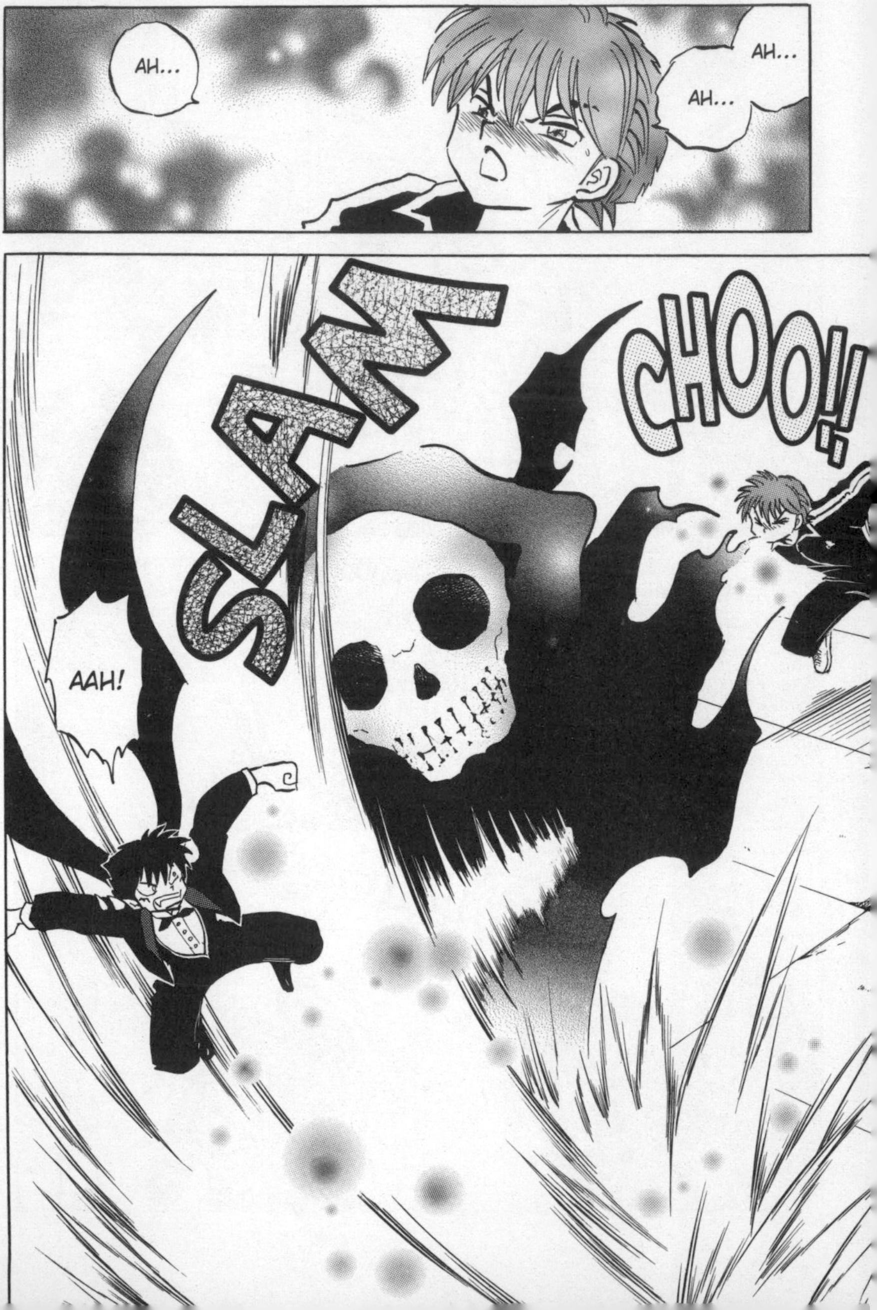
AH... AH...
AH...
CHOO!!
SLAM
AAH!

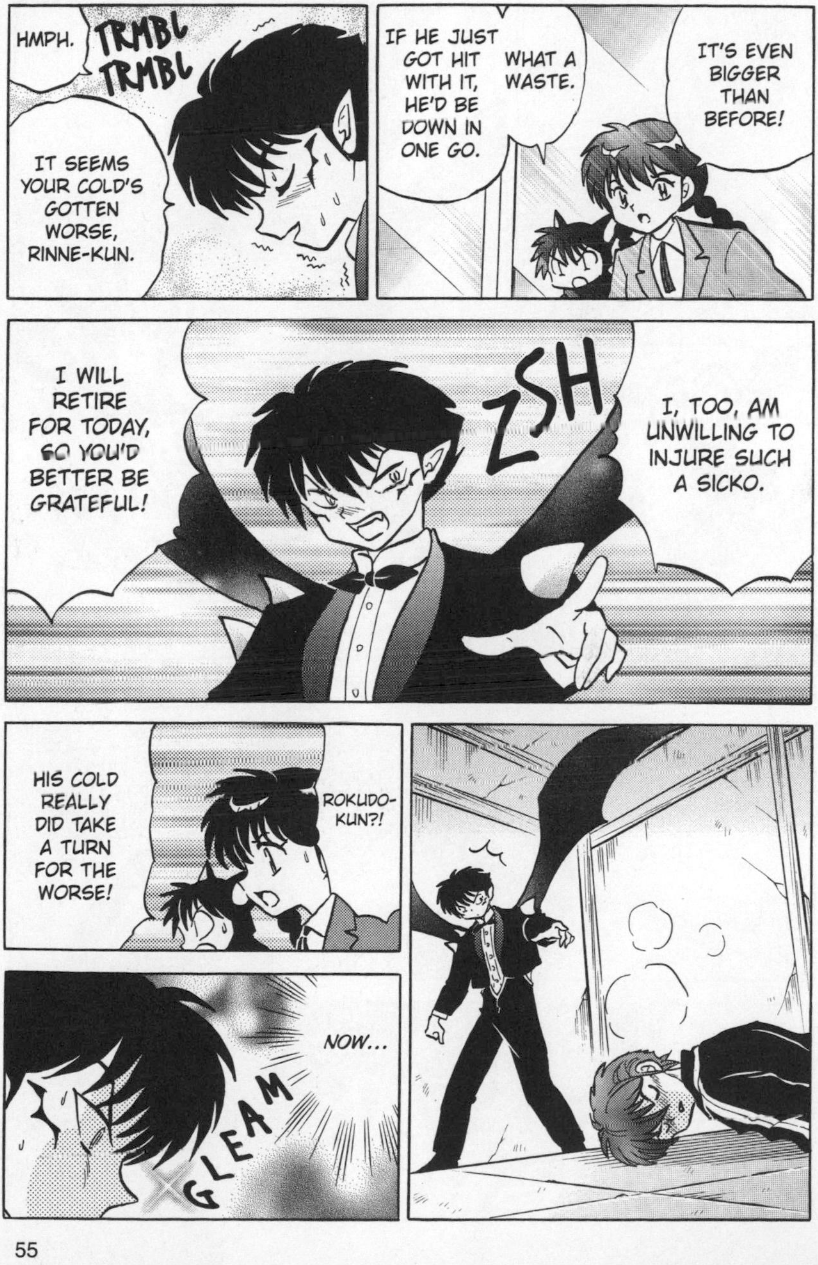
IT'S EVEN BIGGER THAN BEFORE!
WHAT A WASTE.
IF HE JUST GOT HIT WITH IT, HE'D BE DOWN IN ONE GO.
HMPH.
TRMBL TRMBL
IT SEEMS YOUR COLD'S GOTTEN WORSE, RINNE-KUN.
I, TOO, AM UNWILLING TO INJURE SUCH A SICKO.
ZSH
I WILL RETIRE FOR TODAY, SO YOU'D BETTER BE GRATEFUL!
ROKUDO-KUN?!
HIS COLD REALLY DID TAKE A TURN FOR THE WORSE!
NOW...
GLEAM

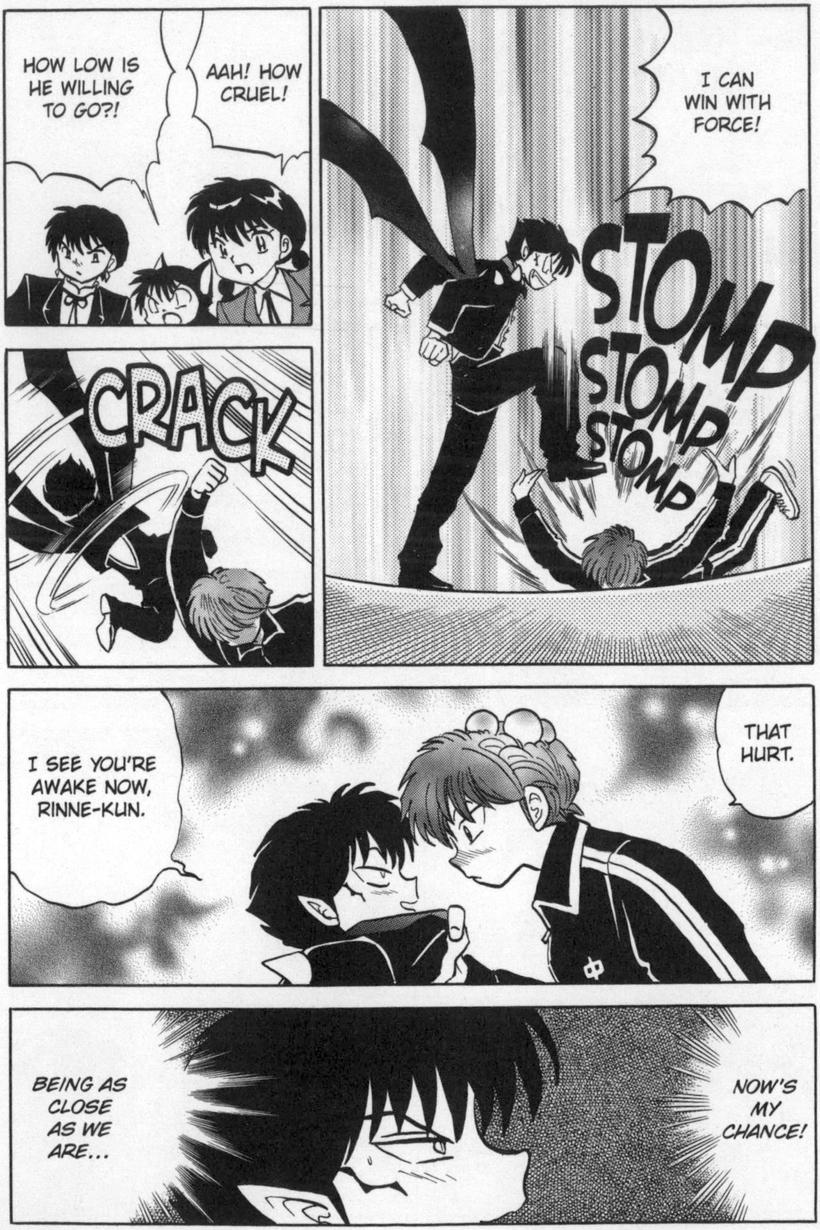
I CAN WIN WITH FORCE!
STOMP
STOMP
STOMP
STOMP
AAH! HOW CRUEL!
HOW LOW IS HE WILLING TO GO?!
CRACK
THAT HURT.
I SEE YOU'RE AWAKE NOW, RINNE-KUN.
NOW'S MY CHANCE!
BEING AS CLOSE AS WE ARE...

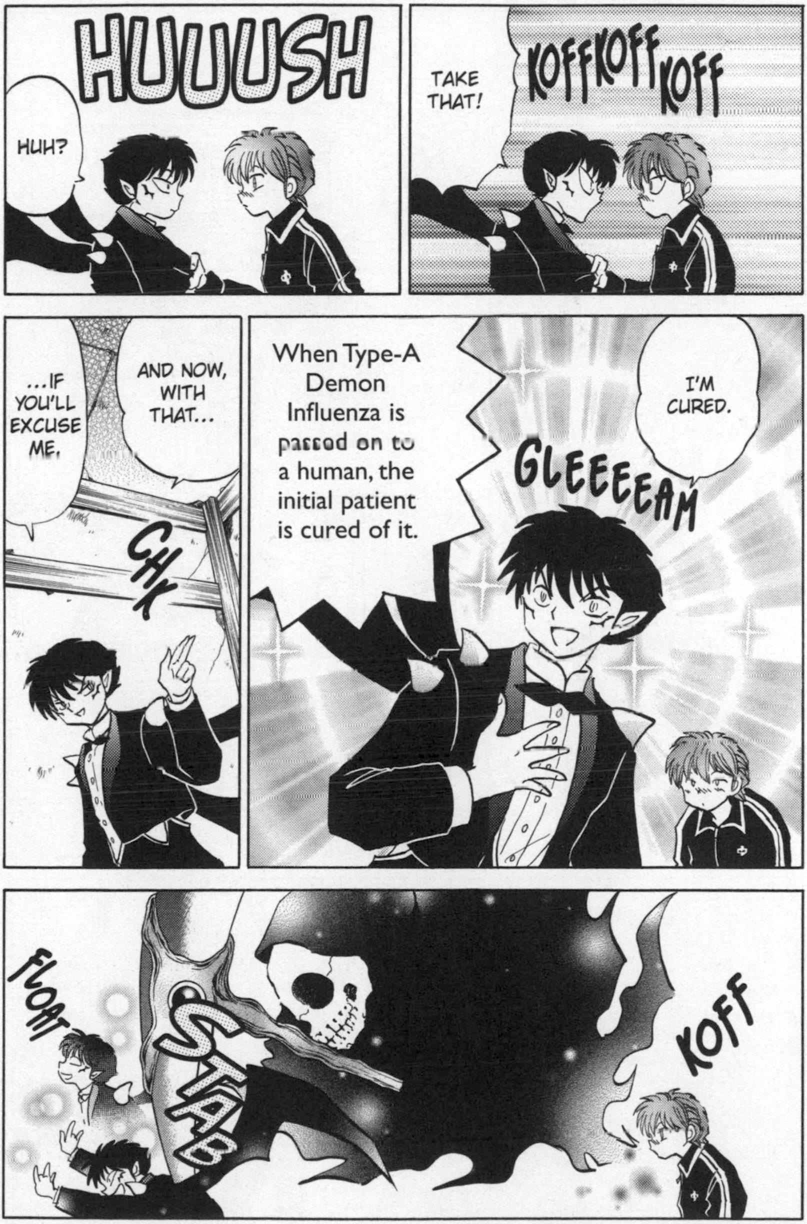
TAKE THAT!
KOFFKOFFKOFF
HUUUSH
HUH?
I'M CURED.
When Type-A Demon Influenza is passed on to a human, the initial patient is cured of it.
GLEEEEEAM
AND NOW, WITH THAT...
...IF YOU'LL EXCUSE ME.
CHK
KOFF
STAB
FLOAT

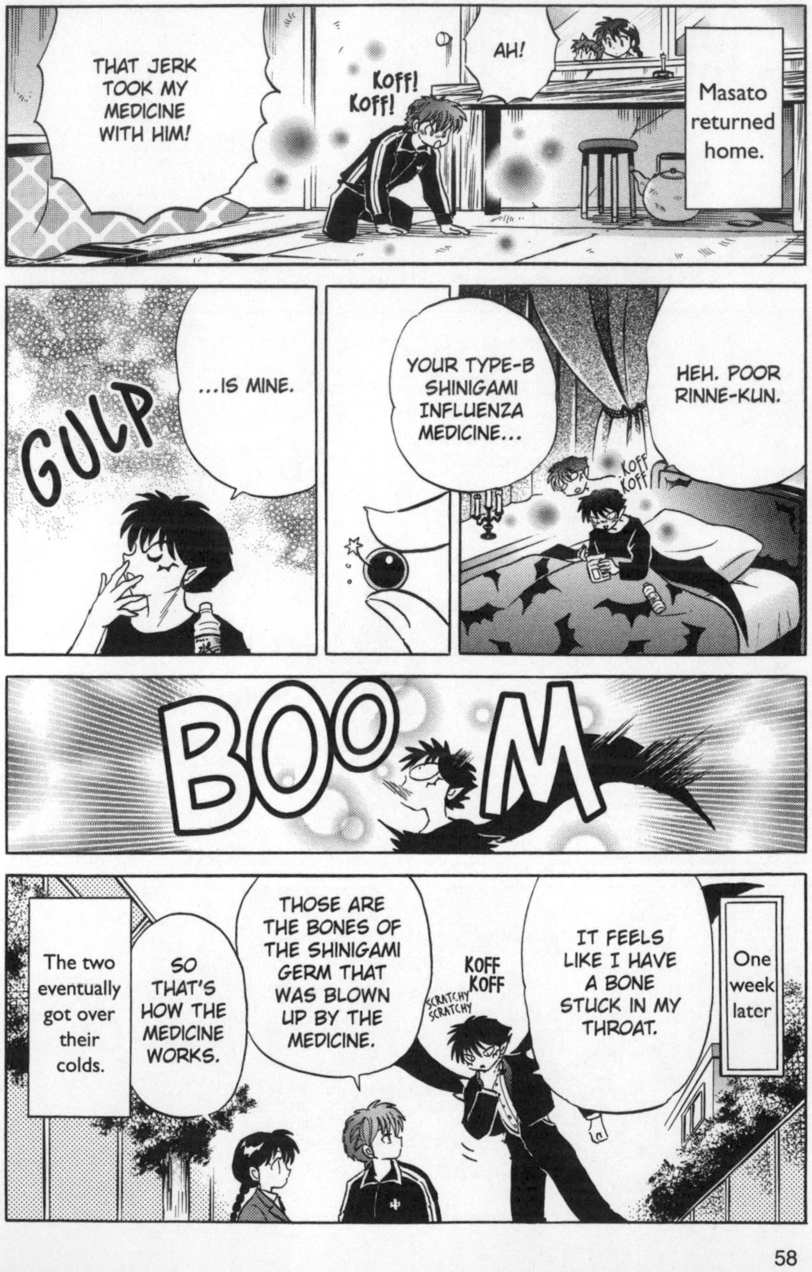
Masato returned home.
AH!
KOFF! KOFF!
THAT JERK TOOK MY MEDICINE WITH HIM!
HEH. POOR RINNE-KUN.
KOFF KOFF
YOUR TYPE-B SHINIGAMI INFLUENZA MEDICINE...
...IS MINE.
GULP
BOOM
One week later
IT FEELS LIKE I HAVE A BONE STUCK IN MY THROAT.
KOFF KOFF
SCRATCHY SCRATCHY
THOSE ARE THE BONES OF THE SHINIGAMI GERM THAT WAS BLOWN UP BY THE MEDICINE.
SO THAT'S HOW THE MEDICINE WORKS.
The two eventually got over their colds.

CHAPTER 182: WHO ARE YOU?!

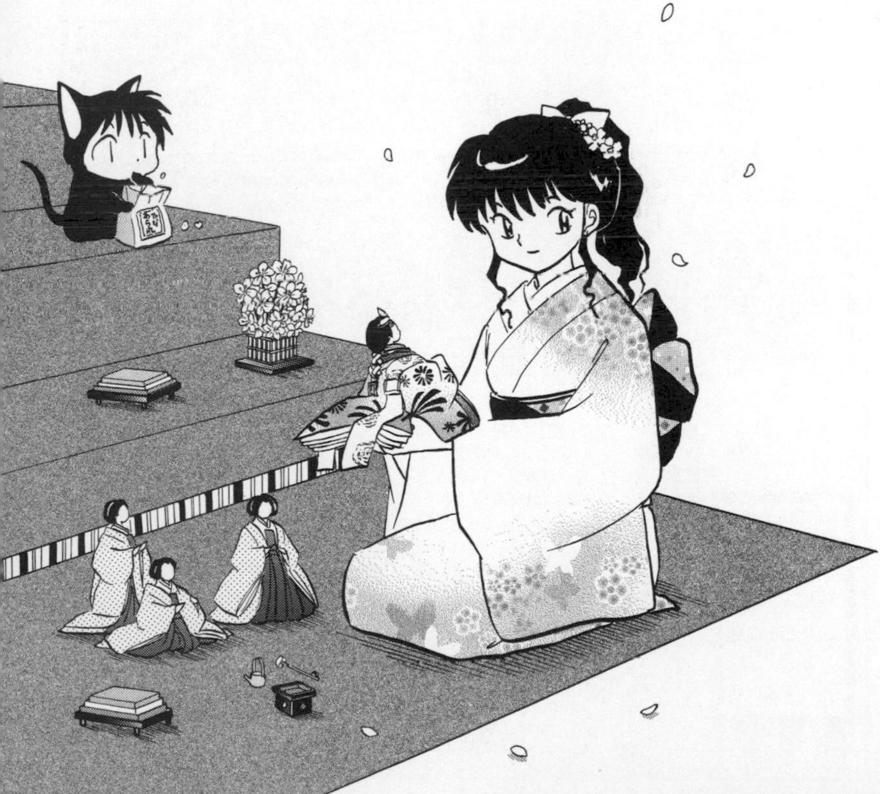

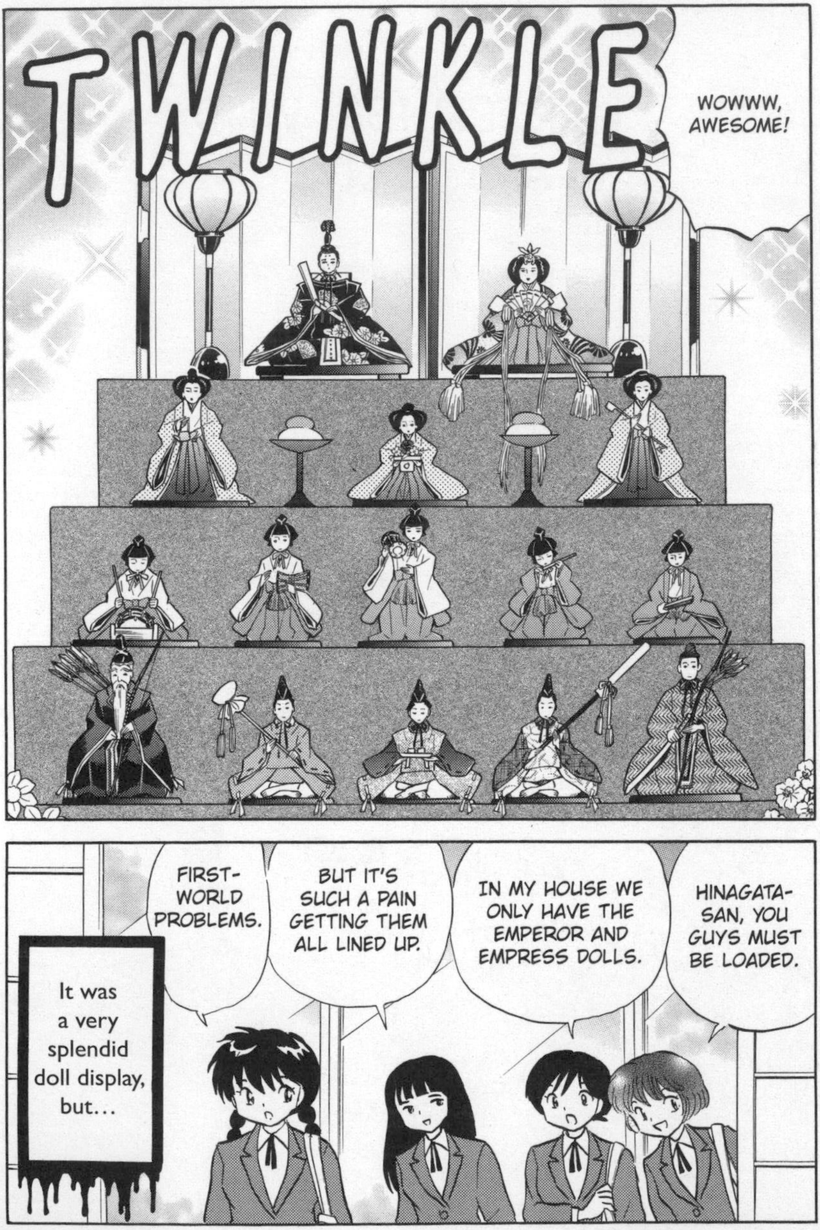
TWINKLE
WOWWW, AWESOME!
HINAGATA-SAN, YOU GUYS MUST BE LOADED.
IN MY HOUSE WE ONLY HAVE THE EMPEROR AND EMPRESS DOLLS.
BUT IT'S SUCH A PAIN GETTING THEM ALL LINED UP.
FIRST-WORLD PROBLEMS.
It was a very splendid doll display, but…

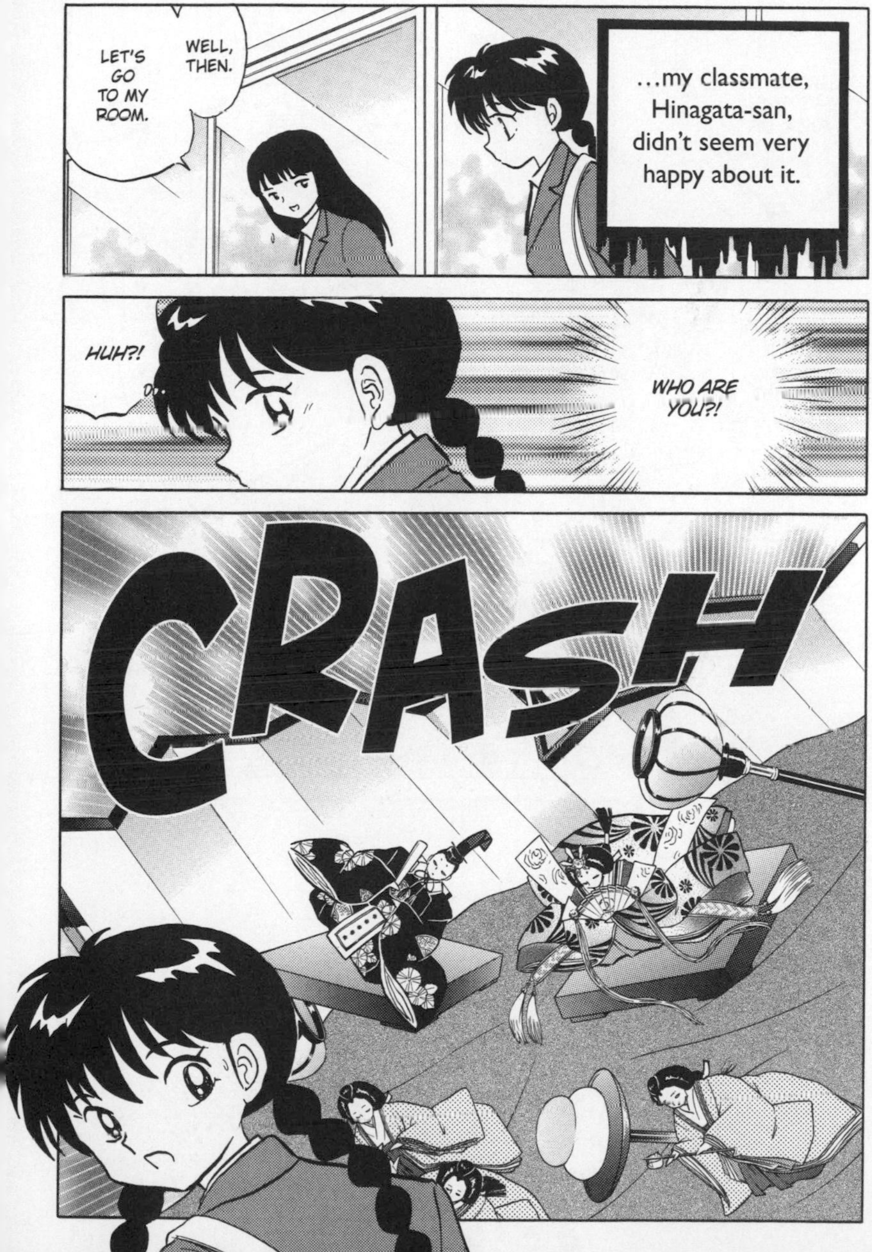
…my classmate, Hinagata-san, didn't seem very happy about it.
WELL, THEN.
LET'S GO TO MY ROOM.
WHO ARE YOU?!
HUH?!
CRASH

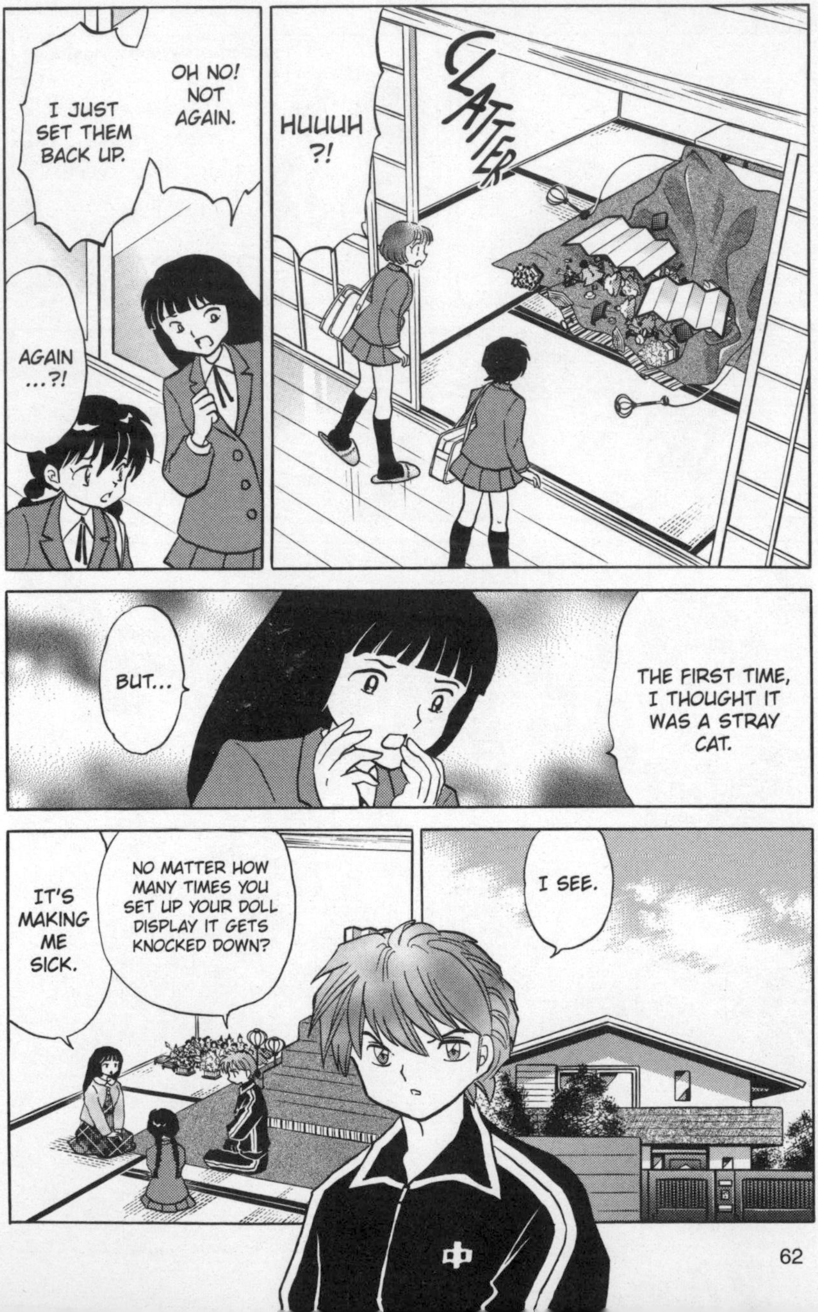
CLATTER
HUUUH ?!
OH NO! NOT AGAIN.
I JUST SET THEM BACK UP.
AGAIN ...?!
THE FIRST TIME, I THOUGHT IT WAS A STRAY CAT.
BUT...
I SEE.
NO MATTER HOW MANY TIMES YOU SET UP YOUR DOLL DISPLAY IT GETS KNOCKED DOWN?
IT'S MAKING ME SICK.
中

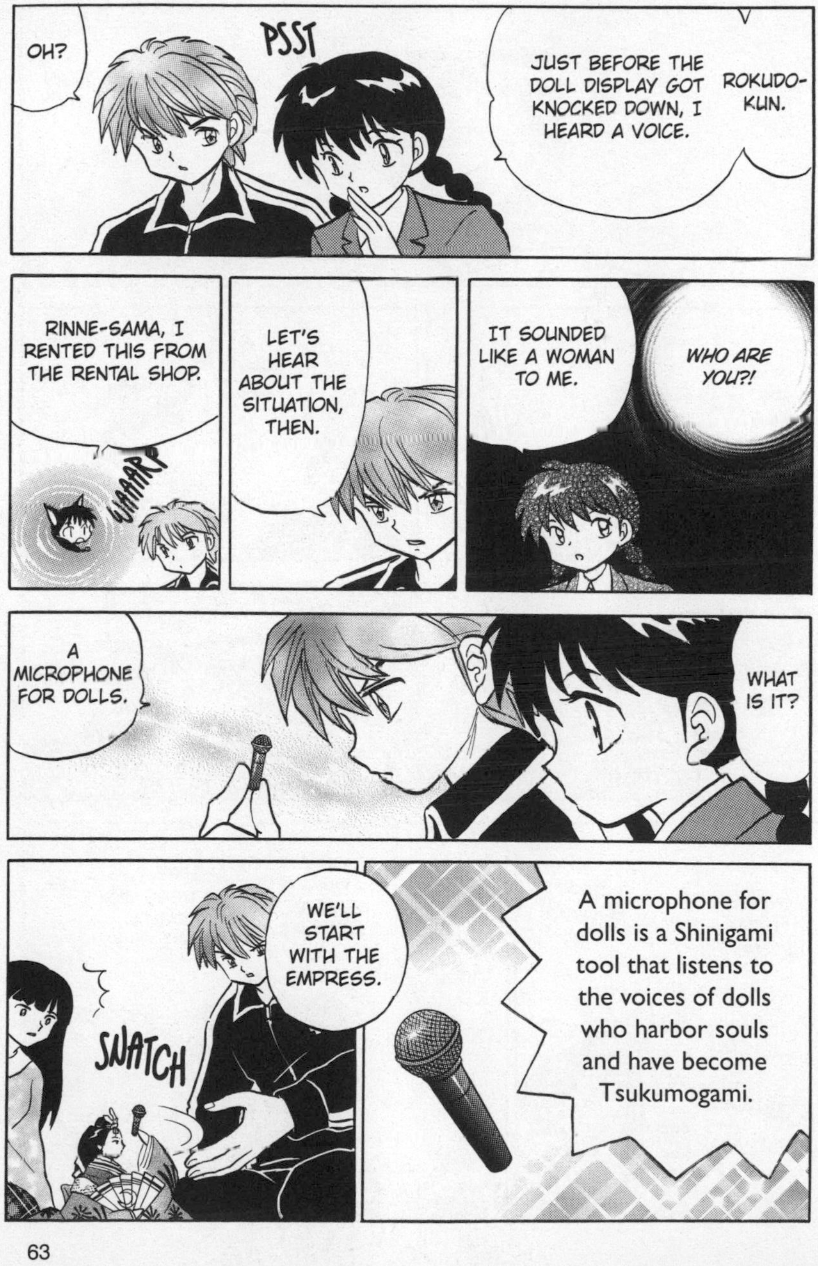
ROKUDO-KUN.
JUST BEFORE THE DOLL DISPLAY GOT KNOCKED DOWN, I HEARD A VOICE.
PSST
OH?
WHO ARE YOU?!
IT SOUNDED LIKE A WOMAN TO ME.
LET'S HEAR ABOUT THE SITUATION, THEN.
RINNE-SAMA, I RENTED THIS FROM THE RENTAL SHOP.
WHAARP
WHAT IS IT?
A MICROPHONE FOR DOLLS.
A microphone for dolls is a Shinigami tool that listens to the voices of dolls who harbor souls and have become Tsukumogami.
WE'LL START WITH THE EMPRESS.
SNATCH

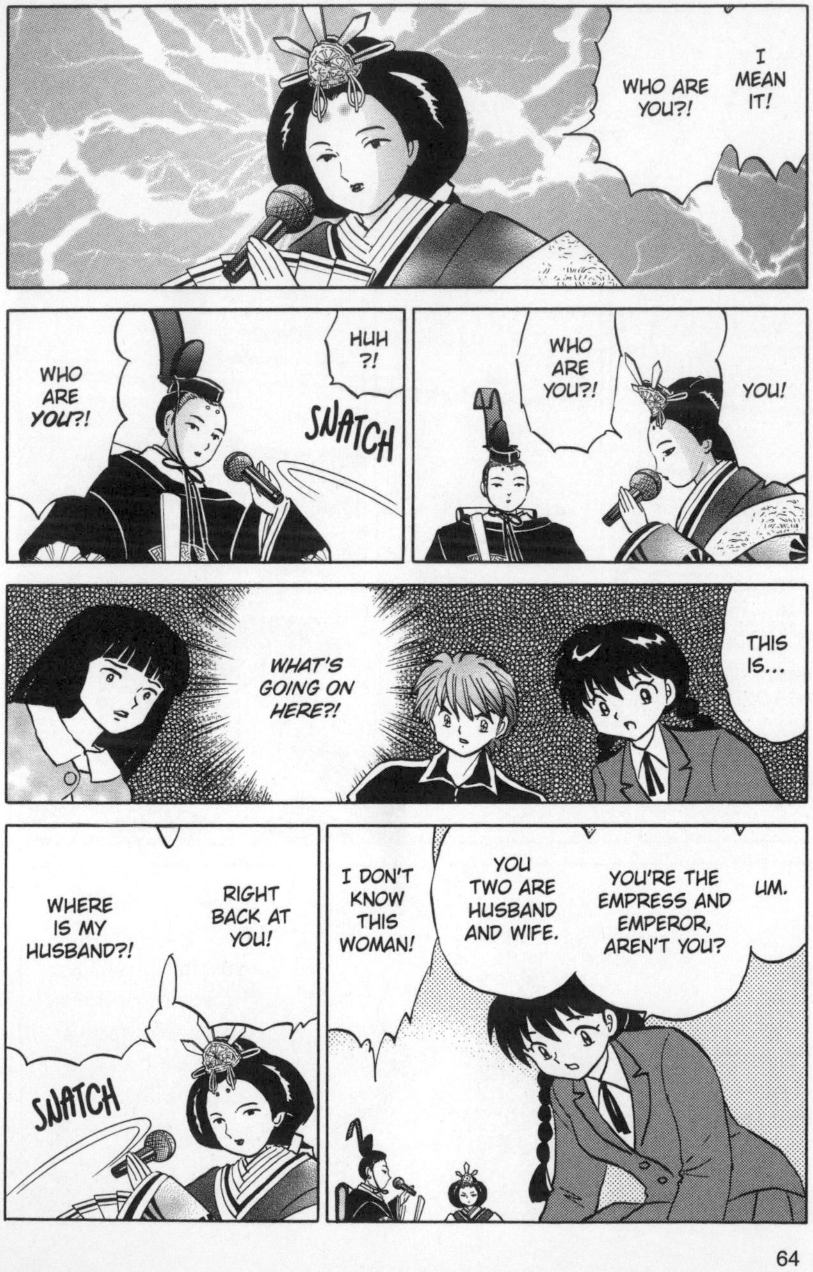
I MEAN IT!
WHO ARE YOU?!
YOU!
WHO ARE YOU?!
HUH ?!
SNATCH
WHO ARE YOU?!
THIS IS...
WHAT'S GOING ON HERE?!
UM.
YOU'RE THE EMPRESS AND EMPEROR, AREN'T YOU?
YOU TWO ARE HUSBAND AND WIFE.
I DON'T KNOW THIS WOMAN!
RIGHT BACK AT YOU!
WHERE IS MY HUSBAND?!
SNATCH

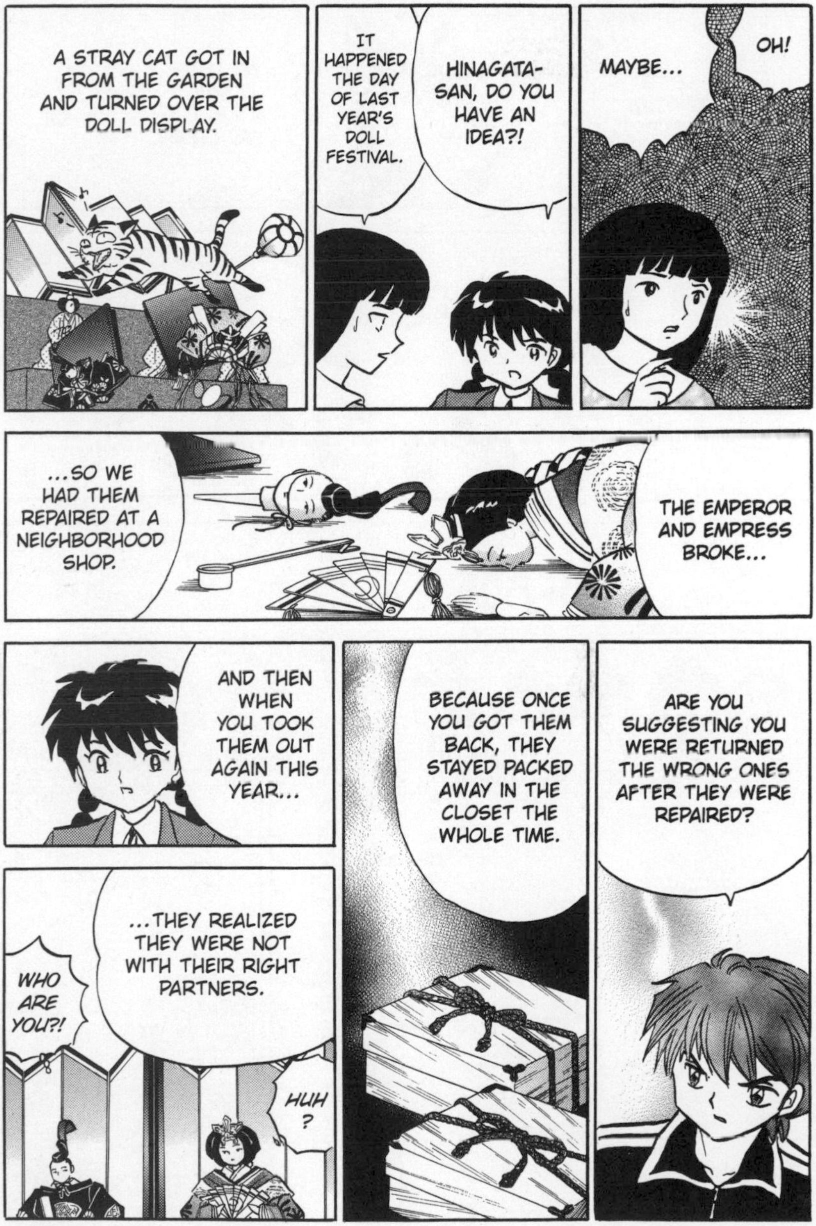
OH!
MAYBE...
HINAGATA-SAN, DO YOU HAVE AN IDEA?!
IT HAPPENED THE DAY OF LAST YEAR'S DOLL FESTIVAL.
A STRAY CAT GOT IN FROM THE GARDEN AND TURNED OVER THE DOLL DISPLAY.
THE EMPEROR AND EMPRESS BROKE...
...SO WE HAD THEM REPAIRED AT A NEIGHBORHOOD SHOP.
ARE YOU SUGGESTING YOU WERE RETURNED THE WRONG ONES AFTER THEY WERE REPAIRED?
BECAUSE ONCE YOU GOT THEM BACK, THEY STAYED PACKED AWAY IN THE CLOSET THE WHOLE TIME.
AND THEN WHEN YOU TOOK THEM OUT AGAIN THIS YEAR...
...THEY REALIZED THEY WERE NOT WITH THEIR RIGHT PARTNERS.
WHO ARE YOU?!
HUH ?

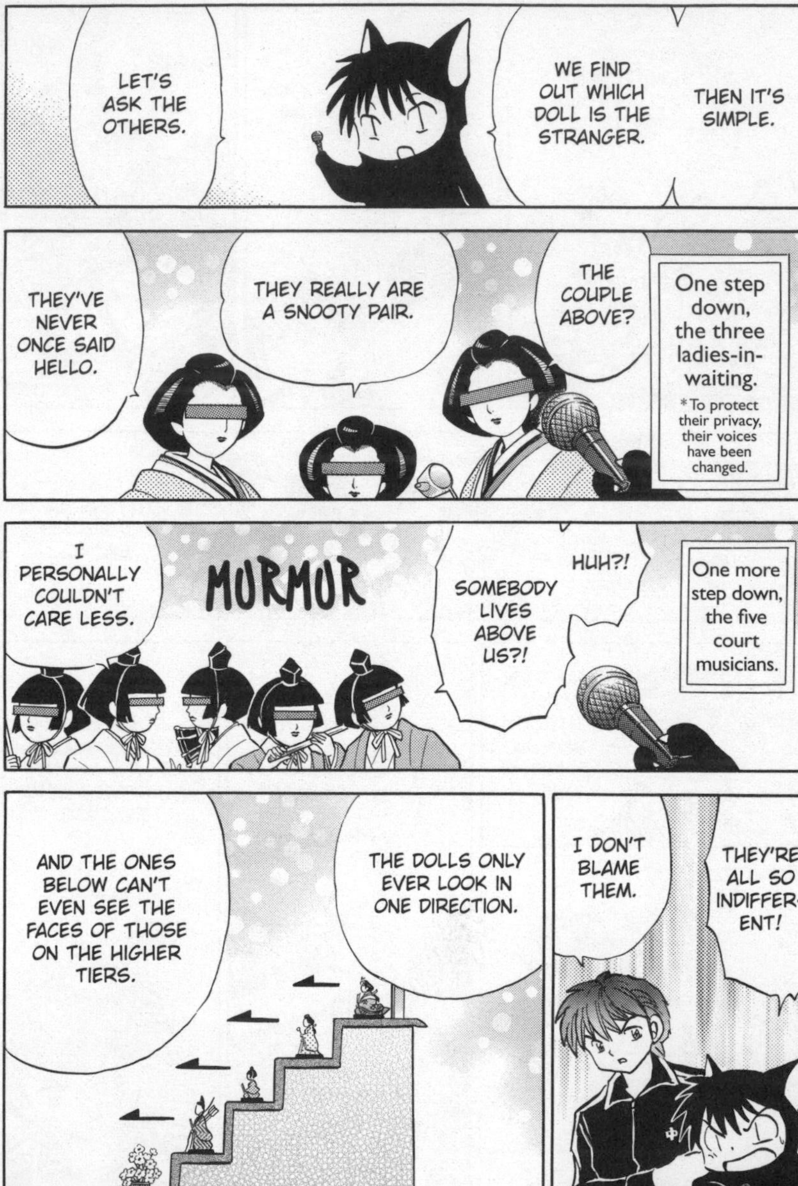
THEN IT'S SIMPLE.
WE FIND OUT WHICH DOLL IS THE STRANGER.
LET'S ASK THE OTHERS.
One step down, the three ladies-in-waiting.
*To protect their privacy, their voices have been changed.
THE COUPLE ABOVE?
THEY REALLY ARE A SNOOTY PAIR.
THEY'VE NEVER ONCE SAID HELLO.
One more step down, the five court musicians.
HUH?!
SOMEBODY LIVES ABOVE US?!
MURMOR
I PERSONALLY COULDN'T CARE LESS.
THEY'RE ALL SO INDIFFER-ENT!
I DON'T BLAME THEM.
THE DOLLS ONLY EVER LOOK IN ONE DIRECTION.
AND THE ONES BELOW CAN'T EVEN SEE THE FACES OF THOSE ON THE HIGHER TIERS.

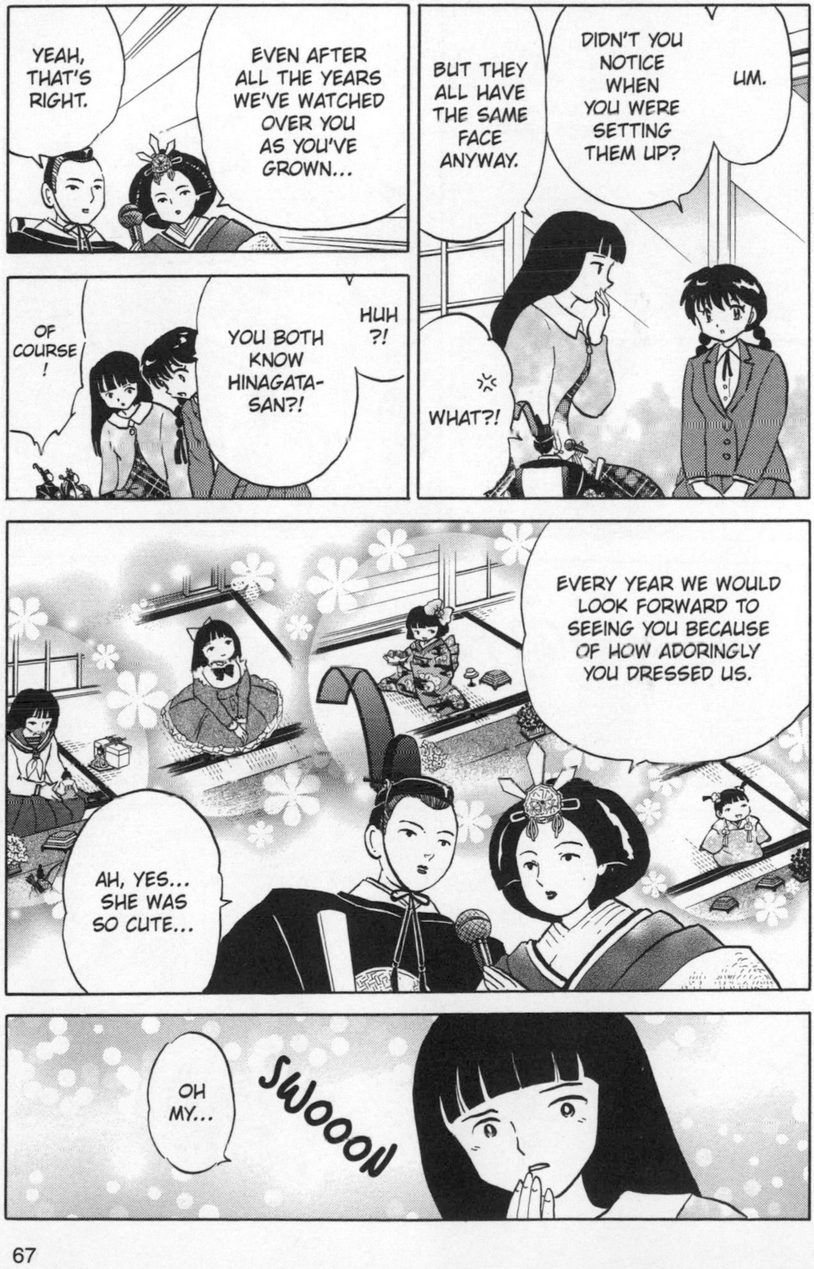
UM.
DIDN'T YOU NOTICE WHEN YOU WERE SETTING THEM UP?
BUT THEY ALL HAVE THE SAME FACE ANYWAY.
WHAT?!
EVEN AFTER ALL THE YEARS WE'VE WATCHED OVER YOU AS YOU'VE GROWN...
YEAH, THAT'S RIGHT.
HUH?!
YOU BOTH KNOW HINAGATA-SAN?!
OF COURSE!
EVERY YEAR WE WOULD LOOK FORWARD TO SEEING YOU BECAUSE OF HOW ADORINGLY YOU DRESSED US.
AH, YES... SHE WAS SO CUTE...
SWOOOON
OH MY...

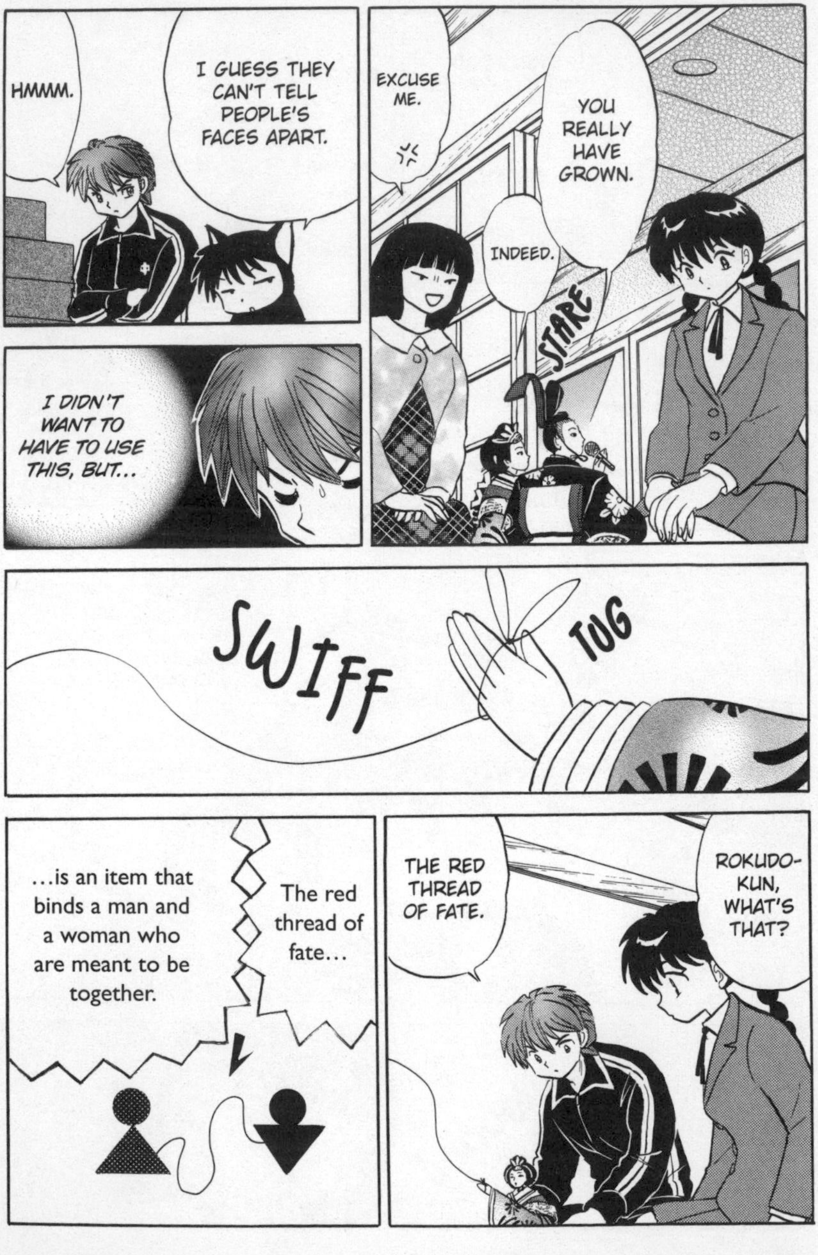
YOU REALLY HAVE GROWN.
EXCUSE ME.
INDEED.
STARE
I GUESS THEY CAN'T TELL PEOPLE'S FACES APART.
HMMM.
I DIDN'T WANT TO HAVE TO USE THIS, BUT...
TUG
SWIFF
ROKUDO-KUN, WHAT'S THAT?
THE RED THREAD OF FATE.
The red thread of fate...
...is an item that binds a man and a woman who are meant to be together.

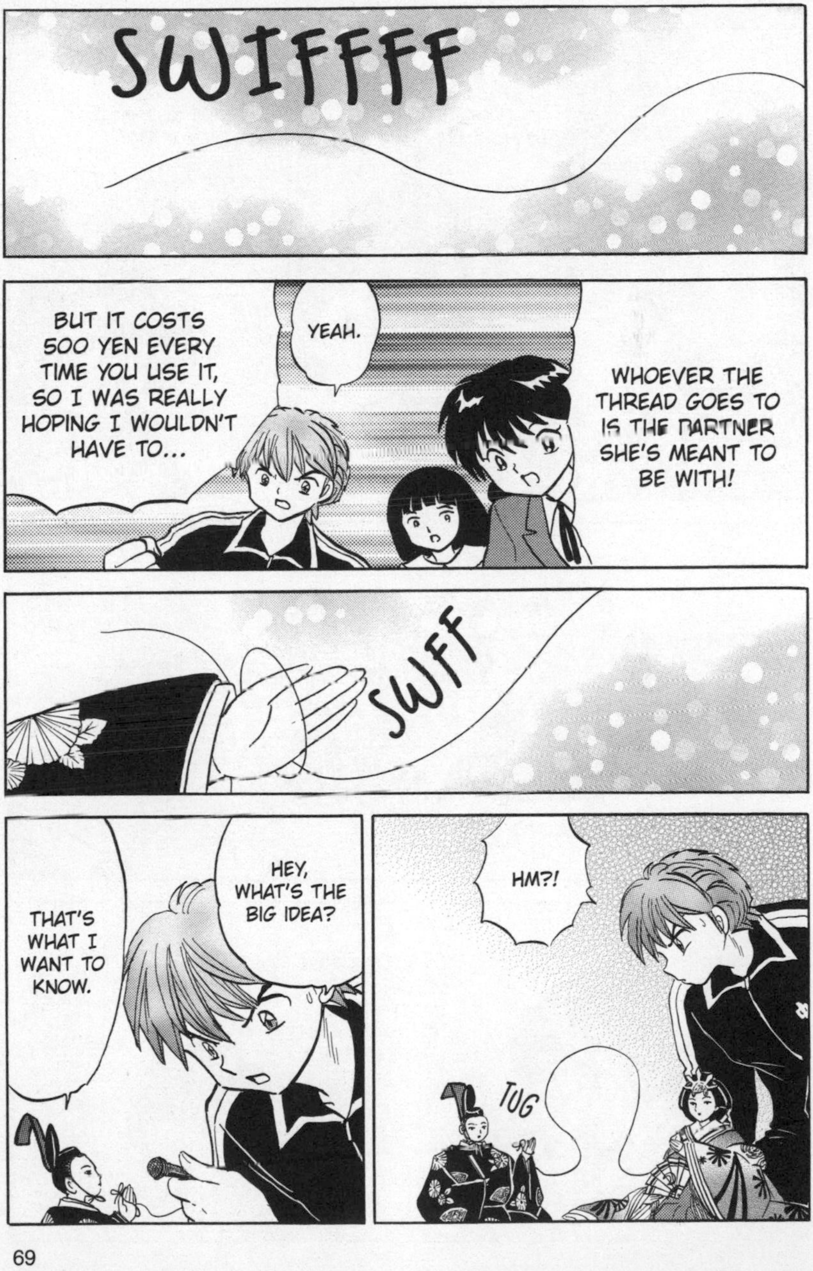
SWIFFFF
WHOEVER THE THREAD GOES TO IS THE PARTNER SHE'S MEANT TO BE WITH!
BUT IT COSTS 500 YEN EVERY TIME YOU USE IT, SO I WAS REALLY HOPING I WOULDN'T HAVE TO...
YEAH.
SWUFF
HM?!
TUG
HEY, WHAT'S THE BIG IDEA?
THAT'S WHAT I WANT TO KNOW.

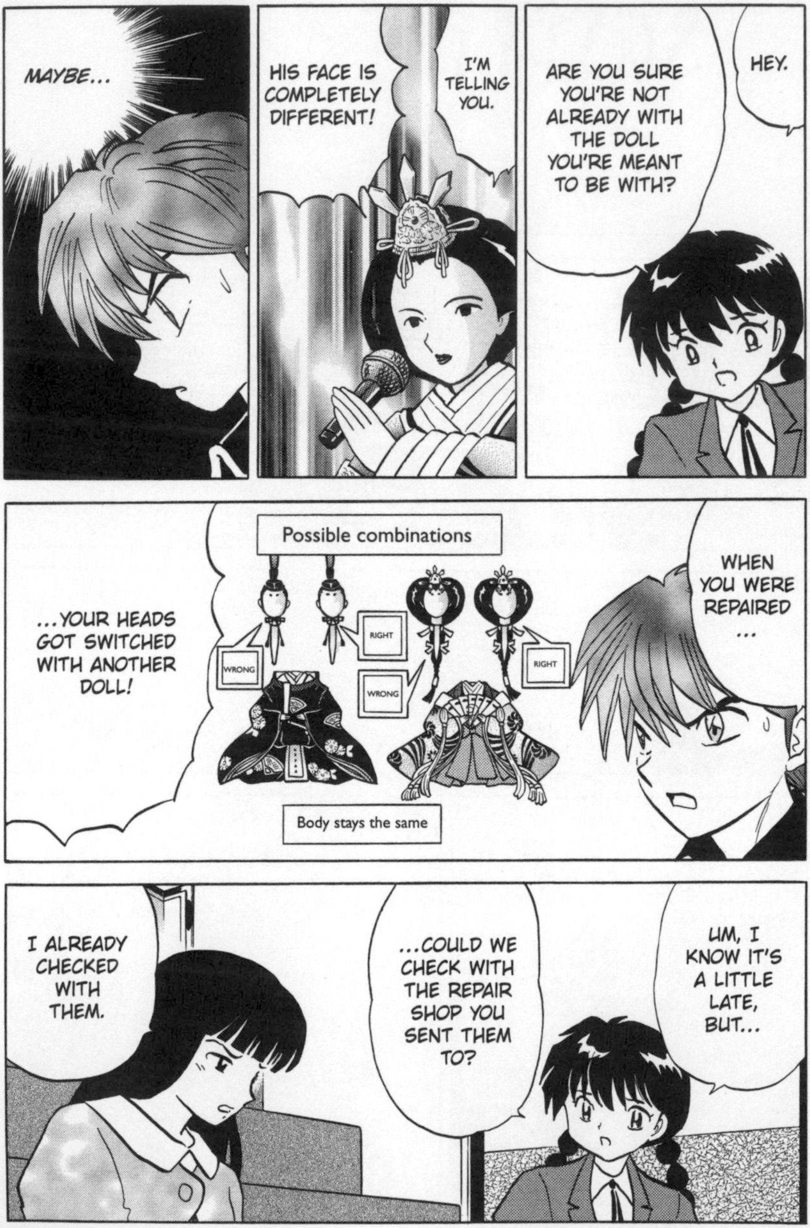
HEY.
ARE YOU SURE YOU'RE NOT ALREADY WITH THE DOLL YOU'RE MEANT TO BE WITH?
I'M TELLING YOU.
HIS FACE IS COMPLETELY DIFFERENT!
MAYBE...
WHEN YOU WERE REPAIRED ...
Possible combinations
RIGHT
RIGHT
WRONG
WRONG
Body stays the same
...YOUR HEADS GOT SWITCHED WITH ANOTHER DOLL!
UM, I KNOW IT'S A LITTLE LATE, BUT...
...COULD WE CHECK WITH THE REPAIR SHOP YOU SENT THEM TO?
I ALREADY CHECKED WITH THEM.

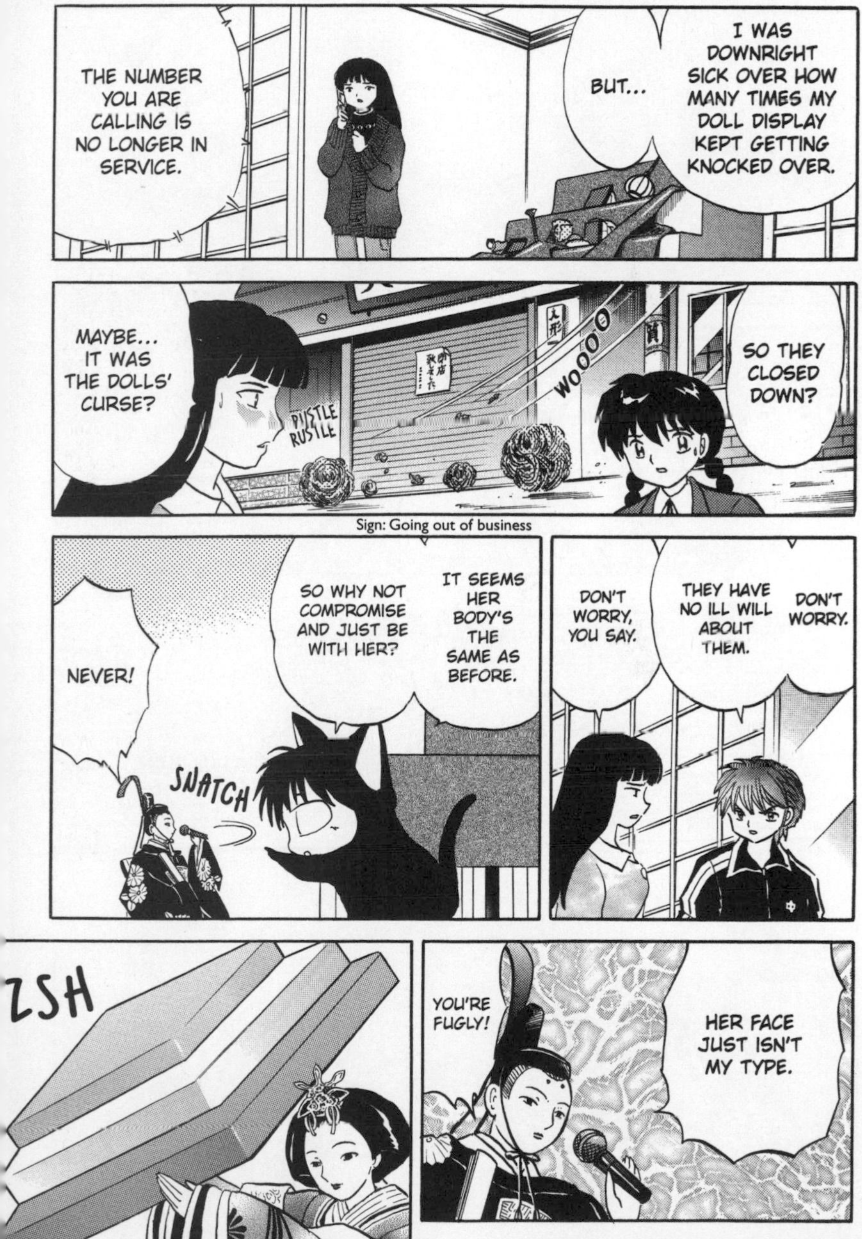
I WAS DOWNRIGHT SICK OVER HOW MANY TIMES MY DOLL DISPLAY KEPT GETTING KNOCKED OVER.
BUT...
THE NUMBER YOU ARE CALLING IS NO LONGER IN SERVICE.
SO THEY CLOSED DOWN?
WOOOO
RUSTLE RUSTLE
MAYBE... IT WAS THE DOLLS' CURSE?
Sign: Going out of business
DON'T WORRY.
THEY HAVE NO ILL WILL ABOUT THEM.
DON'T WORRY, YOU SAY.
IT SEEMS HER BODY'S THE SAME AS BEFORE.
SO WHY NOT COMPROMISE AND JUST BE WITH HER?
NEVER!
SNATCH
HER FACE JUST ISN'T MY TYPE.
YOU'RE FUGLY!
ZSH

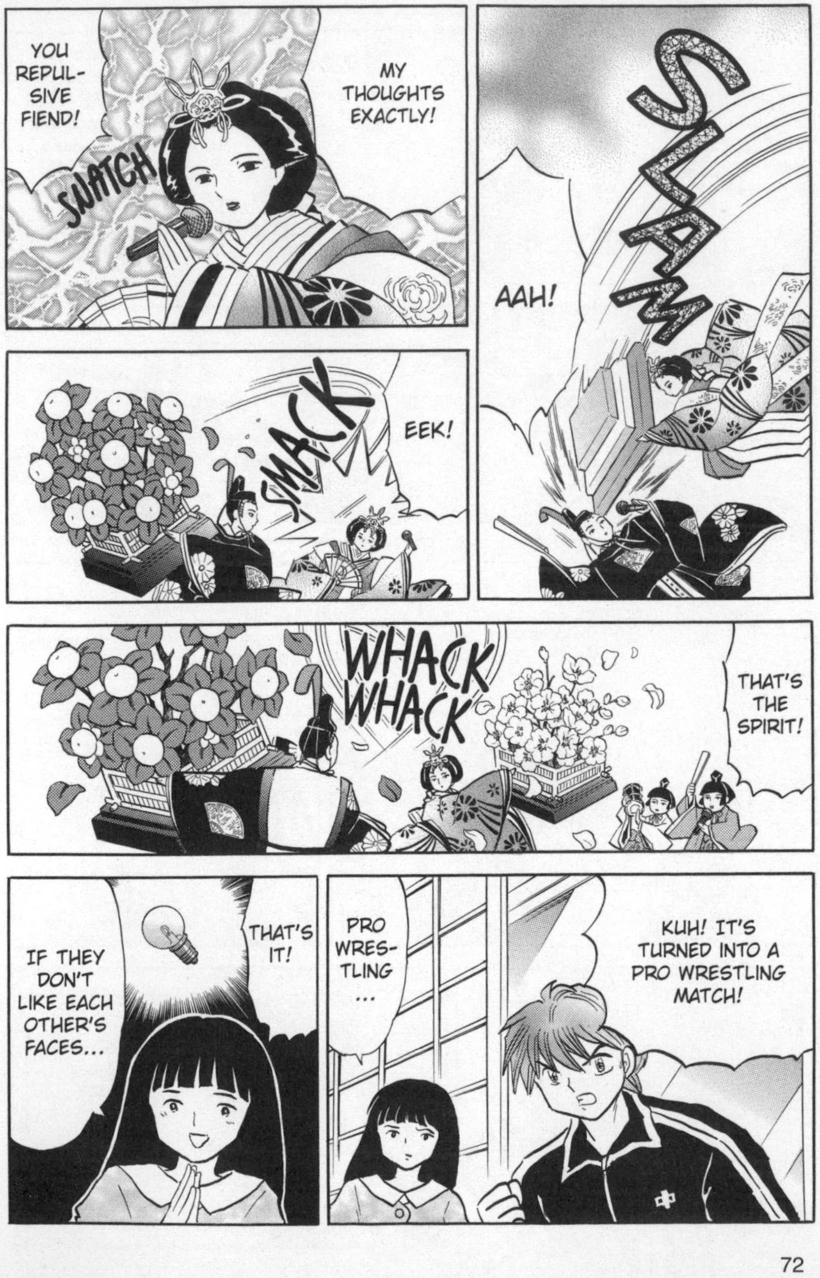
SLAM
AAH!
MY THOUGHTS EXACTLY!
YOU REPULSIVE FIEND!
SWATCH
EEK!
SMACK
THAT'S THE SPIRIT!
WHACK WHACK
KUH! IT'S TURNED INTO A PRO WRESTLING MATCH!
PRO WRESTLING...
THAT'S IT!
IF THEY DON'T LIKE EACH OTHER'S FACES...

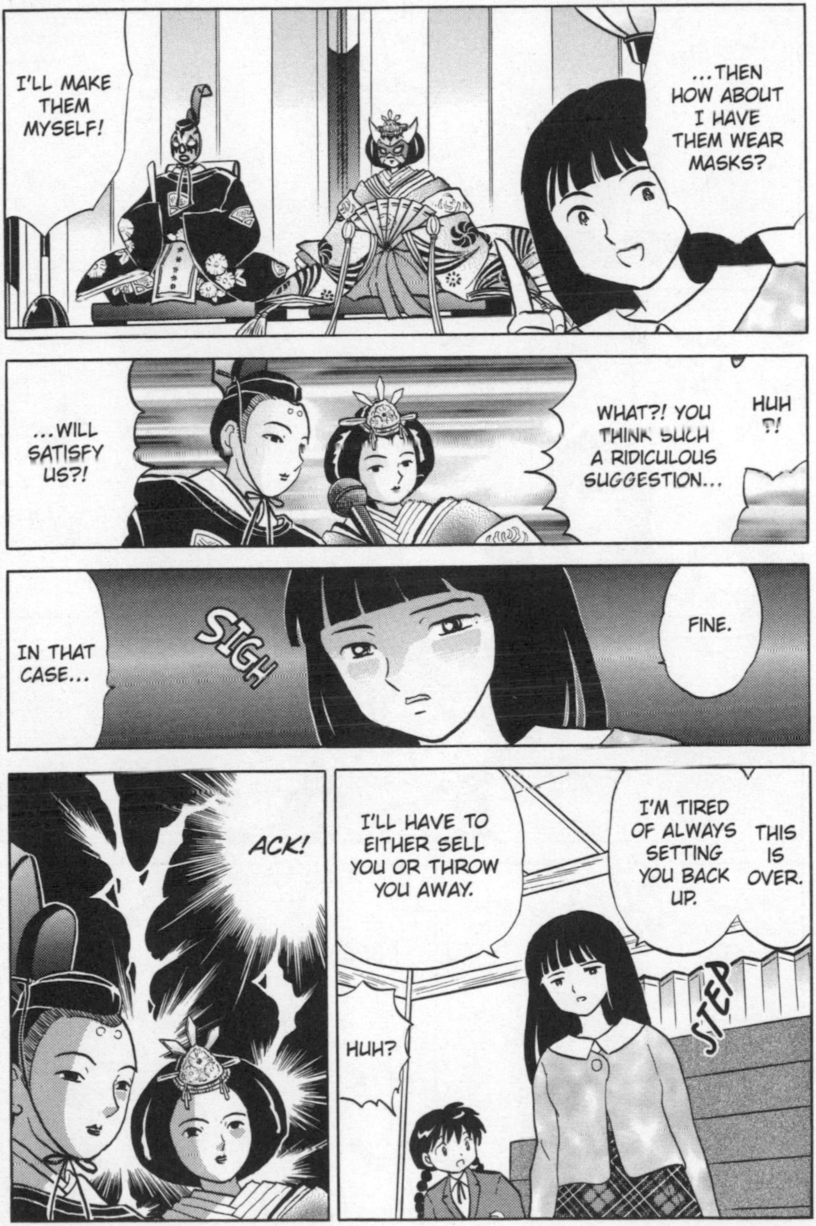
...THEN HOW ABOUT I HAVE THEM WEAR MASKS?
I'LL MAKE THEM MYSELF!
HUH ?!
WHAT?! YOU THINK SUCH A RIDICULOUS SUGGESTION...
...WILL SATISFY US?!
FINE.
SIGH
IN THAT CASE...
THIS IS OVER.
I'M TIRED OF ALWAYS SETTING YOU BACK UP.
I'LL HAVE TO EITHER SELL YOU OR THROW YOU AWAY.
STEP
HUH?
ACK!

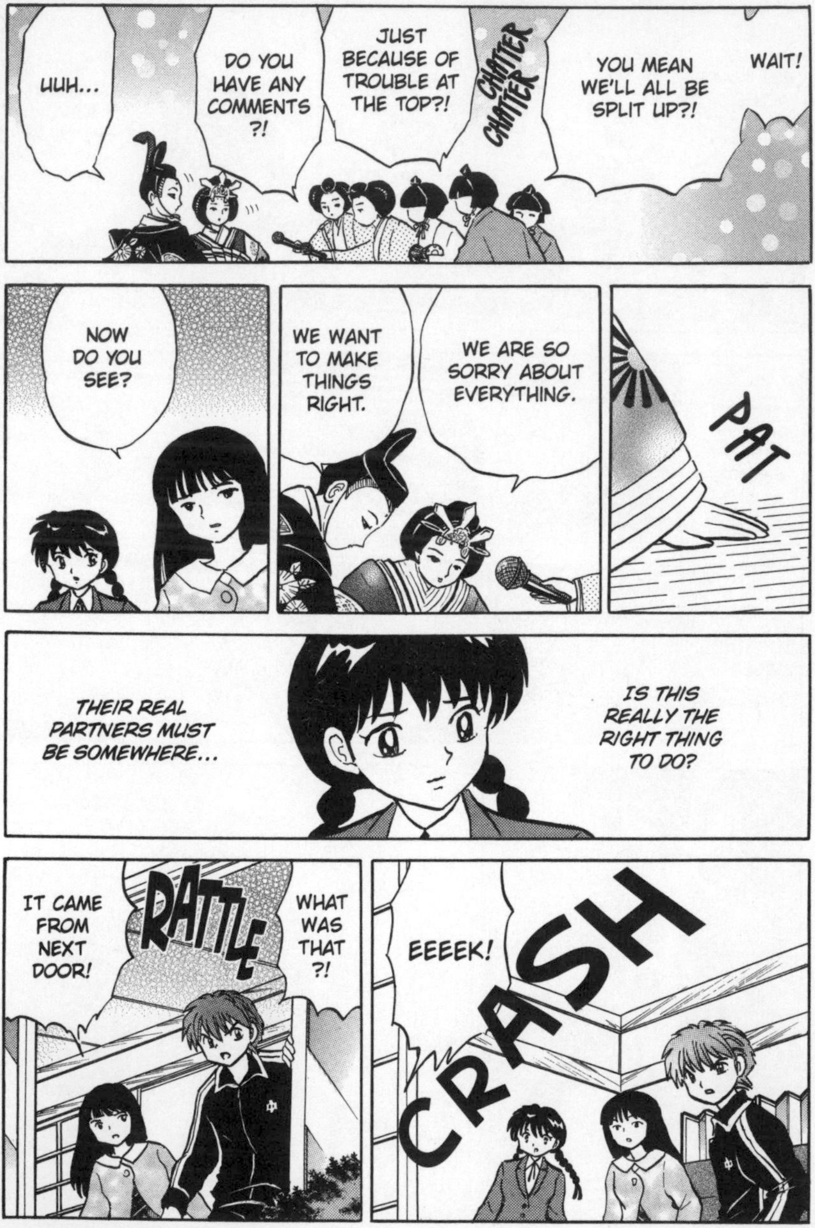

WAIT!
YOU MEAN WE'LL ALL BE SPLIT UP?!
CHATTER CHATTER
JUST BECAUSE OF TROUBLE AT THE TOP?!
DO YOU HAVE ANY COMMENTS ?!
UUH...
PAT
WE ARE SO SORRY ABOUT EVERYTHING.
WE WANT TO MAKE THINGS RIGHT.
NOW DO YOU SEE?
IS THIS REALLY THE RIGHT THING TO DO?
THEIR REAL PARTNERS MUST BE SOMEWHERE...
CRASH
EEEEK!
WHAT WAS THAT ?!
RATTLE
IT CAME FROM NEXT DOOR!

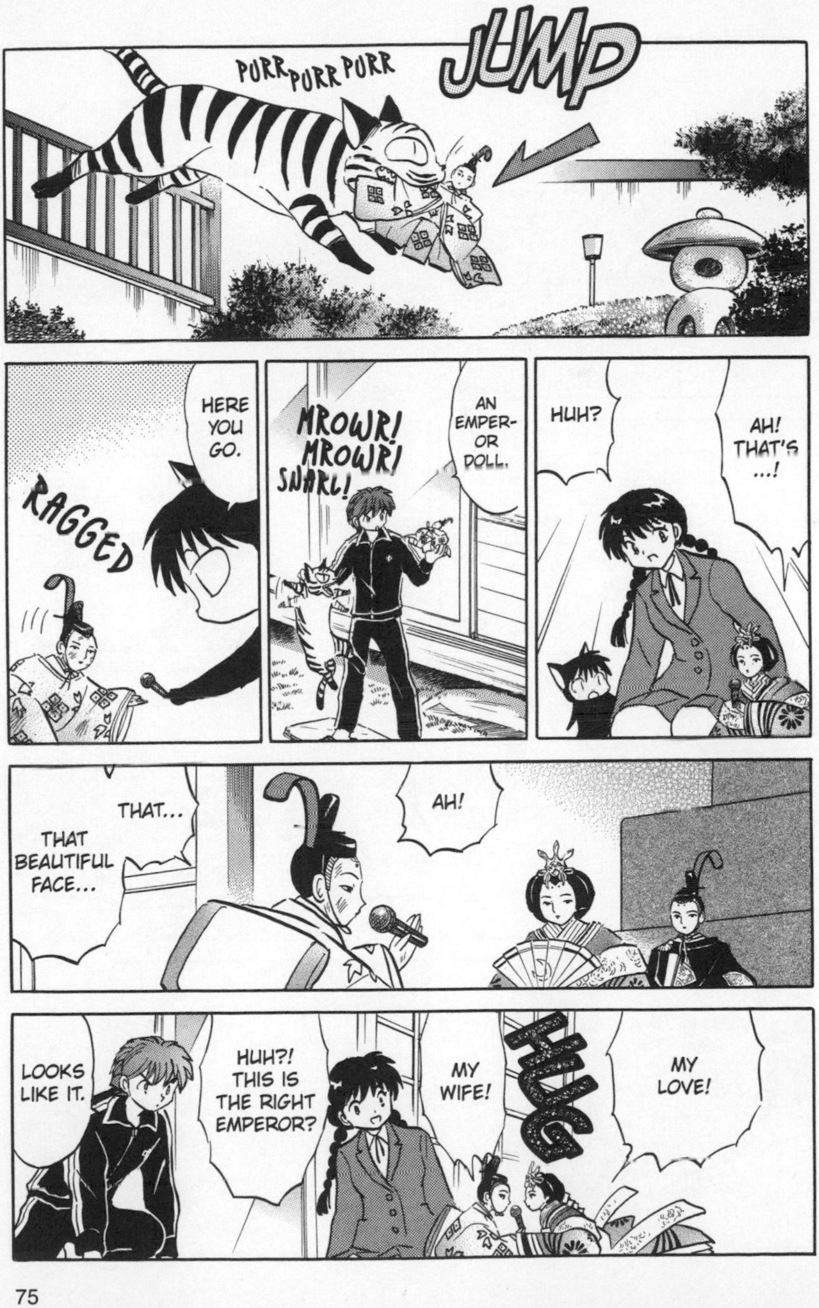
JUMP
PURR PURR PURR
AH! THAT'S ...!
HUH?
AN EMPER-OR DOLL.
MROWR! MROWR! SNARL!
HERE YOU GO.
RAGGED
AH!
THAT...
THAT BEAUTIFUL FACE...
MY LOVE!
HUG
MY WIFE!
HUH?! THIS IS THE RIGHT EMPEROR?
LOOKS LIKE IT.

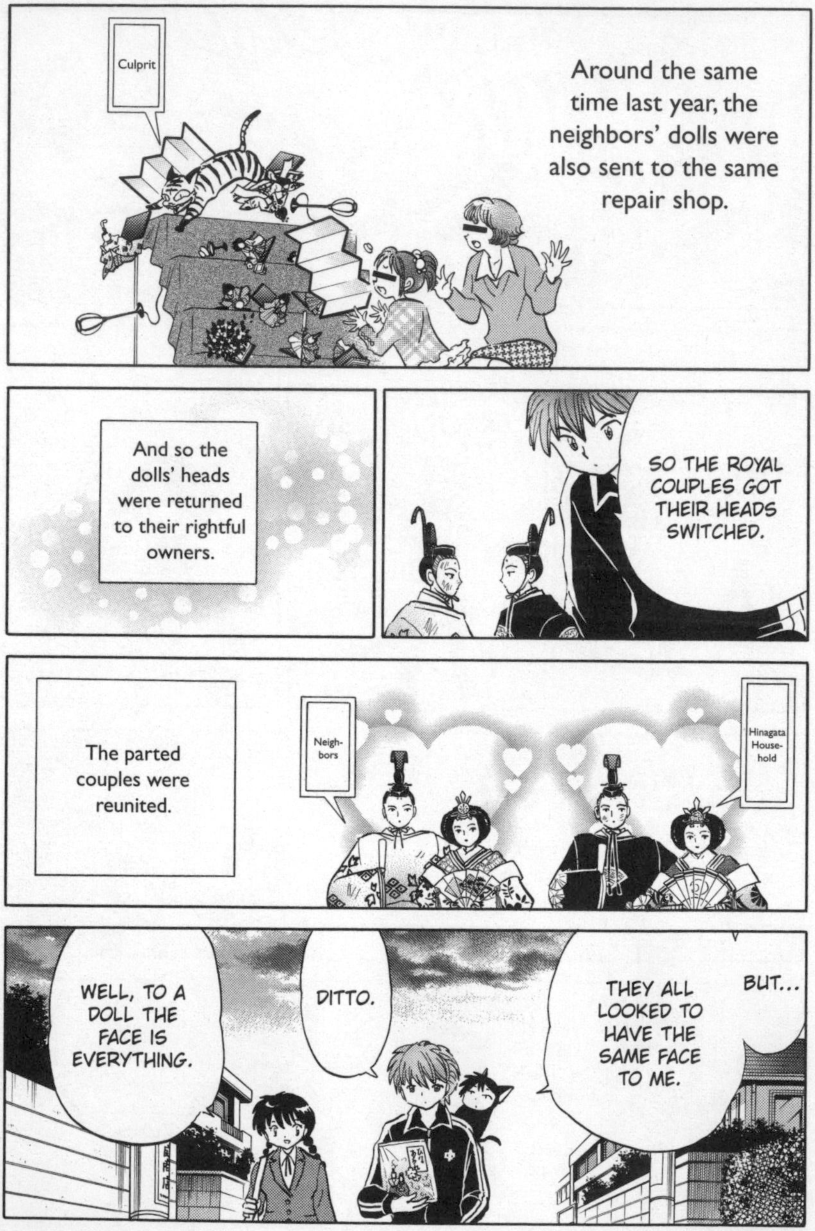
Around the same time last year, the neighbors' dolls were also sent to the same repair shop.
Culprit
SO THE ROYAL COUPLES GOT THEIR HEADS SWITCHED.
And so the dolls' heads were returned to their rightful owners.
Hinagata House-hold
Neigh-bors
The parted couples were reunited.
BUT...
THEY ALL LOOKED TO HAVE THE SAME FACE TO ME.
DITTO.
WELL, TO A DOLL THE FACE IS EVERYTHING.

CHAPTER 183: WINDFALL WAX

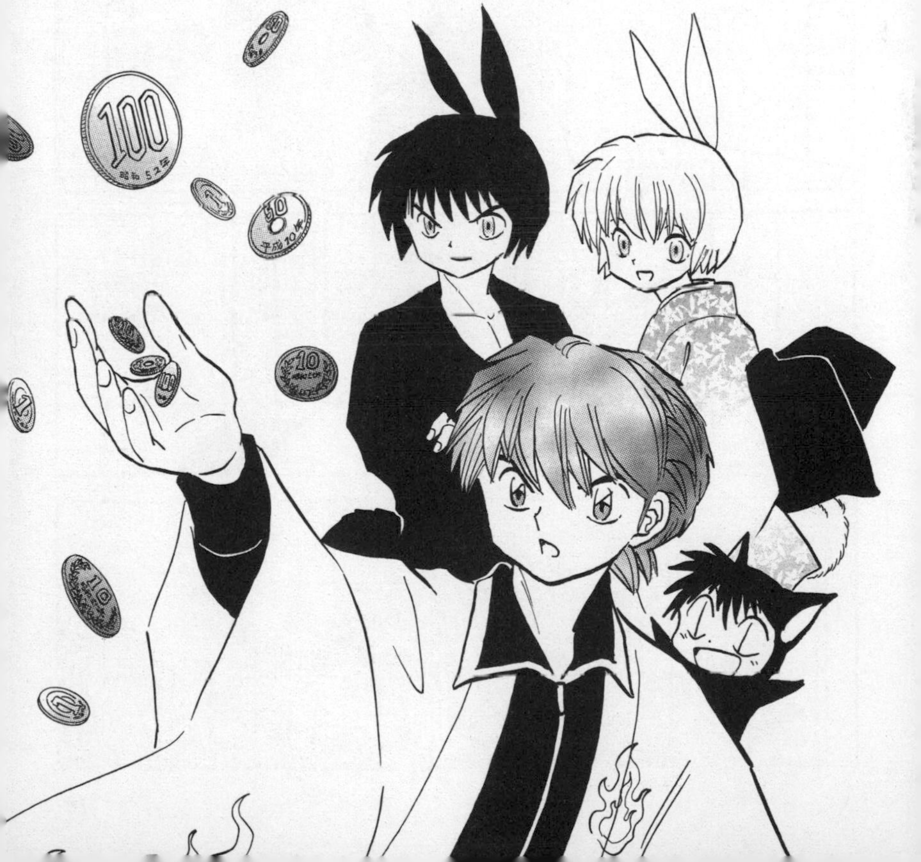

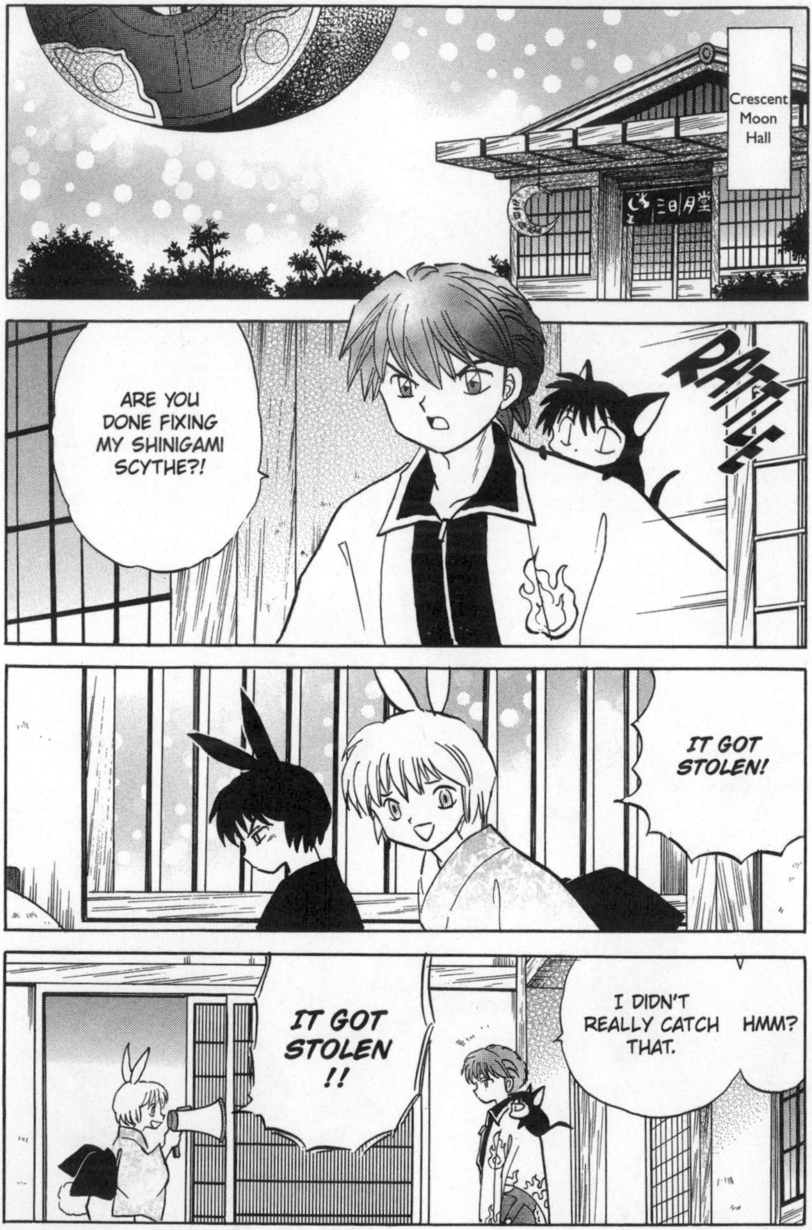
Crescent Moon Hall
三日月堂
RATTLE
ARE YOU DONE FIXING MY SHINIGAMI SCYTHE?!
IT GOT STOLEN!
HMM?
I DIDN'T REALLY CATCH THAT.
IT GOT STOLEN !!

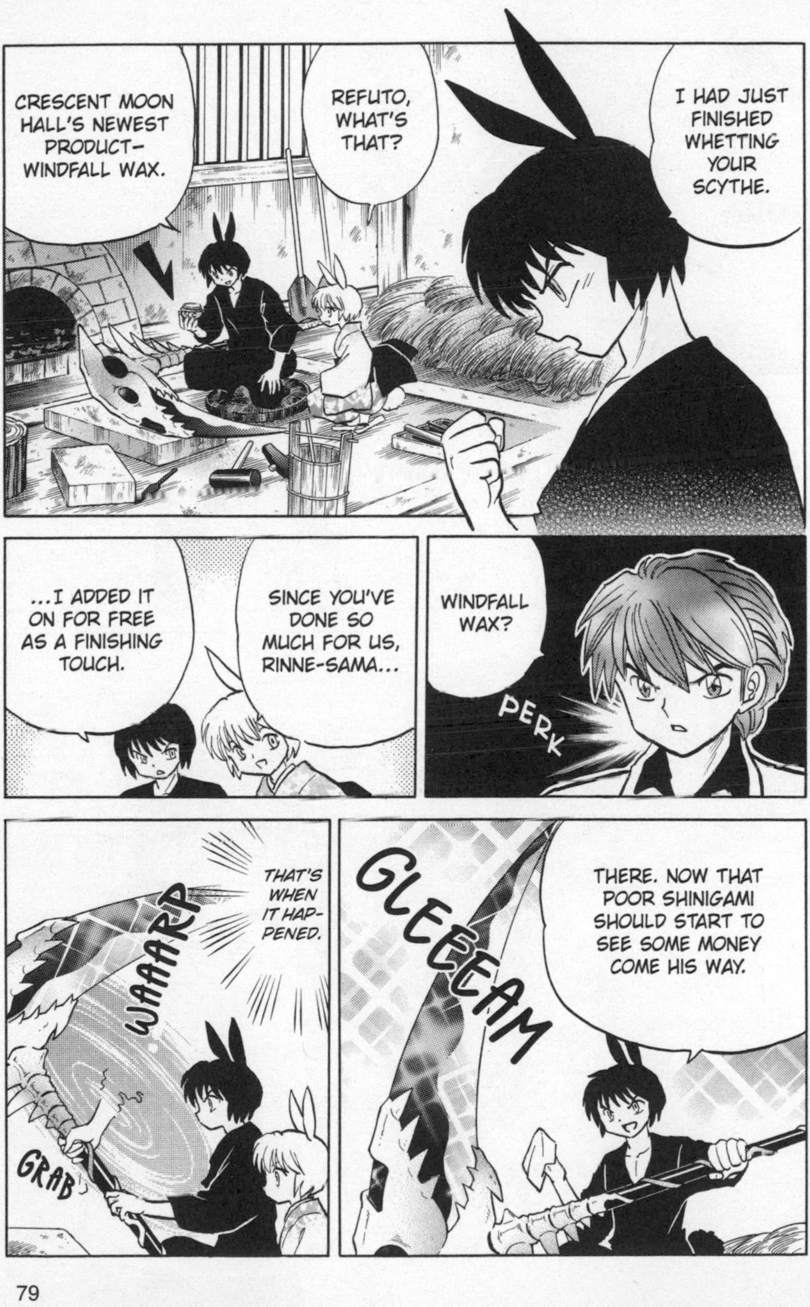
I HAD JUST FINISHED WHETTING YOUR SCYTHE.
REFUTO, WHAT'S THAT?
CRESCENT MOON HALL'S NEWEST PRODUCT— WINDFALL WAX.
WINDFALL WAX?
PERK
SINCE YOU'VE DONE SO MUCH FOR US, RINNE-SAMA...
...I ADDED IT ON FOR FREE AS A FINISHING TOUCH.
THERE. NOW THAT POOR SHINIGAMI SHOULD START TO SEE SOME MONEY COME HIS WAY.
GLEEEAM
THAT'S WHEN IT HAP- PENED.
WAAARP
GRAB

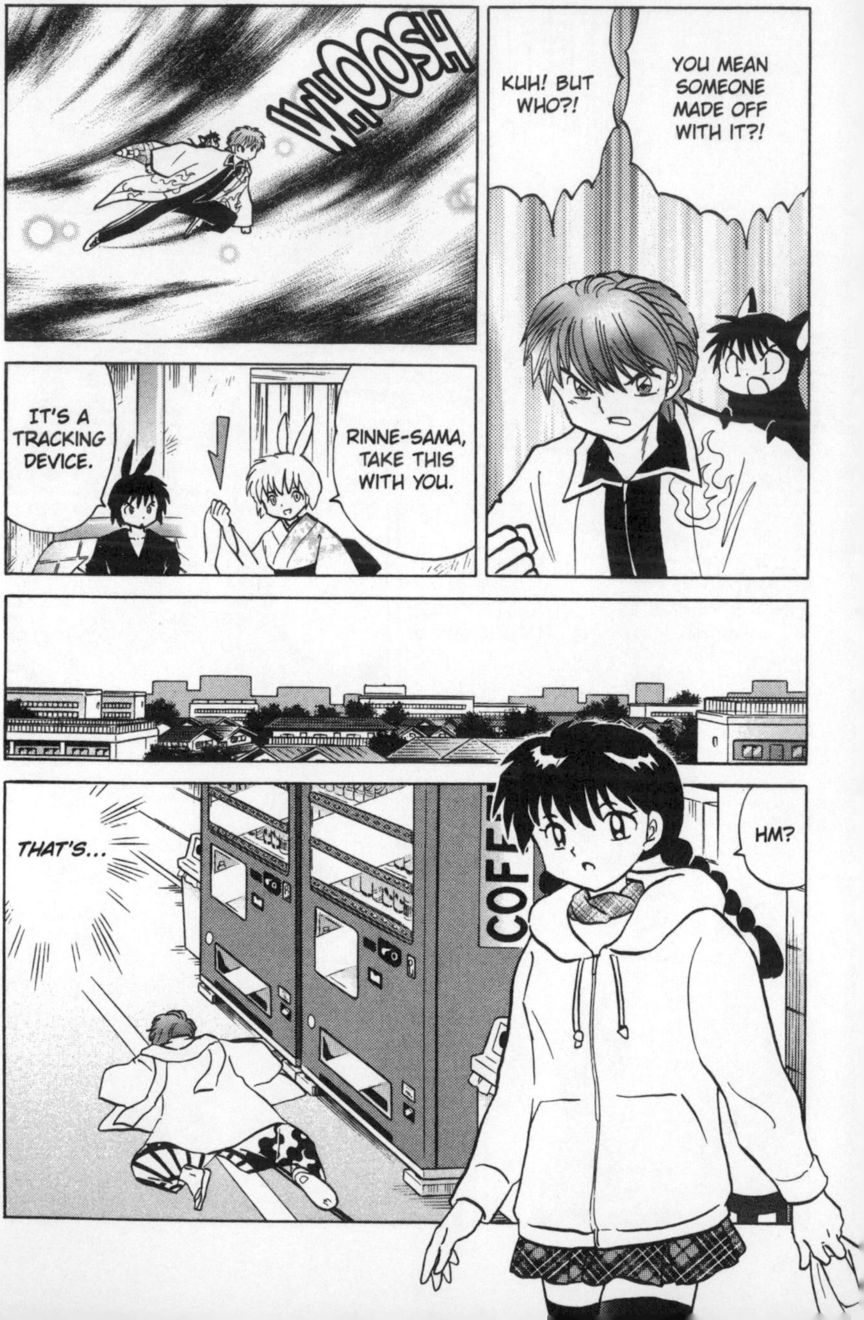
YOU MEAN SOMEONE MADE OFF WITH IT?!
KUH! BUT WHO?!
WHOOSH
RINNE-SAMA, TAKE THIS WITH YOU.
IT'S A TRACKING DEVICE.
HM?
THAT'S...
COFF

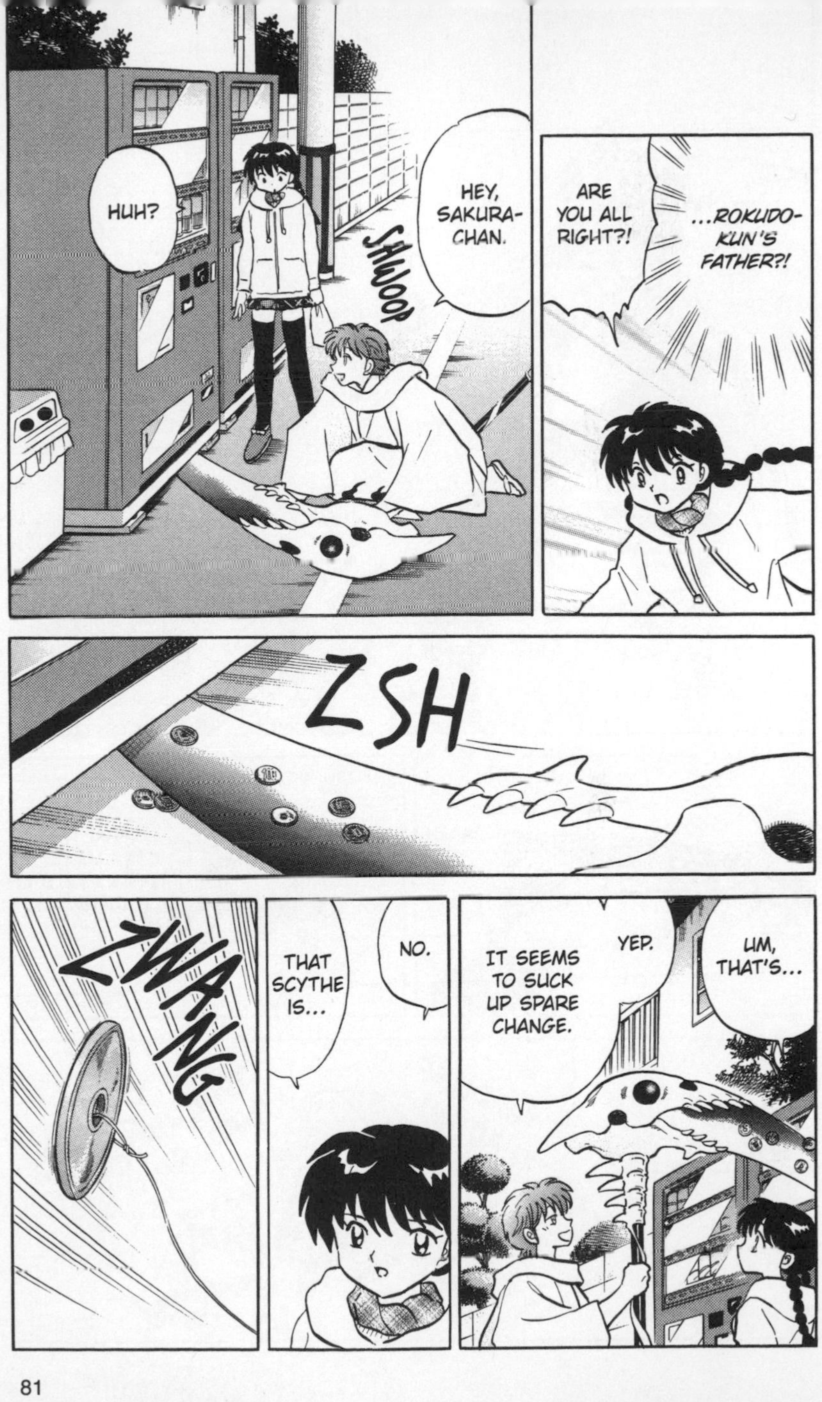
...ROKUDO-KUN'S FATHER?!
ARE YOU ALL RIGHT?!
HEY, SAKURA-CHAN.
SHWOOP
HUH?
ZSH
UM, THAT'S...
YEP.
IT SEEMS TO SUCK UP SPARE CHANGE.
NO.
THAT SCYTHE IS...
ZWANG

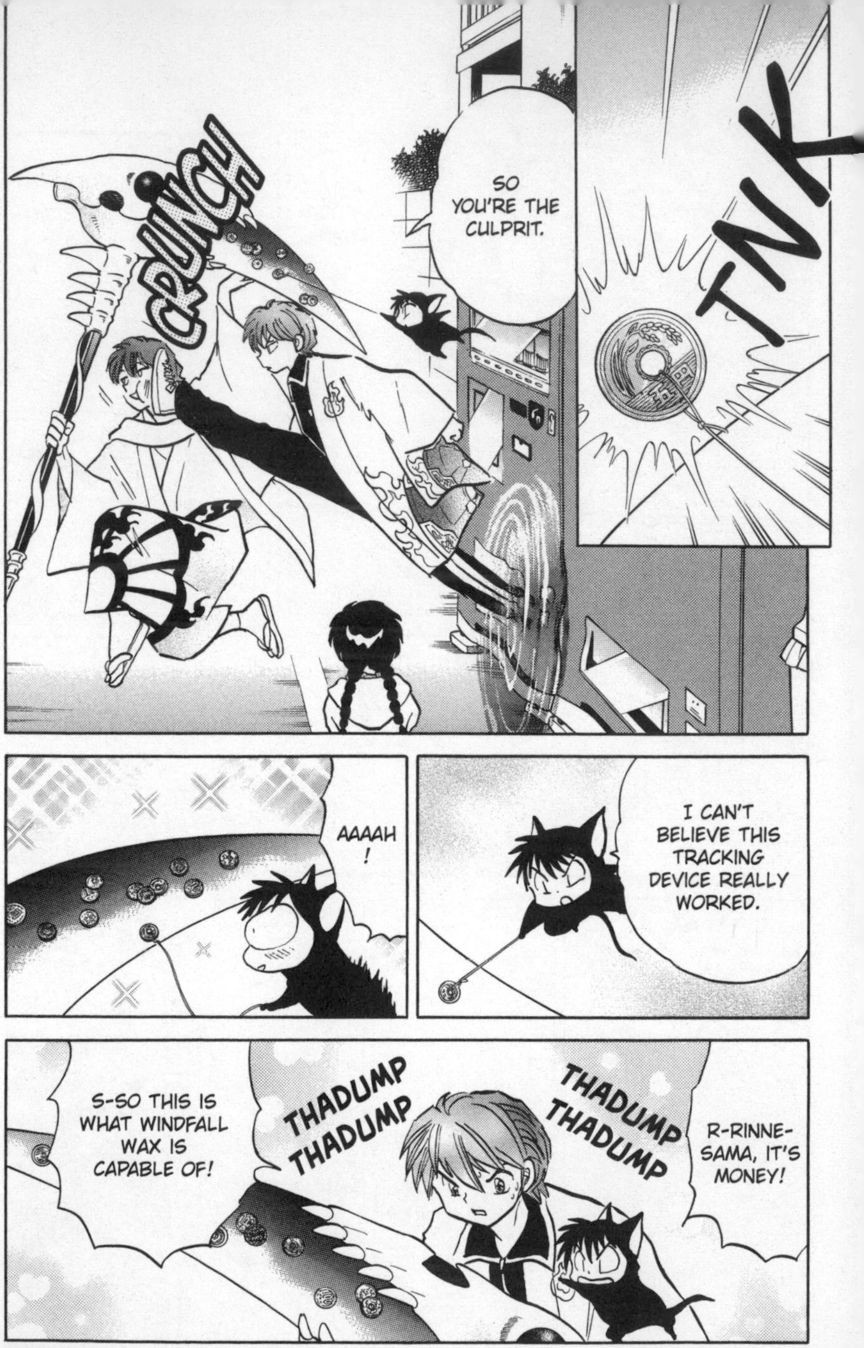
TNK
SO YOU'RE THE CULPRIT.
CRUNCH
I CAN'T BELIEVE THIS TRACKING DEVICE REALLY WORKED.
AAAAH !
R-RINNE-SAMA, IT'S MONEY!
THADUMP THADUMP
THADUMP THADUMP
S-SO THIS IS WHAT WINDFALL WAX IS CAPABLE OF!

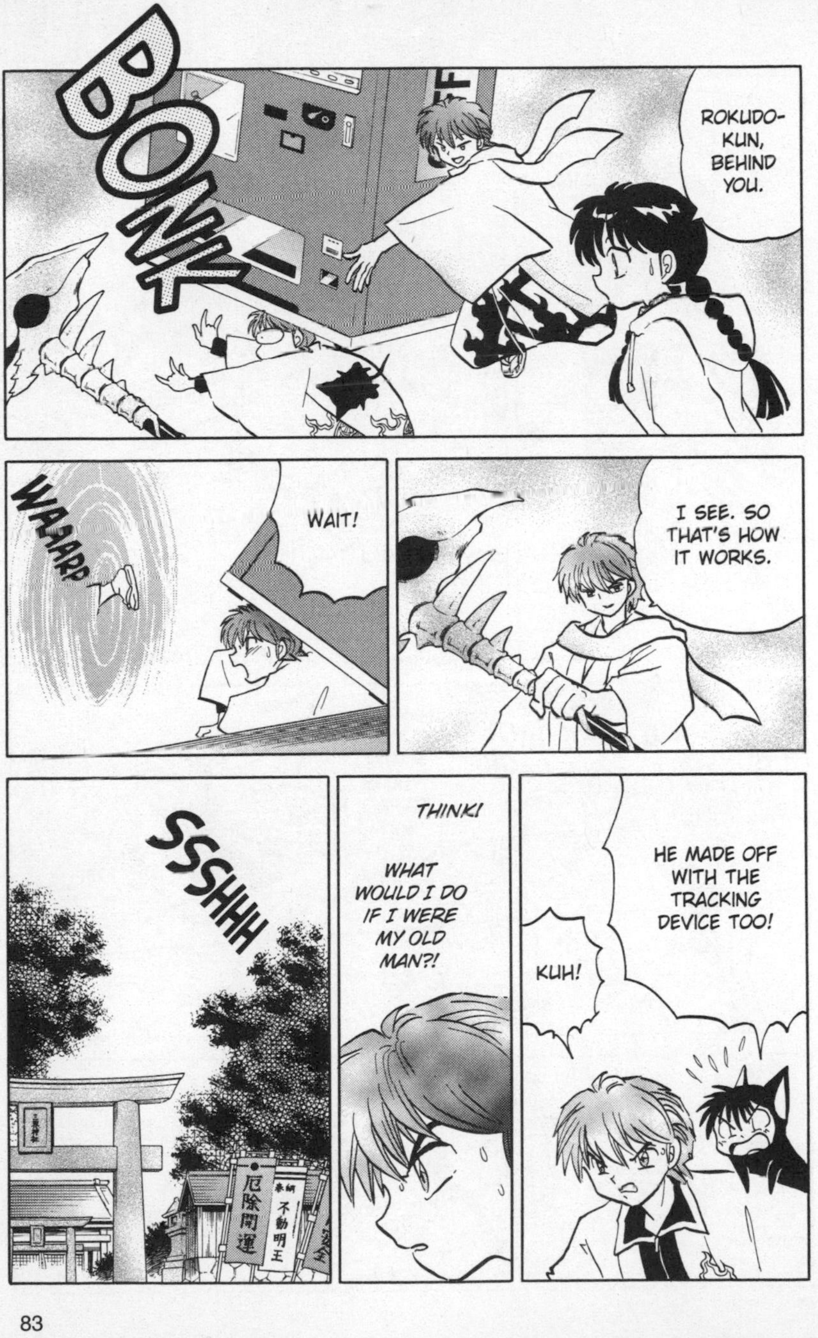
ROKUDO-KUN, BEHIND YOU.
BONK
I SEE. SO THAT'S HOW IT WORKS.
WAIT!
WAAARP
HE MADE OFF WITH THE TRACKING DEVICE TOO!
KUH!
THINK!
WHAT WOULD I DO IF I WERE MY OLD MAN?!
SSHHH
厄除開運
奉納 不動明王

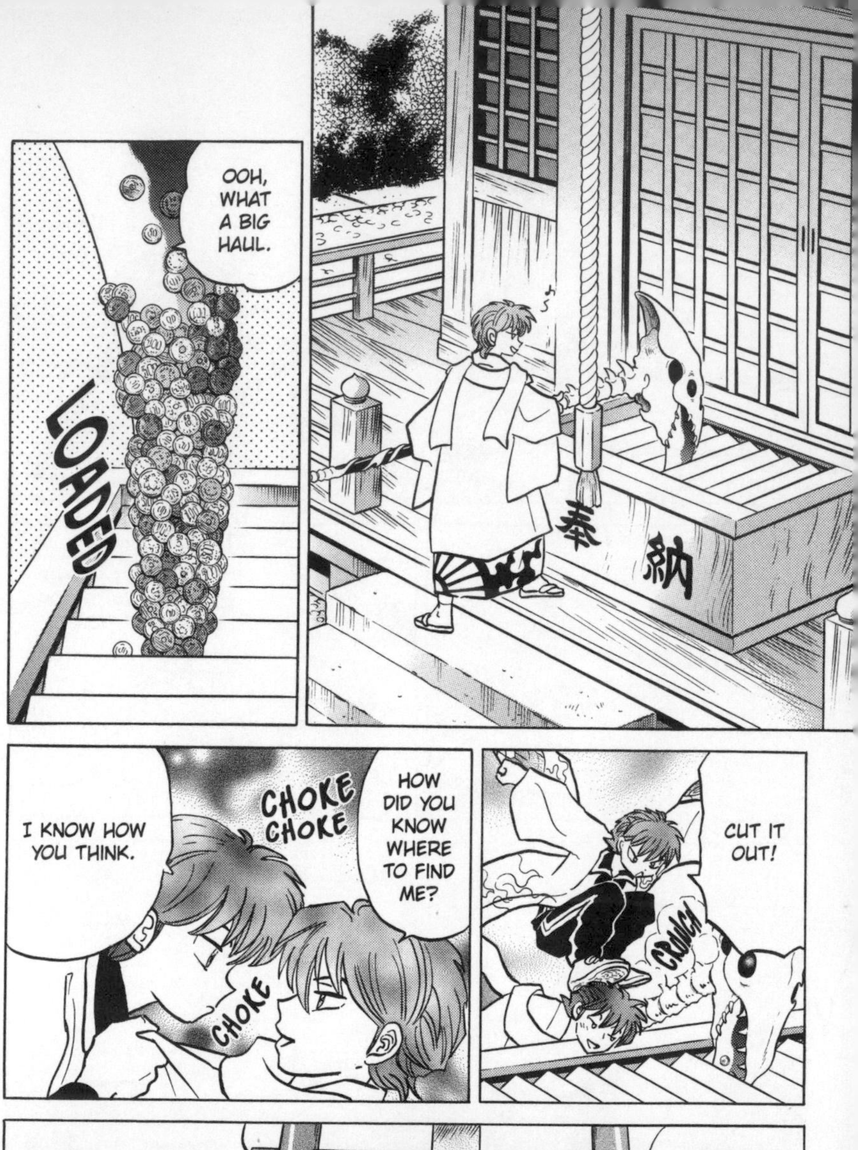
奉納
OOH, WHAT A BIG HAUL.
LOADED
CUT IT OUT!
CRUNCH
HOW DID YOU KNOW WHERE TO FIND ME?
CHOKE CHOKE
I KNOW HOW YOU THINK.
CHOKE
I CAN'T BELIEVE HE'S ACTUALLY HERE.
IT'S TRUE, THIS SHRINE IS THE ONLY PLACE IN THE AREA WHERE YOU CAN GET A LOT OF CHANGE.

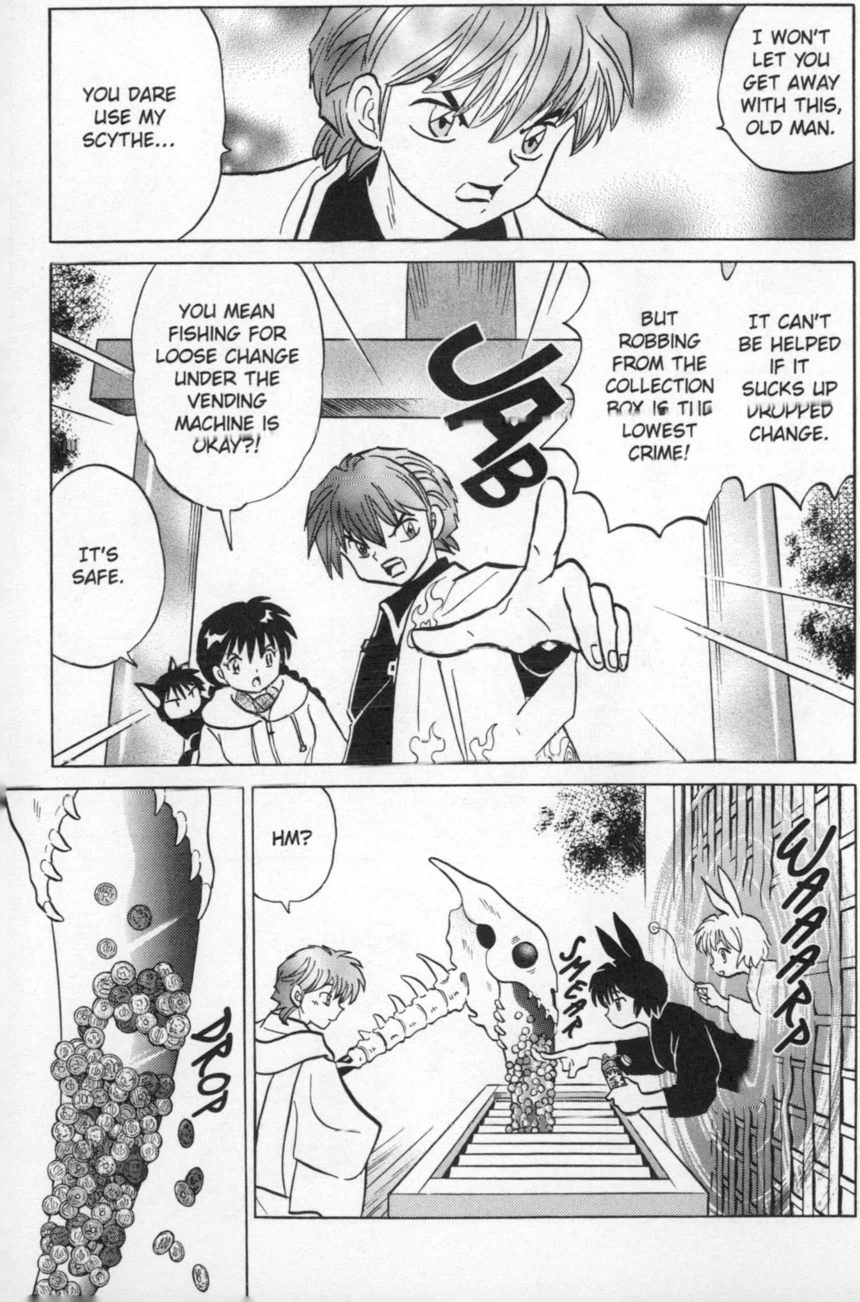
I WON'T LET YOU GET AWAY WITH THIS, OLD MAN.
YOU DARE USE MY SCYTHE...
IT CAN'T BE HELPED IF IT SUCKS UP DROPPED CHANGE.
BUT ROBBING FROM THE COLLECTION BOX IS THE LOWEST CRIME!
JAB
YOU MEAN FISHING FOR LOOSE CHANGE UNDER THE VENDING MACHINE IS OKAY?!
IT'S SAFE.
WAAAARP
SMEAR
HM?
DROP

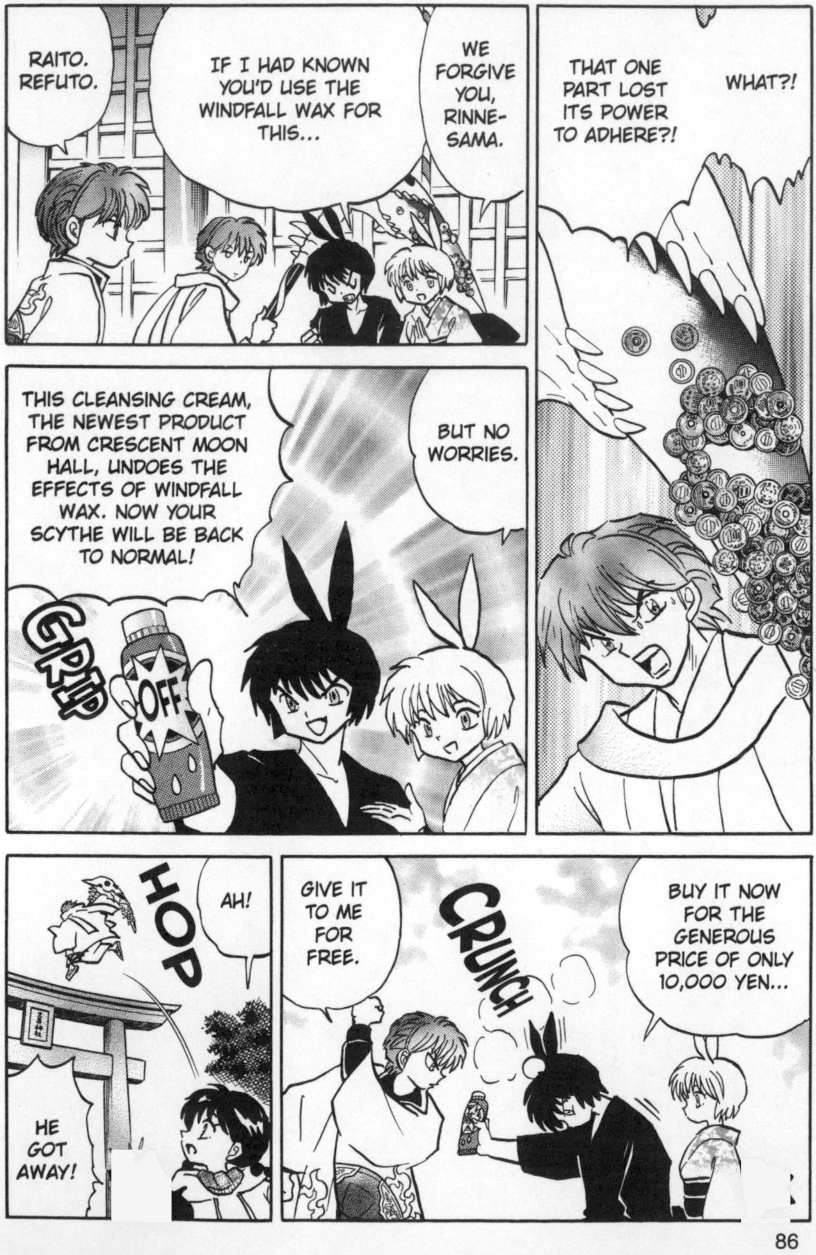
WHAT?!
THAT ONE PART LOST ITS POWER TO ADHERE?!
WE FORGIVE YOU, RINNE-SAMA.
IF I HAD KNOWN YOU'D USE THE WINDFALL WAX FOR THIS...
RAITO. REFUTO.
BUT NO WORRIES.
THIS CLEANSING CREAM, THE NEWEST PRODUCT FROM CRESCENT MOON HALL, UNDOES THE EFFECTS OF WINDFALL WAX. NOW YOUR SCYTHE WILL BE BACK TO NORMAL!
GRIP
OFF
BUY IT NOW FOR THE GENEROUS PRICE OF ONLY 10,000 YEN...
CRUNCH
GIVE IT TO ME FOR FREE.
AH!
HOP
HE GOT AWAY!

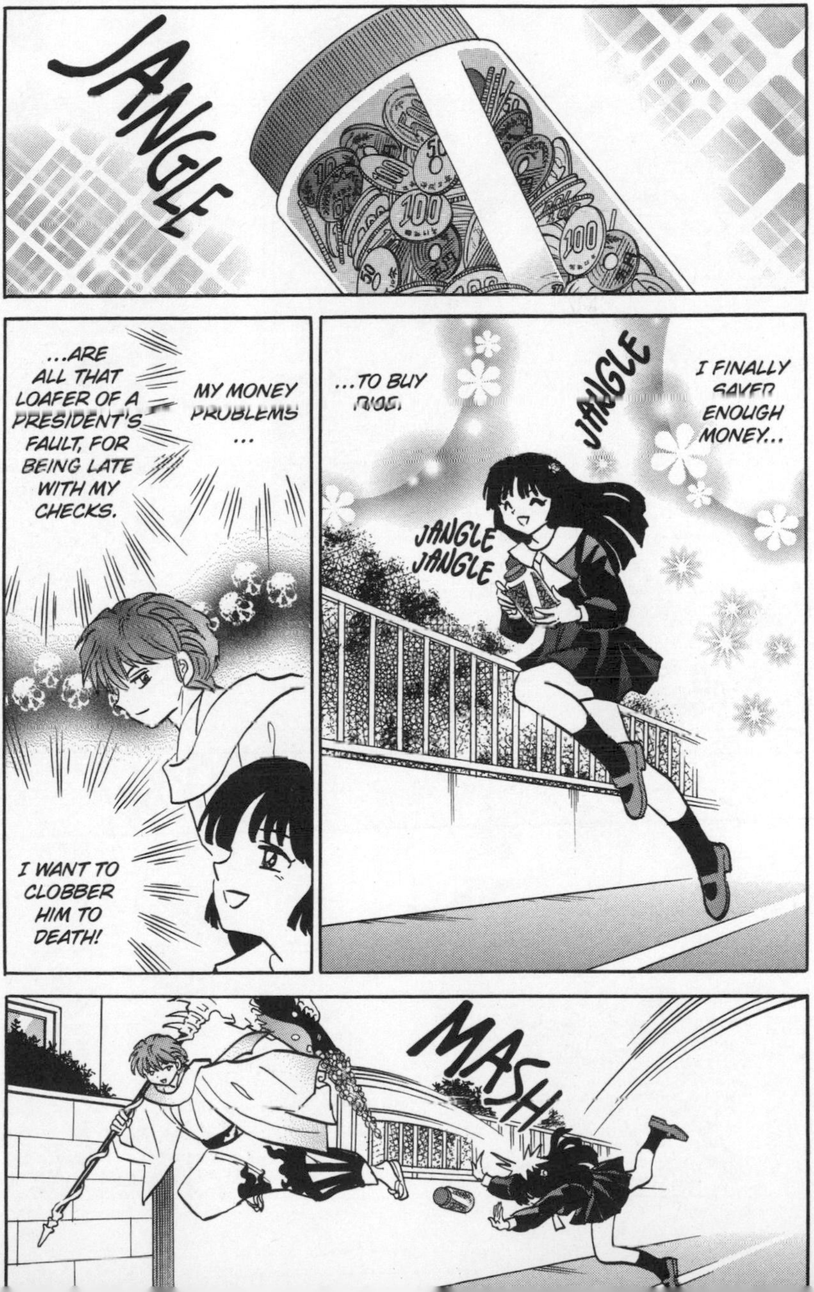
JANGLE
I FINALLY SAVED ENOUGH MONEY...
JANGLE
...TO BUY
JANGLE JANGLE
MY MONEY PROBLEMS...
...ARE ALL THAT LOAFER OF A PRESIDENT'S FAULT, FOR BEING LATE WITH MY CHECKS.
I WANT TO CLOBBER HIM TO DEATH!
MASH

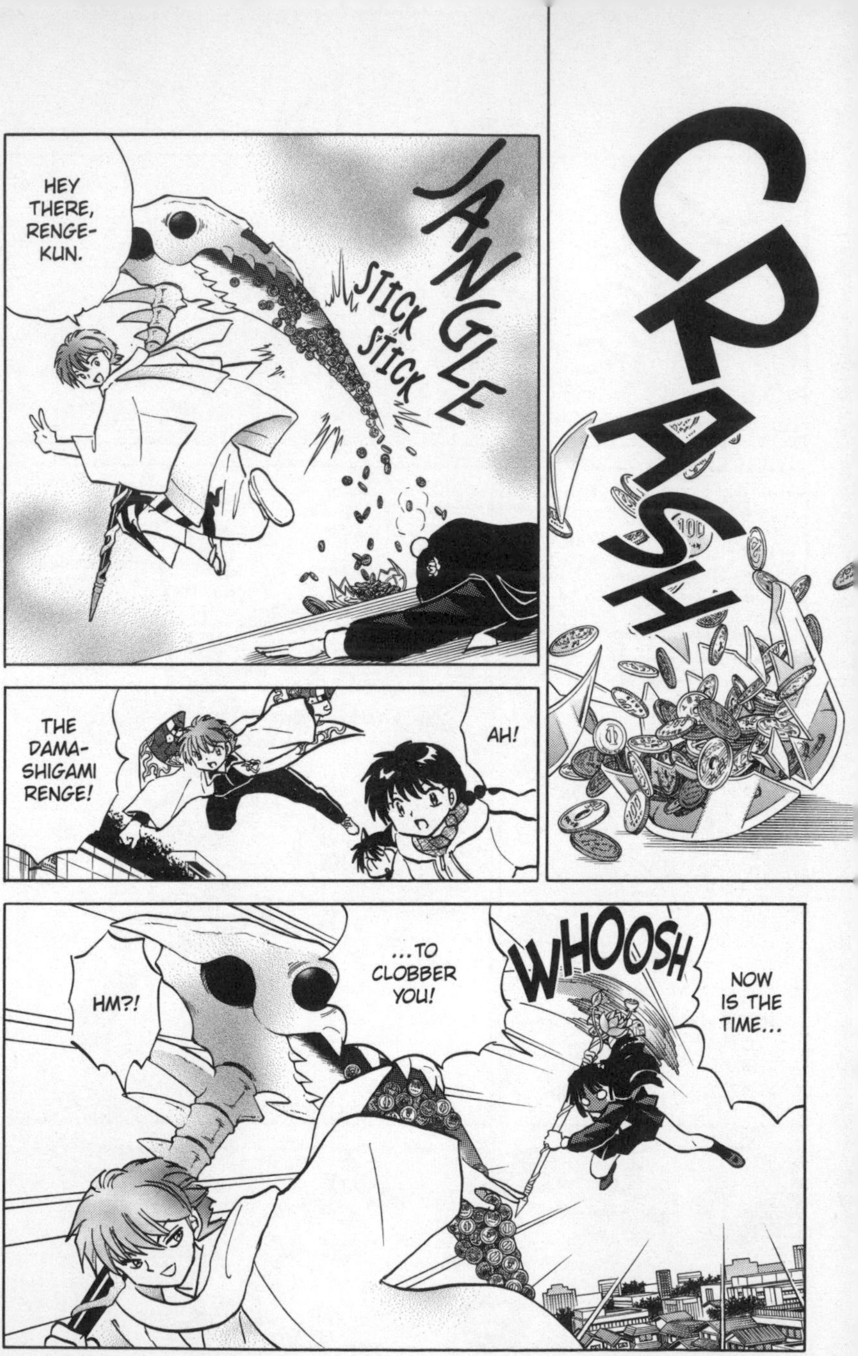
CRASH
JANGLE
STICK STICK
HEY THERE, RENGE-KUN.
AH!
THE DAMA-SHIGAMI RENGE!
NOW IS THE TIME...
WHOOSH
...TO CLOBBER YOU!
HM?!

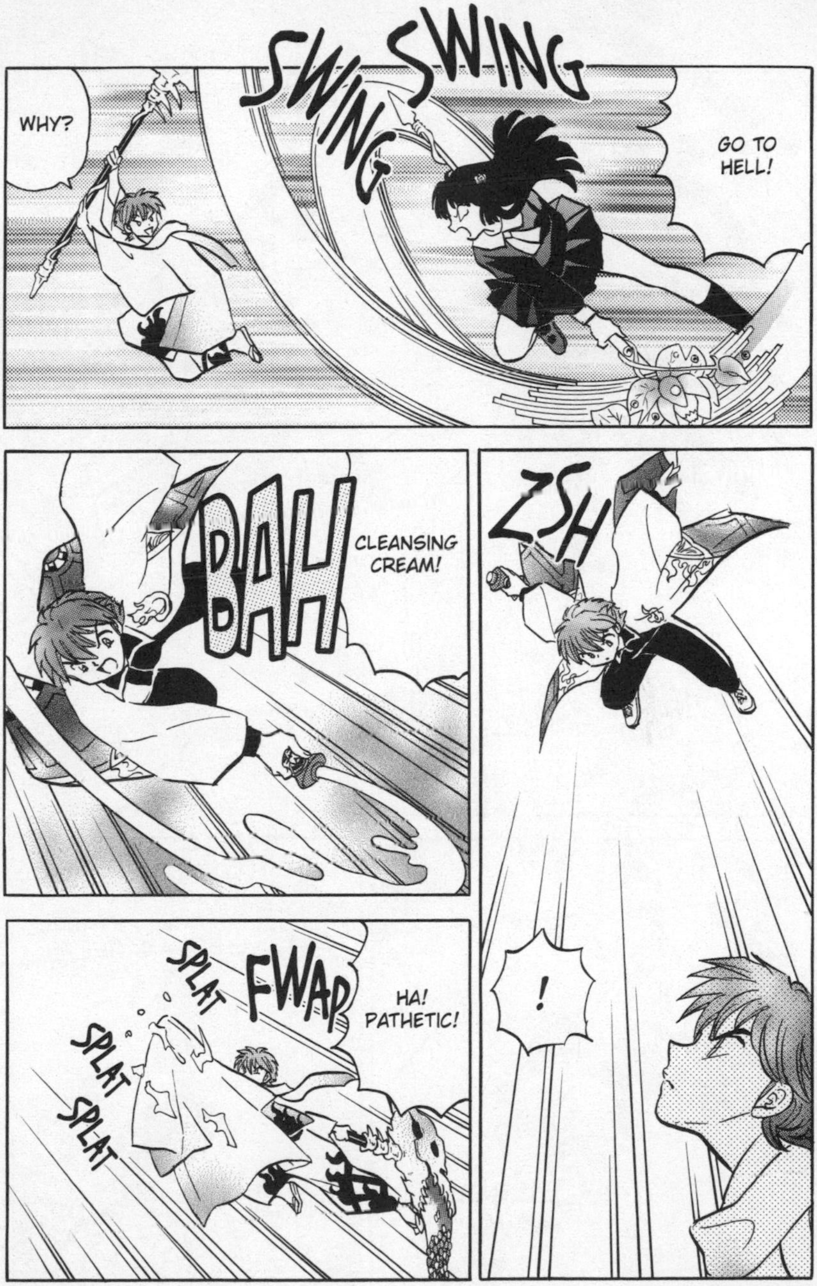
GO TO HELL!
SWING SWING
SWING
WHY?
ZSH
!
CLEANSING CREAM!
BAH
HA! PATHETIC!
FWAP
SPLAT
SPLAT
SPLAT
SPLAT

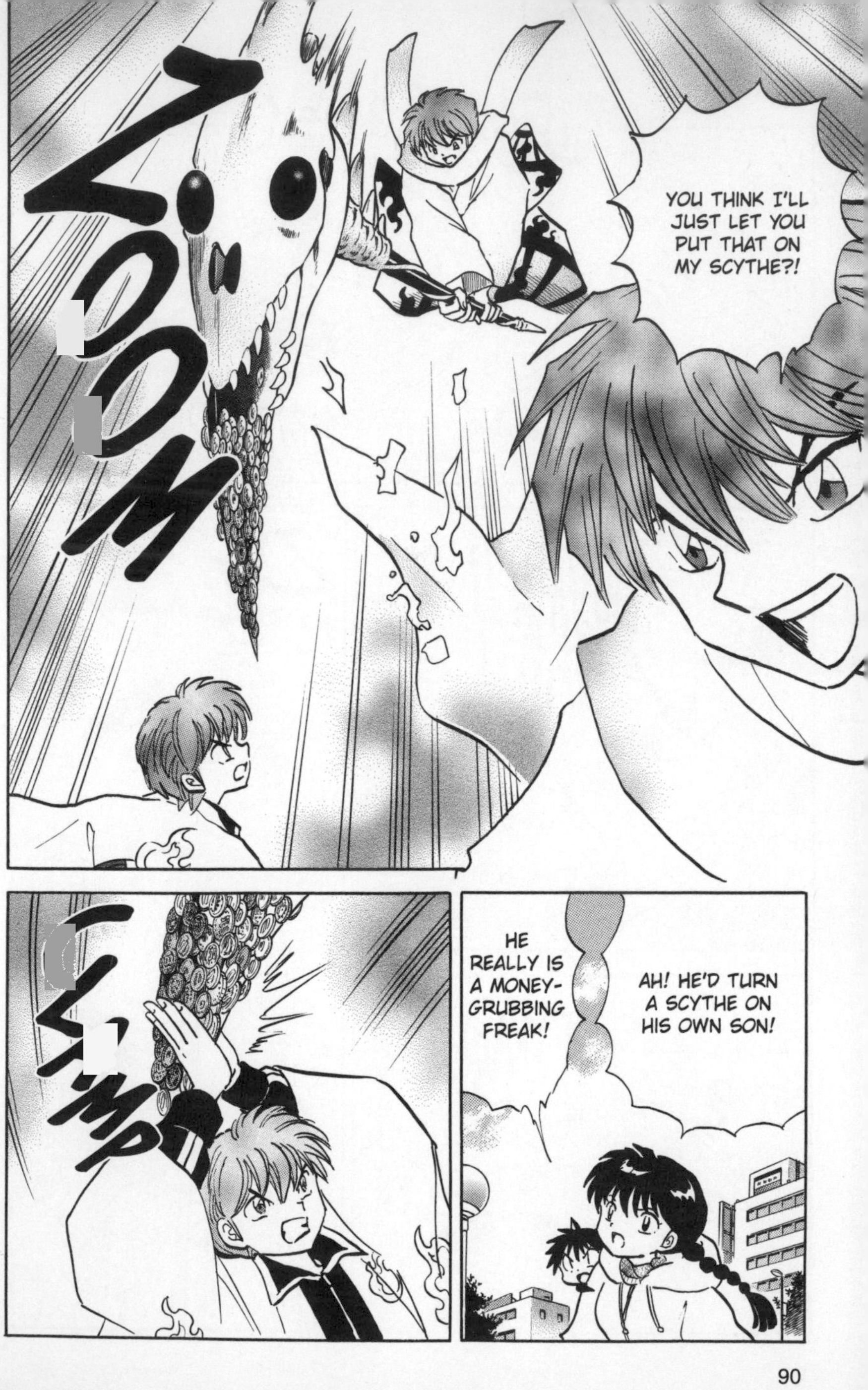
YOU THINK I'LL JUST LET YOU PUT THAT ON MY SCYTHE?!
AH! HE'D TURN A SCYTHE ON HIS OWN SON!
HE REALLY IS A MONEY-GRUBBING FREAK!

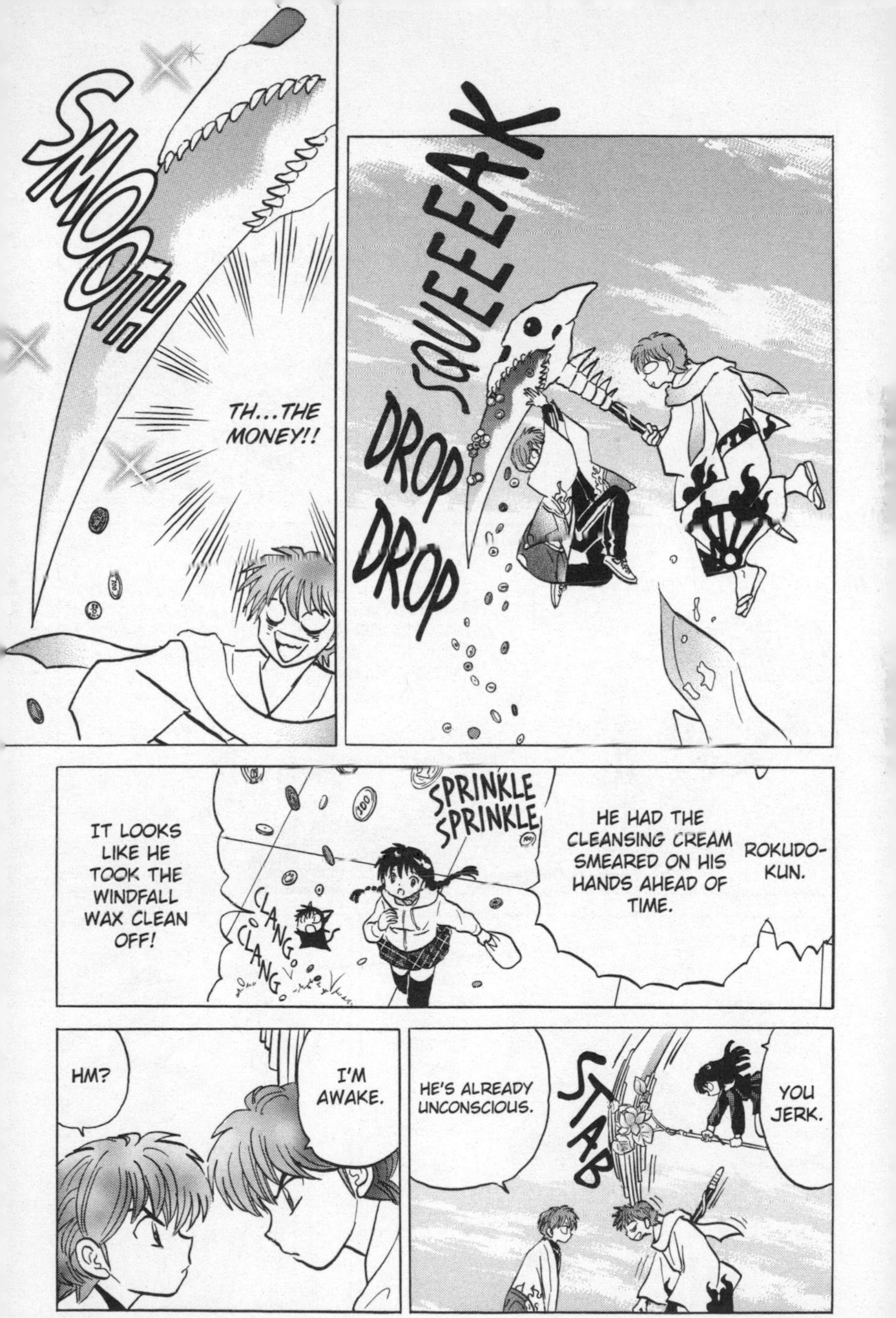
SQUEEEAK
DROP DROP
SMOOOTH
TH...THE MONEY!!
ROKUDO-KUN.
HE HAD THE CLEANSING CREAM SMEARED ON HIS HANDS AHEAD OF TIME.
SPRINKLE SPRINKLE
CLANG CLANG
IT LOOKS LIKE HE TOOK THE WINDFALL WAX CLEAN OFF!
YOU JERK.
STAB
HE'S ALREADY UNCONSCIOUS.
I'M AWAKE.
HM?

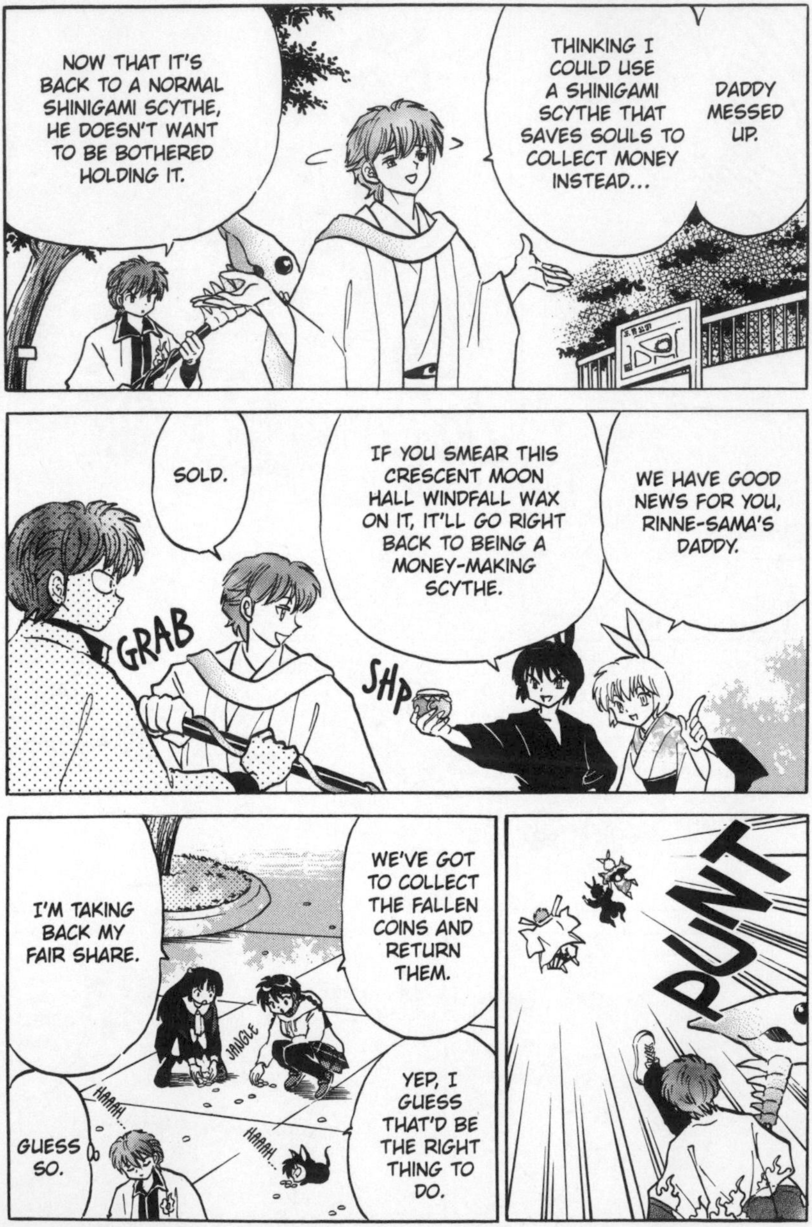
DADDY MESSED UP.
THINKING I COULD USE A SHINIGAMI SCYTHE THAT SAVES SOULS TO COLLECT MONEY INSTEAD...
NOW THAT IT'S BACK TO A NORMAL SHINIGAMI SCYTHE, HE DOESN'T WANT TO BE BOTHERED HOLDING IT.
WE HAVE GOOD NEWS FOR YOU, RINNE-SAMA'S DADDY.
IF YOU SMEAR THIS CRESCENT MOON HALL WINDFALL WAX ON IT, IT'LL GO RIGHT BACK TO BEING A MONEY-MAKING SCYTHE.
SHP
GRAB
SOLD.
PUNT
WE'VE GOT TO COLLECT THE FALLEN COINS AND RETURN THEM.
I'M TAKING BACK MY FAIR SHARE.
JANGLE
YEP, I GUESS THAT'D BE THE RIGHT THING TO DO.
HAAAH...
HAAAH...
GUESS SO.

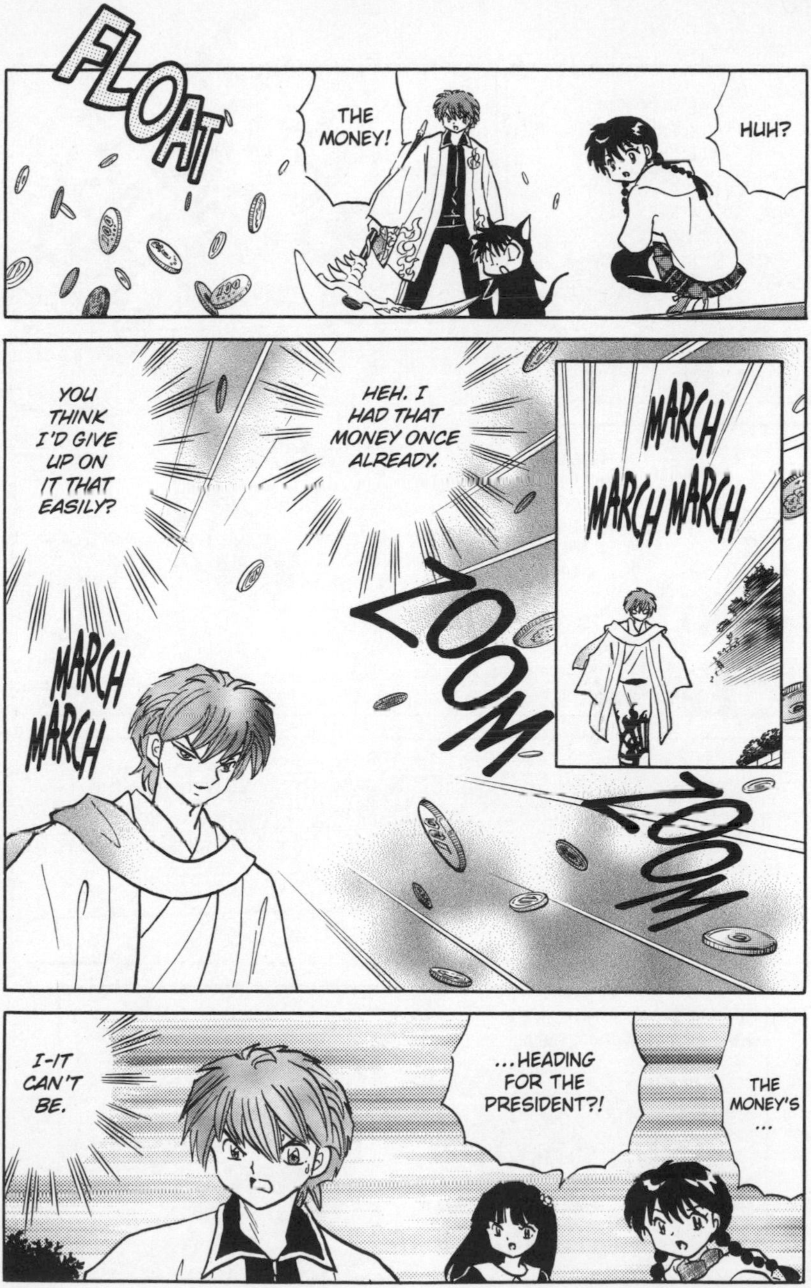
FLOAT
HUH?
THE MONEY!
MARCH
MARCH MARCH
HEH. I HAD THAT MONEY ONCE ALREADY.
YOU THINK I'D GIVE UP ON IT THAT EASILY?
ZOOM
ZOOM
MARCH MARCH
THE MONEY'S...
...HEADING FOR THE PRESIDENT?!
I-IT CAN'T BE.

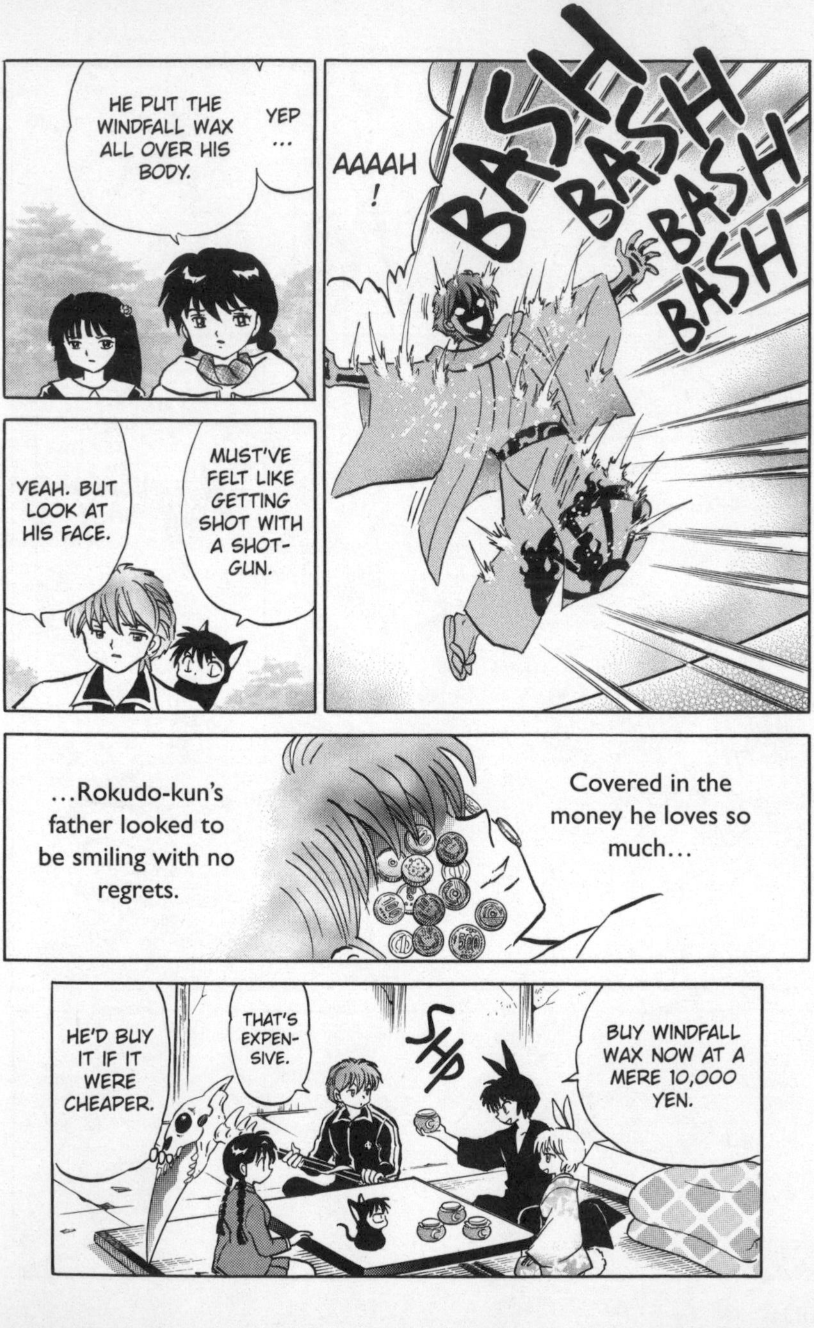
BASH
BASH
BASH
BASH
BASH
AAAAH!
HE PUT THE WINDFALL WAX ALL OVER HIS BODY.
YEP...
MUST'VE FELT LIKE GETTING SHOT WITH A SHOT-GUN.
YEAH. BUT LOOK AT HIS FACE.
Covered in the money he loves so much...
...Rokudo-kun's father looked to be smiling with no regrets.
BUY WINDFALL WAX NOW AT A MERE 10,000 YEN.
SHP
THAT'S EXPEN-SIVE.
HE'D BUY IT IF IT WERE CHEAPER.

CHAPTER 184: AT THE GRADUATION CEREMONY

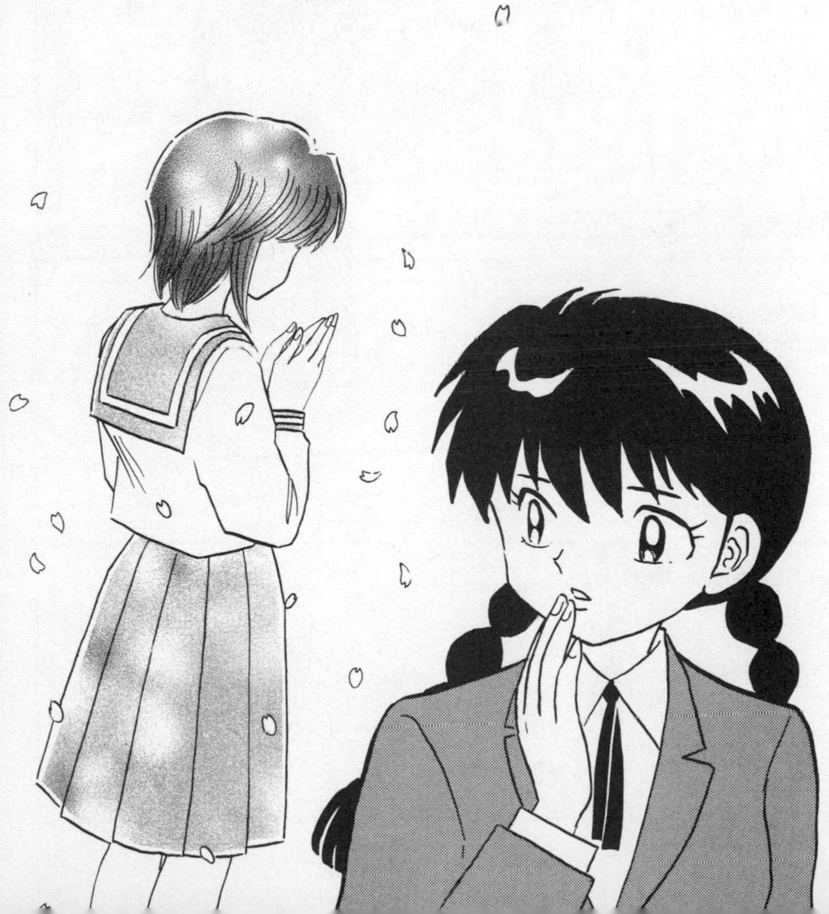

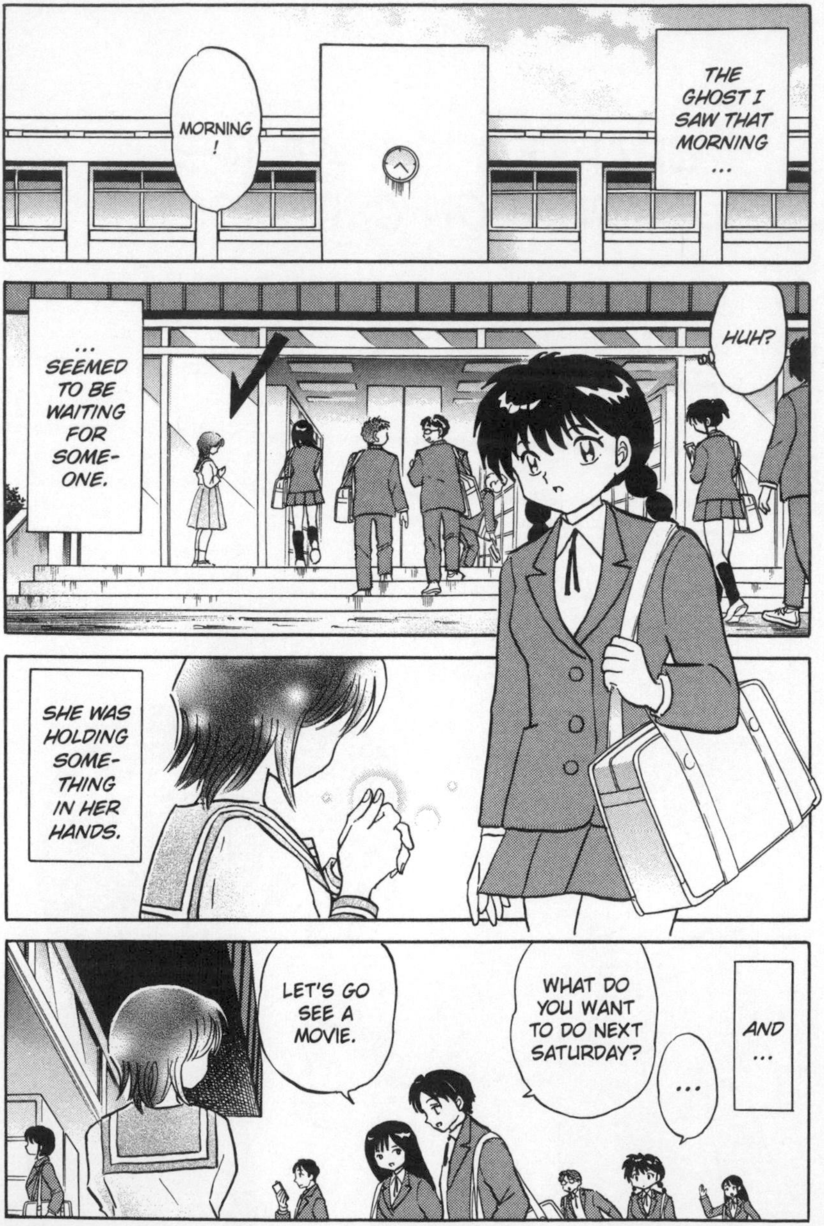
THE GHOST I SAW THAT MORNING ...
MORNING!
HUH?
... SEEMED TO BE WAITING FOR SOME-ONE.
SHE WAS HOLDING SOME-THING IN HER HANDS.
AND ...
...
WHAT DO YOU WANT TO DO NEXT SATURDAY?
LET'S GO SEE A MOVIE.

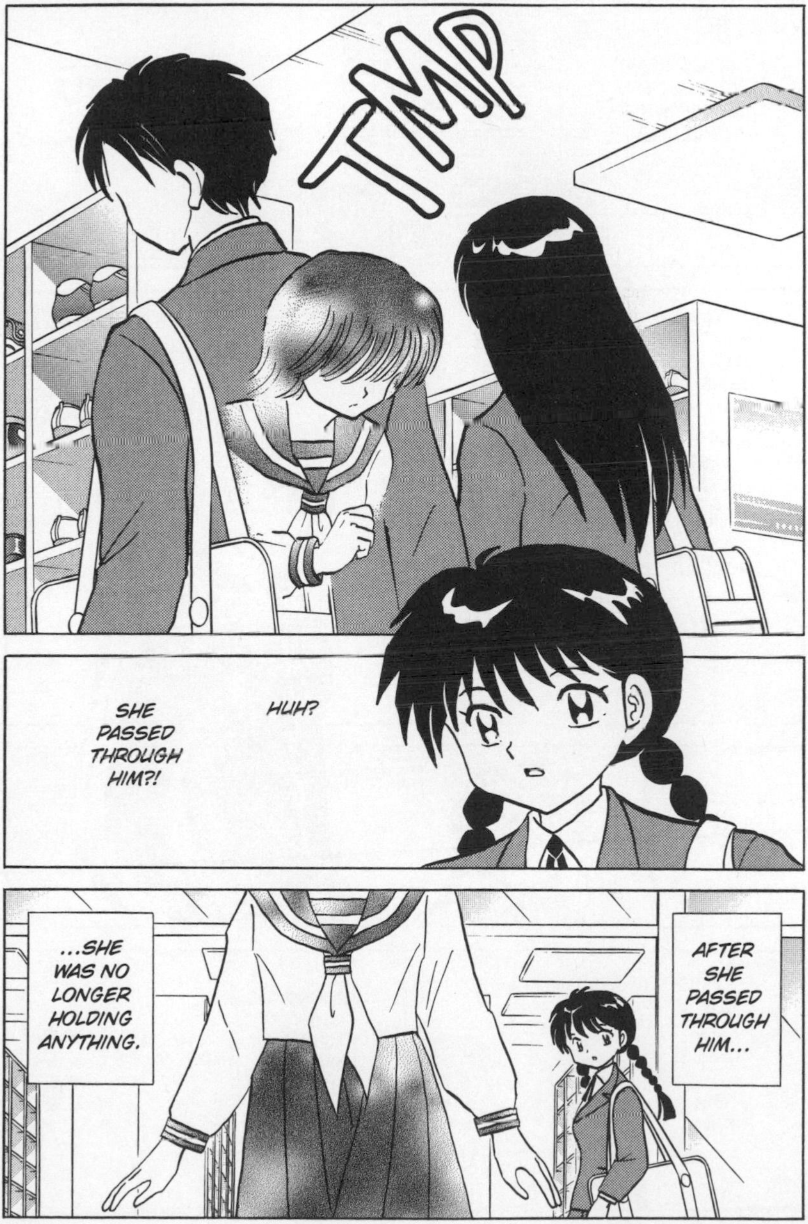
TMP
HUH?
SHE PASSED THROUGH HIM?!
AFTER SHE PASSED THROUGH HIM...
...SHE WAS NO LONGER HOLDING ANYTHING.

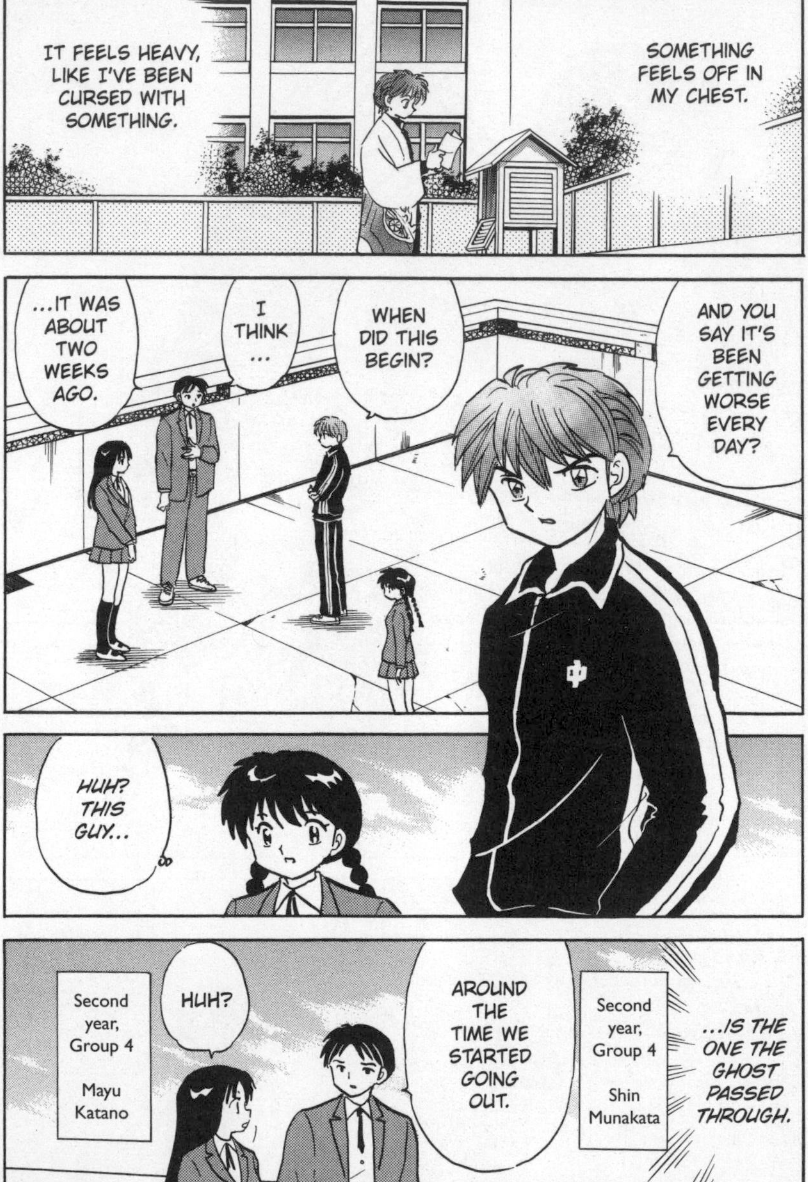
SOMETHING FEELS OFF IN MY CHEST.
IT FEELS HEAVY, LIKE I'VE BEEN CURSED WITH SOMETHING.
AND YOU SAY IT'S BEEN GETTING WORSE EVERY DAY?
WHEN DID THIS BEGIN?
I THINK ...
...IT WAS ABOUT TWO WEEKS AGO.
HUH? THIS GUY...
...IS THE ONE THE GHOST PASSED THROUGH.
Second year, Group 4 Shin Munakata
AROUND THE TIME WE STARTED GOING OUT.
HUH?
Second year, Group 4 Mayu Katano

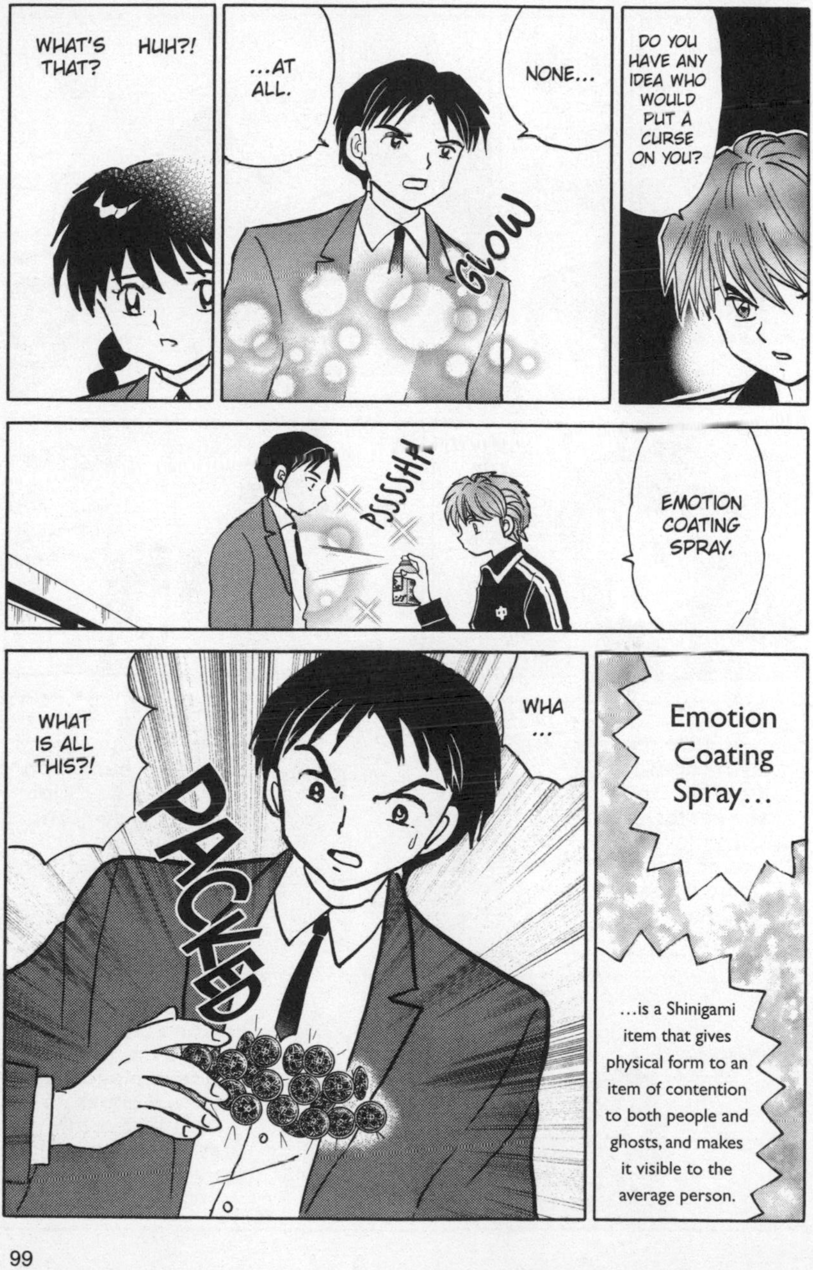
DO YOU HAVE ANY IDEA WHO WOULD PUT A CURSE ON YOU?
NONE...
...AT ALL.
GLOW
HUH?!
WHAT'S THAT?
EMOTION COATING SPRAY.
PSSSSHH
Emotion Coating Spray...
...is a Shinigami item that gives physical form to an item of contention to both people and ghosts, and makes it visible to the average person.
WHA ...
WHAT IS ALL THIS?!
PACKED

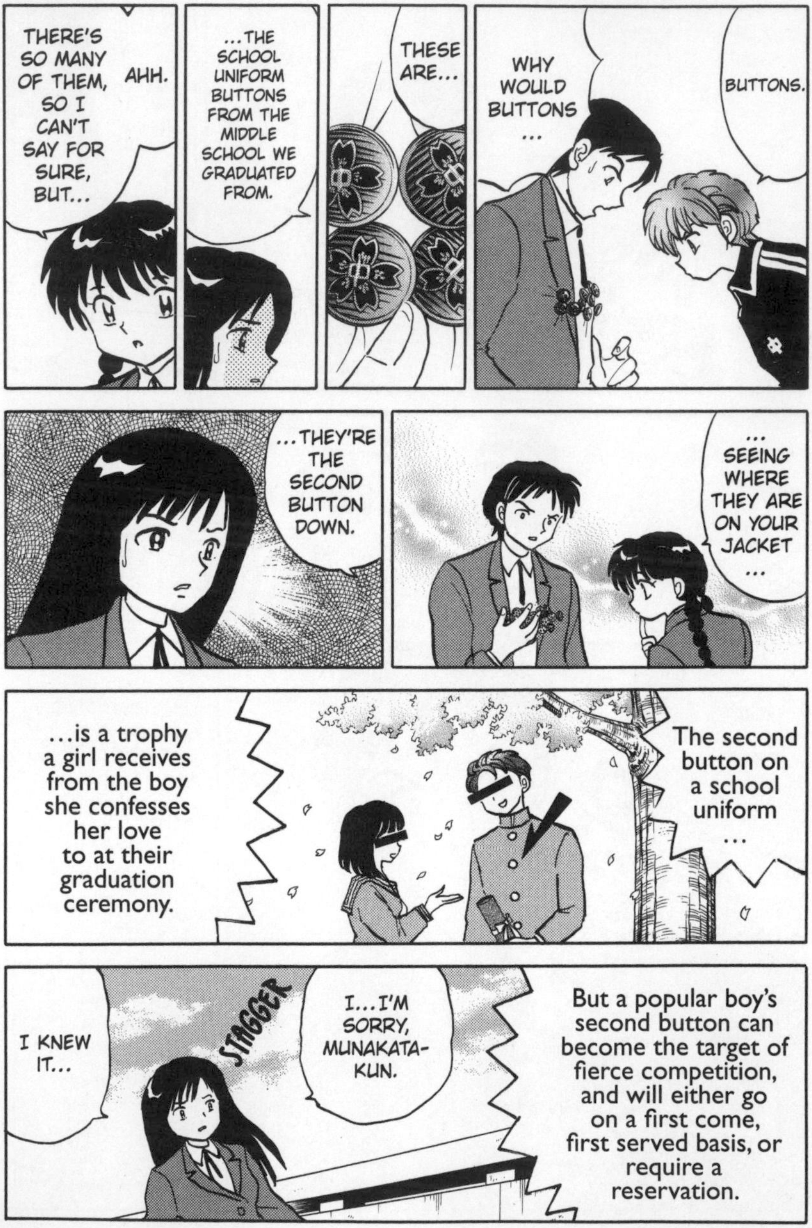
BUTTONS.
WHY WOULD BUTTONS ...
THESE ARE...
...THE SCHOOL UNIFORM BUTTONS FROM THE MIDDLE SCHOOL WE GRADUATED FROM.
AHH.
THERE'S SO MANY OF THEM, SO I CAN'T SAY FOR SURE, BUT...
... SEEING WHERE THEY ARE ON YOUR JACKET ...
...THEY'RE THE SECOND BUTTON DOWN.
The second button on a school uniform ...
...is a trophy a girl receives from the boy she confesses her love to at their graduation ceremony.
But a popular boy's second button can become the target of fierce competition, and will either go on a first come, first served basis, or require a reservation.
I...I'M SORRY, MUNAKATA-KUN.
STAGGER
I KNEW IT...

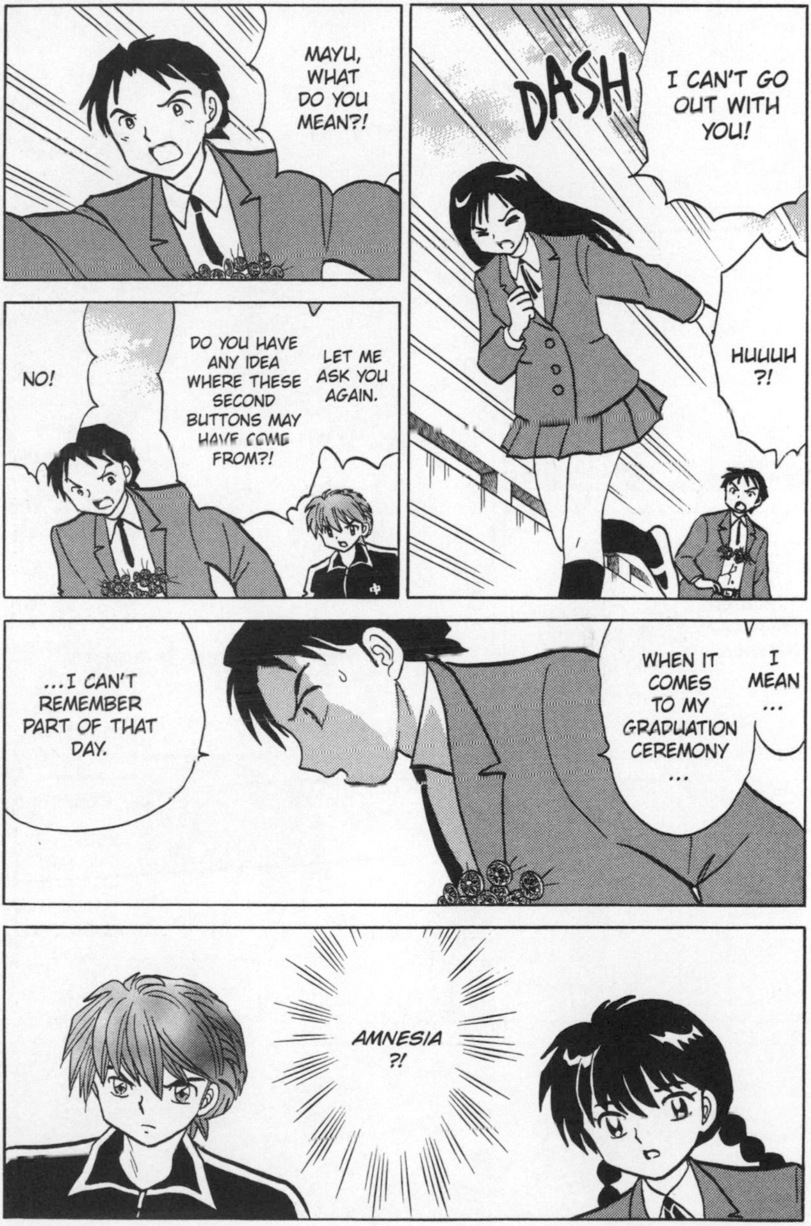
DASH
I CAN'T GO OUT WITH YOU!
HUUUH ?!
MAYU, WHAT DO YOU MEAN?!
LET ME ASK YOU AGAIN.
DO YOU HAVE ANY IDEA WHERE THESE SECOND BUTTONS MAY HAVE COME FROM?!
NO!
I MEAN ...
WHEN IT COMES TO MY GRADUATION CEREMONY ...
...I CAN'T REMEMBER PART OF THAT DAY.
AMNESIA ?!

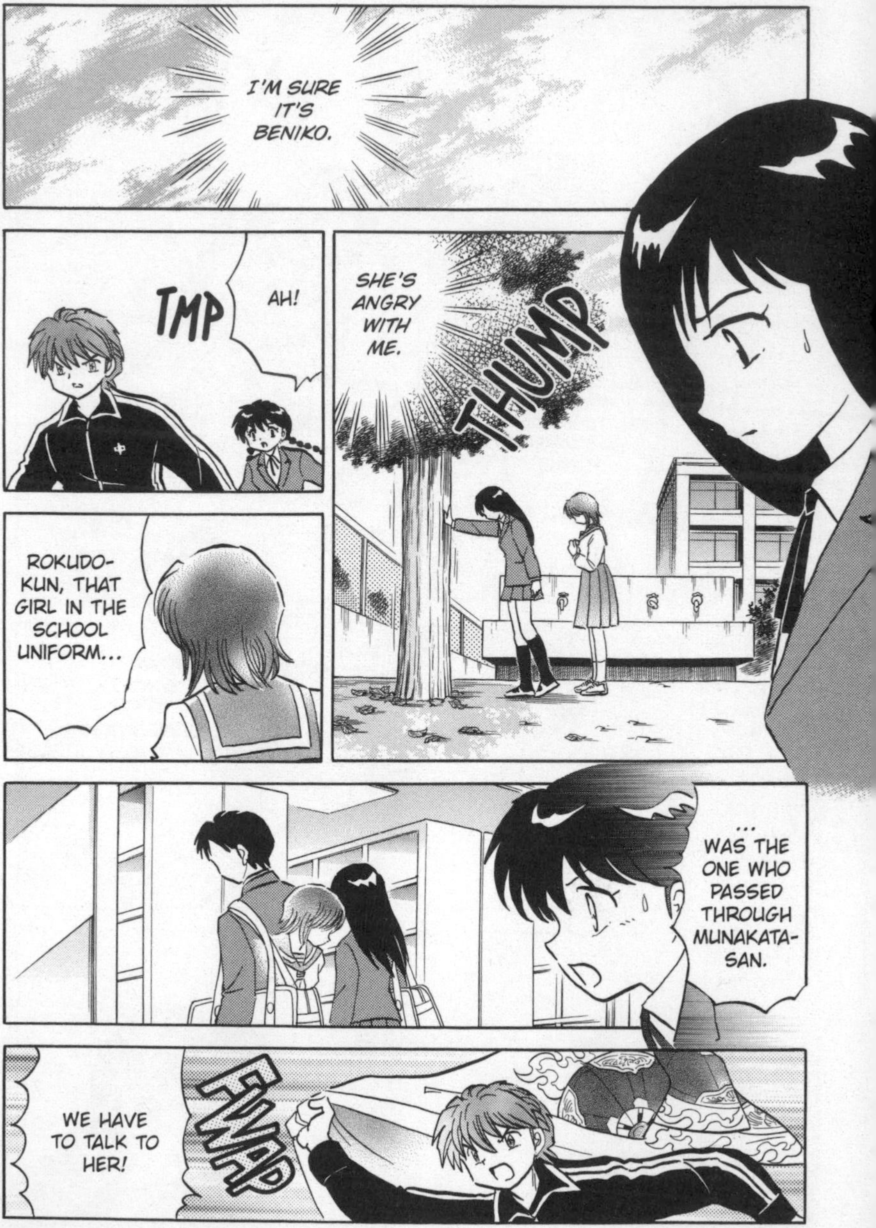

I'M SURE IT'S BENIKO.
SHE'S ANGRY WITH ME.
THUMP
AH!
TMP
ROKUDO-KUN, THAT GIRL IN THE SCHOOL UNIFORM...
... WAS THE ONE WHO PASSED THROUGH MUNAKATA-SAN.
FWAP
WE HAVE TO TALK TO HER!

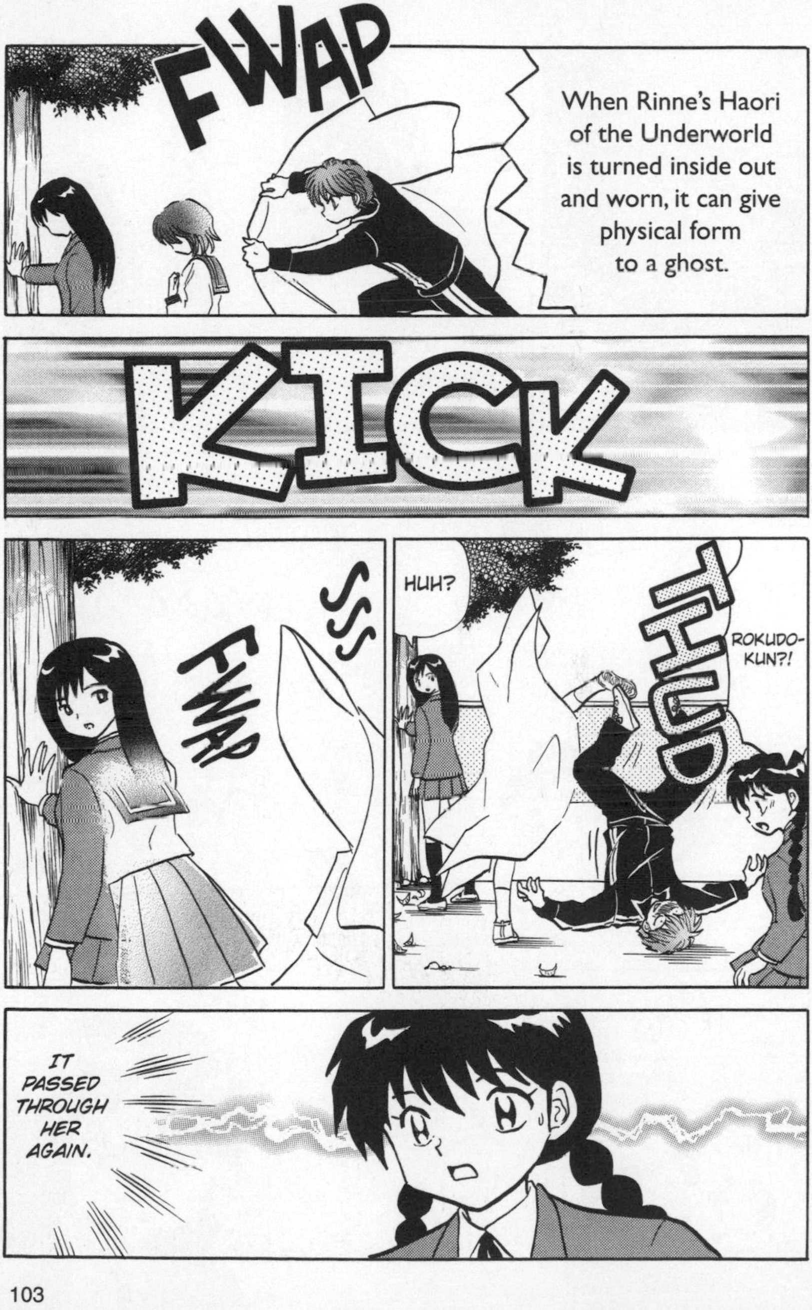
FWAP
When Rinne's Haori of the Underworld is turned inside out and worn, it can give physical form to a ghost.
KICK
THUD
HUH?
ROKUDO-KUN?!
SSS
FWAP
IT PASSED THROUGH HER AGAIN.

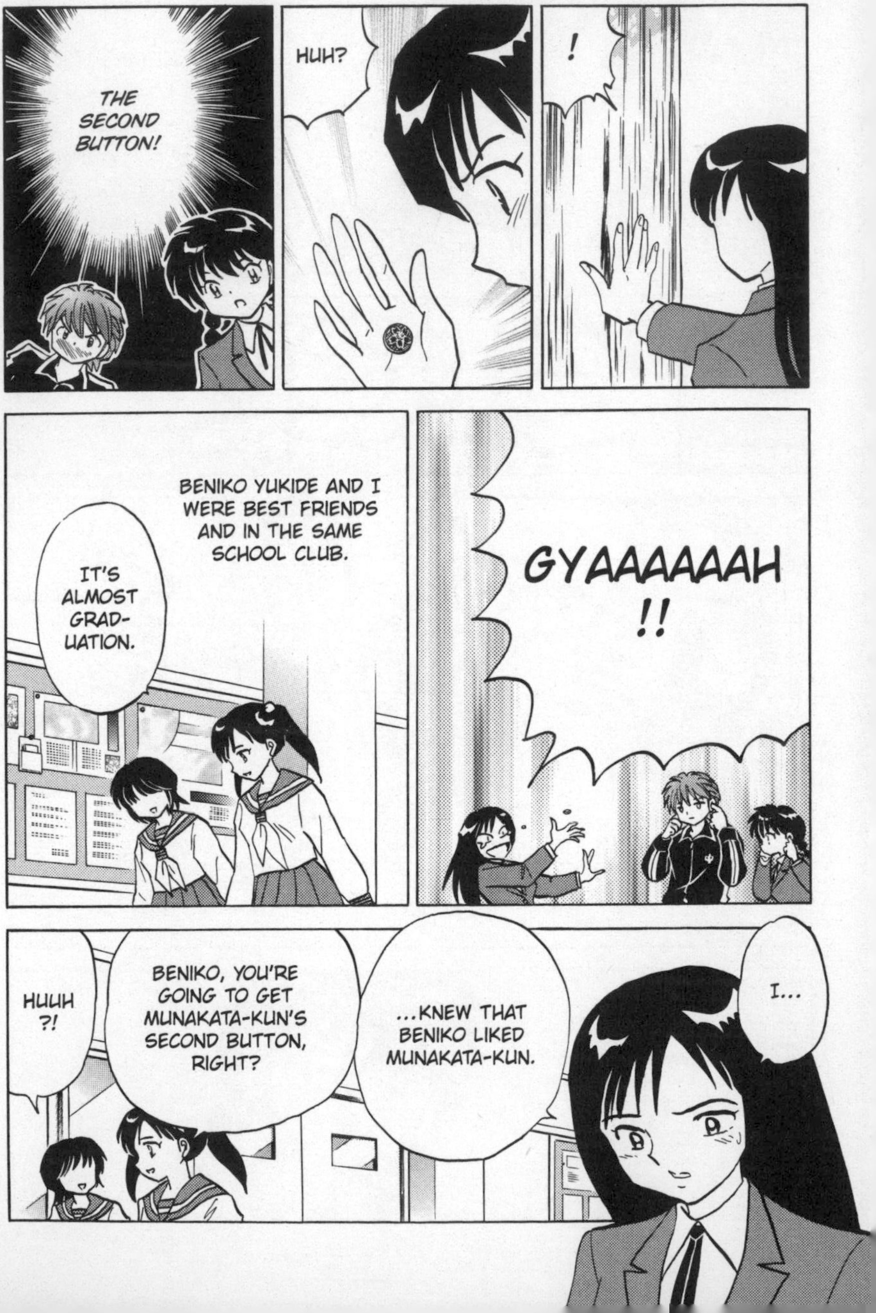
!
HUH?
THE SECOND BUTTON!
GYAAAAAAH !!
BENIKO YUKIDE AND I WERE BEST FRIENDS AND IN THE SAME SCHOOL CLUB.
IT'S ALMOST GRAD-UATION.
I...
...KNEW THAT BENIKO LIKED MUNAKATA-KUN.
BENIKO, YOU'RE GOING TO GET MUNAKATA-KUN'S SECOND BUTTON, RIGHT?
HUUH ?!

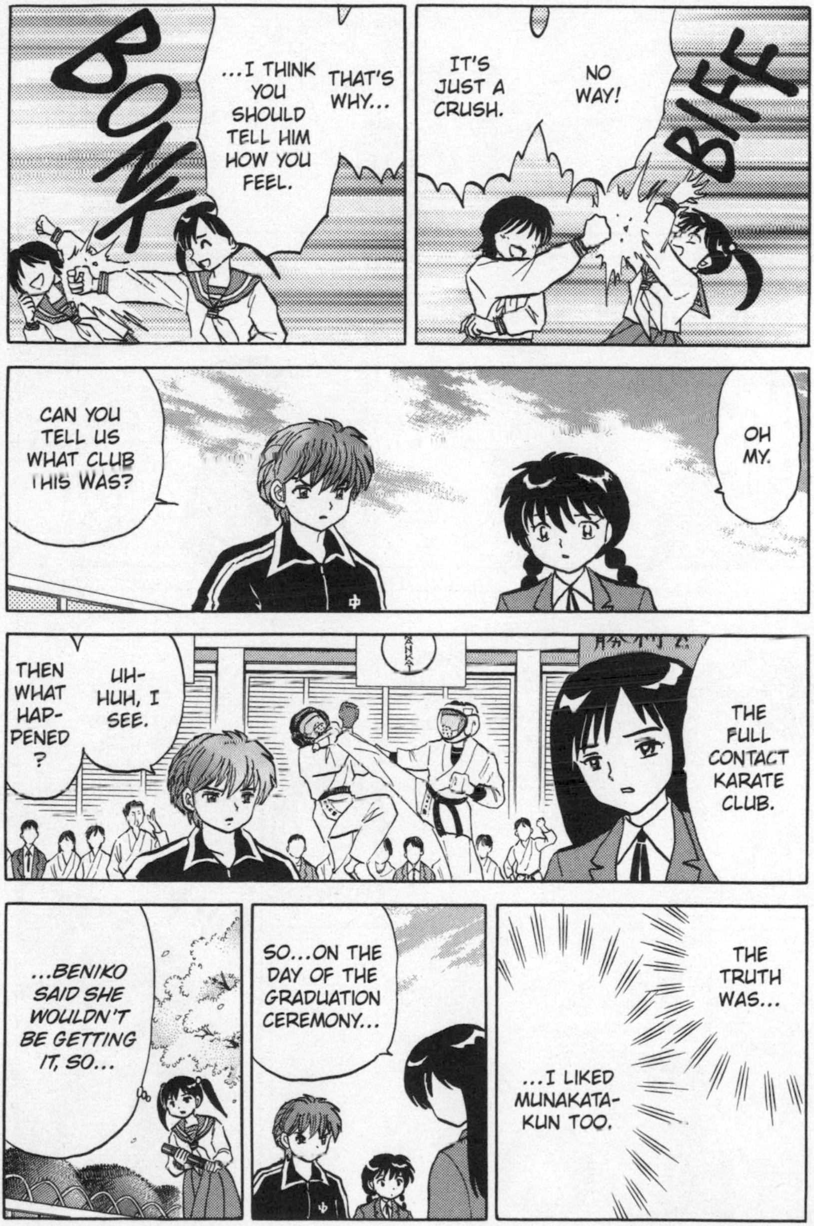
NO WAY!
BIFF
IT'S JUST A CRUSH.
THAT'S WHY...
...I THINK YOU SHOULD TELL HIM HOW YOU FEEL.
BONK
OH MY.
CAN YOU TELL US WHAT CLUB THIS WAS?
THE FULL CONTACT KARATE CLUB.
UH-HUH, I SEE.
THEN WHAT HAPPENED?
THE TRUTH WAS...
...I LIKED MUNAKATA-KUN TOO.
SO...ON THE DAY OF THE GRADUATION CEREMONY...
...BENIKO SAID SHE WOULDN'T BE GETTING IT, SO...

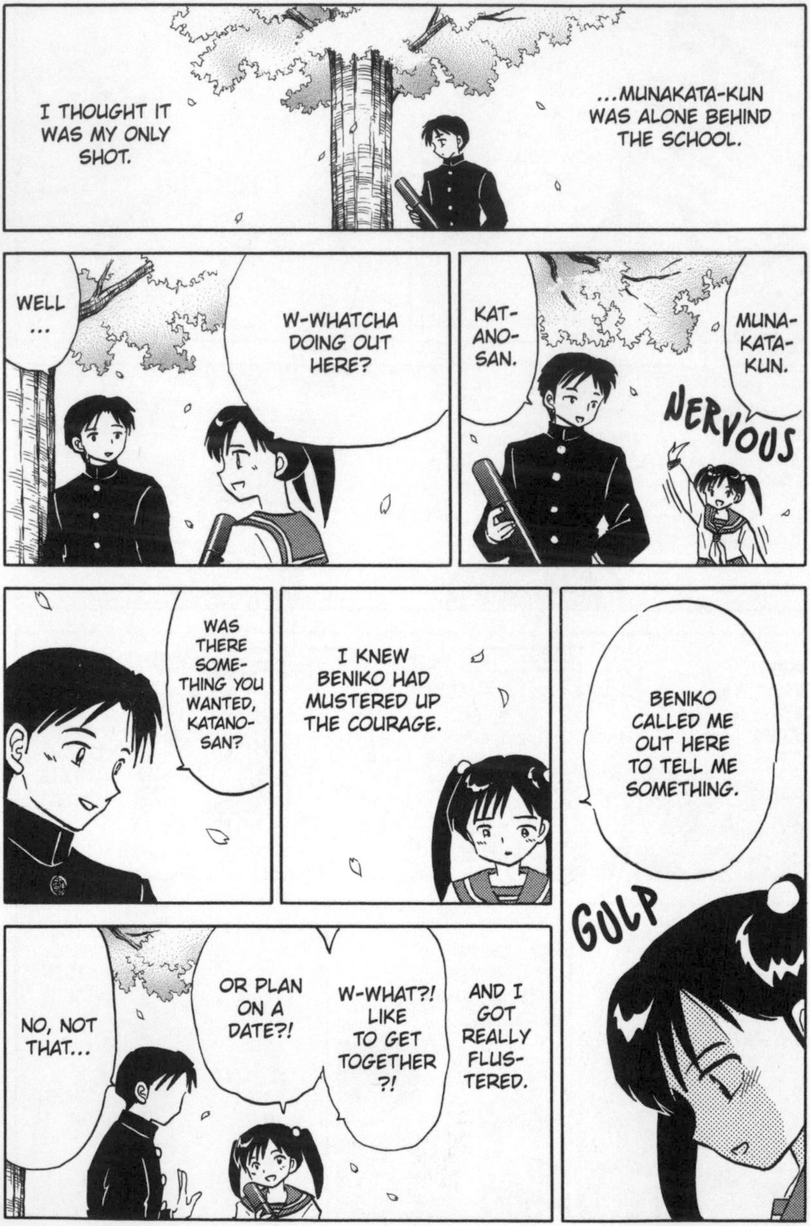
...MUNAKATA-KUN WAS ALONE BEHIND THE SCHOOL.
I THOUGHT IT WAS MY ONLY SHOT.
MUNA-KATA-KUN.
NERVOUS
KAT-ANO-SAN.
W-WHATCHA DOING OUT HERE?
WELL ...
BENIKO CALLED ME OUT HERE TO TELL ME SOMETHING.
GULP
I KNEW BENIKO HAD MUSTERED UP THE COURAGE.
WAS THERE SOME-THING YOU WANTED, KATANO-SAN?
AND I GOT REALLY FLUS-TERED.
W-WHAT?! LIKE TO GET TOGETHER ?!
OR PLAN ON A DATE?!
NO, NOT THAT...

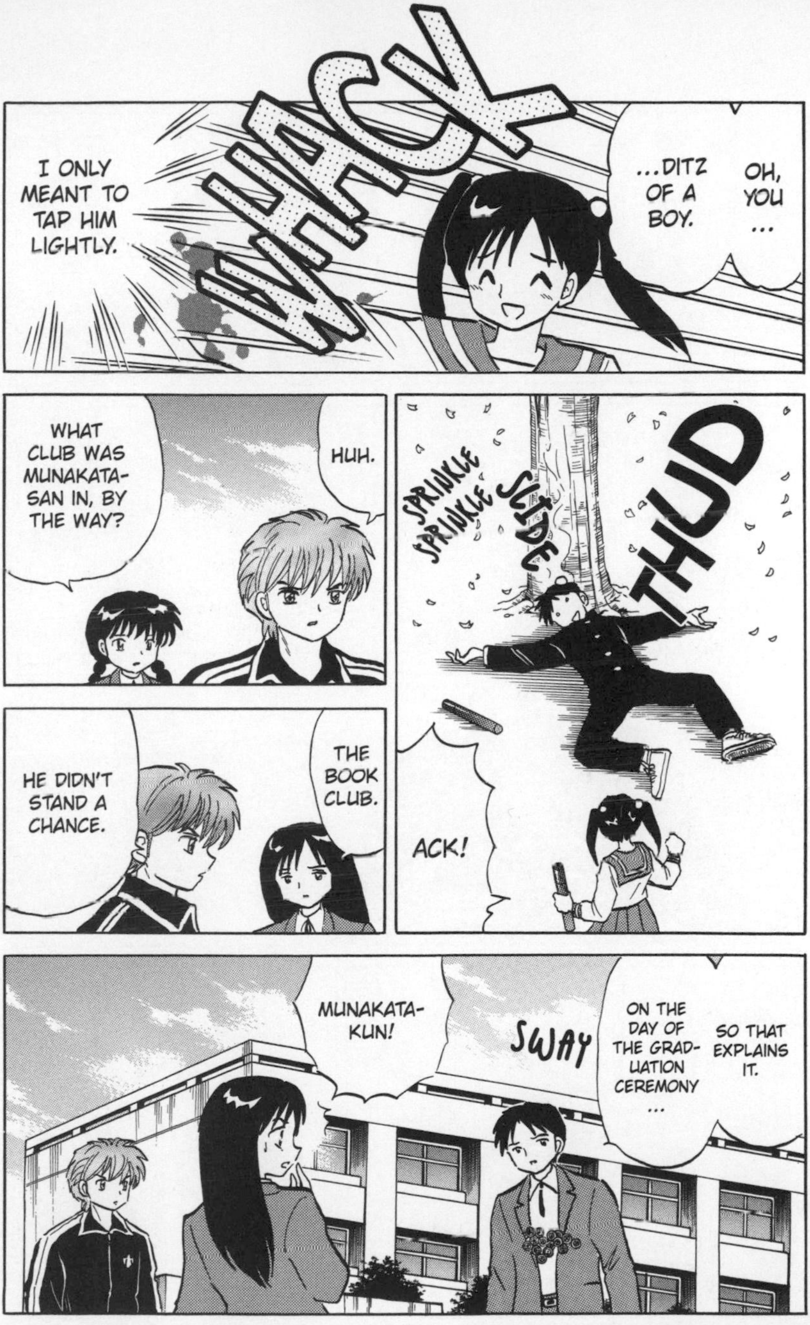

OH, YOU ...
...DITZ OF A BOY.
WHACK
I ONLY MEANT TO TAP HIM LIGHTLY.
THUD
SLIDE
SPRINKLE SPRINKLE
ACK!
HUH.
WHAT CLUB WAS MUNAKATA-SAN IN, BY THE WAY?
THE BOOK CLUB.
HE DIDN'T STAND A CHANCE.
SO THAT EXPLAINS IT.
ON THE DAY OF THE GRAD-UATION CEREMONY ...
SWAY
MUNAKATA-KUN!

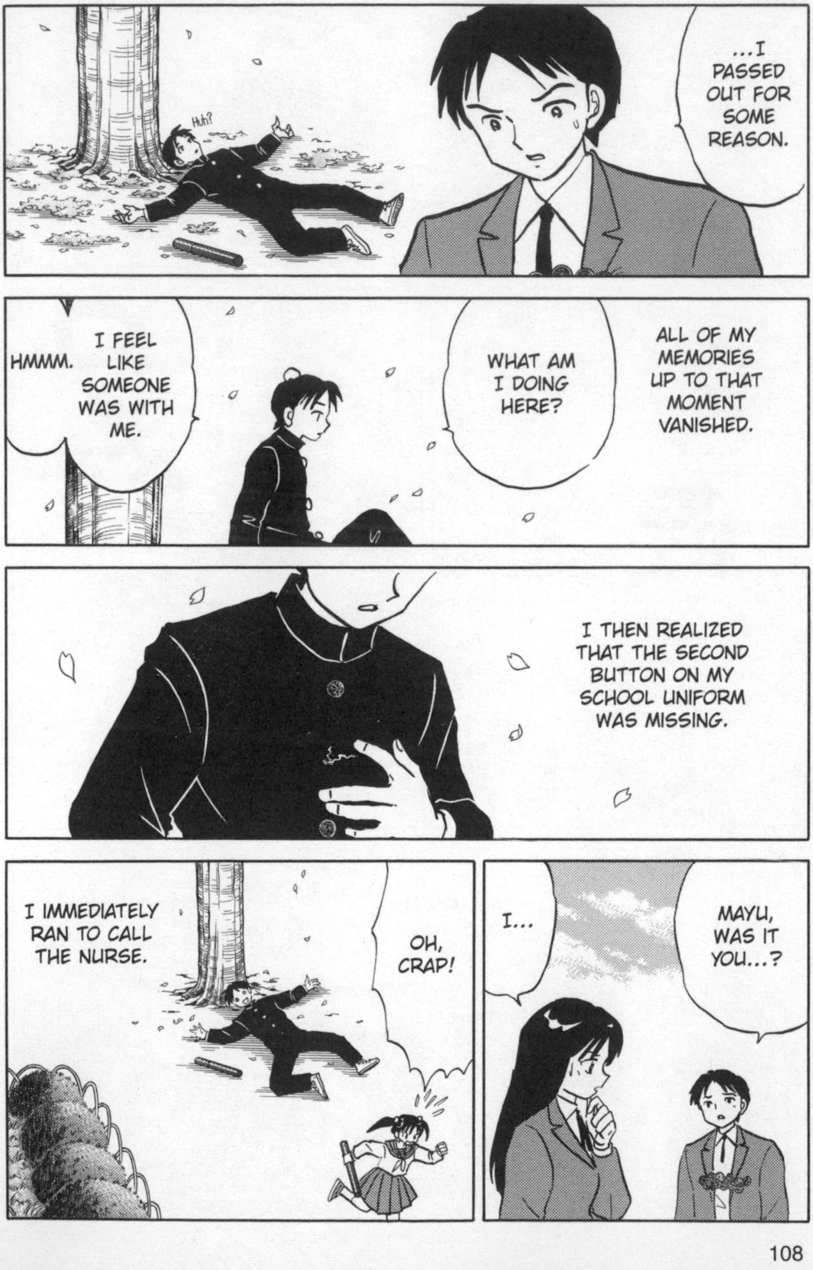
...I PASSED OUT FOR SOME REASON.
Huh?
ALL OF MY MEMORIES UP TO THAT MOMENT VANISHED.
WHAT AM I DOING HERE?
I FEEL LIKE SOMEONE WAS WITH ME.
HMMM.
I THEN REALIZED THAT THE SECOND BUTTON ON MY SCHOOL UNIFORM WAS MISSING.
MAYU, WAS IT YOU...?
I...
OH, CRAP!
I IMMEDIATELY RAN TO CALL THE NURSE.

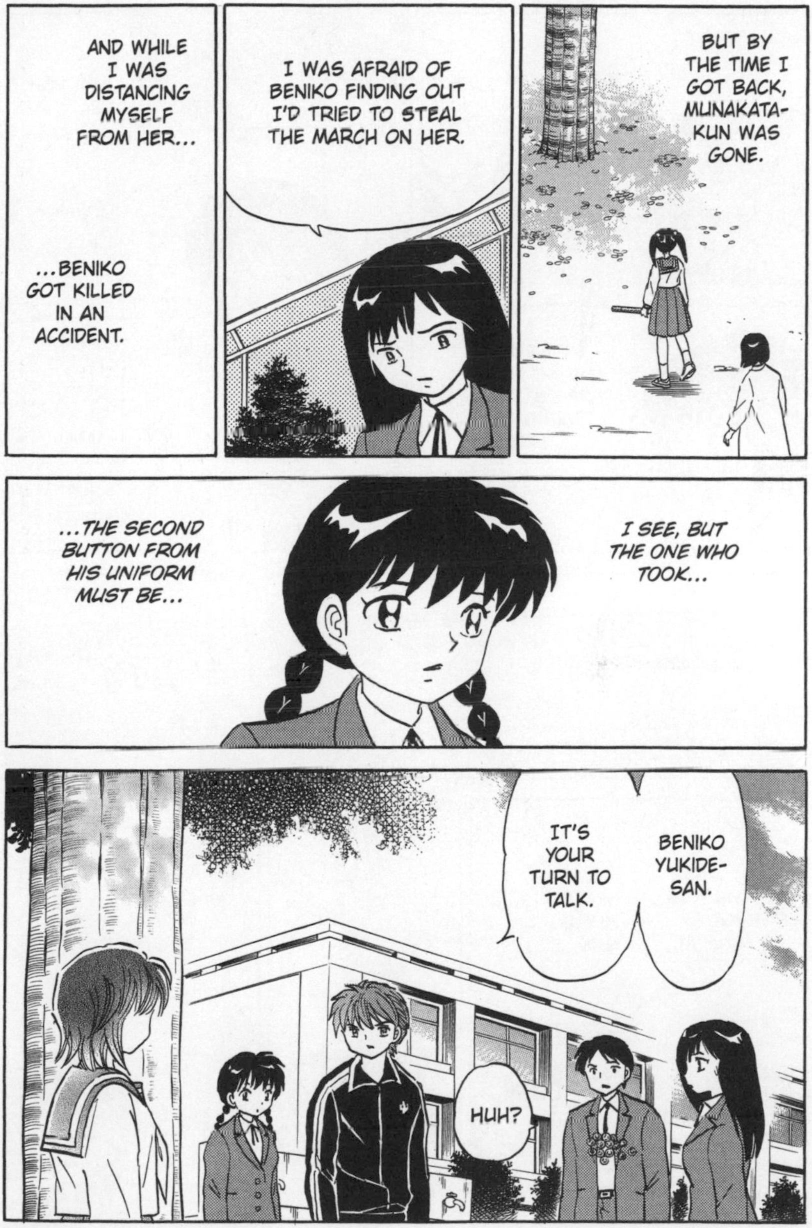
BUT BY THE TIME I GOT BACK, MUNAKATA-KUN WAS GONE.
I WAS AFRAID OF BENIKO FINDING OUT I'D TRIED TO STEAL THE MARCH ON HER.
AND WHILE I WAS DISTANCING MYSELF FROM HER...
...BENIKO GOT KILLED IN AN ACCIDENT.
I SEE, BUT THE ONE WHO TOOK...
...THE SECOND BUTTON FROM HIS UNIFORM MUST BE...
BENIKO YUKIDE-SAN.
IT'S YOUR TURN TO TALK.
HUH?

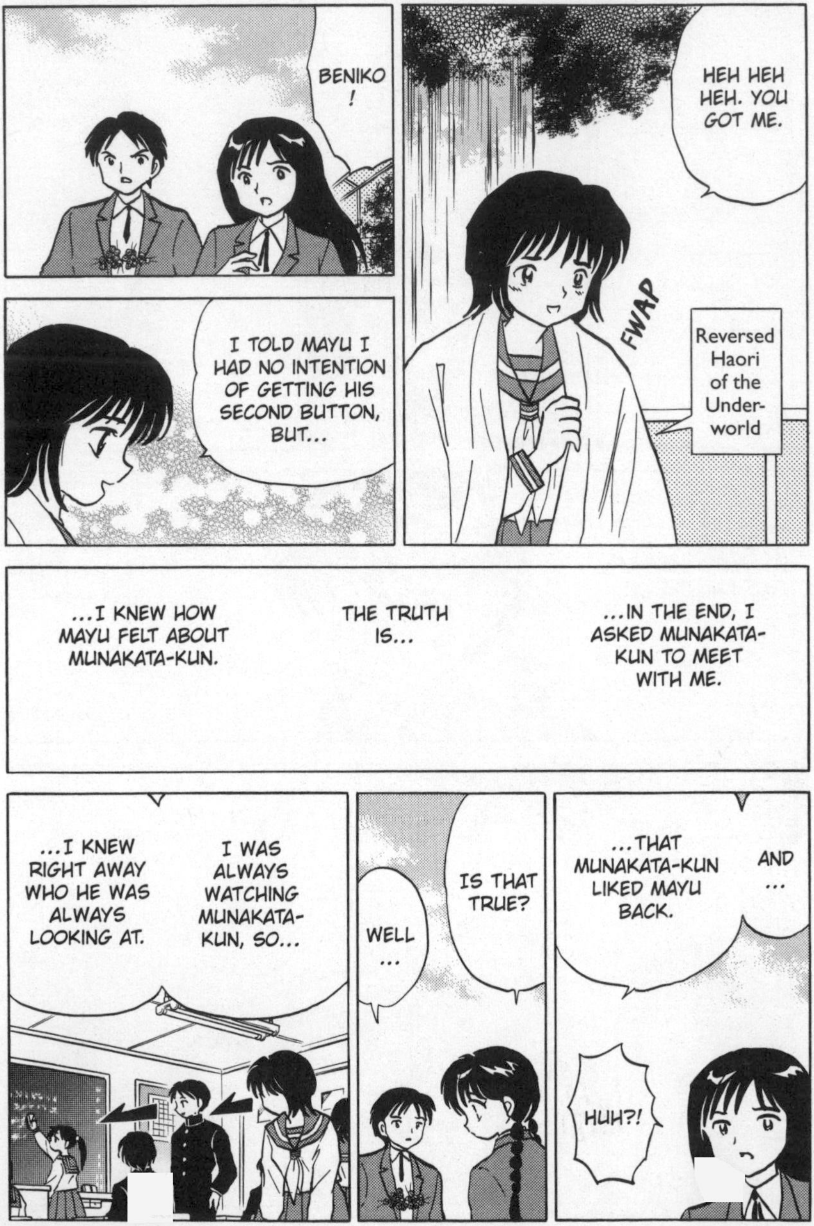
HEH HEH HEH. YOU GOT ME.
FWAP
Reversed Haori of the Underworld
BENIKO!
I TOLD MAYU I HAD NO INTENTION OF GETTING HIS SECOND BUTTON, BUT...
...IN THE END, I ASKED MUNAKATA-KUN TO MEET WITH ME.
THE TRUTH IS...
...I KNEW HOW MAYU FELT ABOUT MUNAKATA-KUN.
AND...
...THAT MUNAKATA-KUN LIKED MAYU BACK.
HUH?!
IS THAT TRUE?
WELL...
I WAS ALWAYS WATCHING MUNAKATA-KUN, SO...
...I KNEW RIGHT AWAY WHO HE WAS ALWAYS LOOKING AT.

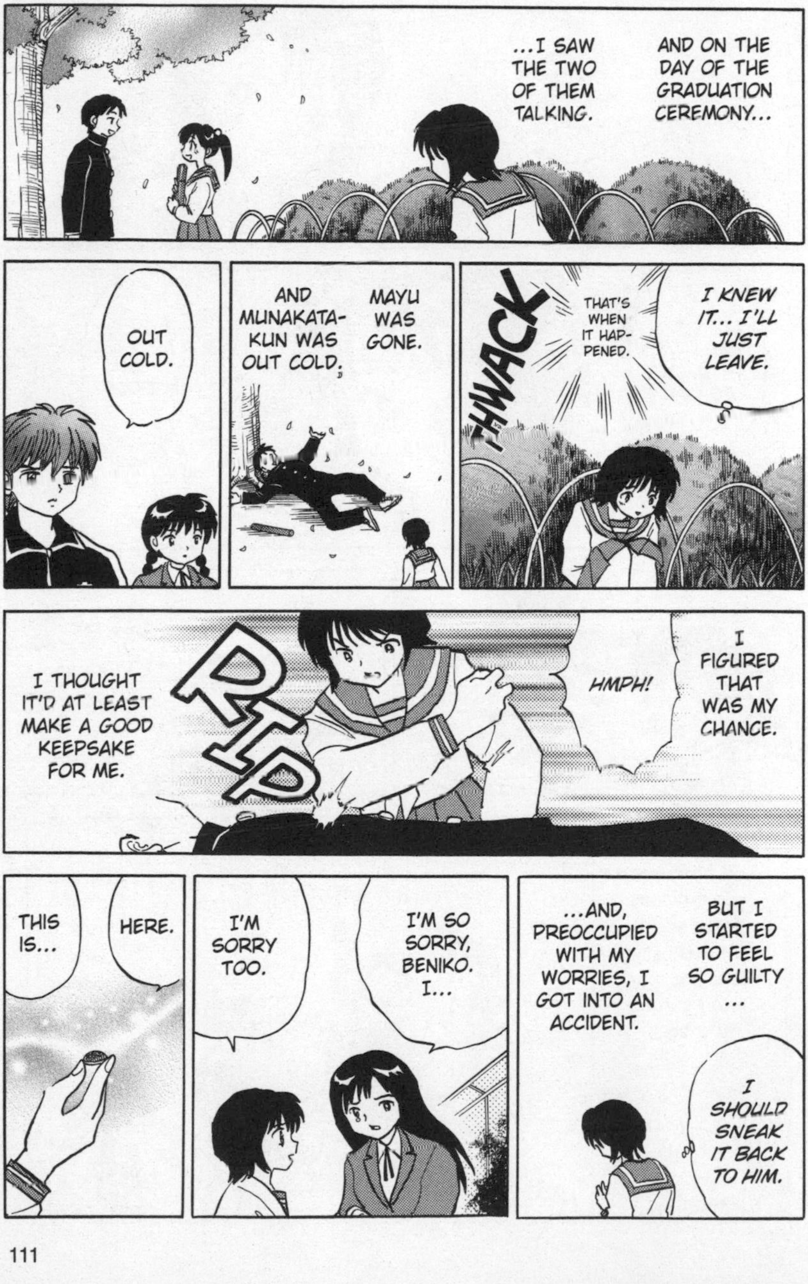
AND ON THE DAY OF THE GRADUATION CEREMONY...
...I SAW THE TWO OF THEM TALKING.
I KNEW IT... I'LL JUST LEAVE.
THAT'S WHEN IT HAPPENED.
THWACK
MAYU WAS GONE.
AND MUNAKATA-KUN WAS OUT COLD.
OUT COLD.
I FIGURED THAT WAS MY CHANCE.
HMPH!
RIP
I THOUGHT IT'D AT LEAST MAKE A GOOD KEEPSAKE FOR ME.
BUT I STARTED TO FEEL SO GUILTY ...
...AND, PREOCCUPIED WITH MY WORRIES, I GOT INTO AN ACCIDENT.
I SHOULD SNEAK IT BACK TO HIM.
I'M SO SORRY, BENIKO. I...
I'M SORRY TOO.
HERE.
THIS IS...

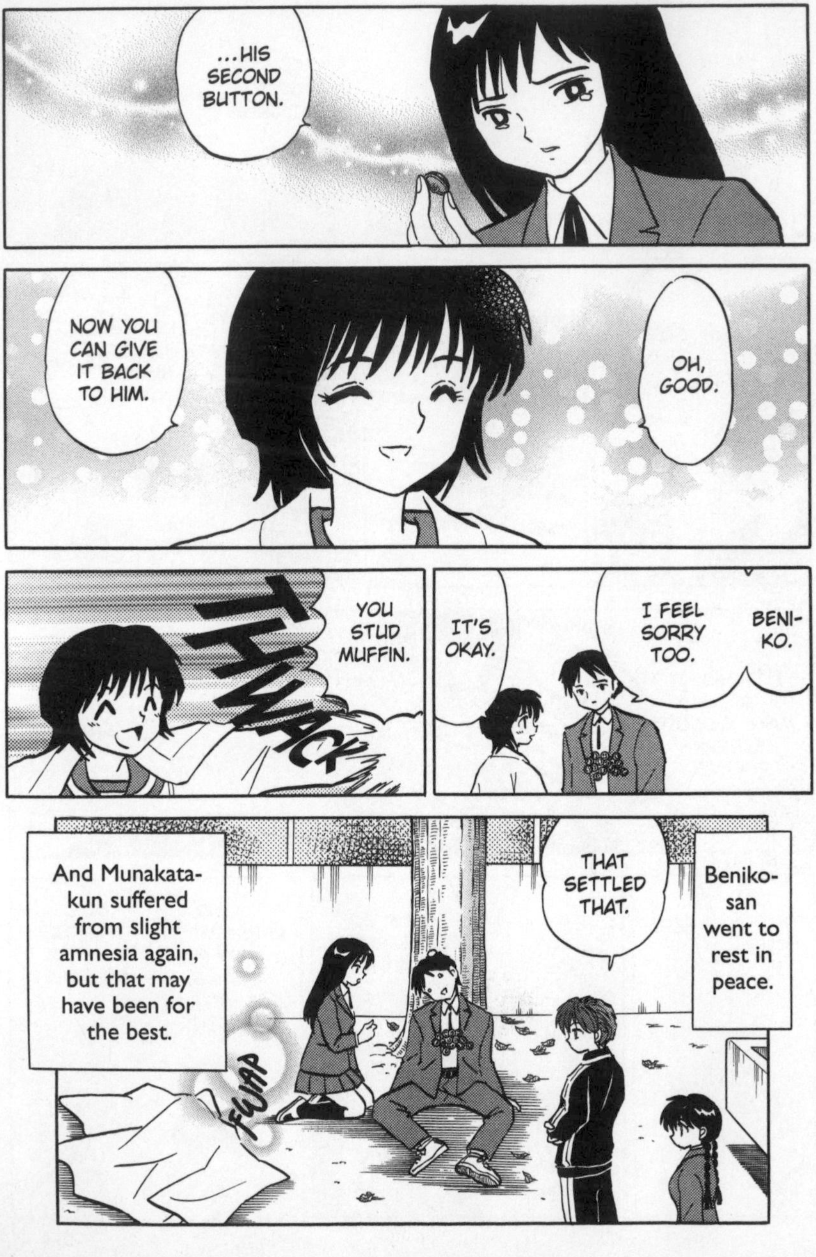
...HIS SECOND BUTTON.
OH, GOOD.
NOW YOU CAN GIVE IT BACK TO HIM.
BENI-KO.
I FEEL SORRY TOO.
IT'S OKAY.
YOU STUD MUFFIN.
THWACK
Beniko-san went to rest in peace.
THAT SETTLED THAT.
And Munakata-kun suffered from slight amnesia again, but that may have been for the best.
FWAP

CHAPTER 185: FORCED PAWNING

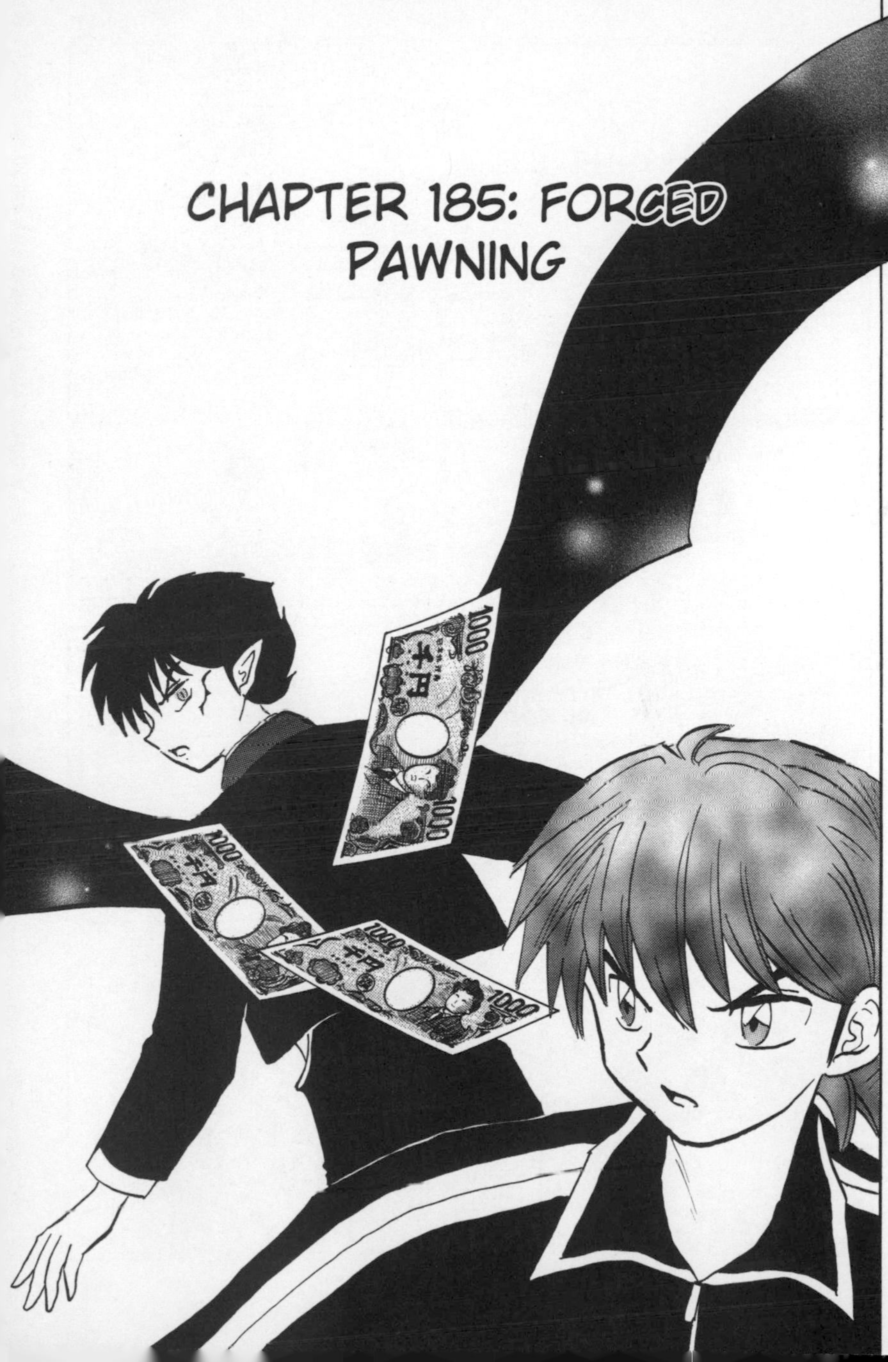

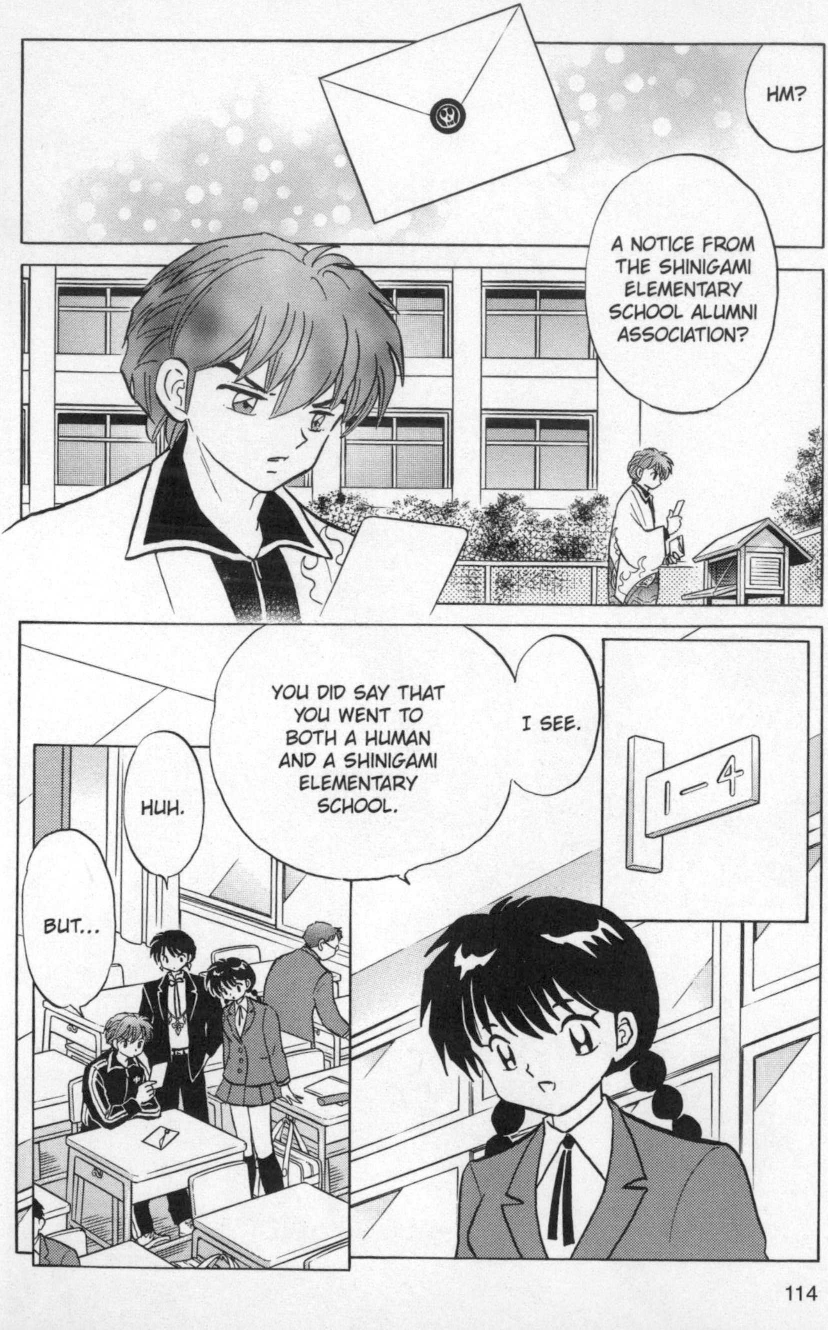
HM?
A NOTICE FROM THE SHINIGAMI ELEMENTARY SCHOOL ALUMNI ASSOCIATION?
1-4
I SEE.
YOU DID SAY THAT YOU WENT TO BOTH A HUMAN AND A SHINIGAMI ELEMENTARY SCHOOL.
HUH.
BUT...

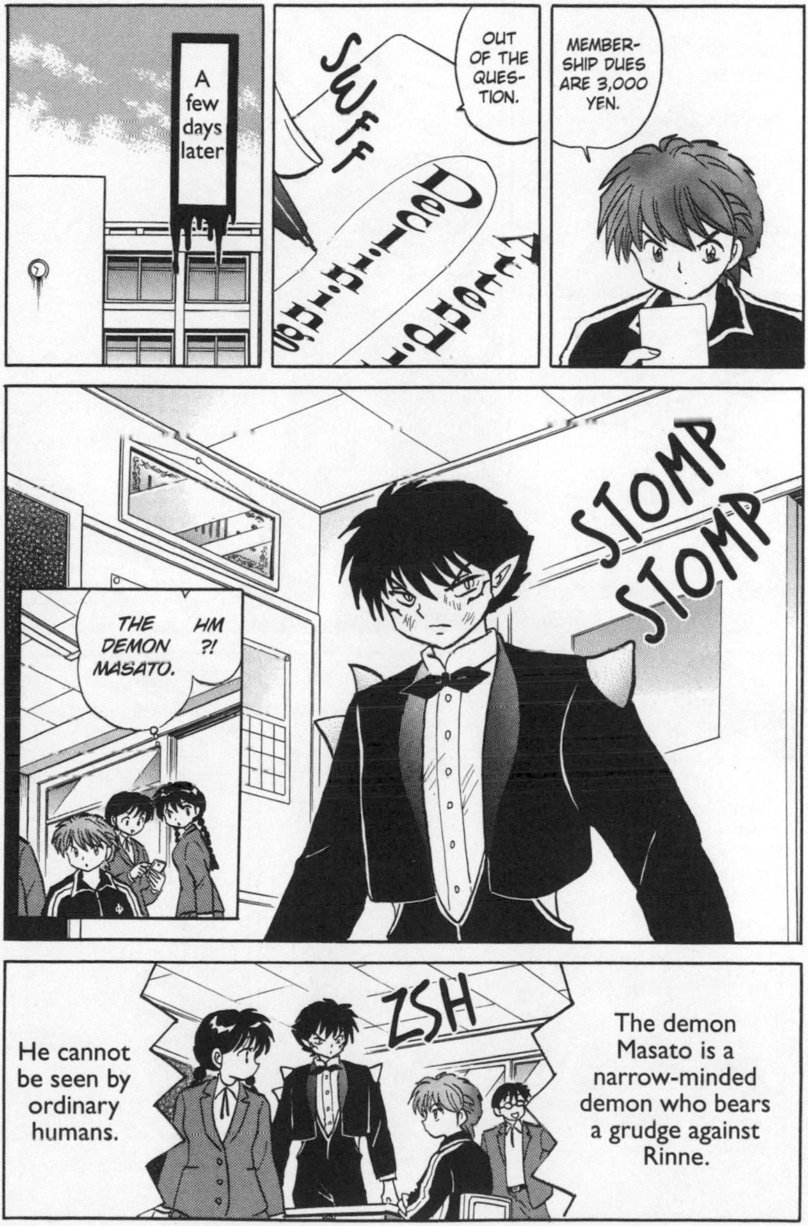
MEMBER-SHIP DUES ARE 3,000 YEN.
OUT OF THE QUES-TION.
SWFF
A few days later
STOMP
STOMP
HM ?!
THE DEMON MASATO.
ZSH
The demon Masato is a narrow-minded demon who bears a grudge against Rinne.
He cannot be seen by ordinary humans.

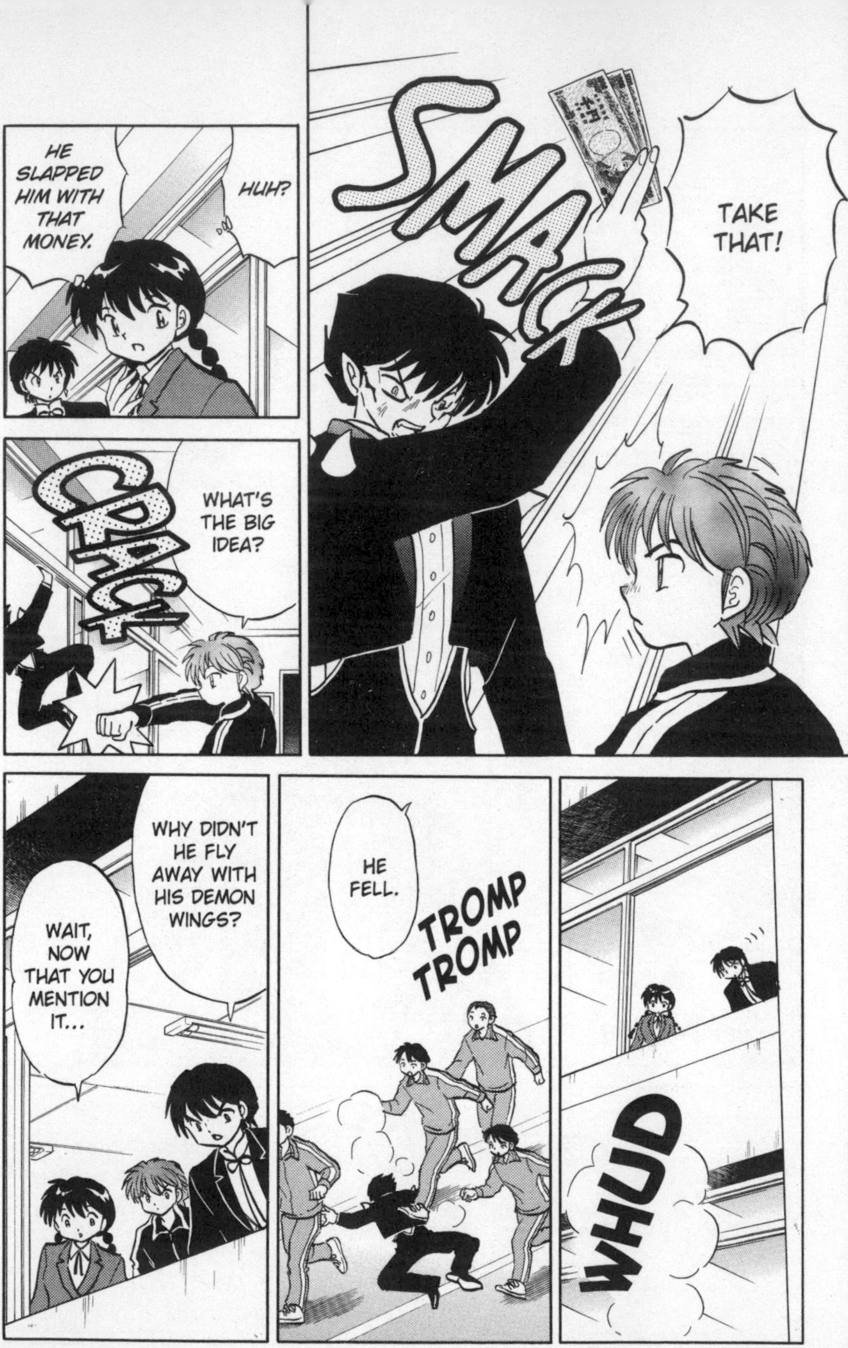
SMACK
TAKE THAT!
HUH?
HE SLAPPED HIM WITH THAT MONEY.
WHAT'S THE BIG IDEA?
CRACK
WHUD
TROMP TROMP
HE FELL.
WHY DIDN'T HE FLY AWAY WITH HIS DEMON WINGS?
WAIT, NOW THAT YOU MENTION IT...

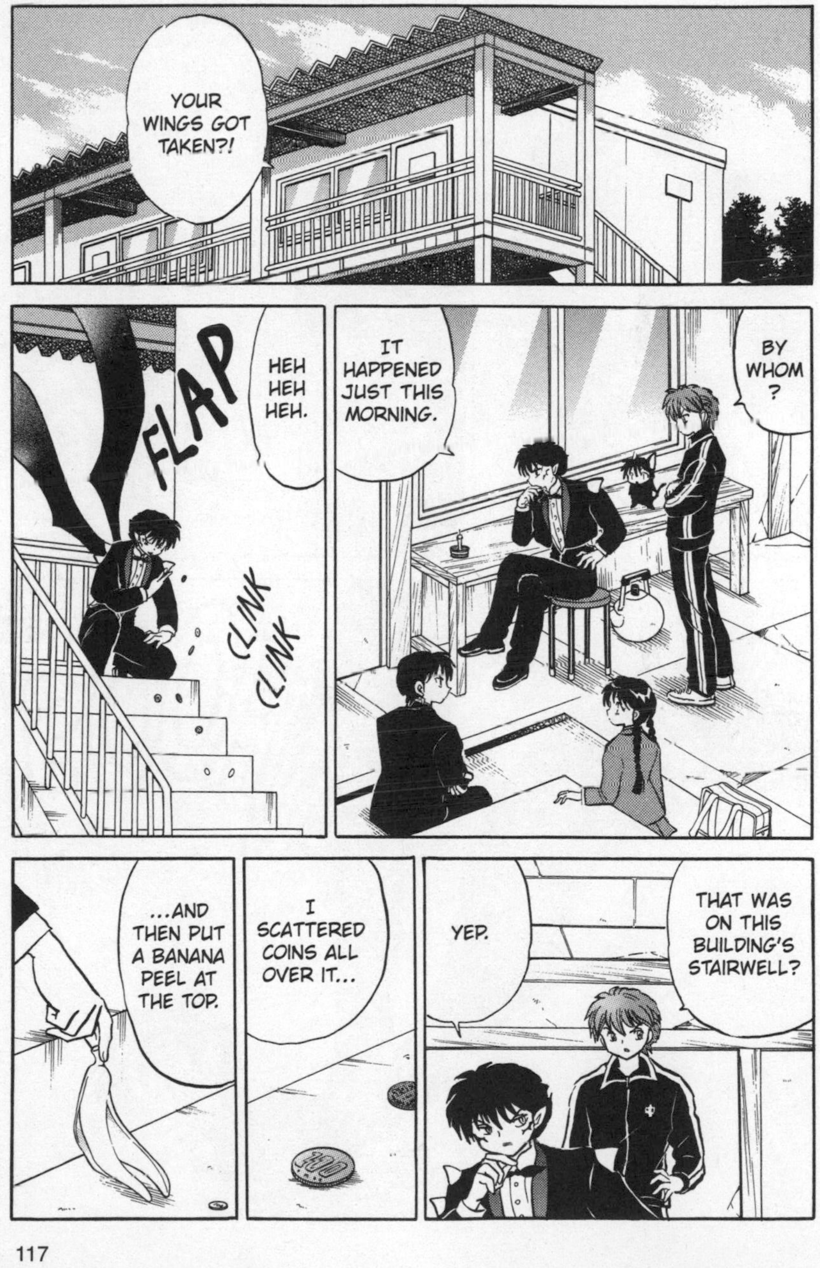
YOUR WINGS GOT TAKEN?!
BY WHOM?
IT HAPPENED JUST THIS MORNING.
HEH HEH HEH.
FLAP
CLINK CLINK
THAT WAS ON THIS BUILDING'S STAIRWELL?
YEP.
I SCATTERED COINS ALL OVER IT...
...AND THEN PUT A BANANA PEEL AT THE TOP.

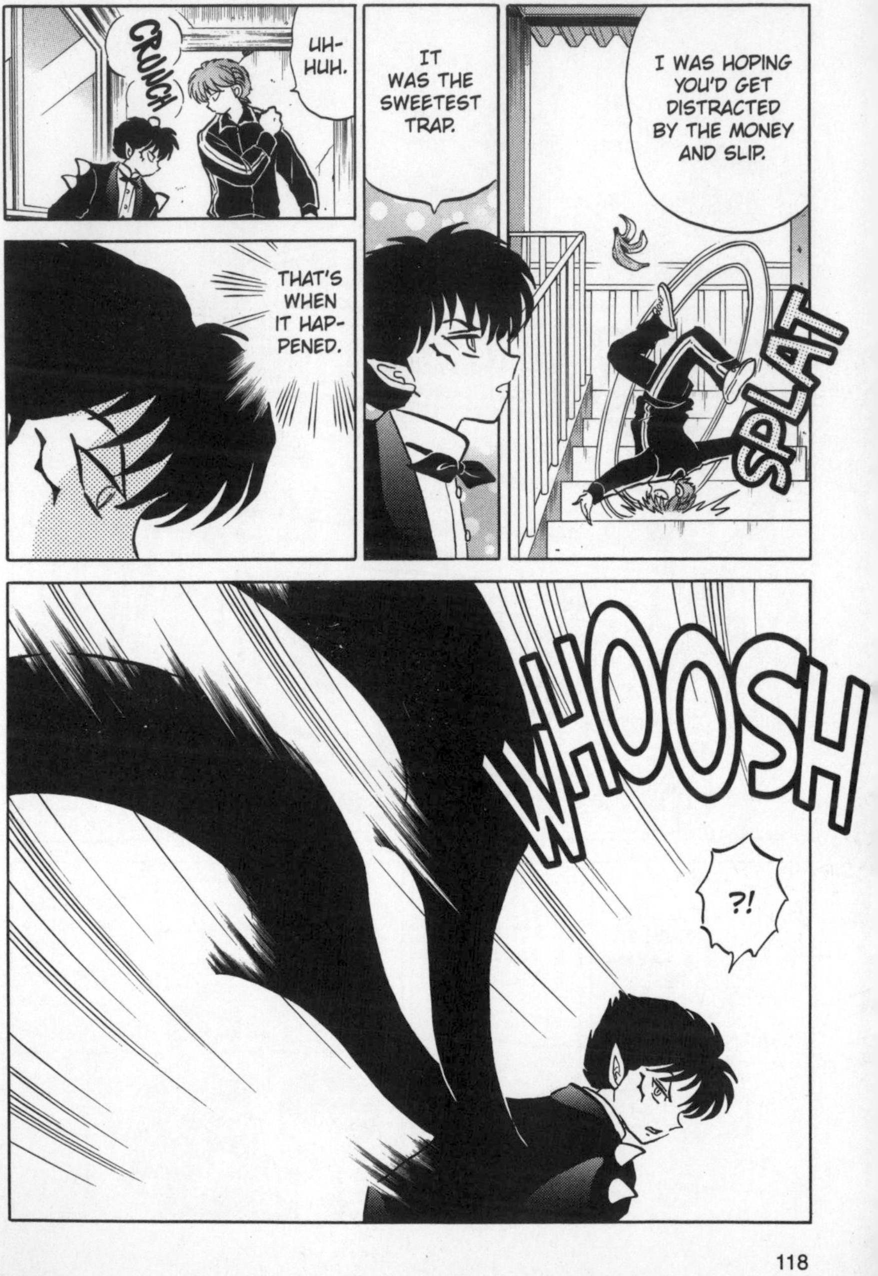
I WAS HOPING YOU'D GET DISTRACTED BY THE MONEY AND SLIP.
SPLAT
IT WAS THE SWEETEST TRAP.
UH-HUH.
CRUNCH
THAT'S WHEN IT HAP-PENED.
WHOOSH
?!

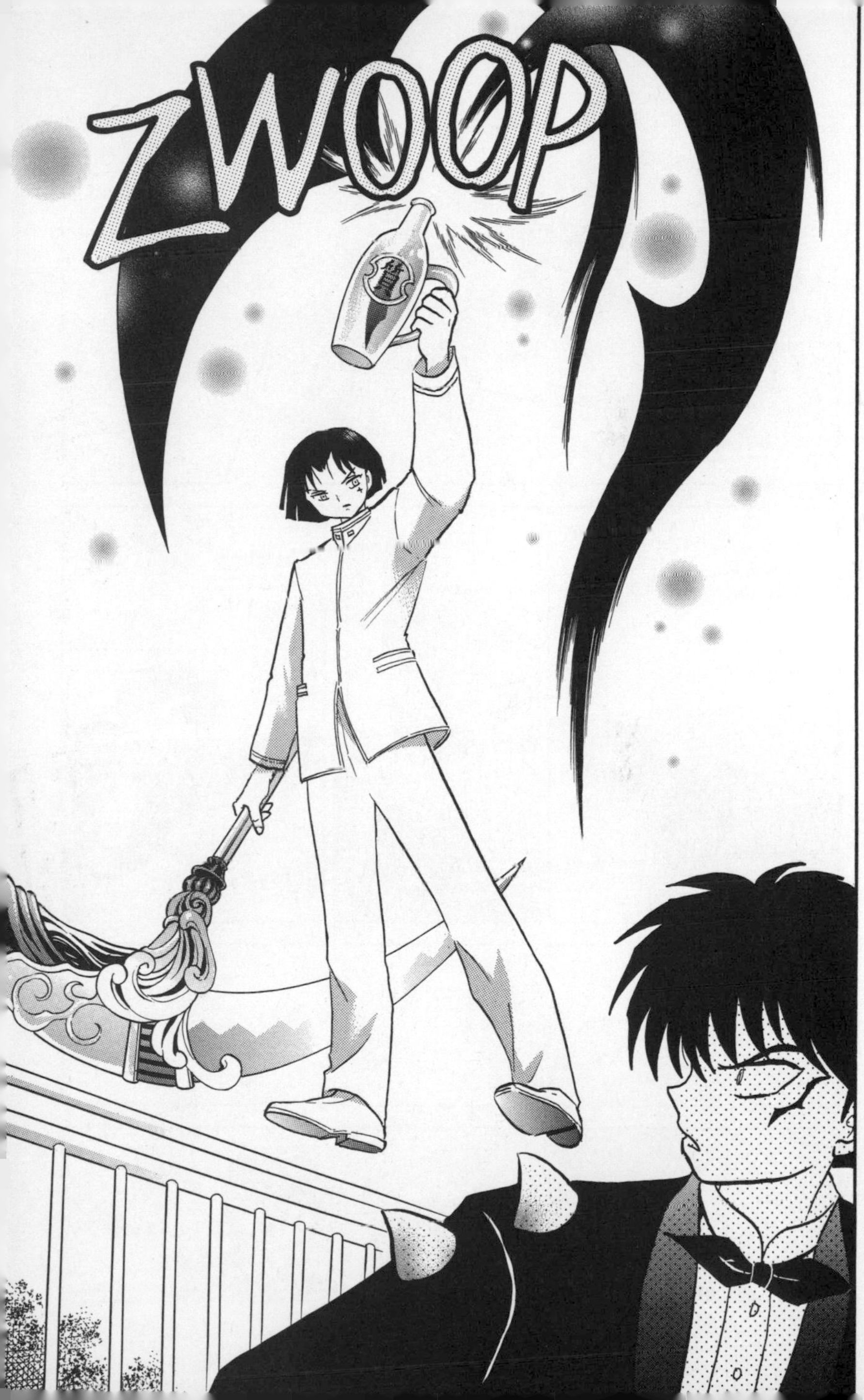
ZWOOP

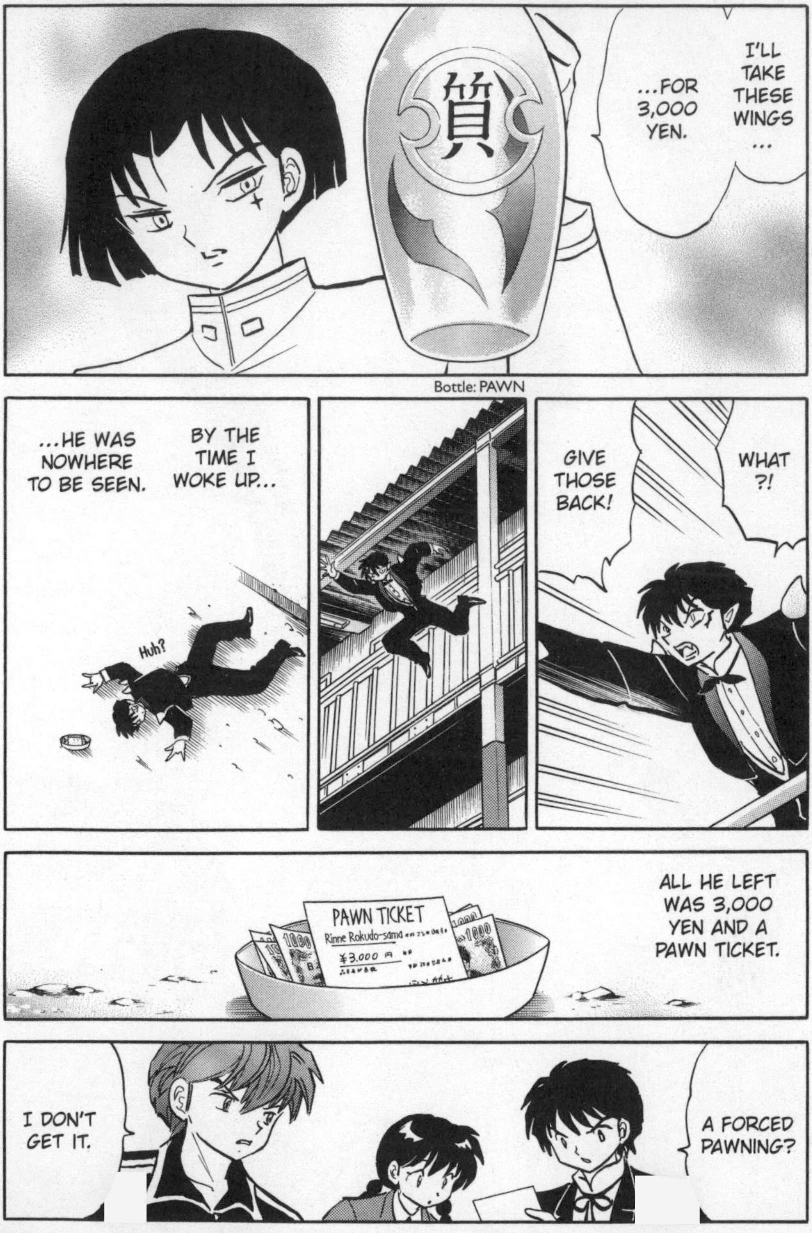
I'LL TAKE THESE WINGS...
...FOR 3,000 YEN.
Bottle: PAWN
WHAT ?!
GIVE THOSE BACK!
BY THE TIME I WOKE UP...
...HE WAS NOWHERE TO BE SEEN.
Huh?
ALL HE LEFT WAS 3,000 YEN AND A PAWN TICKET.
PAWN TICKET
Rinne Rokudo-sama
¥3,000 円
A FORCED PAWNING?
I DON'T GET IT.

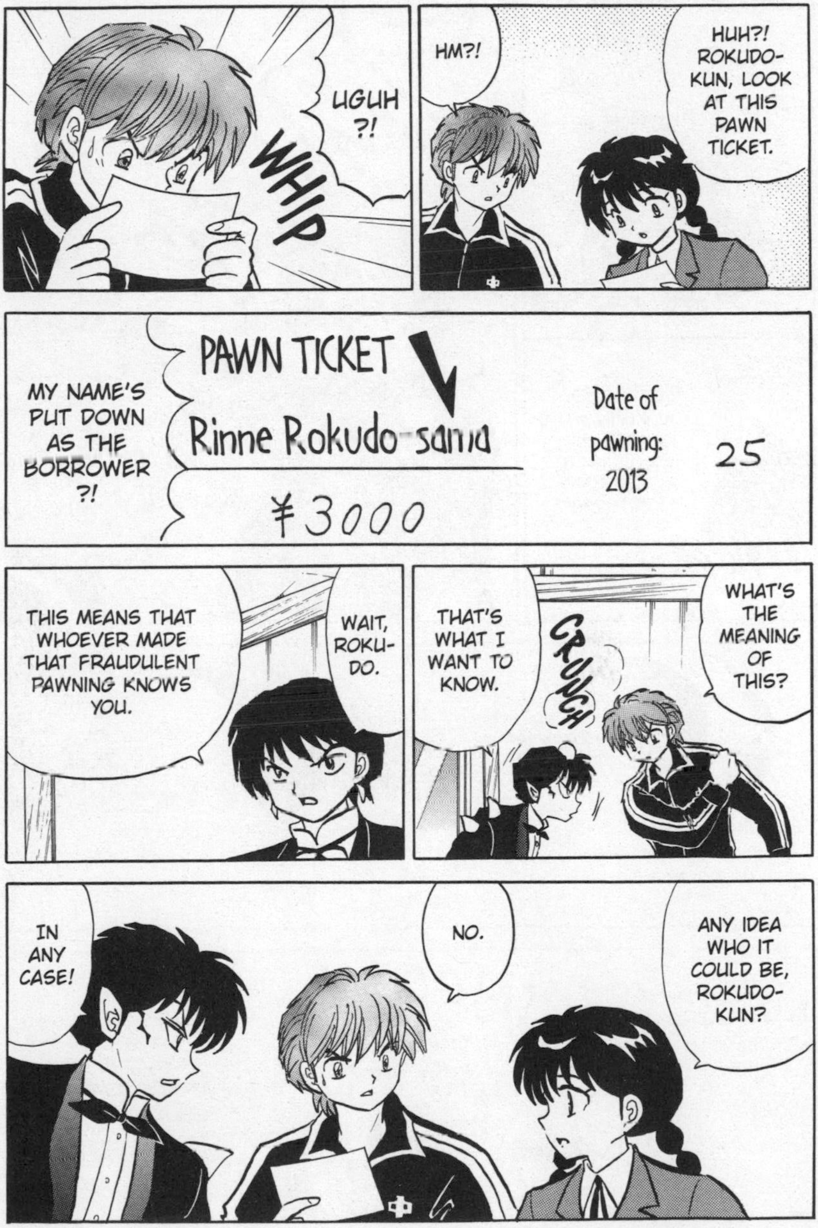
HUH?! ROKUDO-KUN, LOOK AT THIS PAWN TICKET.
HM?!
UGUH ?!
WHIP
Date of pawning: 2013
25
PAWN TICKET
Rinne Rokudo-sama
¥3000
MY NAME'S PUT DOWN AS THE BORROWER ?!
WHAT'S THE MEANING OF THIS?
CRUNCH
THAT'S WHAT I WANT TO KNOW.
WAIT, ROKU-DO.
THIS MEANS THAT WHOEVER MADE THAT FRAUDULENT PAWNING KNOWS YOU.
ANY IDEA WHO IT COULD BE, ROKUDO-KUN?
NO.
IN ANY CASE!

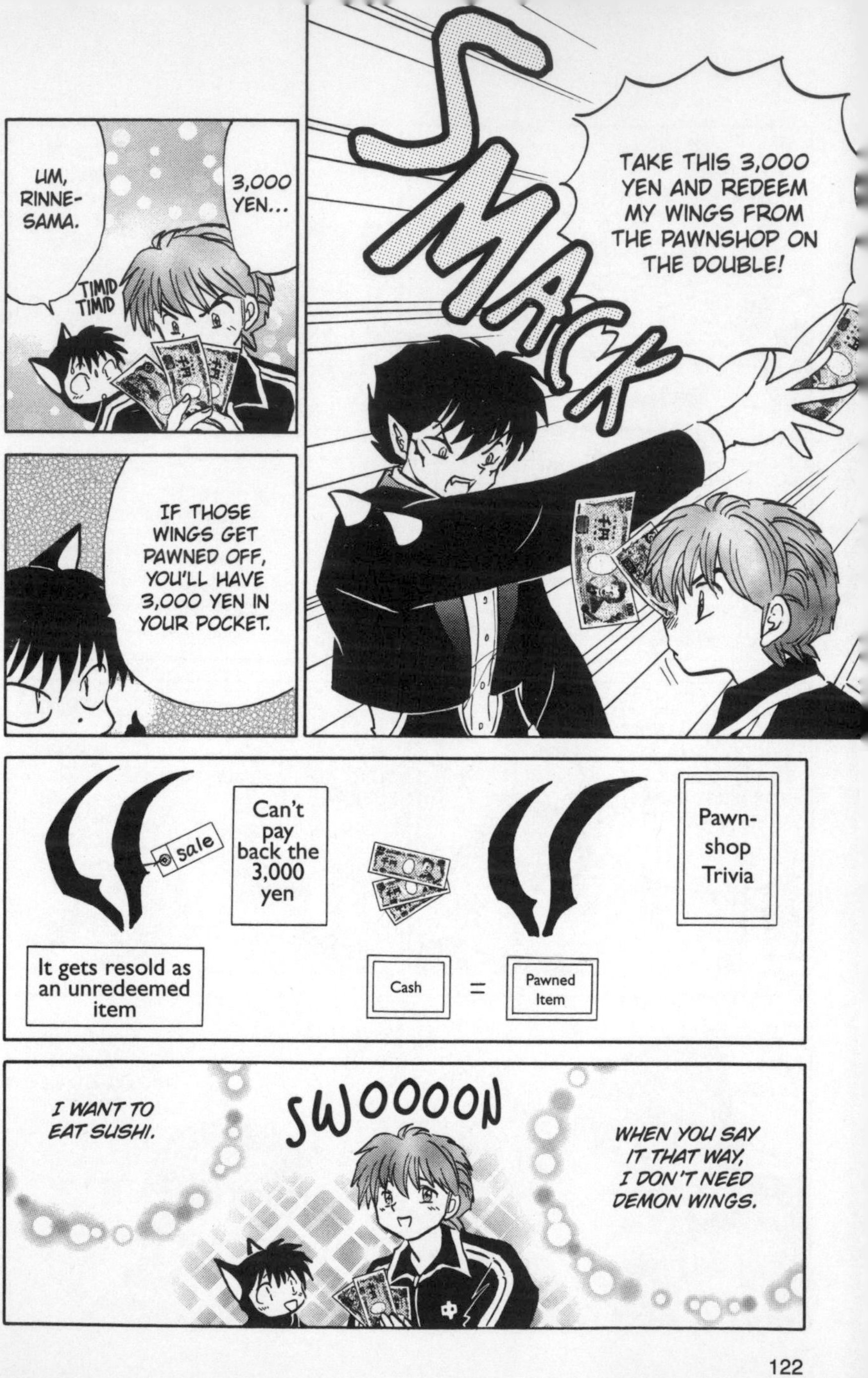
SMACK
TAKE THIS 3,000 YEN AND REDEEM MY WINGS FROM THE PAWNSHOP ON THE DOUBLE!
3,000 YEN...
UM, RINNE-SAMA.
TIMID TIMID
IF THOSE WINGS GET PAWNED OFF, YOU'LL HAVE 3,000 YEN IN YOUR POCKET.
Pawn-shop Trivia
Cash
=
Pawned Item
Can't pay back the 3,000 yen
sale
It gets resold as an unredeemed item
WHEN YOU SAY IT THAT WAY, I DON'T NEED DEMON WINGS.
SWOOOON
I WANT TO EAT SUSHI.

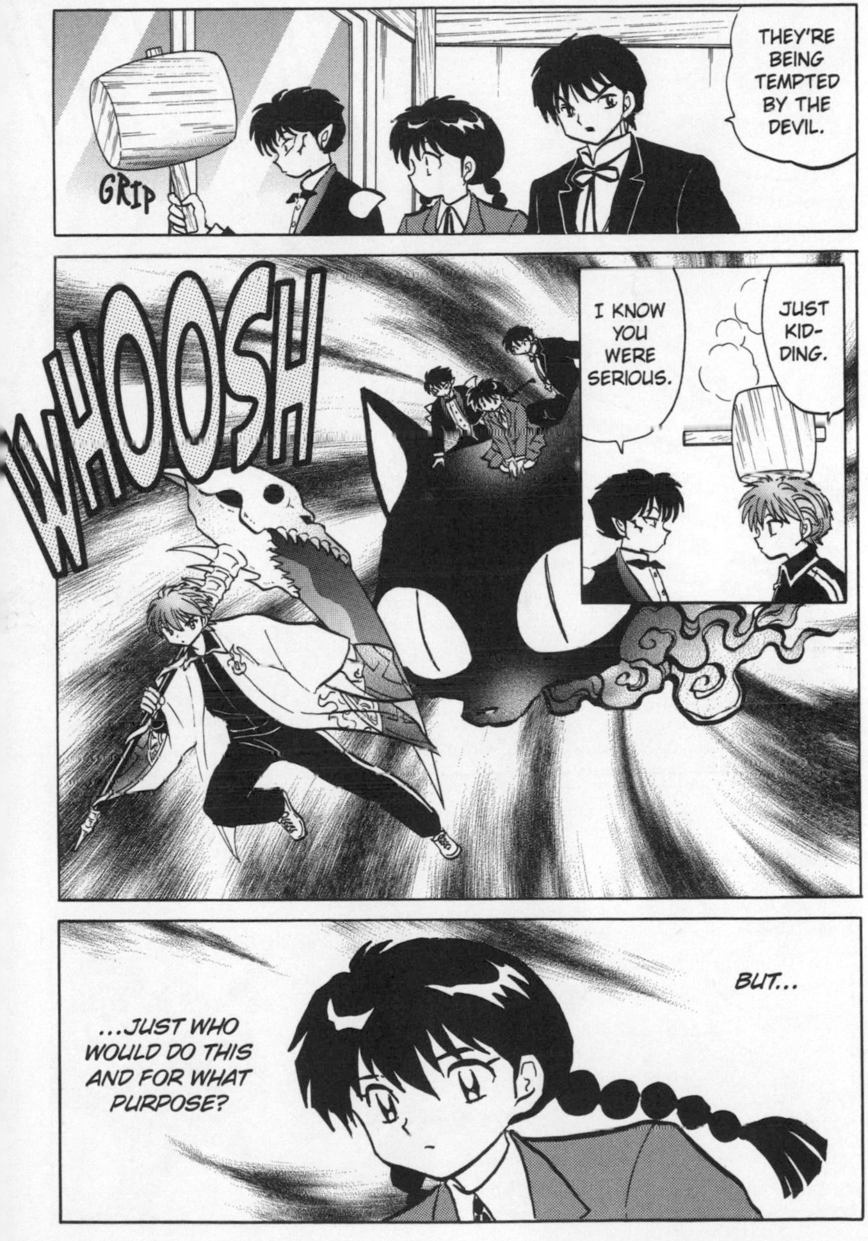
THEY'RE BEING TEMPTED BY THE DEVIL.
GRIP
JUST KID-DING.
I KNOW YOU WERE SERIOUS.
WHOOSH
BUT...
...JUST WHO WOULD DO THIS AND FOR WHAT PURPOSE?

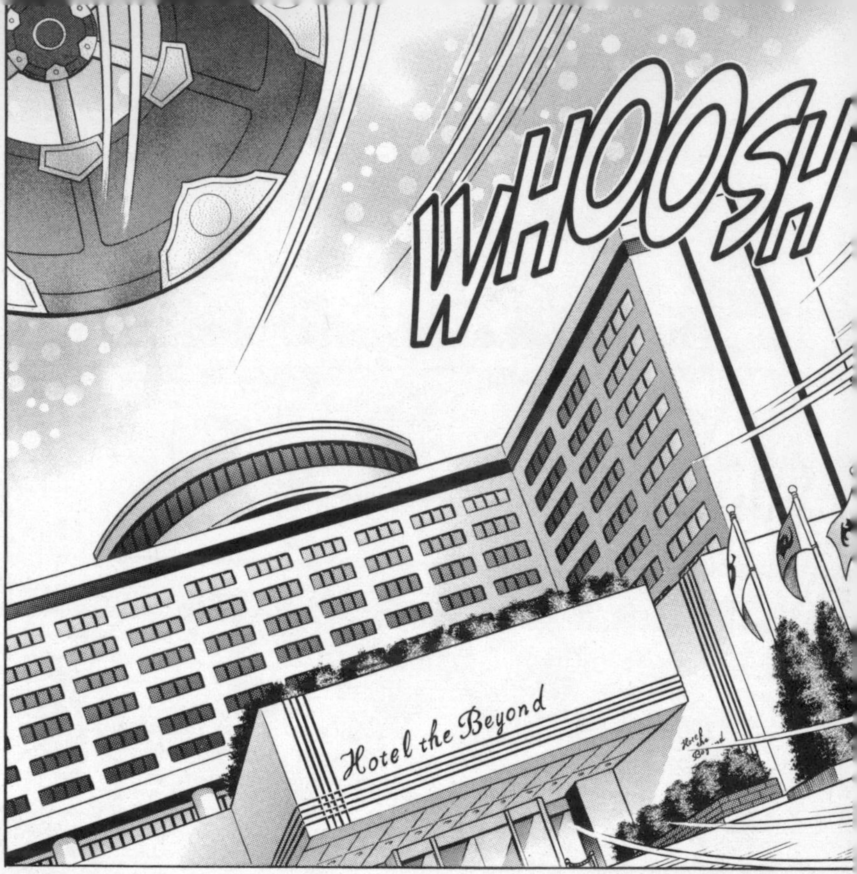
WHOOSH
Hotel the Beyond

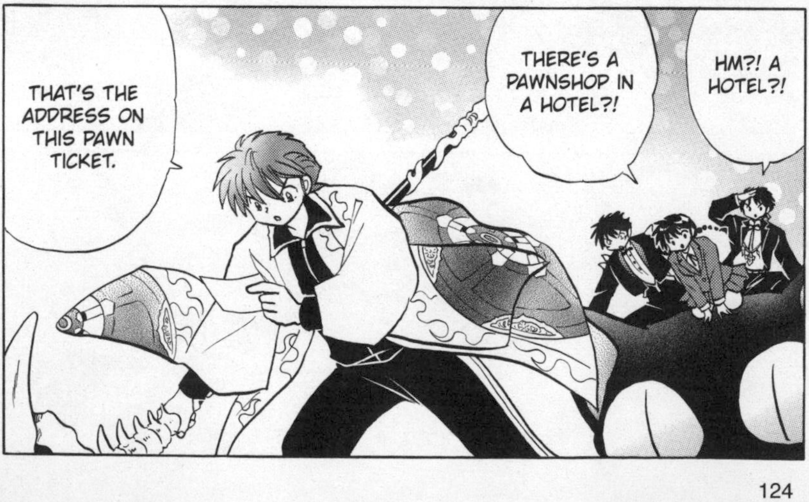
HM?! A HOTEL?!
THERE'S A PAWNSHOP IN A HOTEL?!
THAT'S THE ADDRESS ON THIS PAWN TICKET.

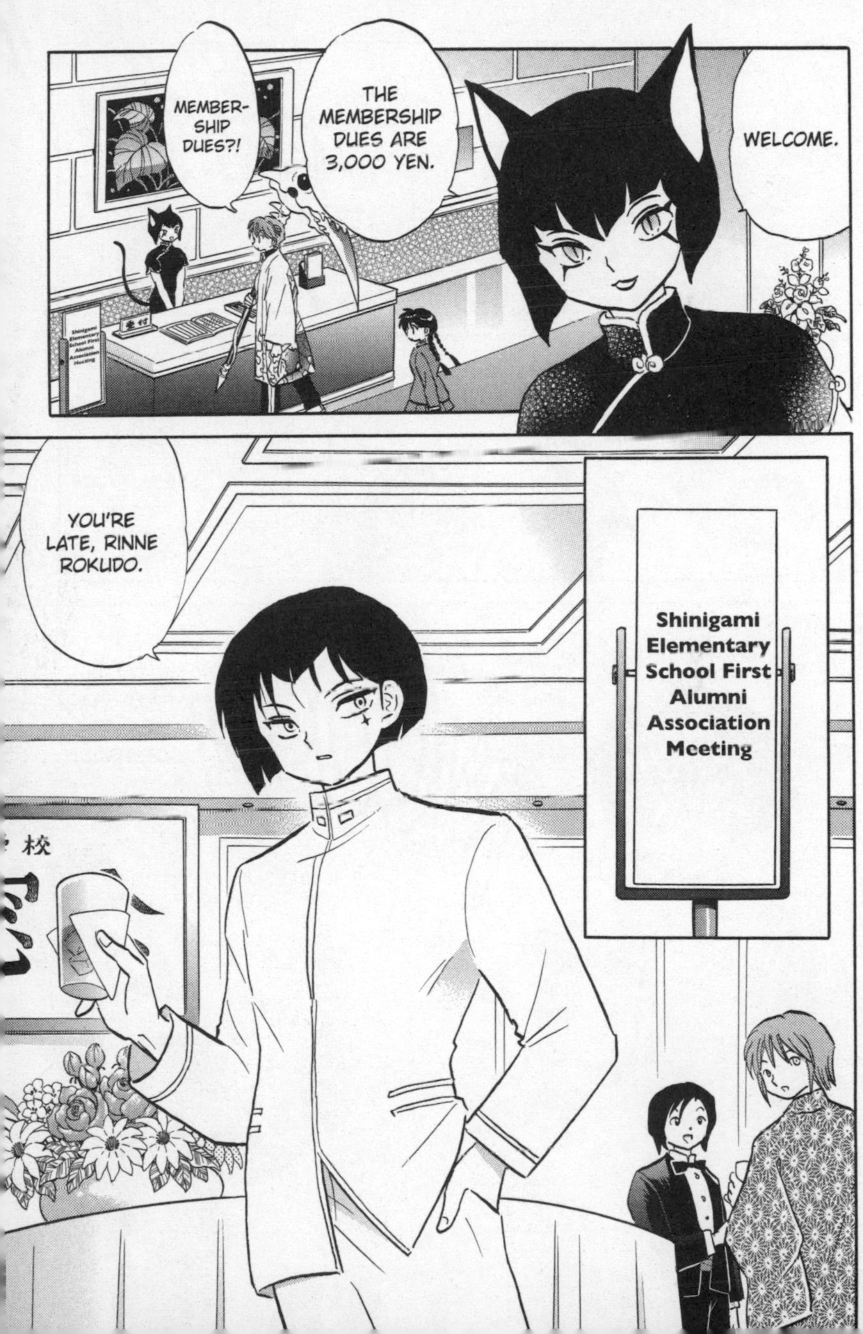
WELCOME.
THE MEMBERSHIP DUES ARE 3,000 YEN.
MEMBER-SHIP DUES?!
Shinigami Elementary School First Alumni Association Meeting
YOU'RE LATE, RINNE ROKUDO.

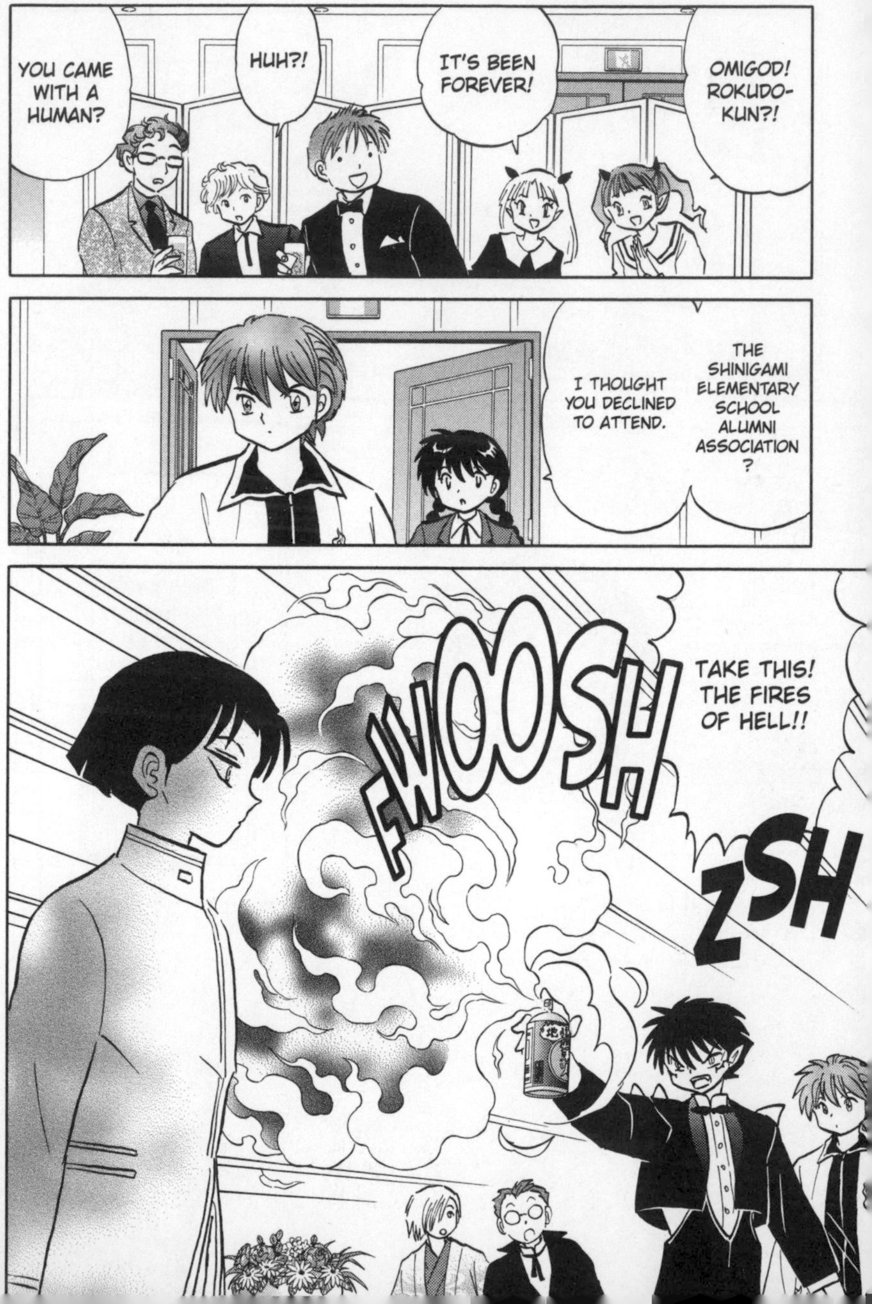
OMIGOD! ROKUDO-KUN?!
IT'S BEEN FOREVER!
HUH?!
YOU CAME WITH A HUMAN?
THE SHINIGAMI ELEMENTARY SCHOOL ALUMNI ASSOCIATION ?
I THOUGHT YOU DECLINED TO ATTEND.
TAKE THIS! THE FIRES OF HELL!!
FWOOSH
ZSH

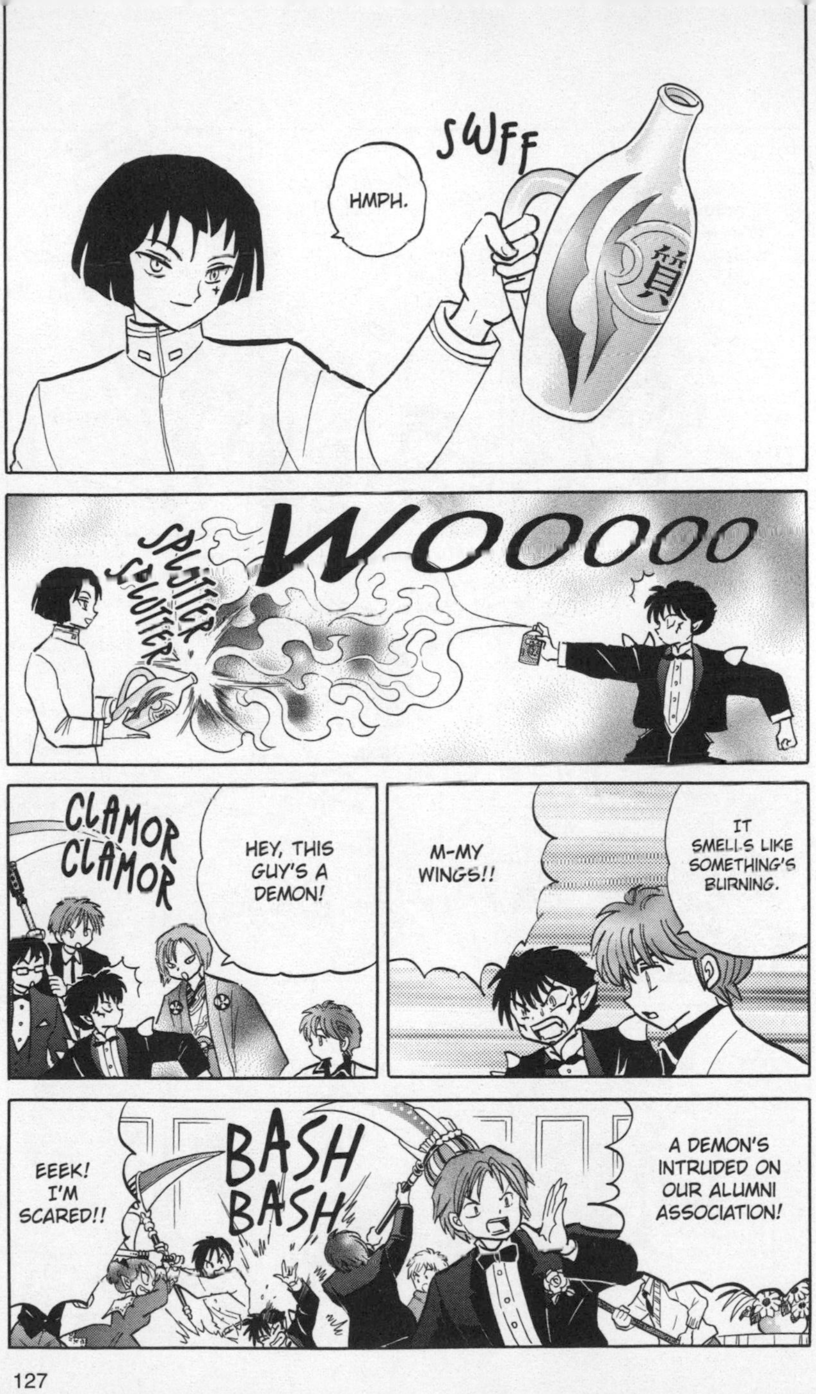
SWFF
HMPH.
WOOOOO
SPLUTTER SPLUTTER
IT SMELLS LIKE SOMETHING'S BURNING.
M-MY WINGS!!
HEY, THIS GUY'S A DEMON!
CLAMOR CLAMOR
A DEMON'S INTRUDED ON OUR ALUMNI ASSOCIATION!
BASH BASH
EEEK! I'M SCARED!!

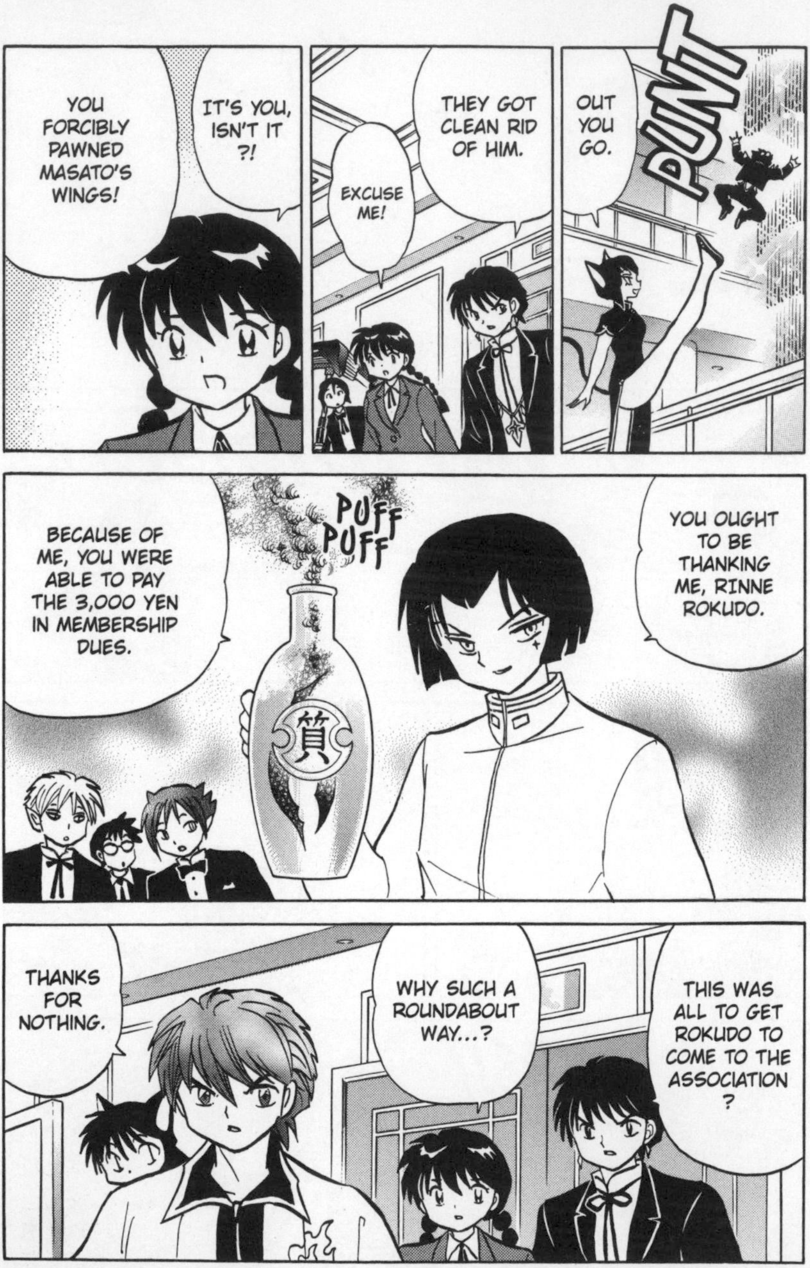
PUNT
OUT YOU GO.
THEY GOT CLEAN RID OF HIM.
EXCUSE ME!
IT'S YOU, ISN'T IT ?!
YOU FORCIBLY PAWNED MASATO'S WINGS!
YOU OUGHT TO BE THANKING ME, RINNE ROKUDO.
PUFF PUFF
BECAUSE OF ME, YOU WERE ABLE TO PAY THE 3,000 YEN IN MEMBERSHIP DUES.
THIS WAS ALL TO GET ROKUDO TO COME TO THE ASSOCIATION ?
WHY SUCH A ROUNDABOUT WAY...?
THANKS FOR NOTHING.

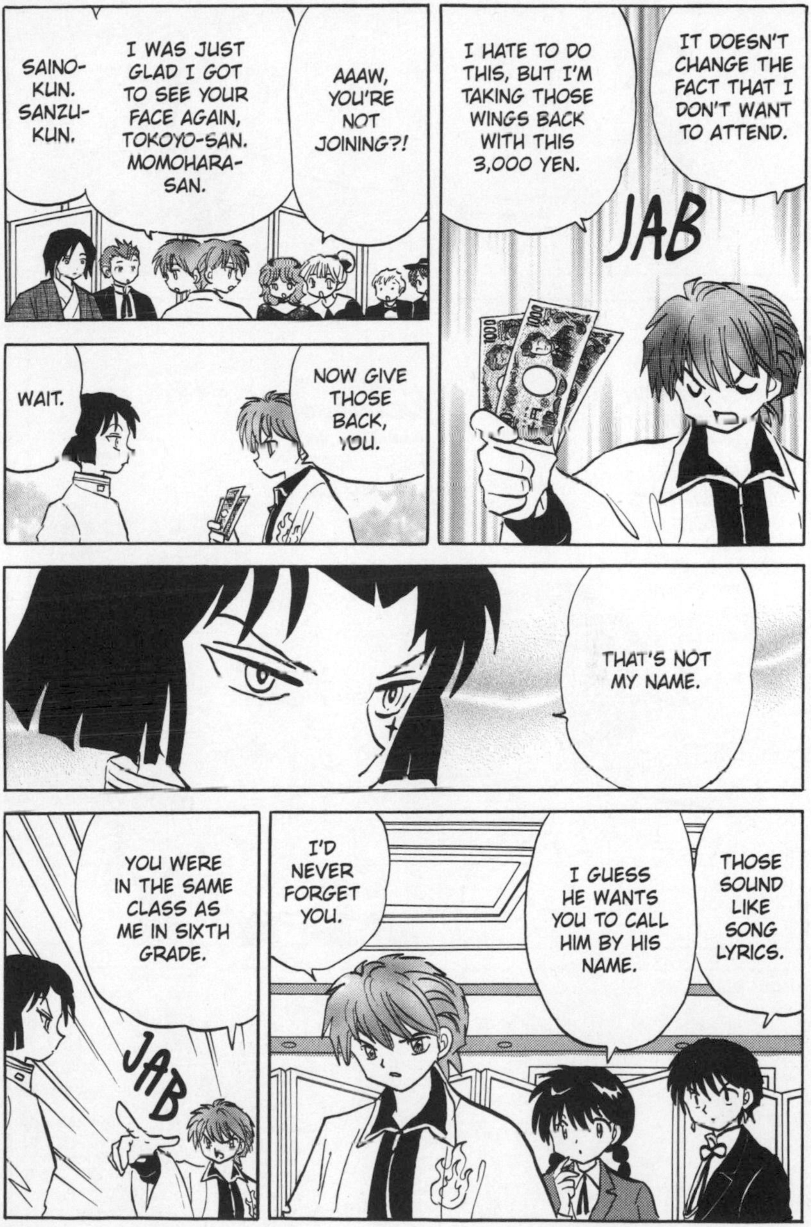
IT DOESN'T CHANGE THE FACT THAT I DON'T WANT TO ATTEND.
I HATE TO DO THIS, BUT I'M TAKING THOSE WINGS BACK WITH THIS 3,000 YEN.
JAB
AAAW, YOU'RE NOT JOINING?!
I WAS JUST GLAD I GOT TO SEE YOUR FACE AGAIN, TOKOYO-SAN. MOMOHARA-SAN.
SAINO-KUN. SANZU-KUN.
NOW GIVE THOSE BACK, YOU.
WAIT.
THAT'S NOT MY NAME.
THOSE SOUND LIKE SONG LYRICS.
I GUESS HE WANTS YOU TO CALL HIM BY HIS NAME.
I'D NEVER FORGET YOU.
YOU WERE IN THE SAME CLASS AS ME IN SIXTH GRADE.
JAB

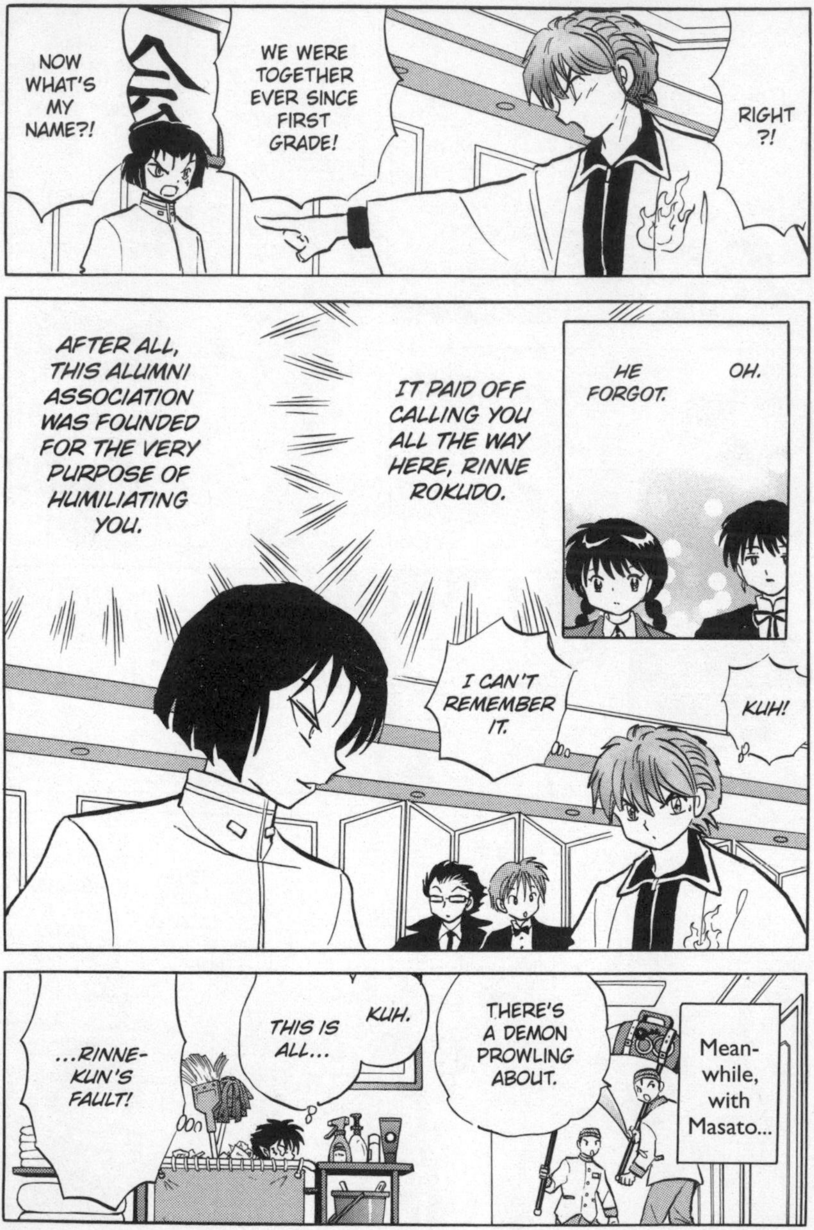
RIGHT ?!
WE WERE TOGETHER EVER SINCE FIRST GRADE!
NOW WHAT'S MY NAME?!
IT PAID OFF CALLING YOU ALL THE WAY HERE, RINNE ROKUDO.
AFTER ALL, THIS ALUMNI ASSOCIATION WAS FOUNDED FOR THE VERY PURPOSE OF HUMILIATING YOU.
I CAN'T REMEMBER IT.
KUH!
OH.
HE FORGOT.
Mean-while, with Masato...
THERE'S A DEMON PROWLING ABOUT.
KUH.
THIS IS ALL...
...RINNE-KUN'S FAULT!

CHAPTER 186: THE FEARSOME OUTDOOR TRAINING

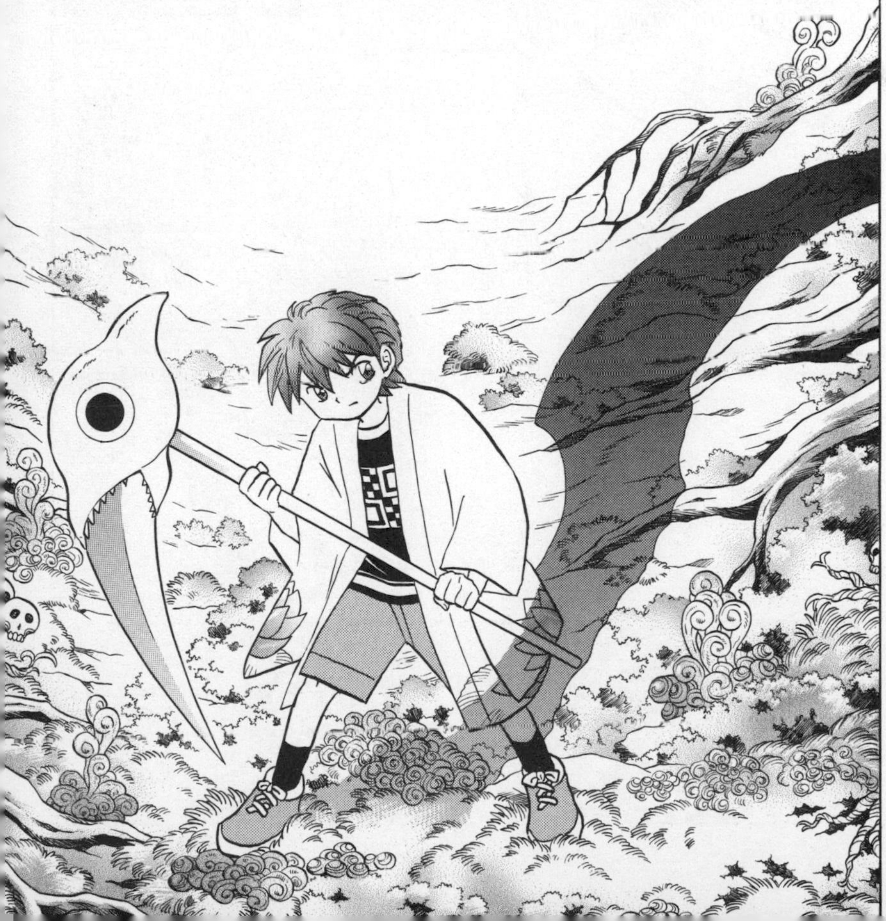

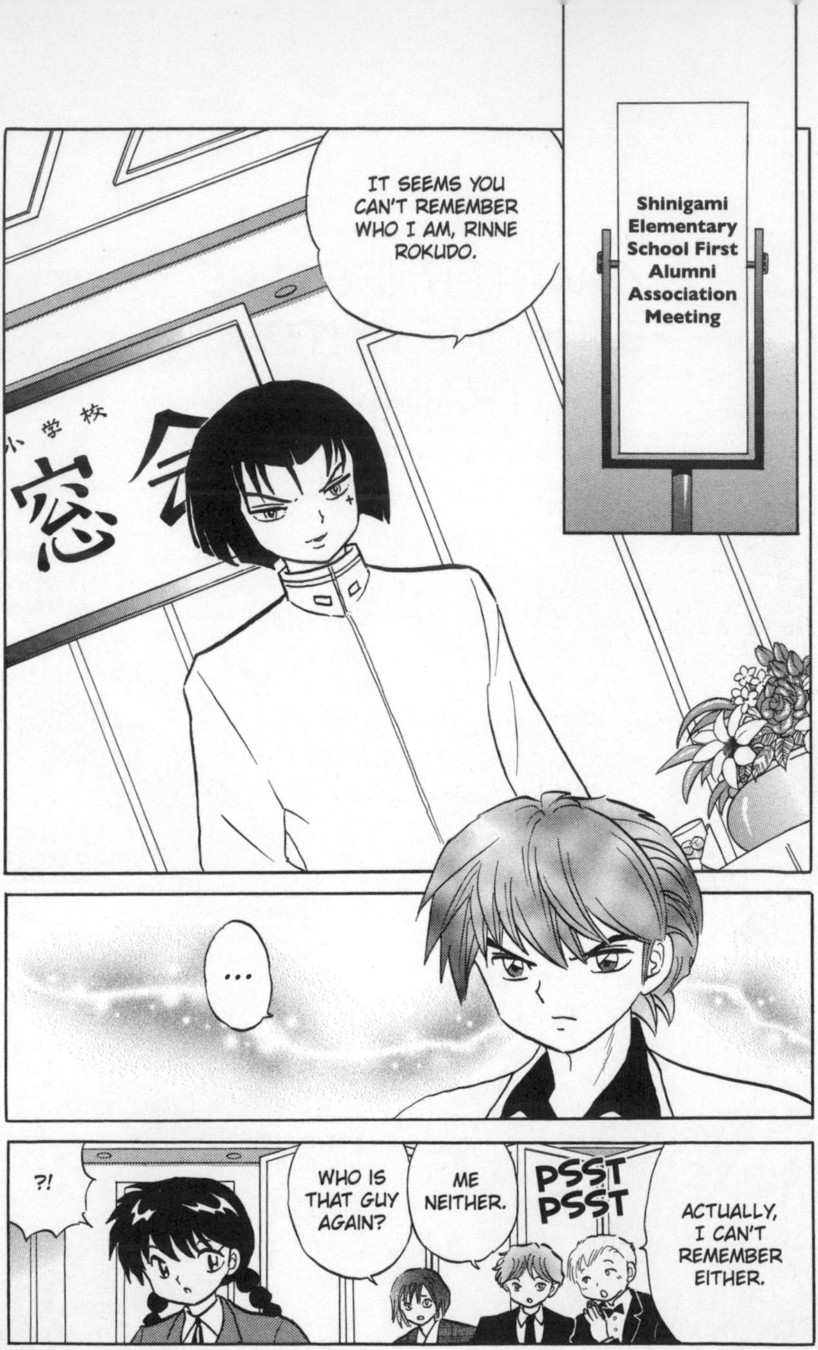
Shinigami Elementary School First Alumni Association Meeting
IT SEEMS YOU CAN'T REMEMBER WHO I AM, RINNE ROKUDO.
小学校
...
ACTUALLY, I CAN'T REMEMBER EITHER.
PSST PSST
ME NEITHER.
WHO IS THAT GUY AGAIN?
?!

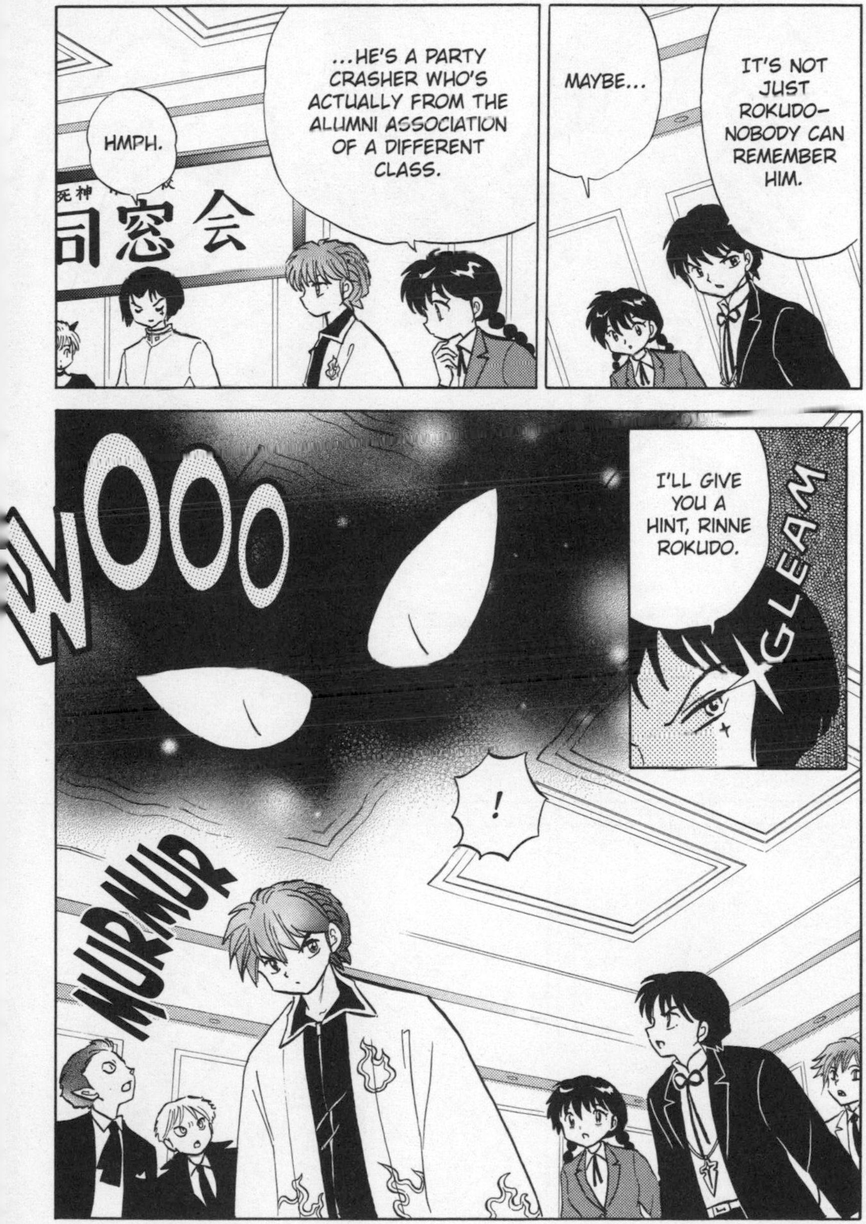
IT'S NOT JUST ROKUDO-NOBODY CAN REMEMBER HIM.
MAYBE...
...HE'S A PARTY CRASHER WHO'S ACTUALLY FROM THE ALUMNI ASSOCIATION OF A DIFFERENT CLASS.
HMPH.
死神
同窓会
I'LL GIVE YOU A HINT, RINNE ROKUDO.
GLEAM
WOOOO
!
MURMUR

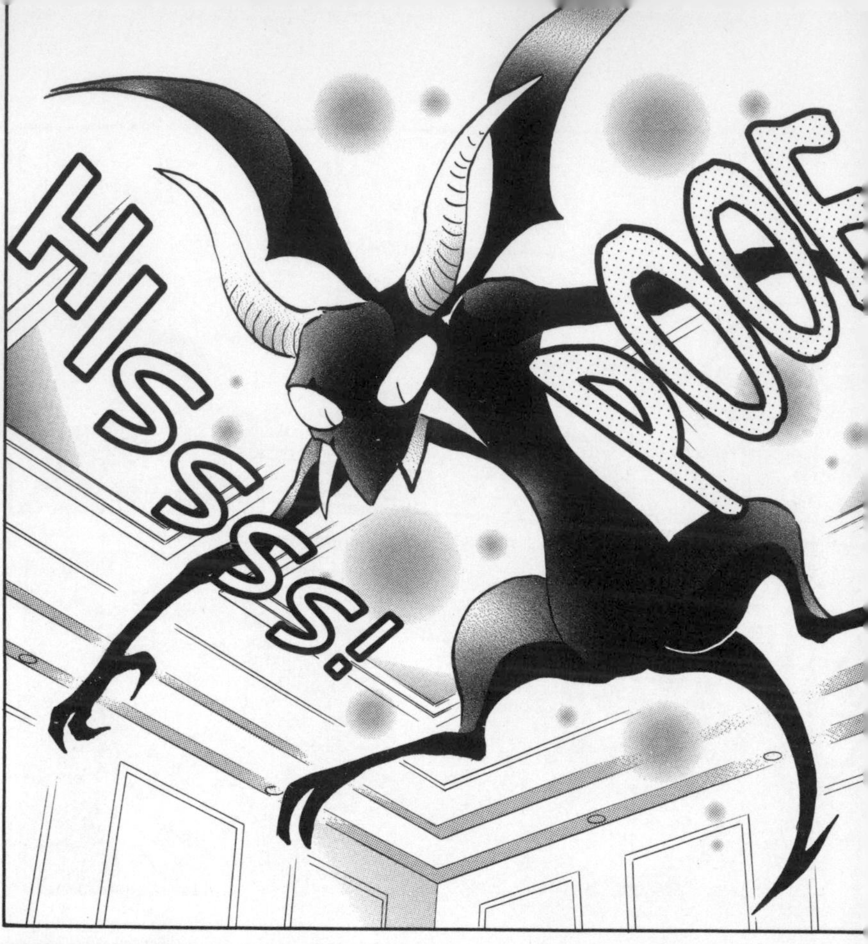
HISSSS!
POOF

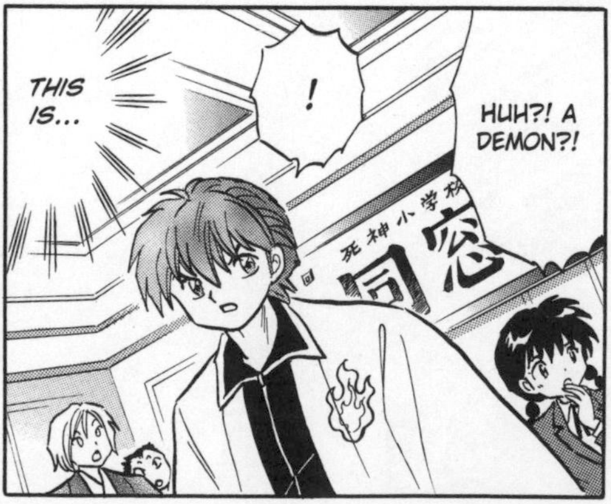
HUH?! A DEMON?!
!
THIS IS...
死神小学校
同窓

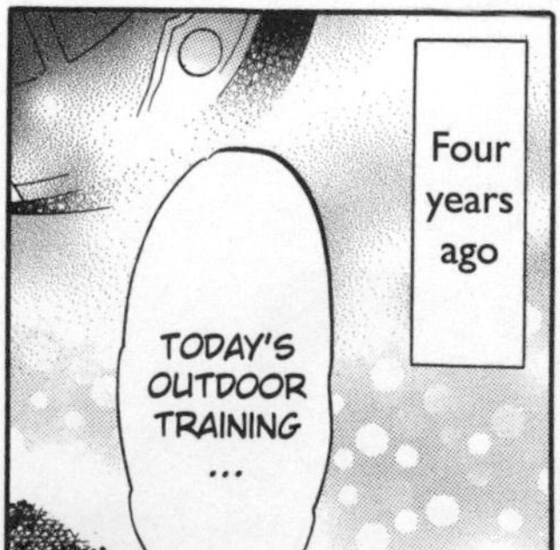
Four years ago
TODAY'S OUTDOOR TRAINING ...

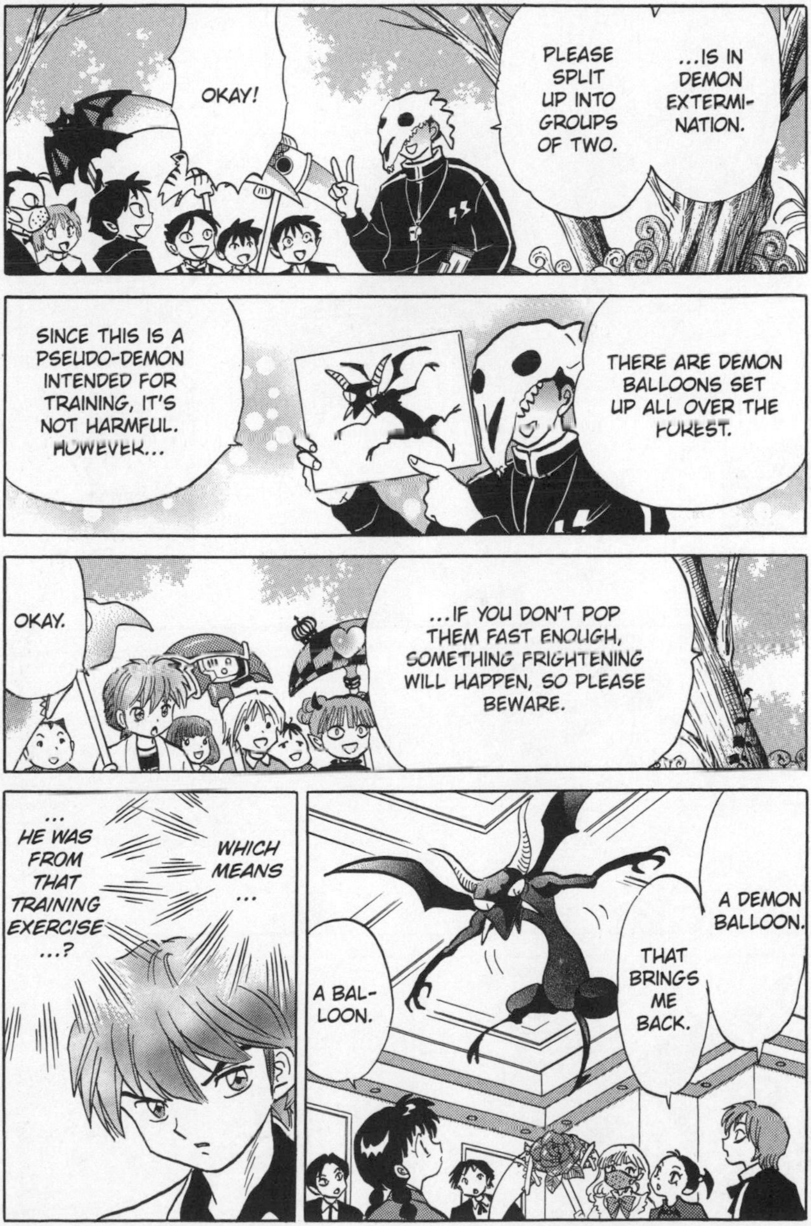
...IS IN DEMON EXTERMINATION.
PLEASE SPLIT UP INTO GROUPS OF TWO.
OKAY!
THERE ARE DEMON BALLOONS SET UP ALL OVER THE FOREST.
SINCE THIS IS A PSEUDO-DEMON INTENDED FOR TRAINING, IT'S NOT HARMFUL. HOWEVER...
...IF YOU DON'T POP THEM FAST ENOUGH, SOMETHING FRIGHTENING WILL HAPPEN, SO PLEASE BEWARE.
OKAY.
A DEMON BALLOON.
THAT BRINGS ME BACK.
A BAL-LOON.
WHICH MEANS ...
... HE WAS FROM THAT TRAINING EXERCISE ...?

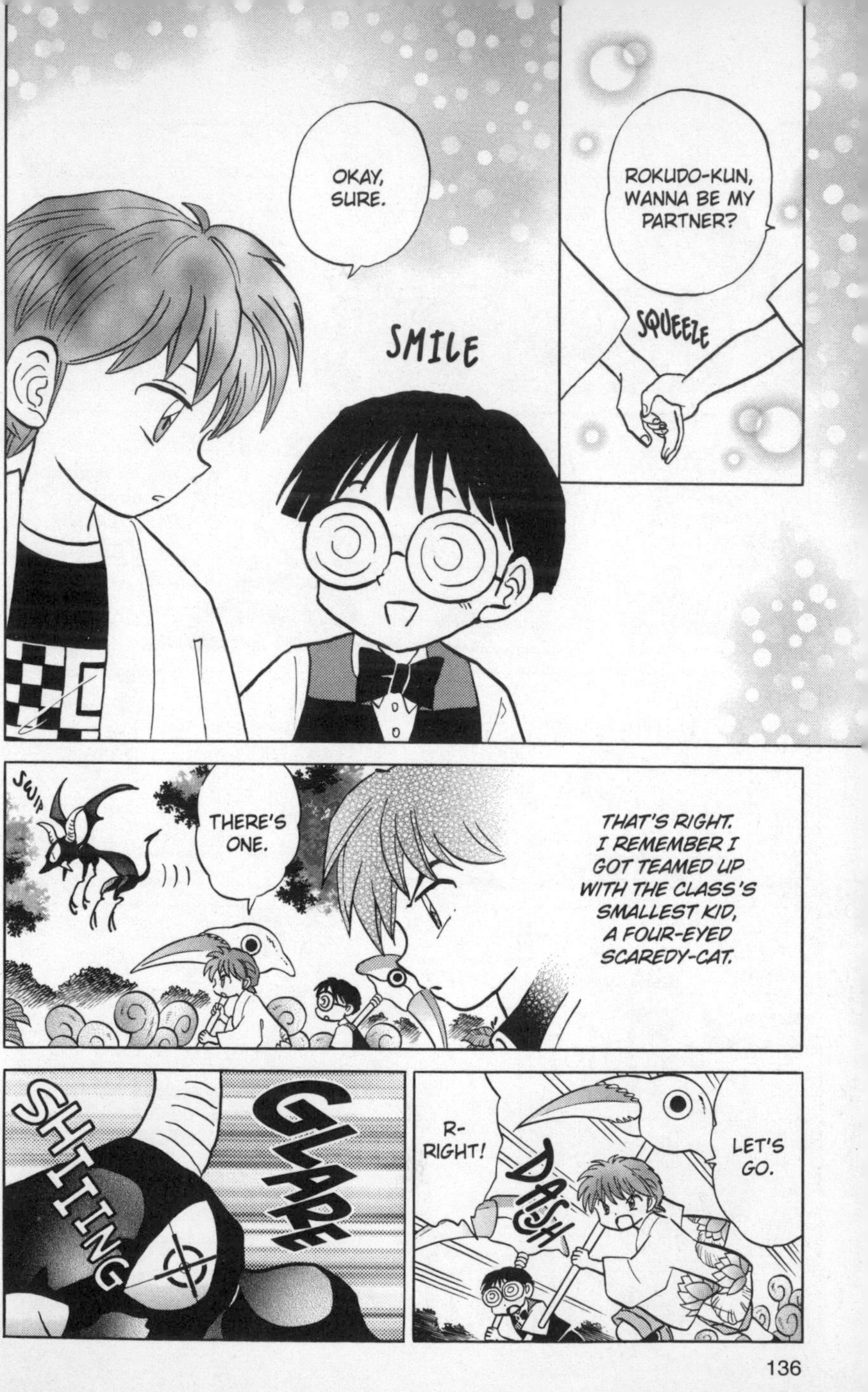
ROKUDO-KUN, WANNA BE MY PARTNER?
SQUEEZE
OKAY, SURE.
SMILE
THAT'S RIGHT. I REMEMBER I GOT TEAMED UP WITH THE CLASS'S SMALLEST KID, A FOUR-EYED SCAREDY-CAT.
THERE'S ONE.
SWIP
LET'S GO.
DASH
R-RIGHT!
GLARE
SHIING

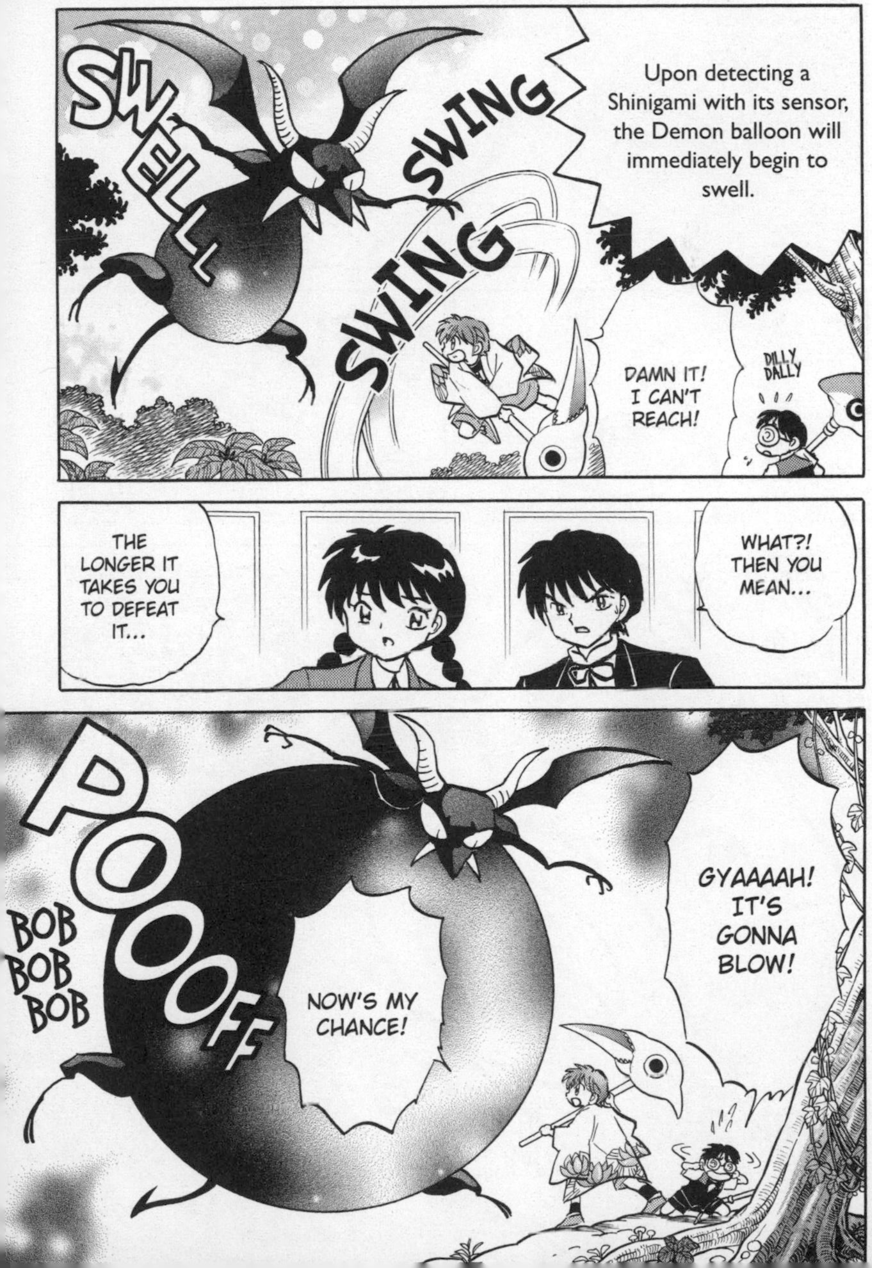
Upon detecting a Shinigami with its sensor, the Demon balloon will immediately begin to swell.
DILLY DALLY
DAMN IT! I CAN'T REACH!
SWING SWING
SWELL
WHAT?! THEN YOU MEAN...
THE LONGER IT TAKES YOU TO DEFEAT IT...
GYAAAAH! IT'S GONNA BLOW!
NOW'S MY CHANCE!
POOOFF
BOB BOB BOB

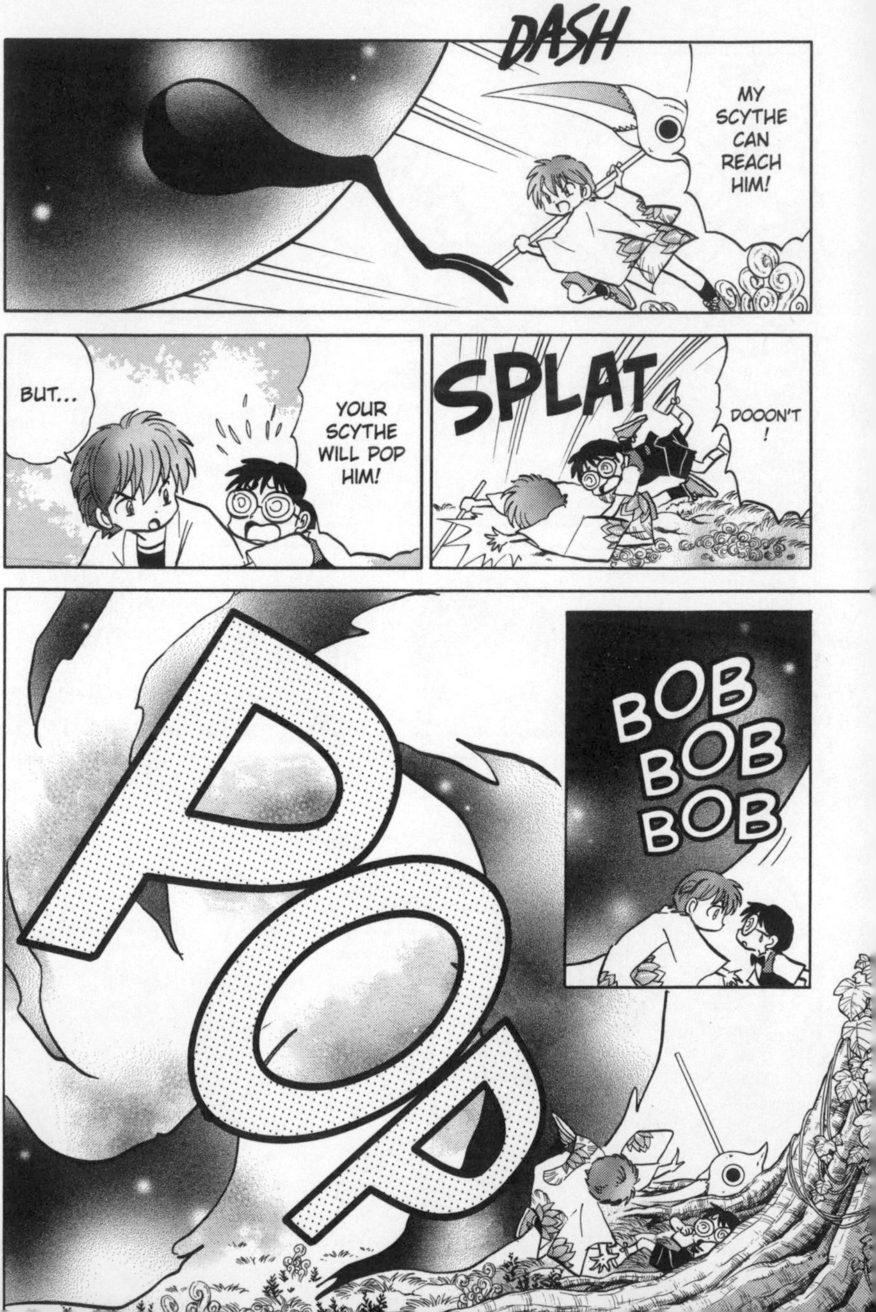
DASH
MY SCYTHE CAN REACH HIM!
SPLAT
DOOON'T!
YOUR SCYTHE WILL POP HIM!
BUT...
BOB BOB BOB
POP

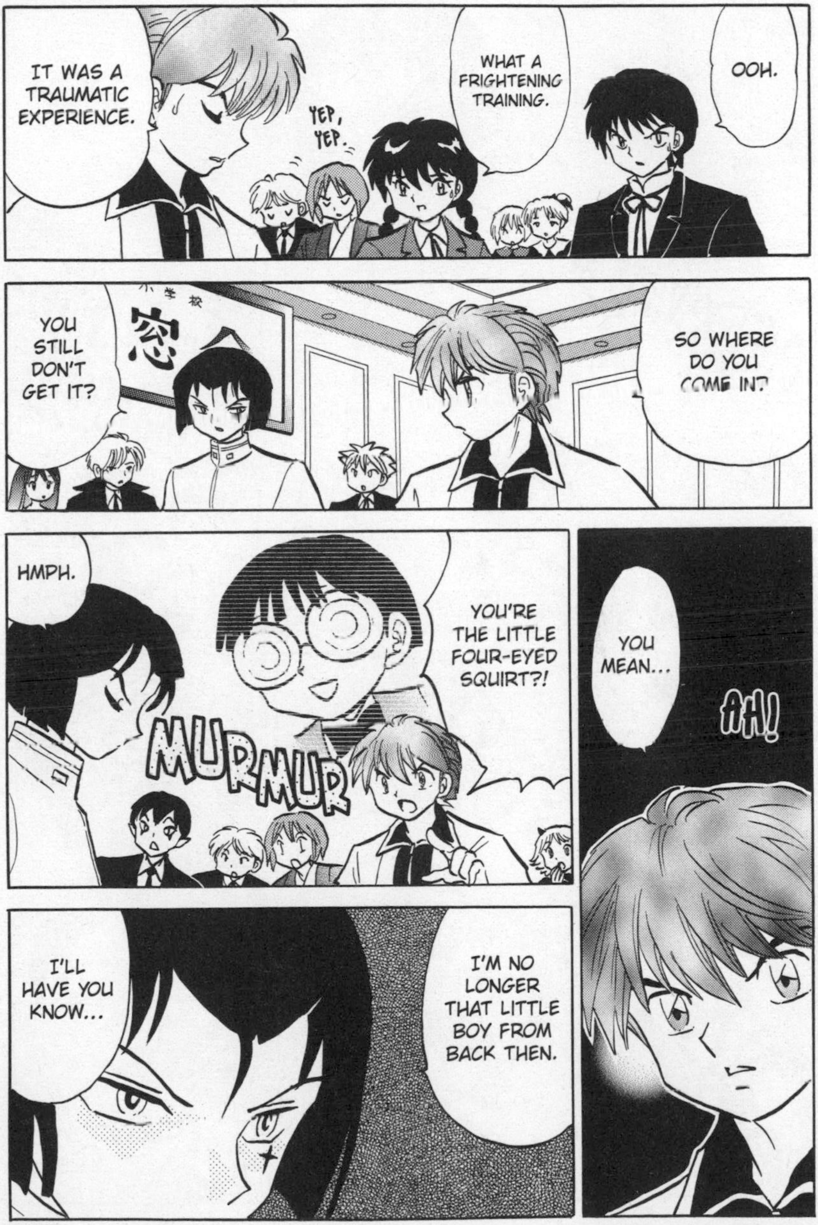
OOH.
WHAT A FRIGHTENING TRAINING.
YEP, YEP.
IT WAS A TRAUMATIC EXPERIENCE.
SO WHERE DO YOU COME IN?
小学校
窓
YOU STILL DON'T GET IT?
YOU MEAN...
AH!
YOU'RE THE LITTLE FOUR-EYED SQUIRT?!
HMPH.
MURMUR
I'LL HAVE YOU KNOW...
I'M NO LONGER THAT LITTLE BOY FROM BACK THEN.

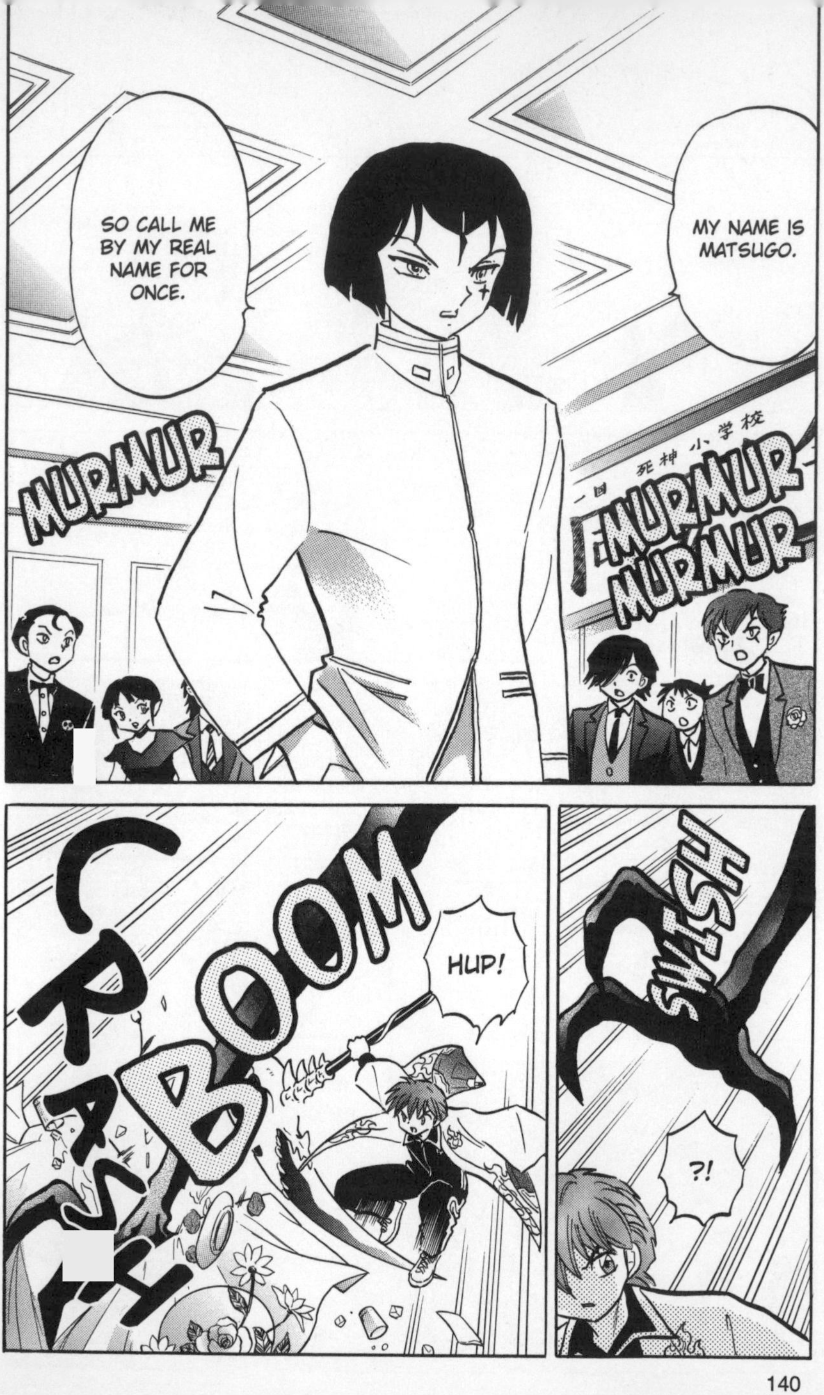
MY NAME IS MATSUGO.
SO CALL ME BY MY REAL NAME FOR ONCE.
死神小学校
MURMUR MURMUR
MURMUR
SWISH
?!
HUP!
BOOM
CRASH

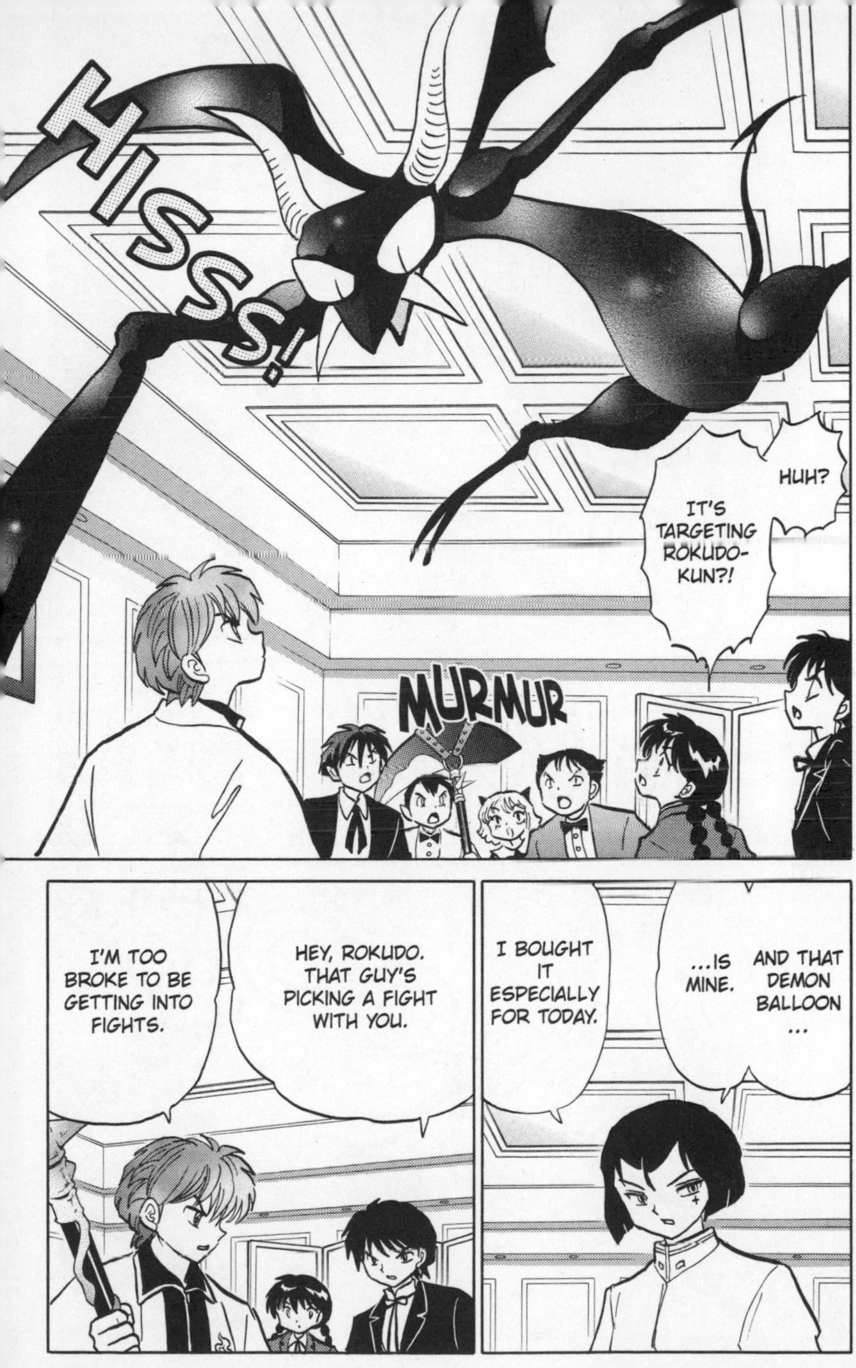
HISSS!
HUH?
IT'S TARGETING ROKUDO-KUN?!
MURMUR
AND THAT DEMON BALLOON ...
...IS MINE.
I BOUGHT IT ESPECIALLY FOR TODAY.
HEY, ROKUDO. THAT GUY'S PICKING A FIGHT WITH YOU.
I'M TOO BROKE TO BE GETTING INTO FIGHTS.

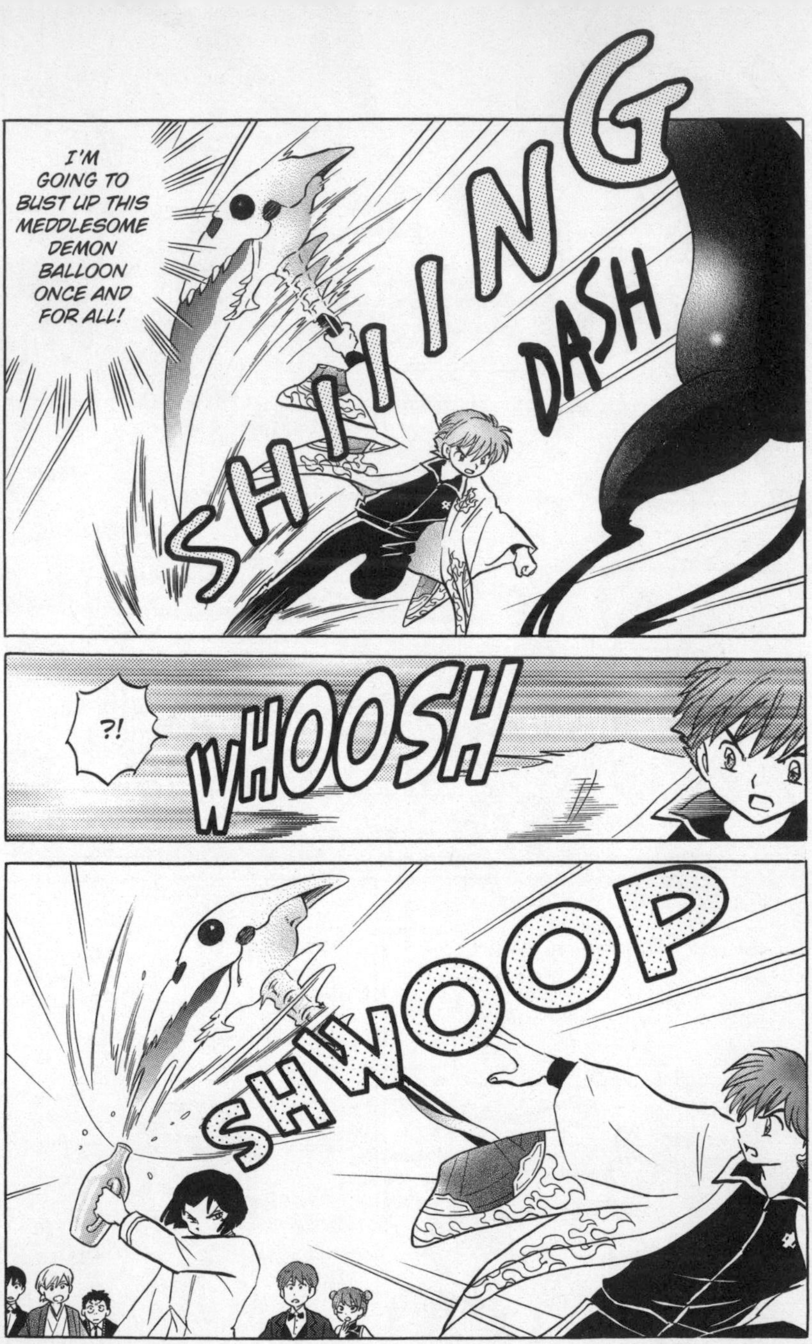
SHIIING
DASH
I'M GOING TO BUST UP THIS MEDDLESOME DEMON BALLOON ONCE AND FOR ALL!
WHOOSH
?!
SHWOOP

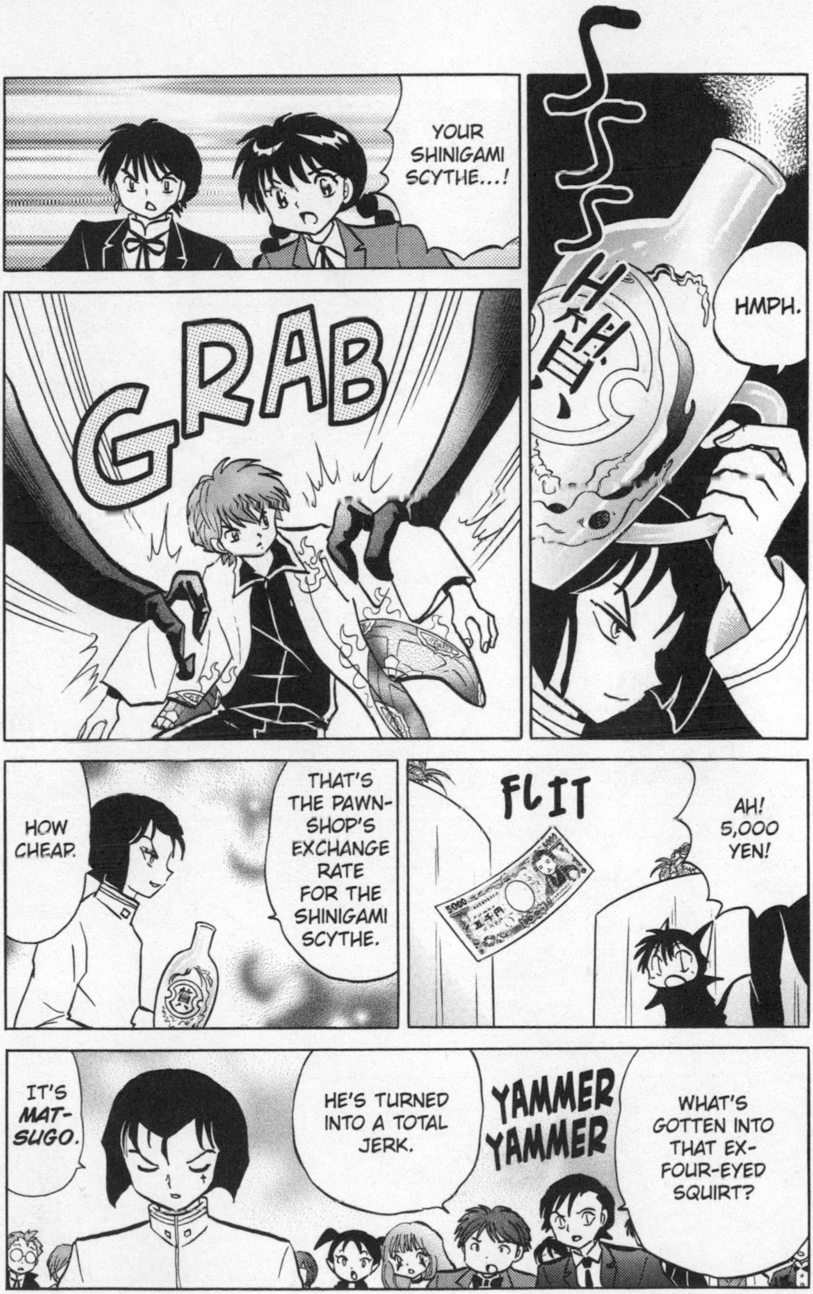
HMPH.
YOUR SHINIGAMI SCYTHE...!
GRAB
FLIT
AH! 5,000 YEN!
THAT'S THE PAWN-SHOP'S EXCHANGE RATE FOR THE SHINIGAMI SCYTHE.
HOW CHEAP.
WHAT'S GOTTEN INTO THAT EX-FOUR-EYED SQUIRT?
YAMMER YAMMER
HE'S TURNED INTO A TOTAL JERK.
IT'S *MATSUGO*.

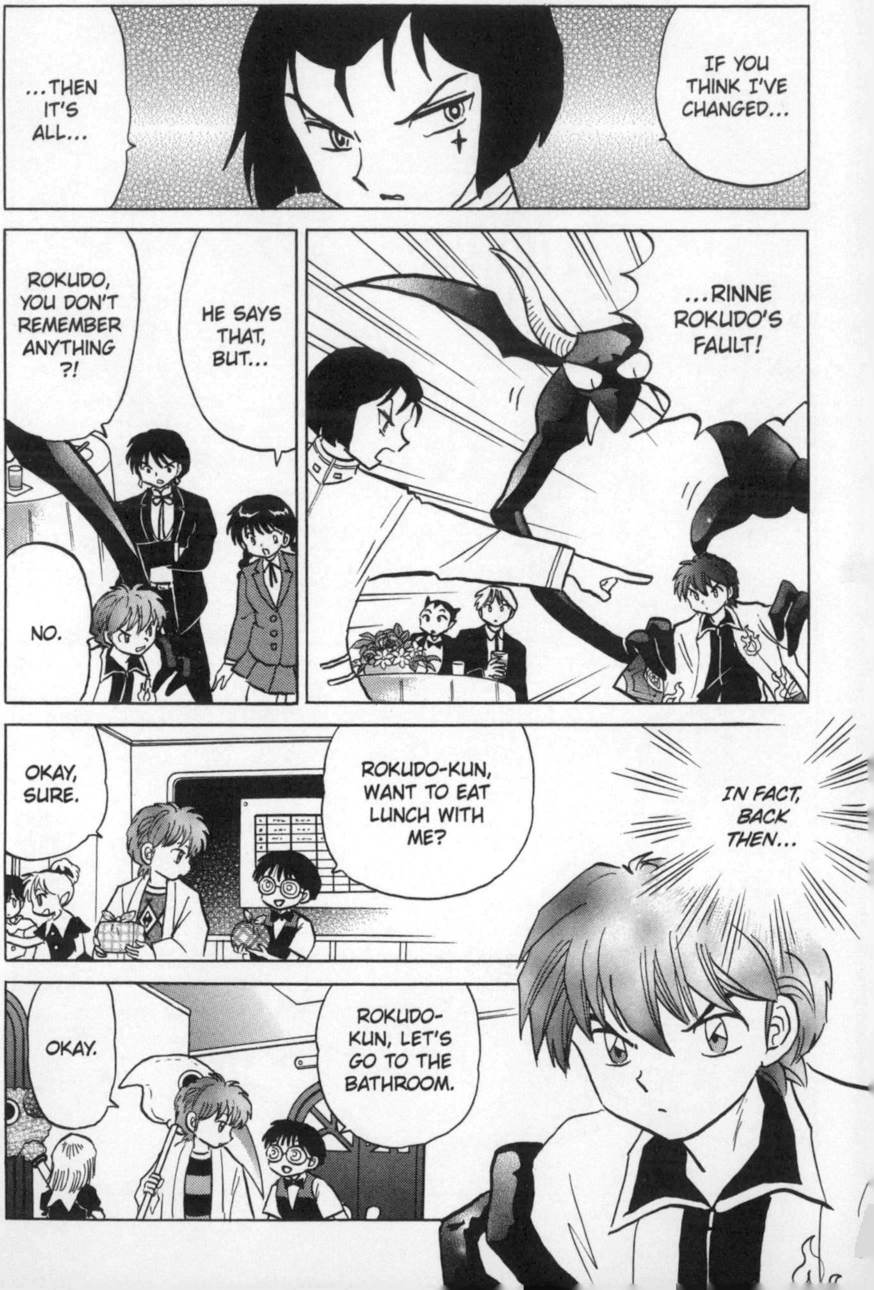
IF YOU THINK I'VE CHANGED...
...THEN IT'S ALL...
...RINNE ROKUDO'S FAULT!
HE SAYS THAT, BUT...
ROKUDO, YOU DON'T REMEMBER ANYTHING?!
NO.
IN FACT, BACK THEN...
ROKUDO-KUN, WANT TO EAT LUNCH WITH ME?
OKAY, SURE.
ROKUDO-KUN, LET'S GO TO THE BATHROOM.
OKAY.

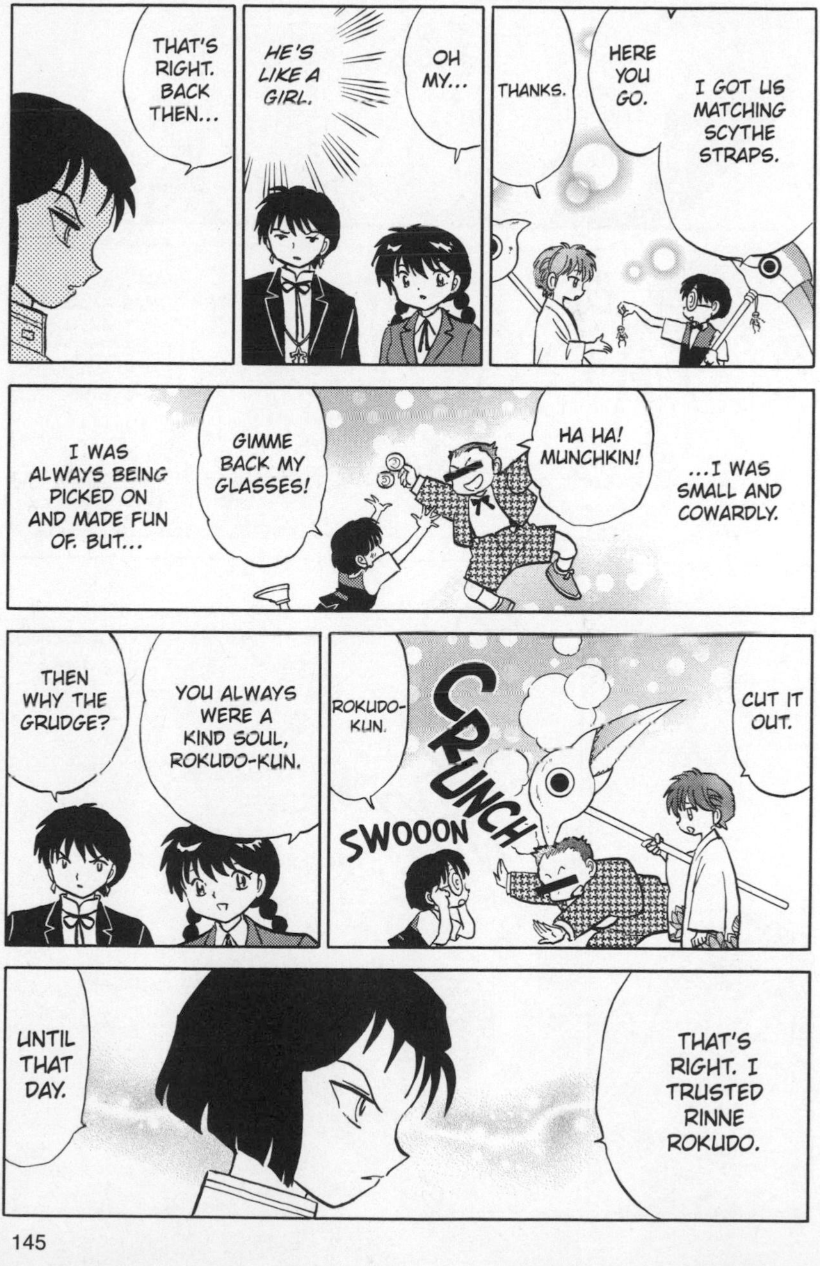
I GOT US MATCHING SCYTHE STRAPS.
HERE YOU GO.
THANKS.
OH MY...
HE'S LIKE A GIRL.
THAT'S RIGHT. BACK THEN...
...I WAS SMALL AND COWARDLY.
HA HA! MUNCHKIN!
GIMME BACK MY GLASSES!
I WAS ALWAYS BEING PICKED ON AND MADE FUN OF. BUT...
CUT IT OUT.
CRUNCH
SWOOON
ROKUDO-KUN.
YOU ALWAYS WERE A KIND SOUL, ROKUDO-KUN.
THEN WHY THE GRUDGE?
THAT'S RIGHT. I TRUSTED RINNE ROKUDO.
UNTIL THAT DAY.

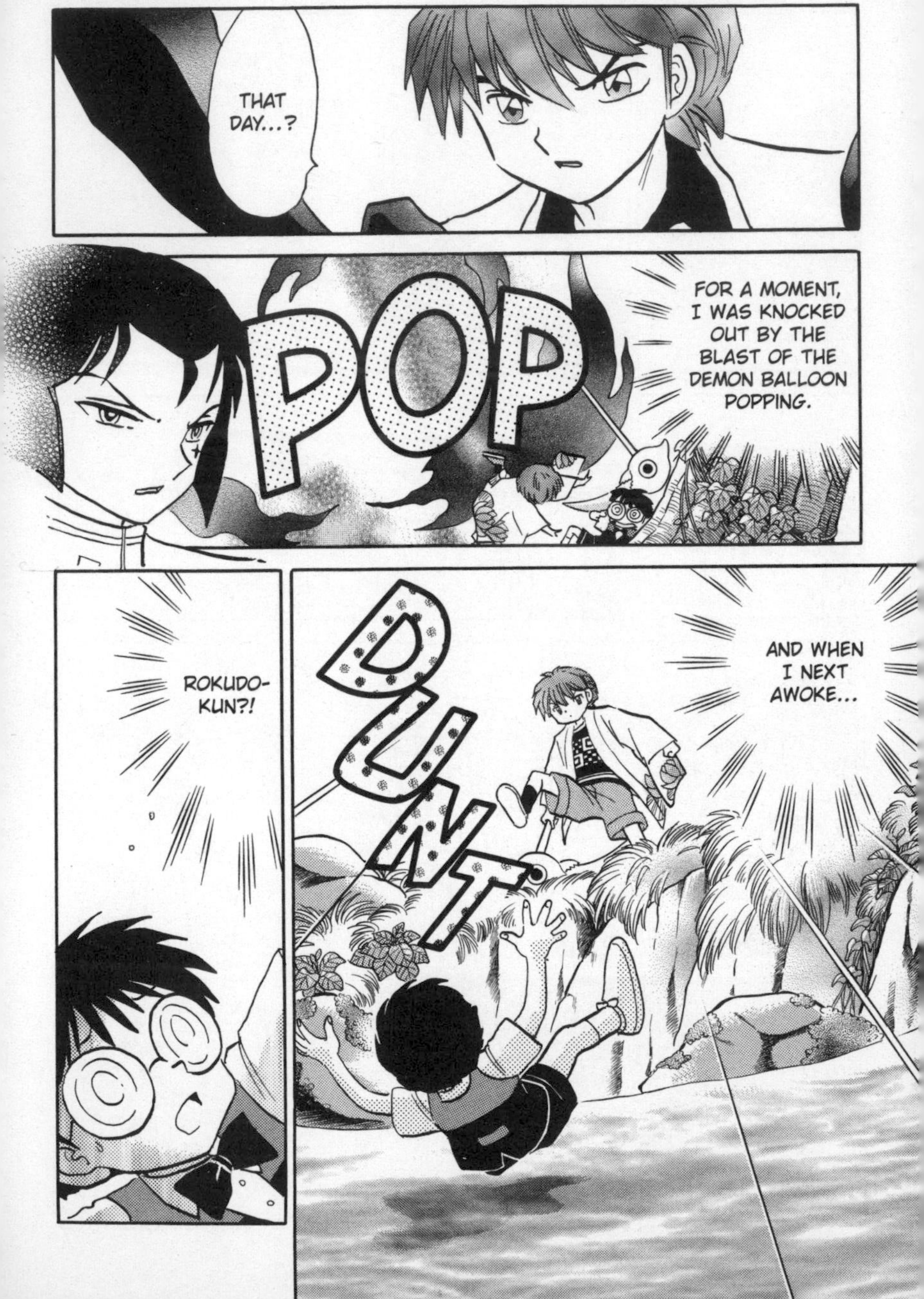
THAT DAY...?
FOR A MOMENT, I WAS KNOCKED OUT BY THE BLAST OF THE DEMON BALLOON POPPING.
POP
AND WHEN I NEXT AWOKE...
DUNT
ROKUDO-KUN?!

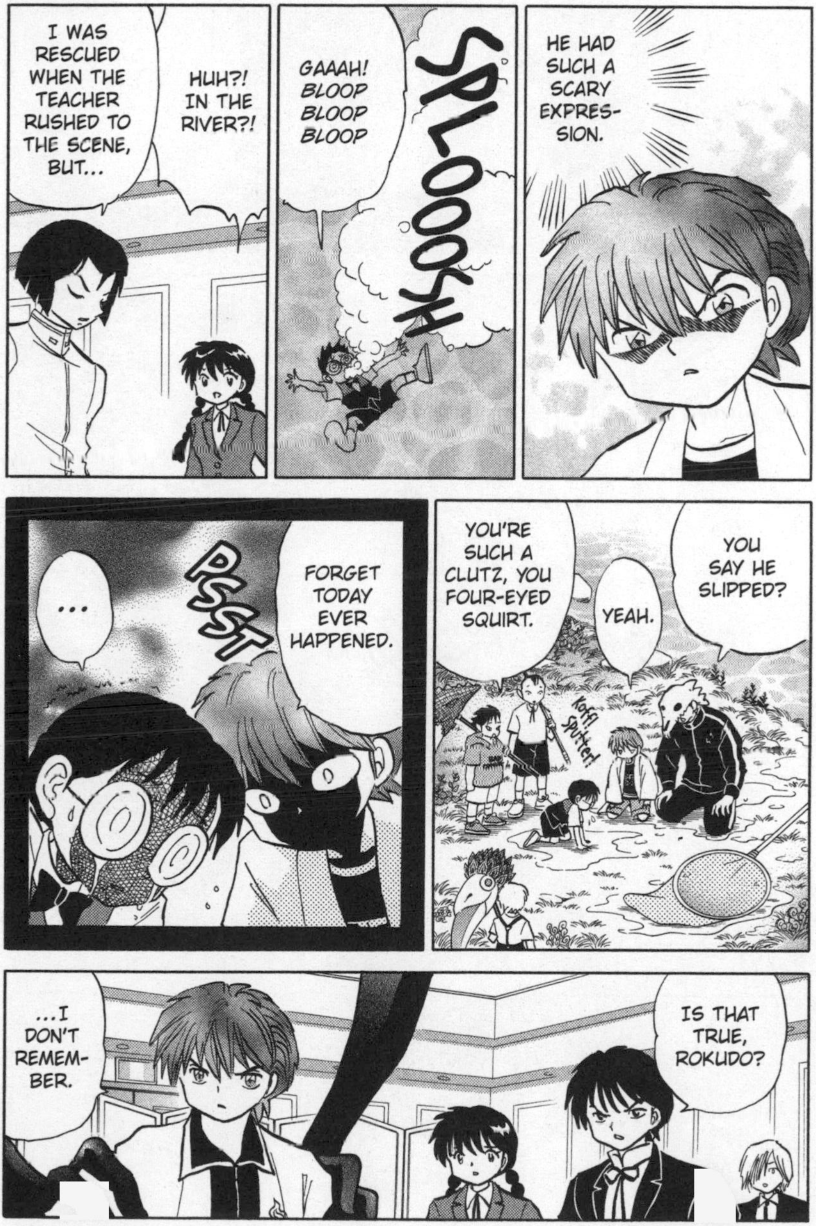
HE HAD SUCH A SCARY EXPRES-SION.
SPLOOOSH
GAAAH! BLOOP BLOOP BLOOP
HUH?! IN THE RIVER?!
I WAS RESCUED WHEN THE TEACHER RUSHED TO THE SCENE, BUT...
YOU SAY HE SLIPPED?
YEAH.
YOU'RE SUCH A CLUTZ, YOU FOUR-EYED SQUIRT.
Koff! Sputter!
FORGET TODAY EVER HAPPENED.
PSST
...
IS THAT TRUE, ROKUDO?
...I DON'T REMEM-BER.

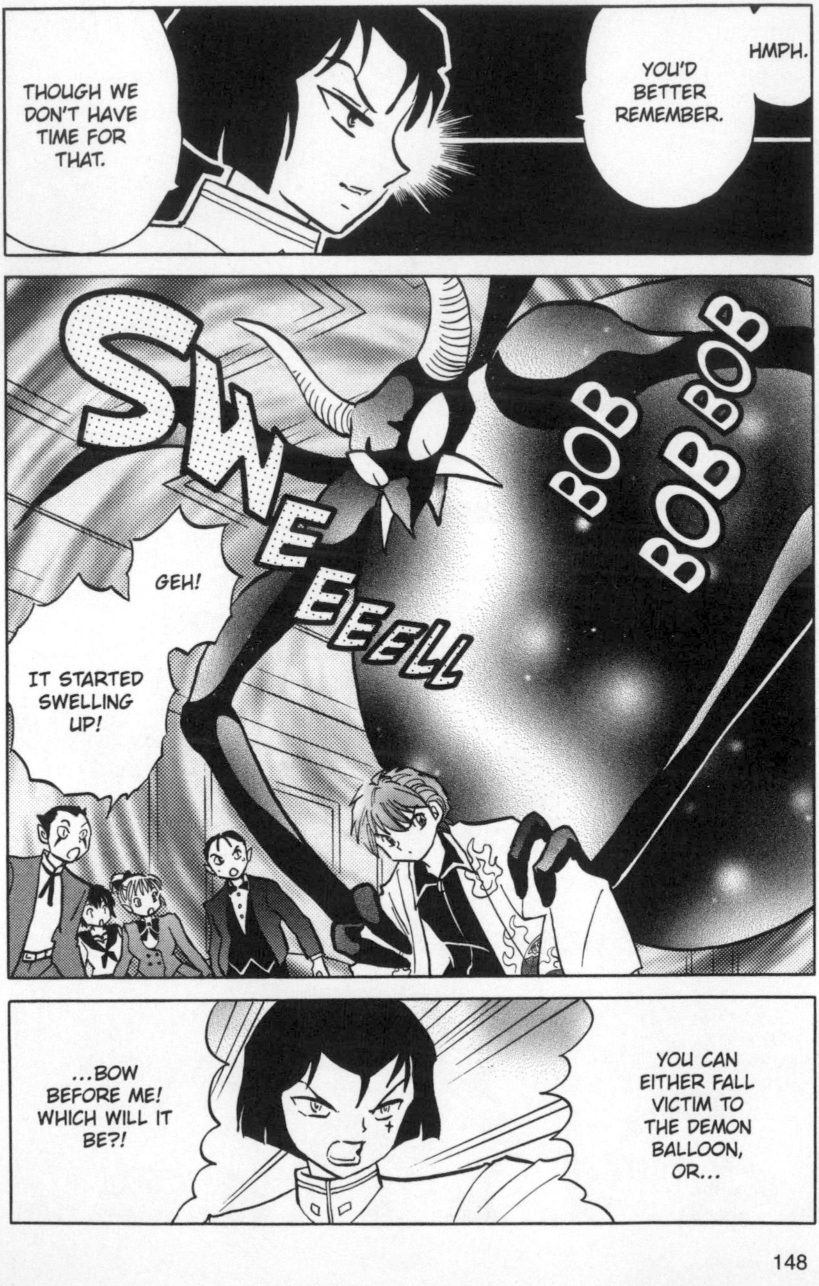
HMPH.
YOU'D BETTER REMEMBER.
THOUGH WE DON'T HAVE TIME FOR THAT.
BOB BOB BOB BOB
SWEEEELL
GEH!
IT STARTED SWELLING UP!
YOU CAN EITHER FALL VICTIM TO THE DEMON BALLOON, OR...
...BOW BEFORE ME! WHICH WILL IT BE?!

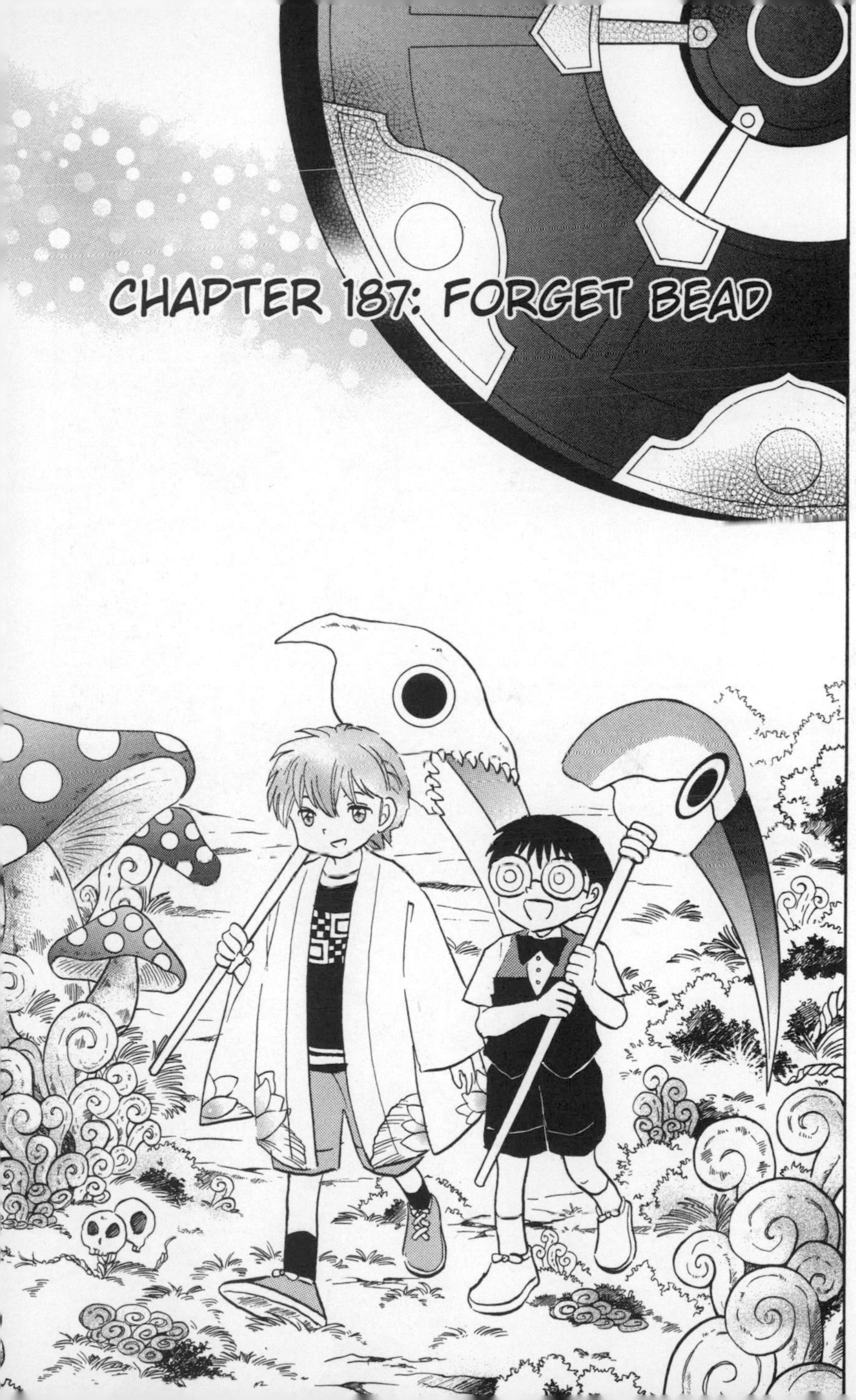
CHAPTER 187: FORGET BEAD

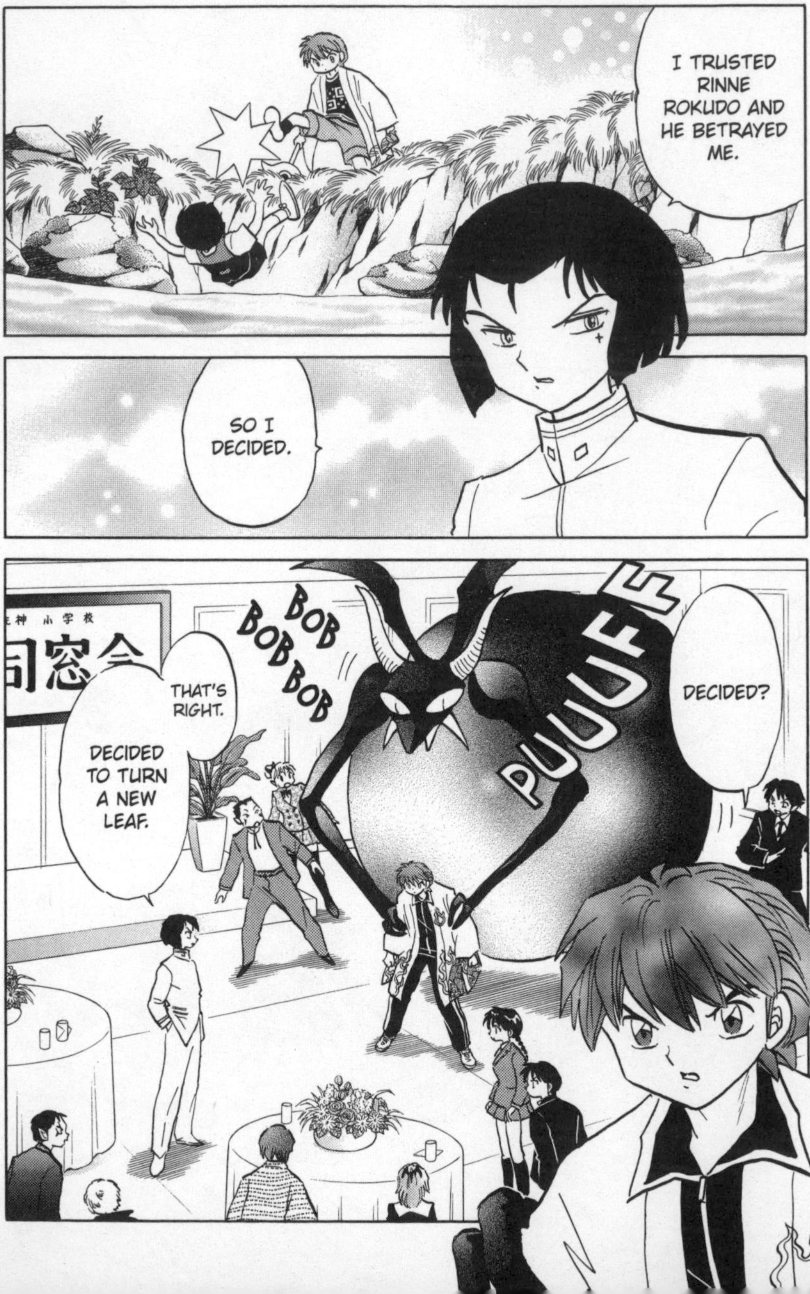
I TRUSTED RINNE ROKUDO AND HE BETRAYED ME.
SO I DECIDED.
DECIDED?
PUUUFF
BOB BOB BOB
THAT'S RIGHT.
DECIDED TO TURN A NEW LEAF.
同窓会

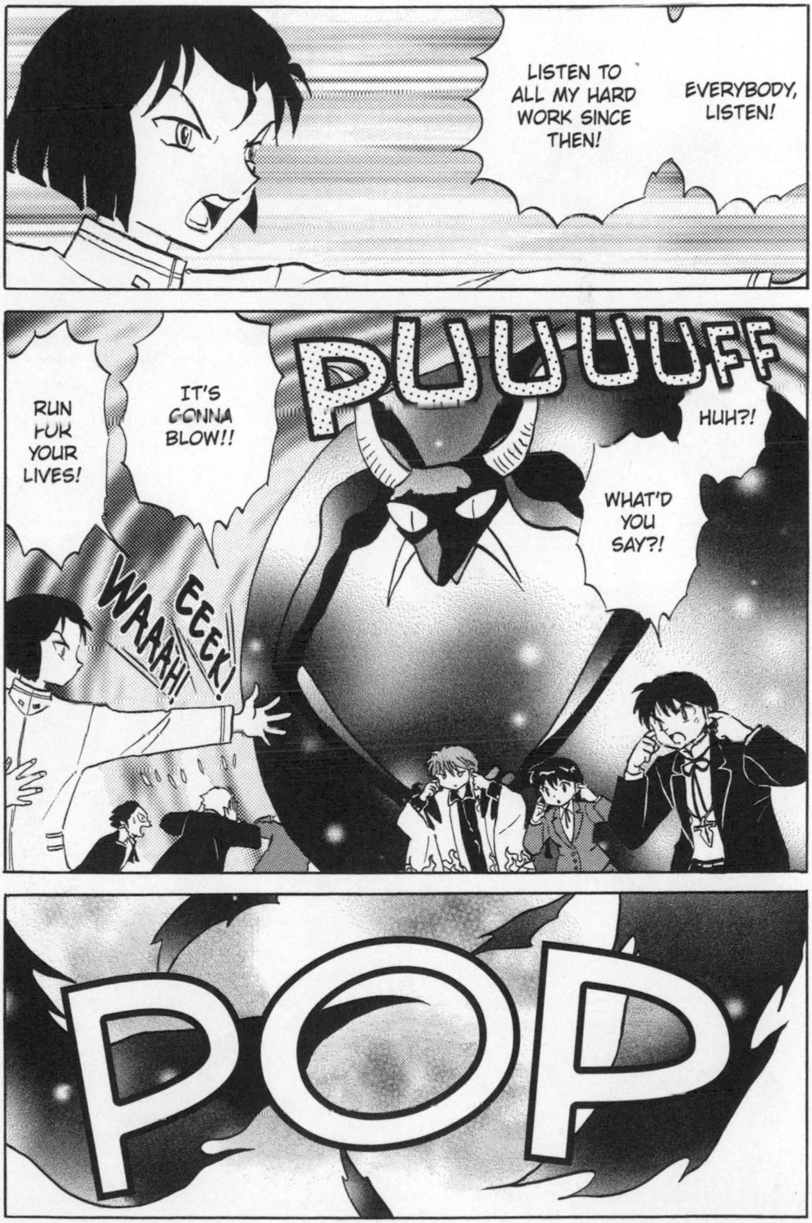
EVERYBODY, LISTEN!
LISTEN TO ALL MY HARD WORK SINCE THEN!
PUUUUFF
HUH?!
WHAT'D YOU SAY?!
IT'S GONNA BLOW!!
RUN FOR YOUR LIVES!
EEEK!
WAAAH!
POP

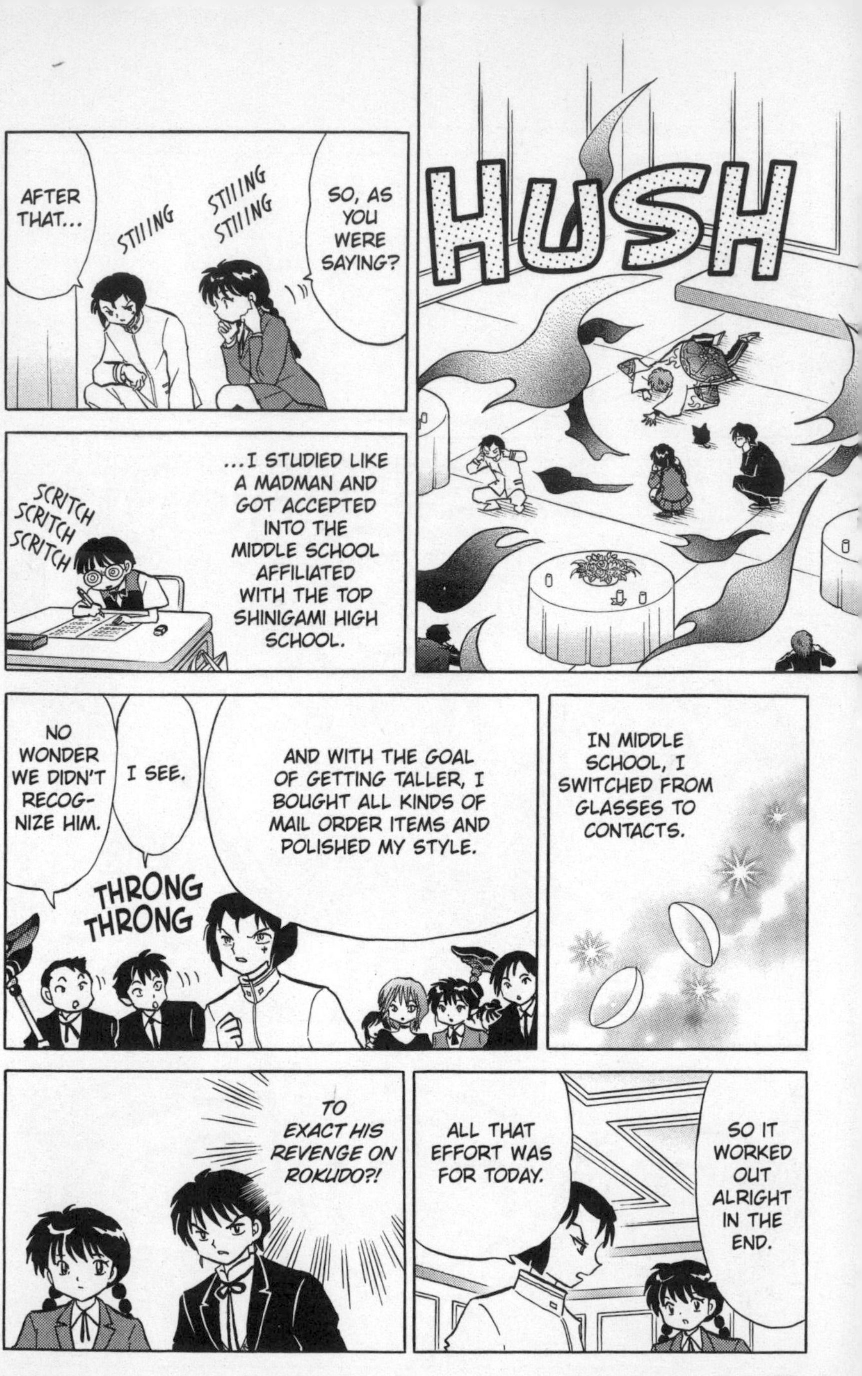
HUSH
SO, AS YOU WERE SAYING?
STIIING STIIING
STIIING
AFTER THAT...
...I STUDIED LIKE A MADMAN AND GOT ACCEPTED INTO THE MIDDLE SCHOOL AFFILIATED WITH THE TOP SHINIGAMI HIGH SCHOOL.
SCRITCH SCRITCH SCRITCH
IN MIDDLE SCHOOL, I SWITCHED FROM GLASSES TO CONTACTS.
AND WITH THE GOAL OF GETTING TALLER, I BOUGHT ALL KINDS OF MAIL ORDER ITEMS AND POLISHED MY STYLE.
I SEE.
NO WONDER WE DIDN'T RECOG-NIZE HIM.
THRONG THRONG
SO IT WORKED OUT ALRIGHT IN THE END.
ALL THAT EFFORT WAS FOR TODAY.
TO EXACT HIS REVENGE ON ROKUDO?!

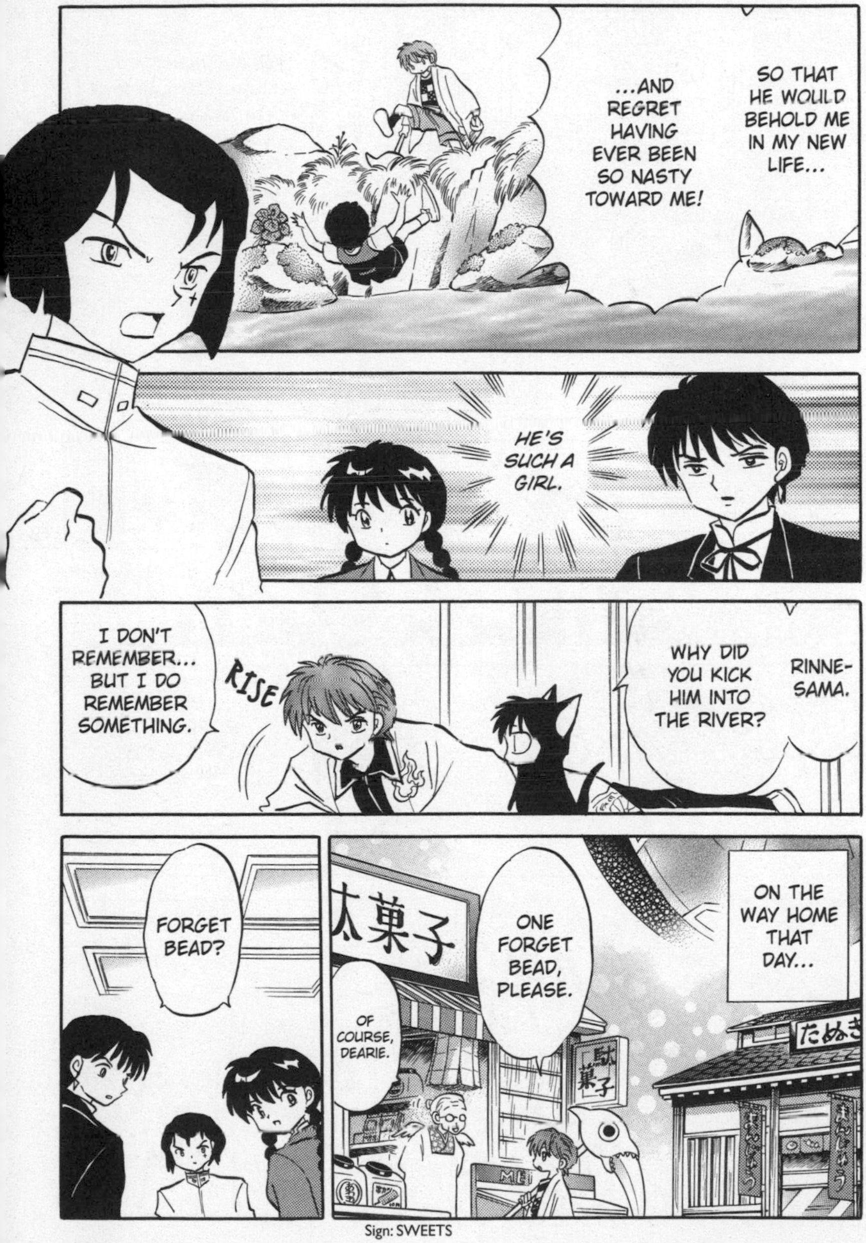
SO THAT HE WOULD BEHOLD ME IN MY NEW LIFE...
...AND REGRET HAVING EVER BEEN SO NASTY TOWARD ME!
HE'S SUCH A GIRL.
RINNE-SAMA.
WHY DID YOU KICK HIM INTO THE RIVER?
RISE
I DON'T REMEMBER... BUT I DO REMEMBER SOMETHING.
ON THE WAY HOME THAT DAY...
たぬき
駄菓子
ONE FORGET BEAD, PLEASE.
OF COURSE, DEARIE.
FORGET BEAD?

Sign: SWEETS

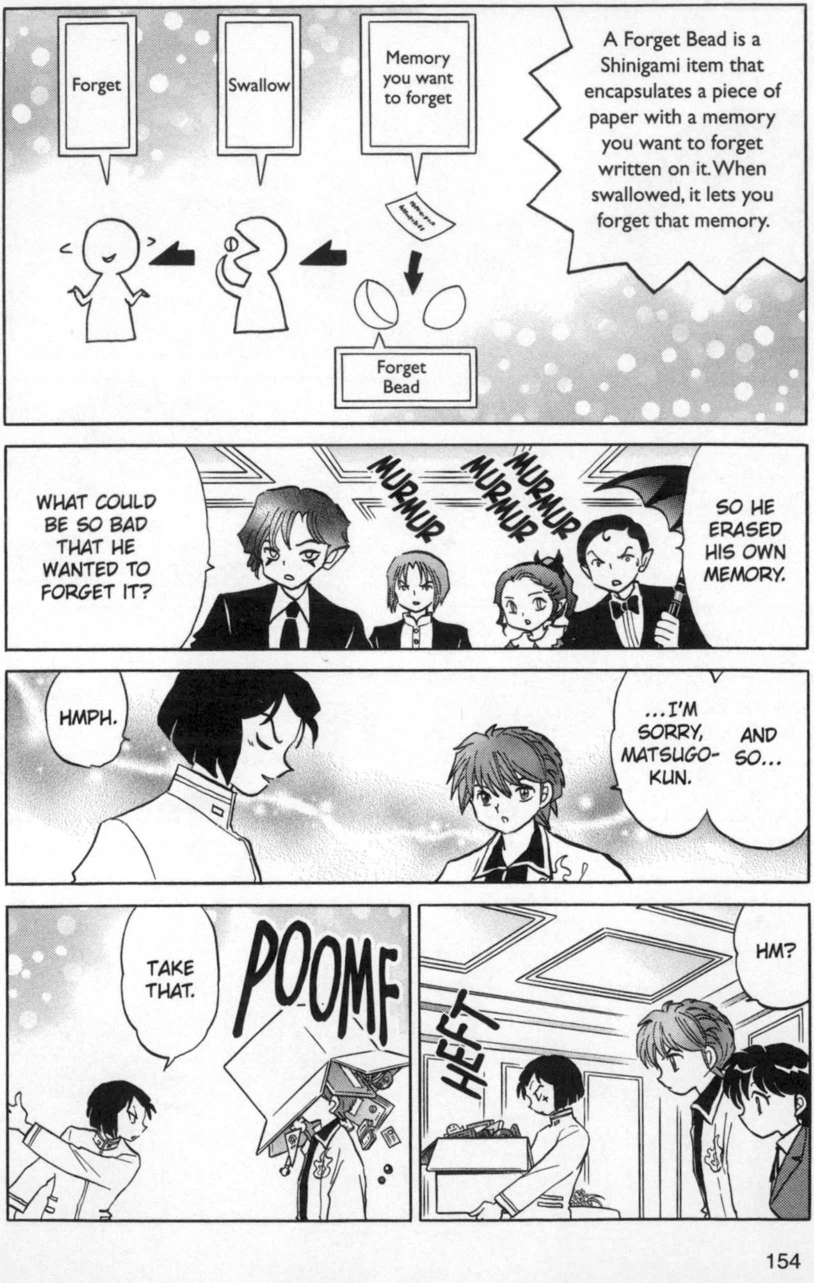

A Forget Bead is a Shinigami item that encapsulates a piece of paper with a memory you want to forget written on it. When swallowed, it lets you forget that memory.
Memory you want to forget
Forget Bead
Swallow
Forget
SO HE ERASED HIS OWN MEMORY.
MURMUR MURMUR
MURMUR
WHAT COULD BE SO BAD THAT HE WANTED TO FORGET IT?
AND SO...
...I'M SORRY, MATSUGO-KUN.
HMPH.
HM?
HEFT
POOMF
TAKE THAT.

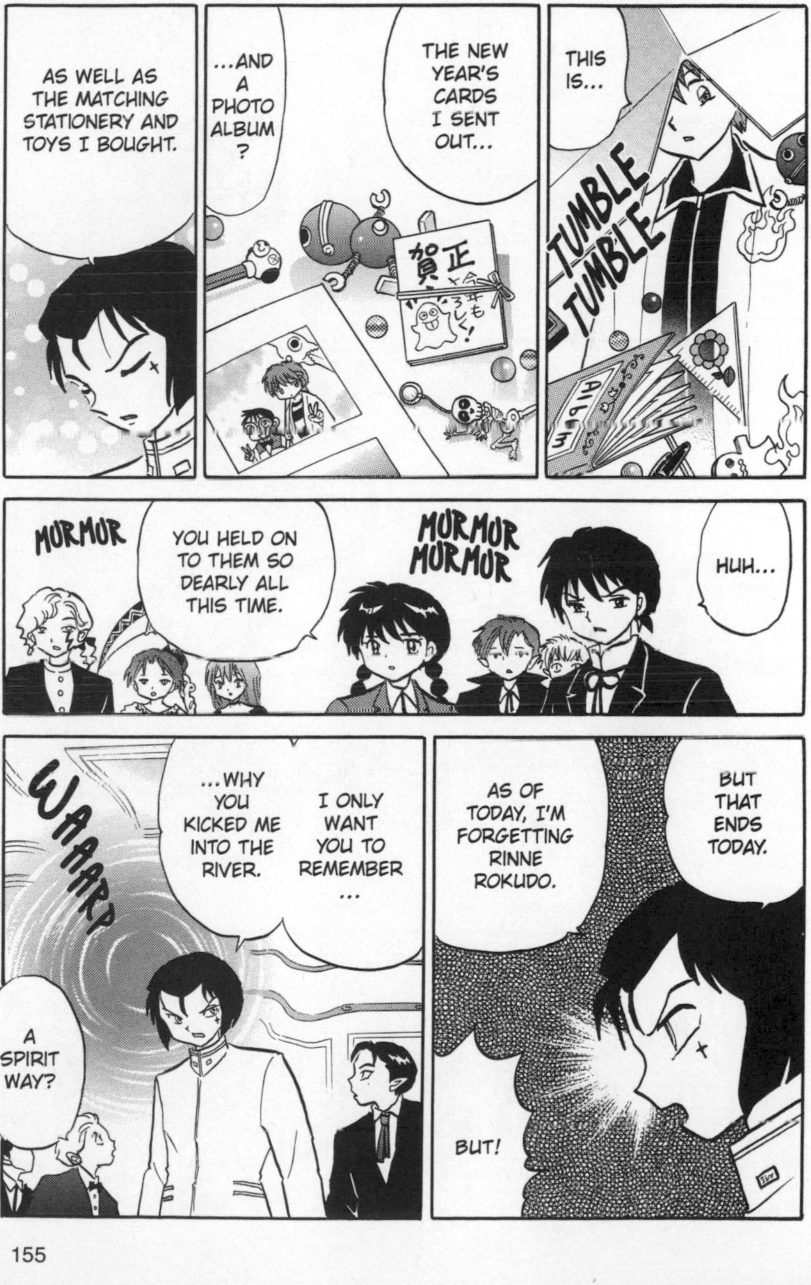
THIS IS...
TUMBLE TUMBLE
THE NEW YEAR'S CARDS I SENT OUT...
賀正
...AND A PHOTO ALBUM ?
AS WELL AS THE MATCHING STATIONERY AND TOYS I BOUGHT.
HUH...
MURMUR MURMUR
YOU HELD ON TO THEM SO DEARLY ALL THIS TIME.
MURMUR
BUT THAT ENDS TODAY.
AS OF TODAY, I'M FORGETTING RINNE ROKUDO.
BUT!
I ONLY WANT YOU TO REMEMBER ...
...WHY YOU KICKED ME INTO THE RIVER.
WHAARP
A SPIRIT WAY?

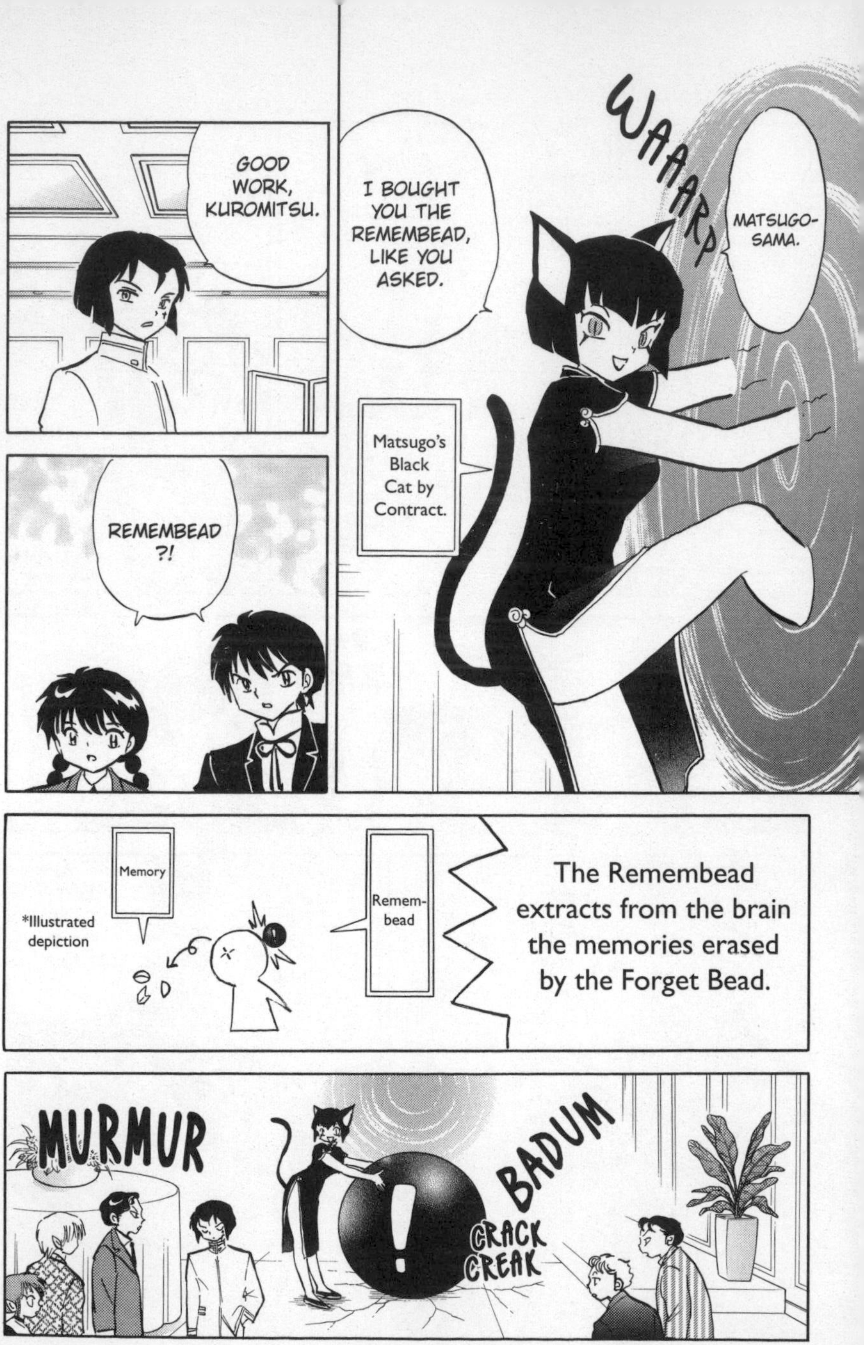
WAAARP
MATSUGO-SAMA.
I BOUGHT YOU THE REMEMBEAD, LIKE YOU ASKED.
Matsugo's Black Cat by Contract.
GOOD WORK, KUROMITSU.
REMEMBEAD ?!
The Remembead extracts from the brain the memories erased by the Forget Bead.
Remem-bead
Memory
*Illustrated depiction
BADUM
CRACK CREAK
MURMUR

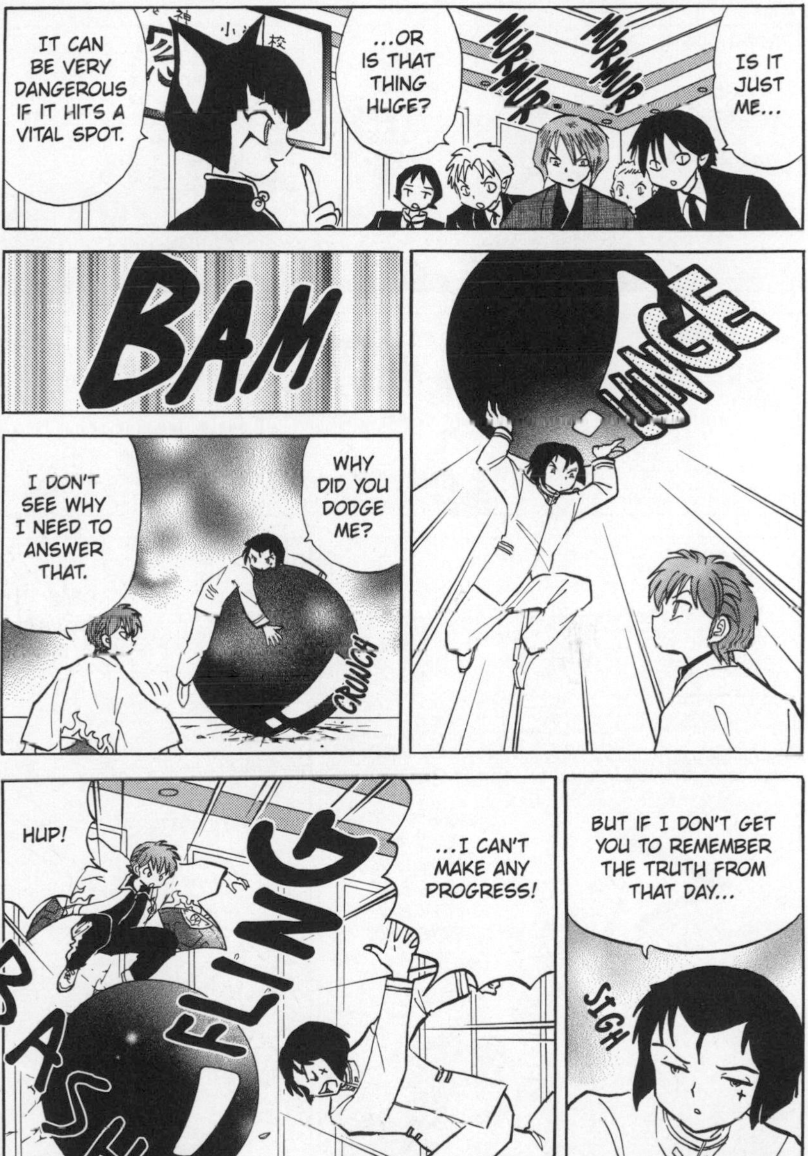
IS IT JUST ME...
MURMUR
MURMUR
...OR IS THAT THING HUGE?
IT CAN BE VERY DANGEROUS IF IT HITS A VITAL SPOT.
LUNGE
BAM
WHY DID YOU DODGE ME?
I DON'T SEE WHY I NEED TO ANSWER THAT.
CRUNCH
BUT IF I DON'T GET YOU TO REMEMBER THE TRUTH FROM THAT DAY...
SIGH
...I CAN'T MAKE ANY PROGRESS!
FLING
HUP!
BASH!

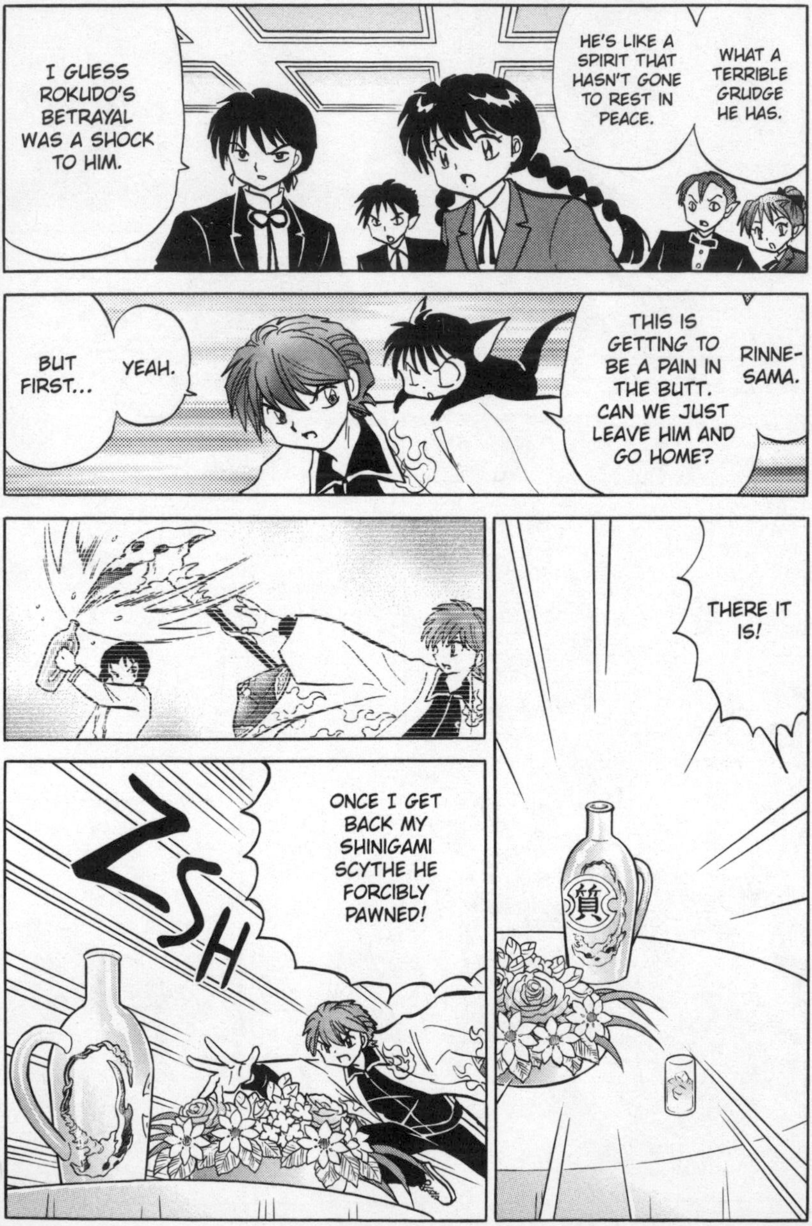
WHAT A TERRIBLE GRUDGE HE HAS.
HE'S LIKE A SPIRIT THAT HASN'T GONE TO REST IN PEACE.
I GUESS ROKUDO'S BETRAYAL WAS A SHOCK TO HIM.
RINNE-SAMA.
THIS IS GETTING TO BE A PAIN IN THE BUTT. CAN WE JUST LEAVE HIM AND GO HOME?
YEAH.
BUT FIRST...
THERE IT IS!
ONCE I GET BACK MY SHINIGAMI SCYTHE HE FORCIBLY PAWNED!
ZSH

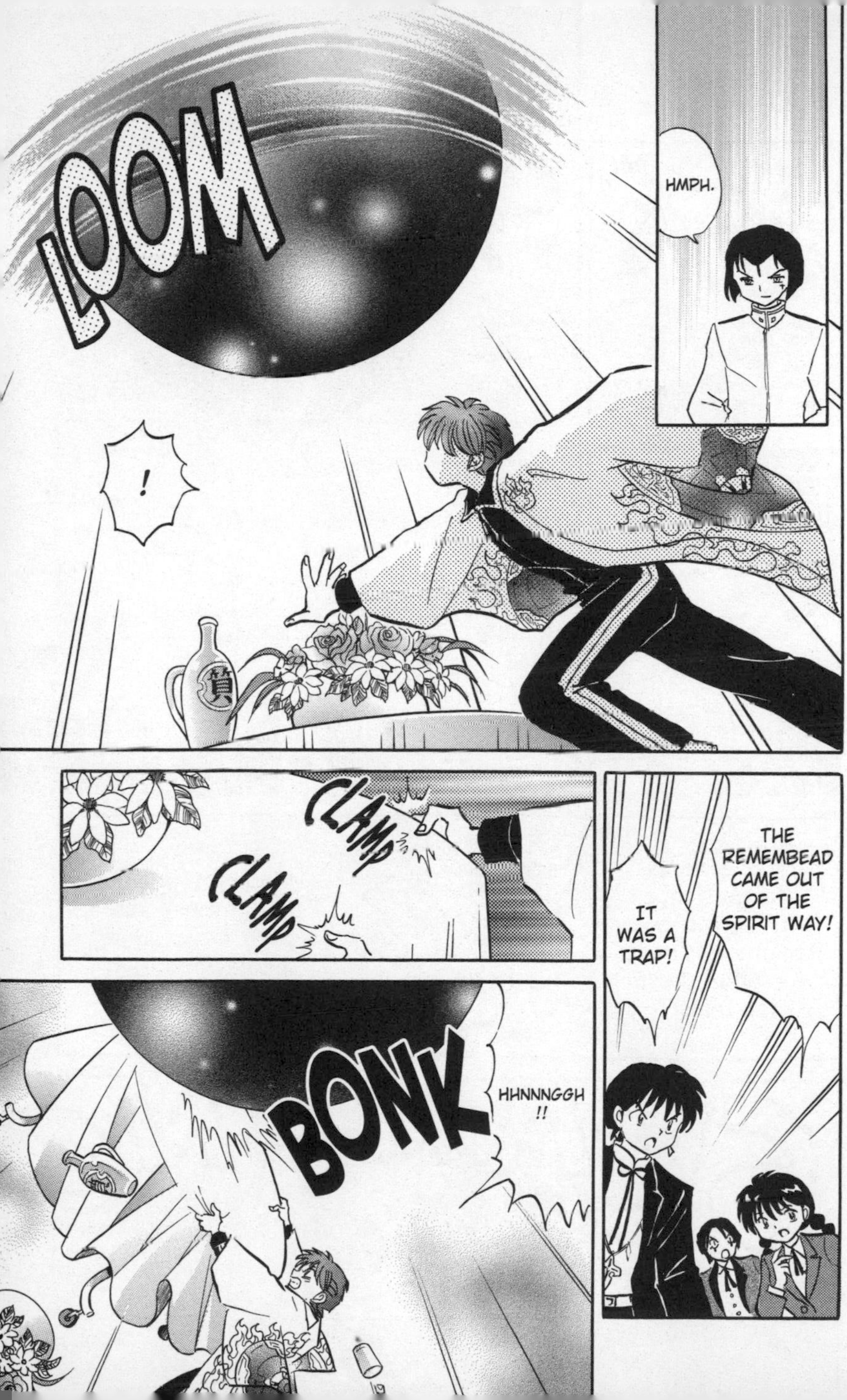
HMPH.
LOOM
!
THE REMEMBEAD CAME OUT OF THE SPIRIT WAY!
IT WAS A TRAP!
CLAMP
CLAMP
BONK
HHNNNGGH !!

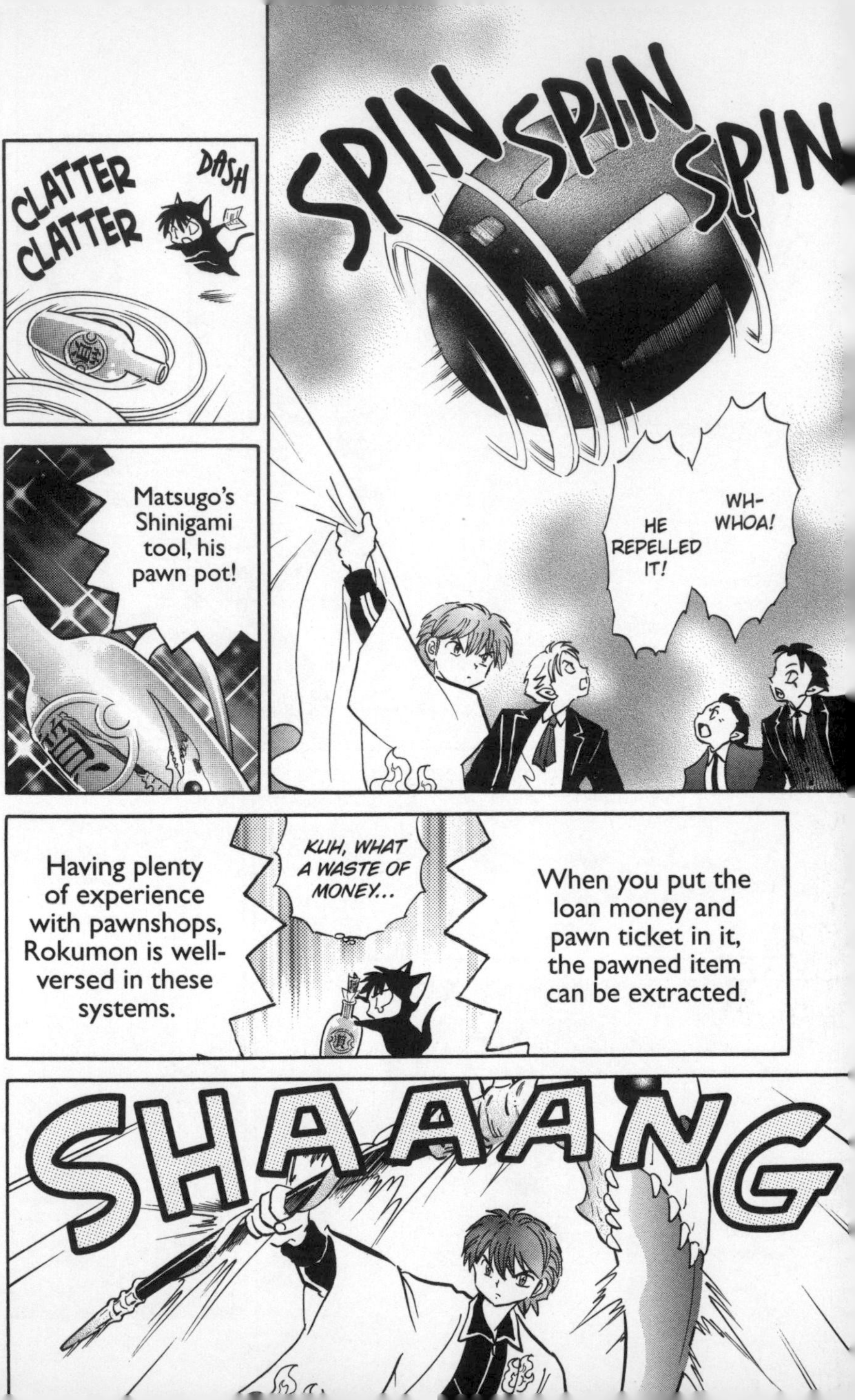
SPIN SPIN SPIN
WH- WHOA!
HE REPELLED IT!
DASH
CLATTER CLATTER
Matsugo's Shinigami tool, his pawn pot!
When you put the loan money and pawn ticket in it, the pawned item can be extracted.
KUH, WHAT A WASTE OF MONEY...
Having plenty of experience with pawnshops, Rokumon is well-versed in these systems.
SHAAANG

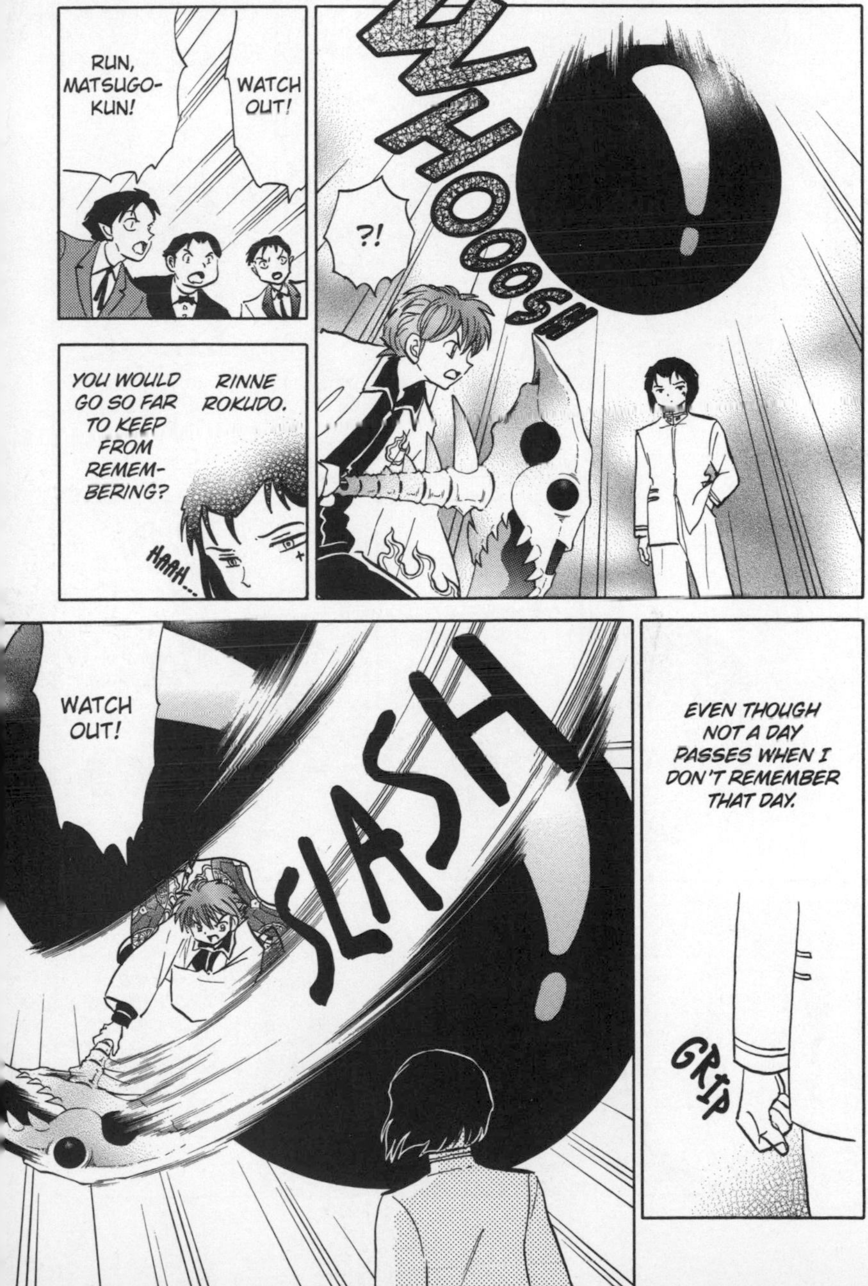
WHOOOSH
?!
WATCH OUT!
RUN, MATSUGO-KUN!
RINNE ROKUDO.
YOU WOULD GO SO FAR TO KEEP FROM REMEMBERING?
HAAH...
EVEN THOUGH NOT A DAY PASSES WHEN I DON'T REMEMBER THAT DAY.
GRIP
SLASH
WATCH OUT!

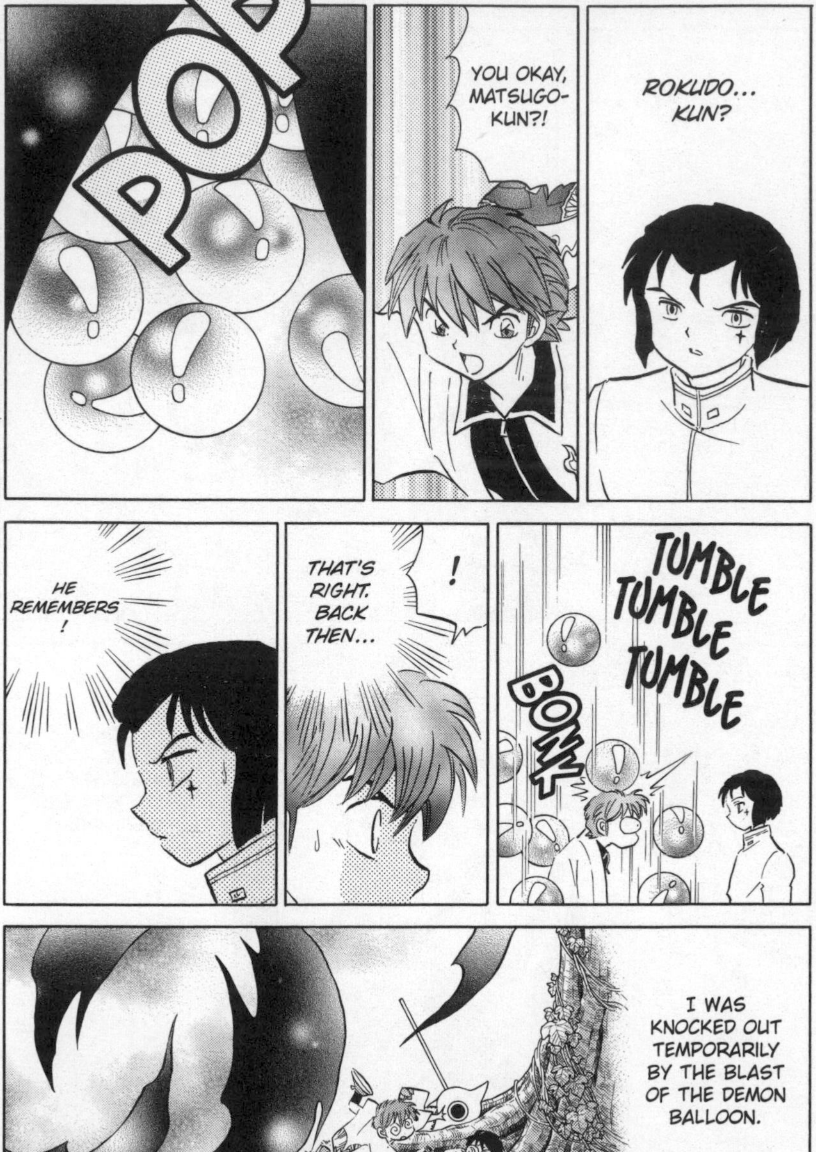
ROKUDO... KUN?
YOU OKAY, MATSUGO-KUN?!
POP
POP
TUMBLE
TUMBLE
TUMBLE
BONK
!
THAT'S RIGHT. BACK THEN...
HE REMEMBERS!
I WAS KNOCKED OUT TEMPORARILY BY THE BLAST OF THE DEMON BALLOON.

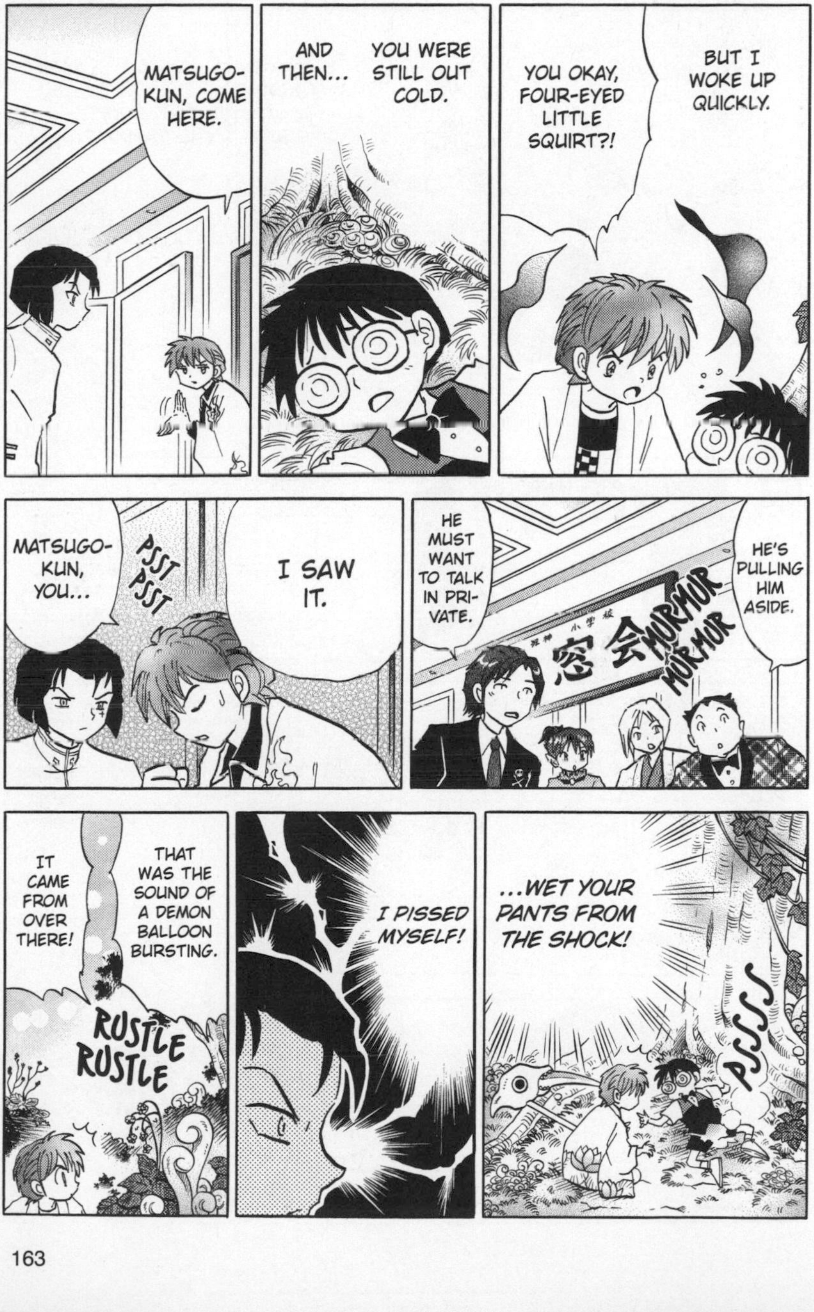
BUT I WOKE UP QUICKLY.
YOU OKAY, FOUR-EYED LITTLE SQUIRT?!
YOU WERE STILL OUT COLD.
AND THEN…
MATSUGO-KUN, COME HERE.
HE'S PULLING HIM ASIDE.
MURMUR MURMUR
窓会
HE MUST WANT TO TALK IN PRIVATE.
I SAW IT.
PSST PSST
MATSUGO-KUN, YOU…
…WET YOUR PANTS FROM THE SHOCK!
PSSSS
I PISSED MYSELF!
THAT WAS THE SOUND OF A DEMON BALLOON BURSTING.
IT CAME FROM OVER THERE!
RUSTLE RUSTLE

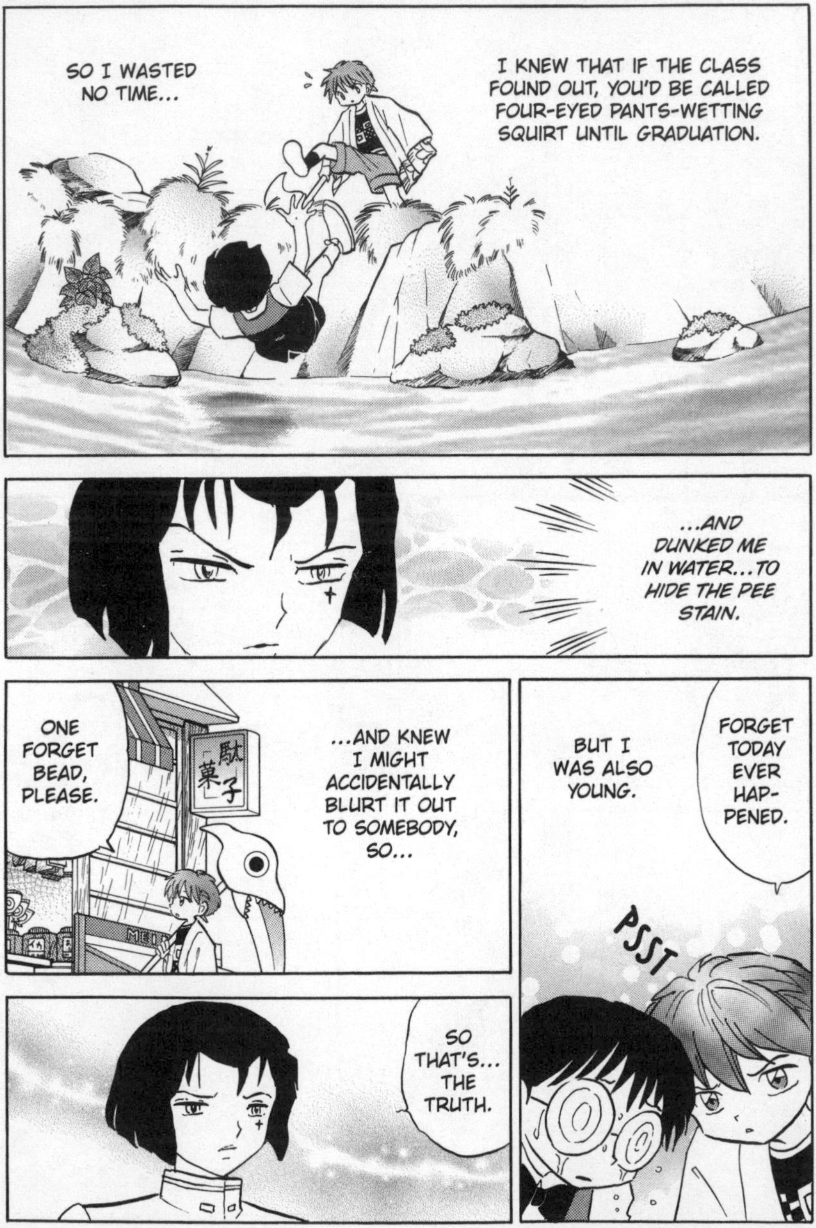
I KNEW THAT IF THE CLASS FOUND OUT, YOU'D BE CALLED FOUR-EYED PANTS-WETTING SQUIRT UNTIL GRADUATION.
SO I WASTED NO TIME...
...AND DUNKED ME IN WATER...TO HIDE THE PEE STAIN.
FORGET TODAY EVER HAP-PENED.
BUT I WAS ALSO YOUNG.
PSST
...AND KNEW I MIGHT ACCIDENTALLY BLURT IT OUT TO SOMEBODY, SO...
ONE FORGET BEAD, PLEASE.
駄菓子
SO THAT'S... THE TRUTH.

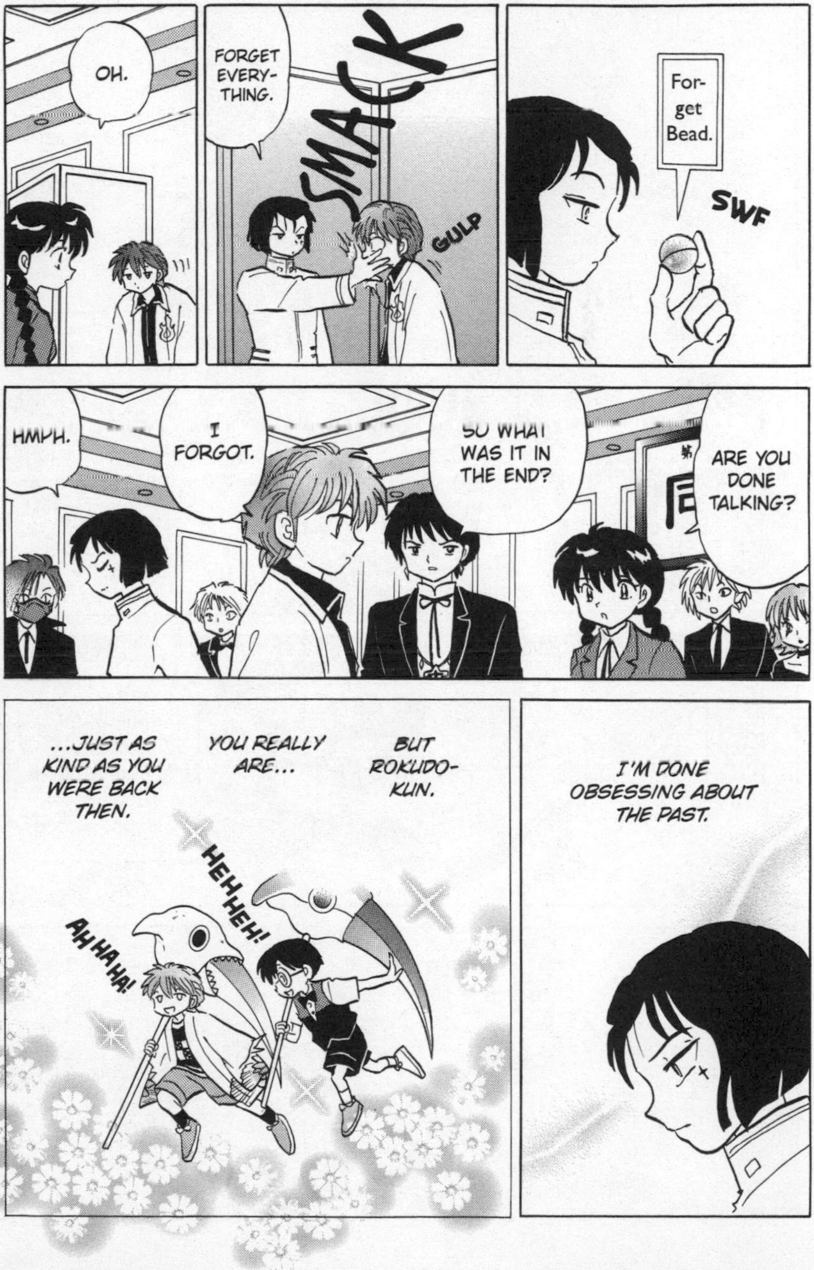
For-get Bead.
SWF
FORGET EVERY-THING.
SMACK
GULP
OH.
ARE YOU DONE TALKING?
SO WHAT WAS IT IN THE END?
I FORGOT.
HMPH.
I'M DONE OBSESSING ABOUT THE PAST.
BUT ROKUDO-KUN.
YOU REALLY ARE...
...JUST AS KIND AS YOU WERE BACK THEN.
HEH HEH!
AH HA HA!

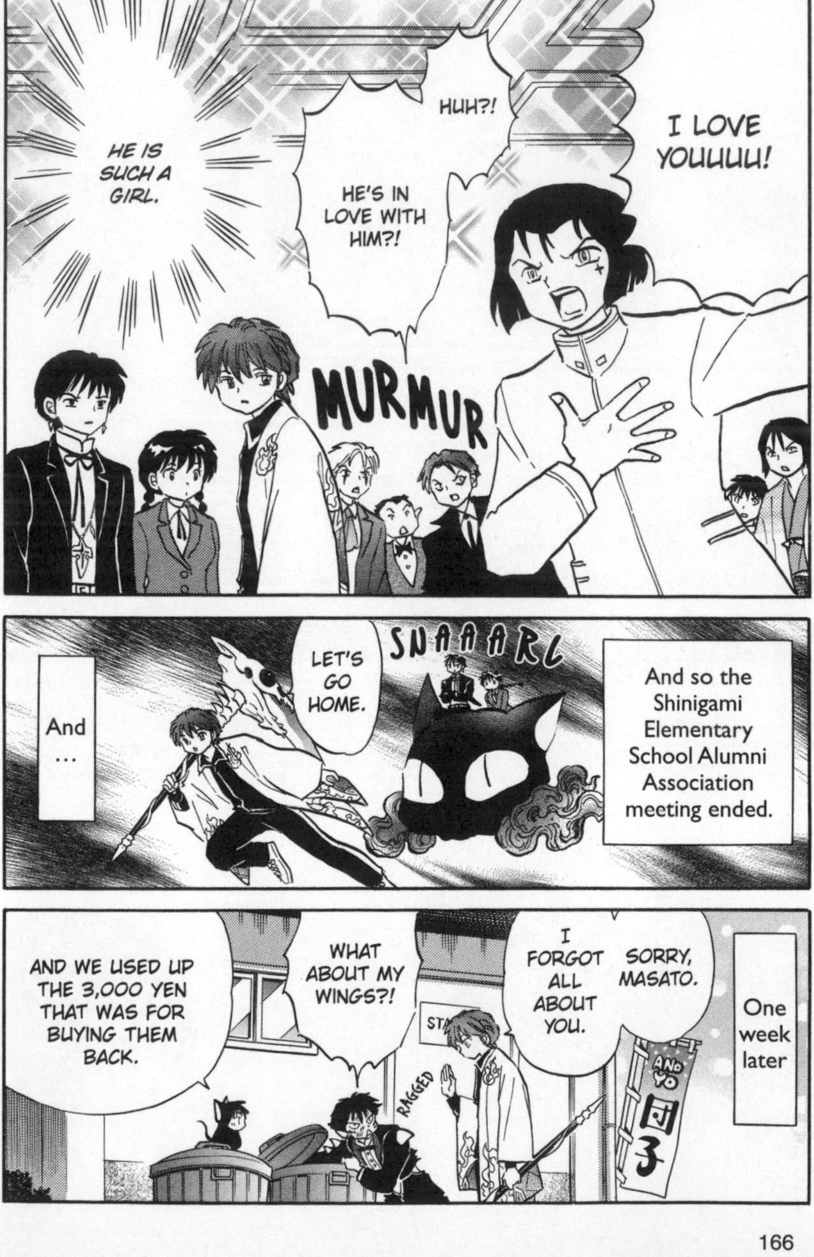
I LOVE YOUUUU!
HUH?!
HE'S IN LOVE WITH HIM?!
MURMUR
HE IS SUCH A GIRL.
And so the Shinigami Elementary School Alumni Association meeting ended.
SNAAARL
LET'S GO HOME.
And ...
One week later
ANO YO
SORRY, MASATO.
I FORGOT ALL ABOUT YOU.
WHAT ABOUT MY WINGS?!
RAGGED
AND WE USED UP THE 3,000 YEN THAT WAS FOR BUYING THEM BACK.

CHAPTER 188: THE FANCY CHOKER

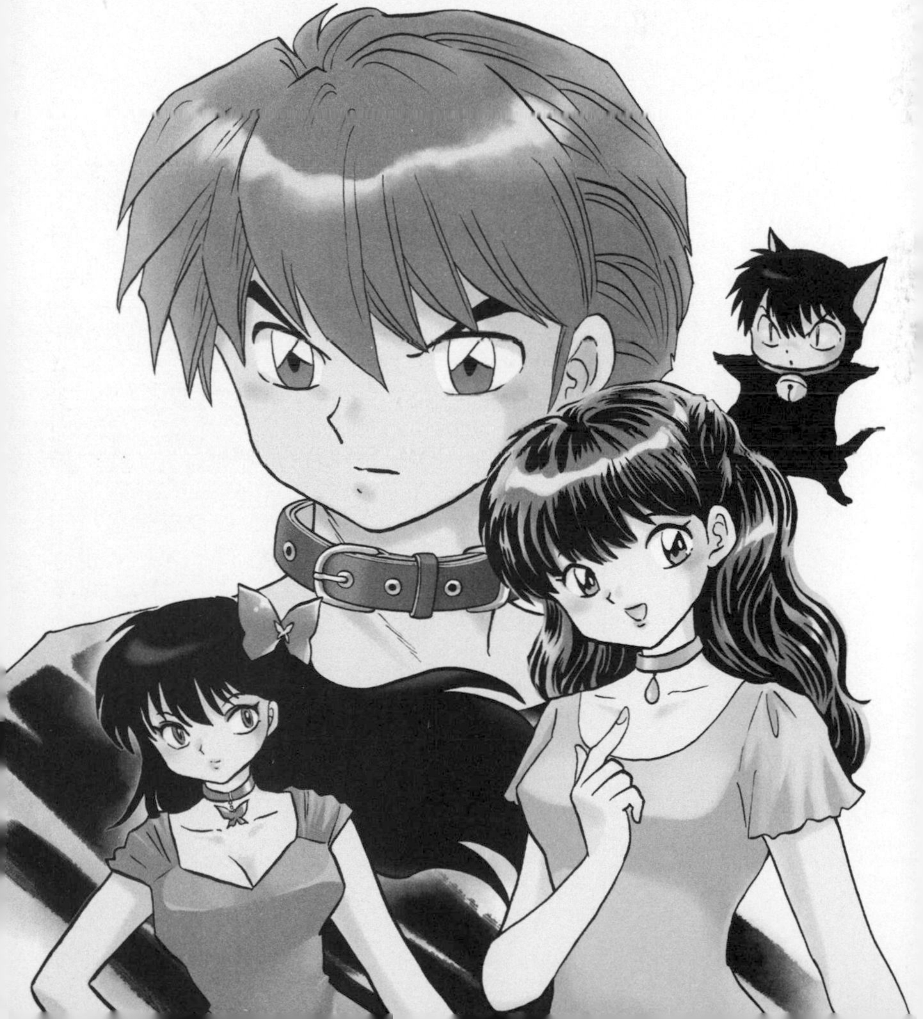

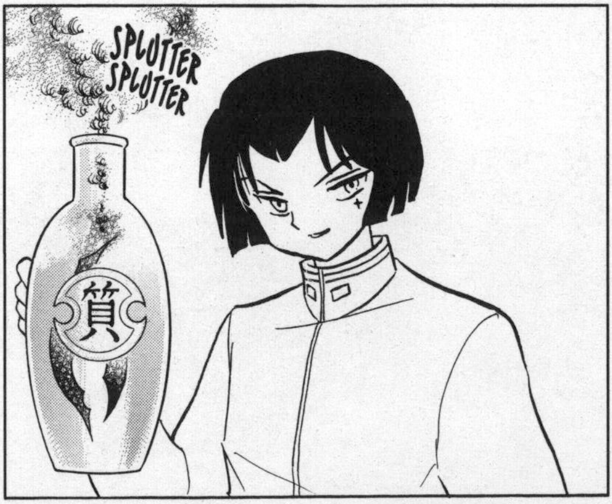
SPLUTTER
SPLUTTER

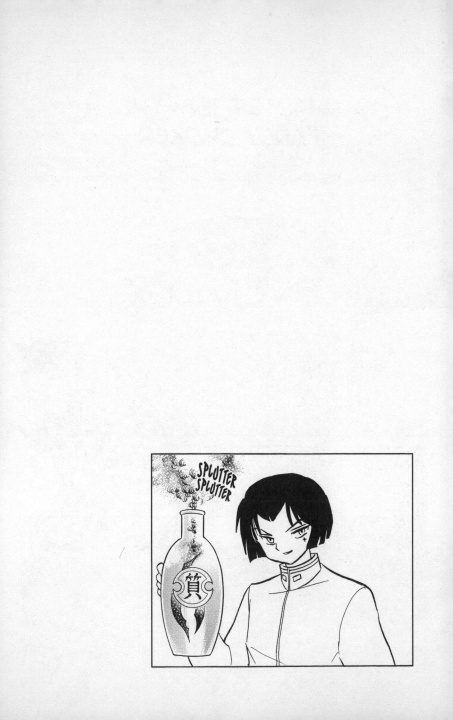

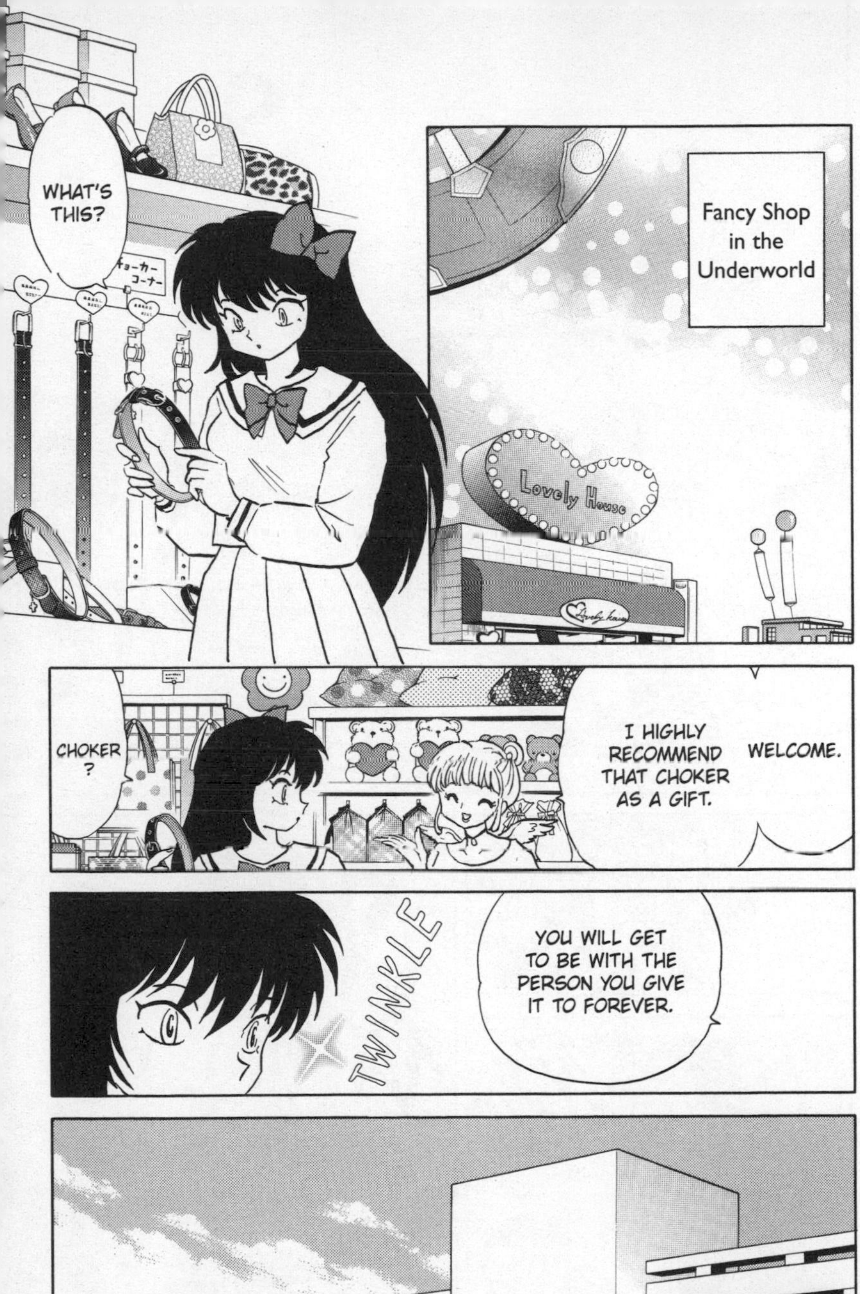
Fancy Shop in the Underworld
Lovely House
WHAT'S THIS?
WELCOME.
I HIGHLY RECOMMEND THAT CHOKER AS A GIFT.
CHOKER ?
YOU WILL GET TO BE WITH THE PERSON YOU GIVE IT TO FOREVER.
TWINKLE

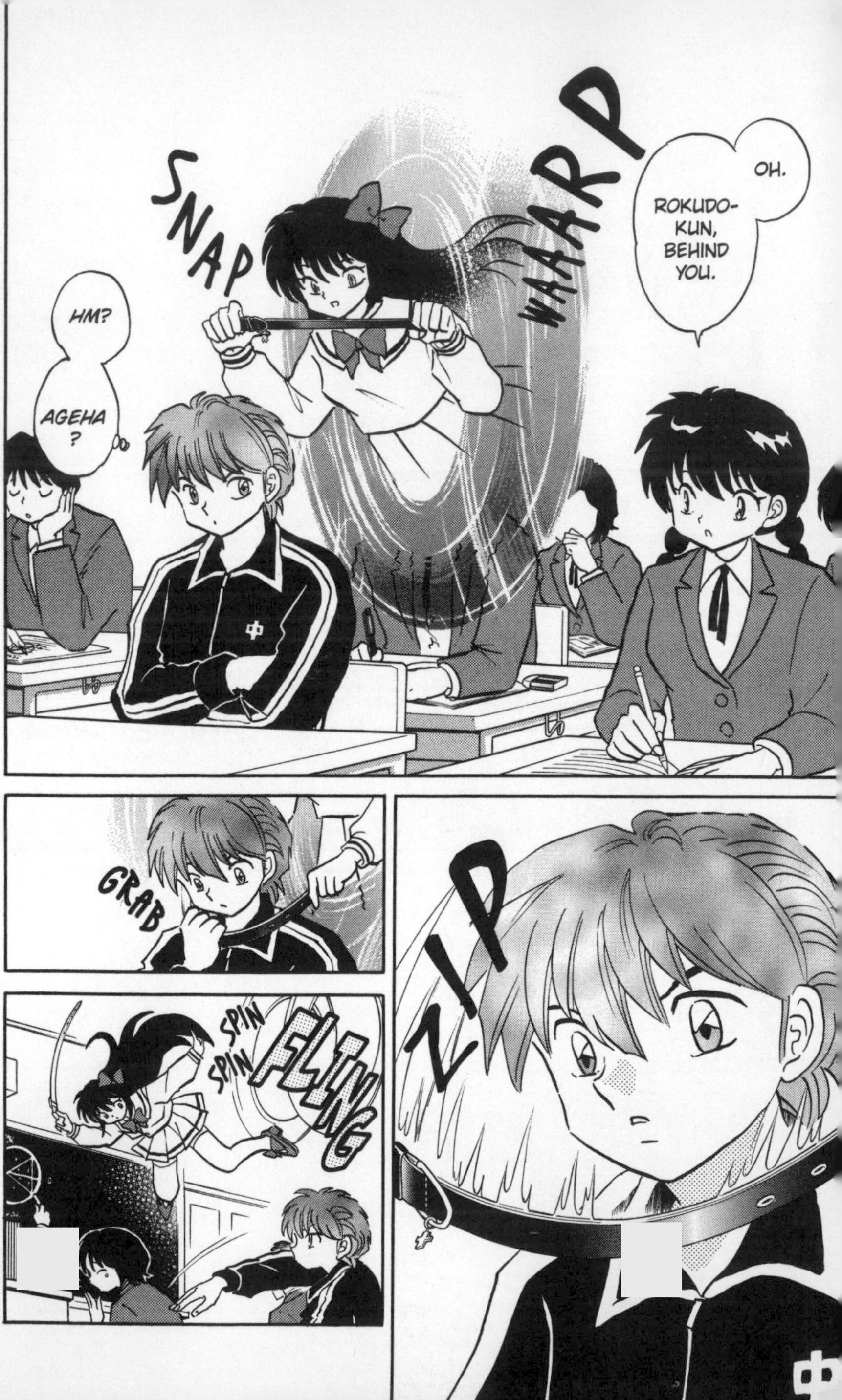
OH.
ROKUDO-KUN, BEHIND YOU.
WHAARP
SNAP
HM?
AGEHA?
ZIP
GRAB
SPIN SPIN
FLING

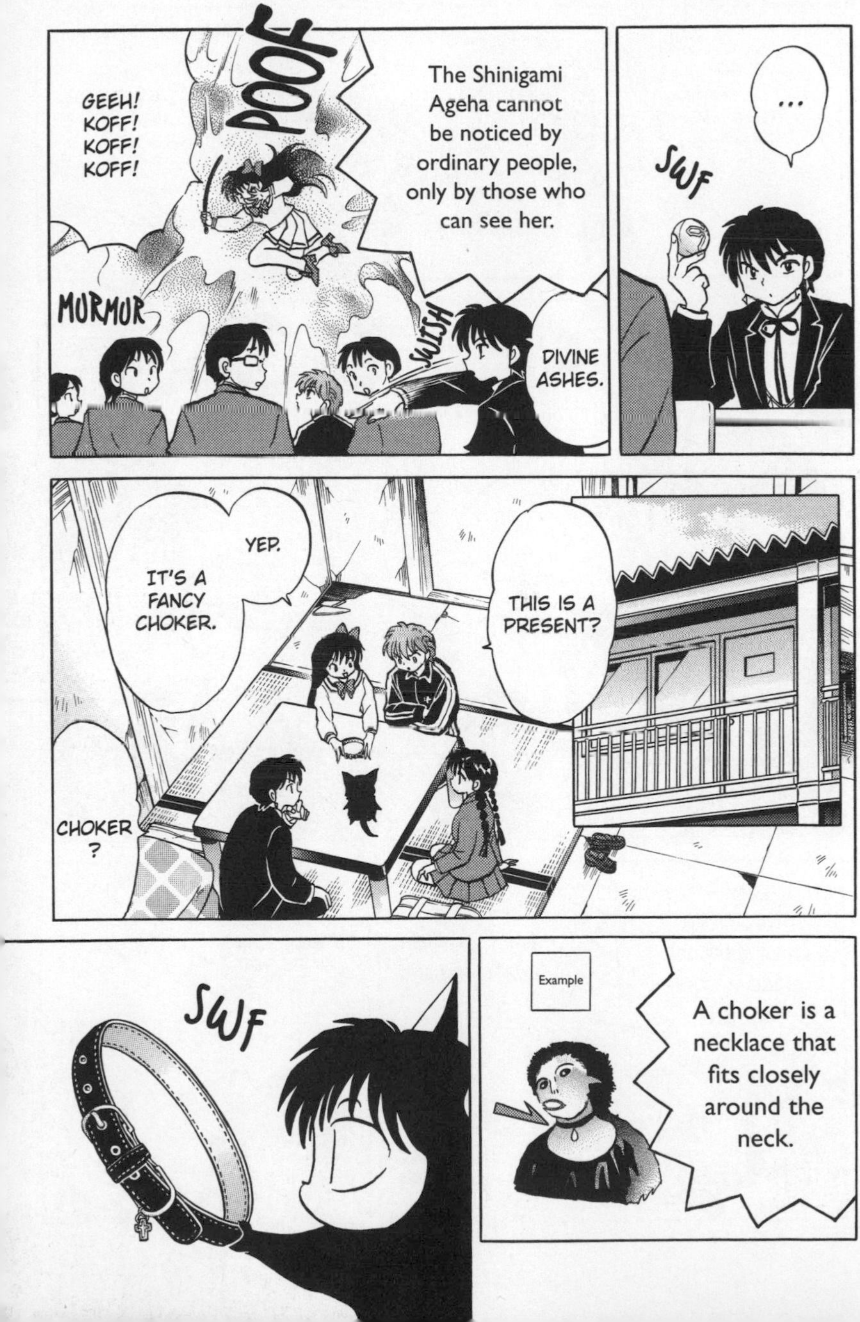
...
SWF
DIVINE ASHES.
SWISH
The Shinigami Ageha cannot be noticed by ordinary people, only by those who can see her.
POOF
GEEH! KOFF! KOFF! KOFF!
MURMUR
THIS IS A PRESENT?
YEP.
IT'S A FANCY CHOKER.
CHOKER ?
Example
A choker is a necklace that fits closely around the neck.
SWF

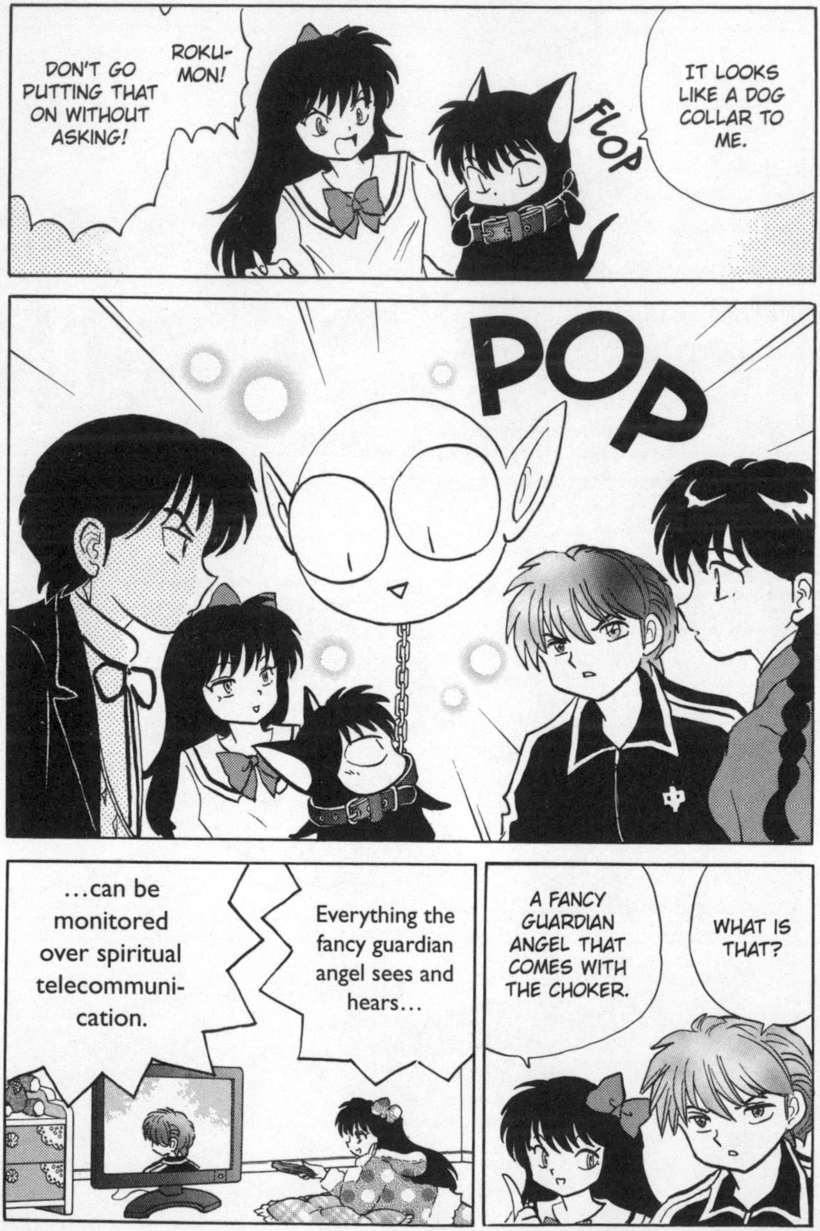
IT LOOKS LIKE A DOG COLLAR TO ME.
FLOP
ROKU-MON!
DON'T GO PUTTING THAT ON WITHOUT ASKING!
POP
WHAT IS THAT?
A FANCY GUARDIAN ANGEL THAT COMES WITH THE CHOKER.
Everything the fancy guardian angel sees and hears…
…can be monitored over spiritual telecommuni-cation.

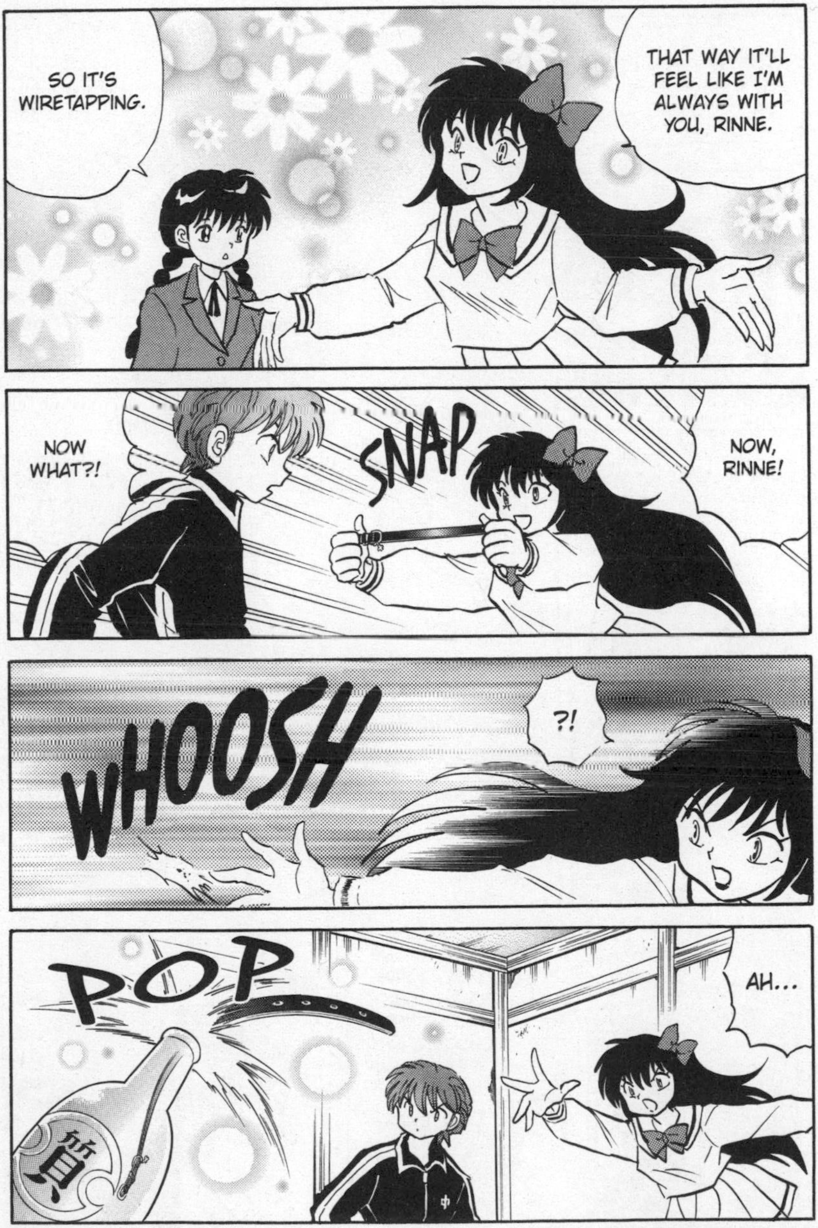
THAT WAY IT'LL FEEL LIKE I'M ALWAYS WITH YOU, RINNE.
SO IT'S WIRETAPPING.
NOW, RINNE!
SNAP
NOW WHAT?!
?!
WHOOSH
AH...
POP

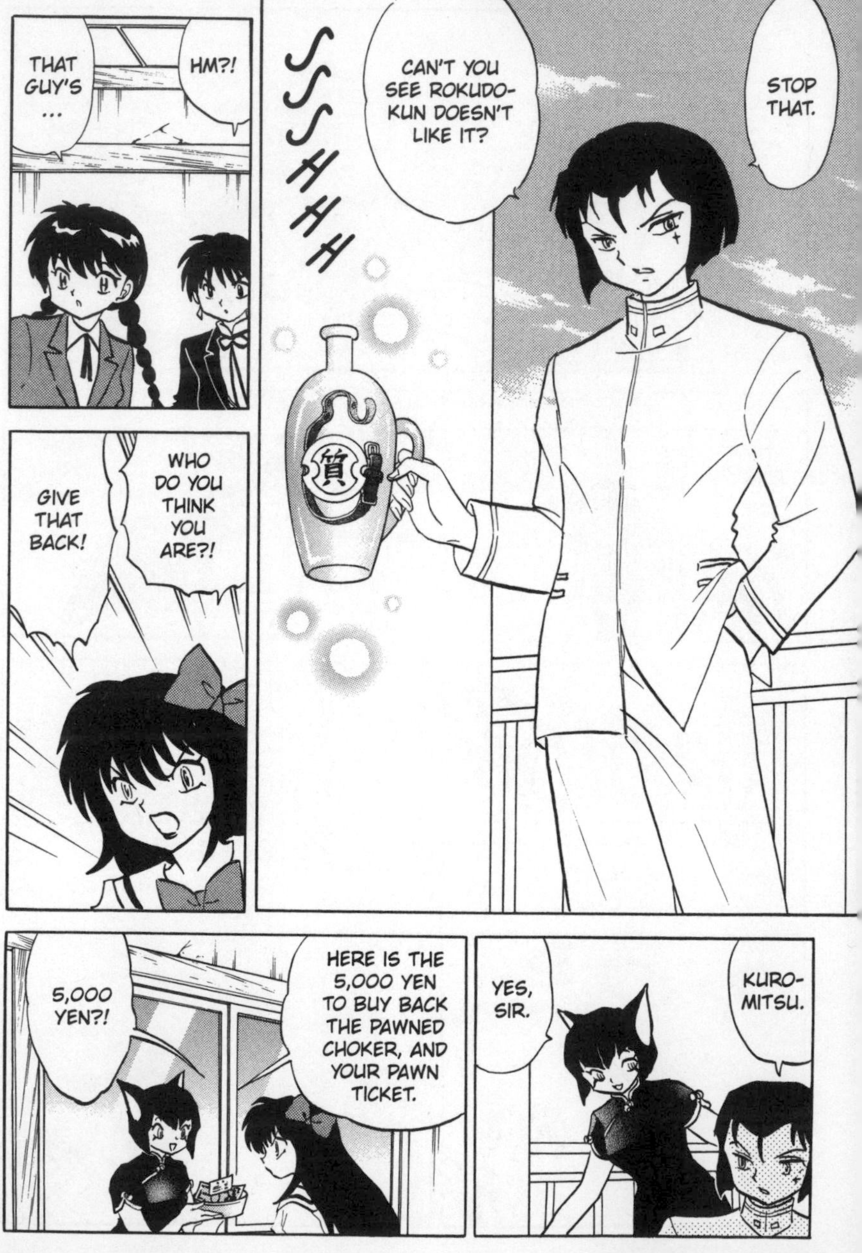
STOP THAT.
CAN'T YOU SEE ROKUDO-KUN DOESN'T LIKE IT?
SSSHHHH
質
HM?!
THAT GUY'S ...
WHO DO YOU THINK YOU ARE?!
GIVE THAT BACK!
KURO-MITSU.
YES, SIR.
HERE IS THE 5,000 YEN TO BUY BACK THE PAWNED CHOKER, AND YOUR PAWN TICKET.
5,000 YEN?!

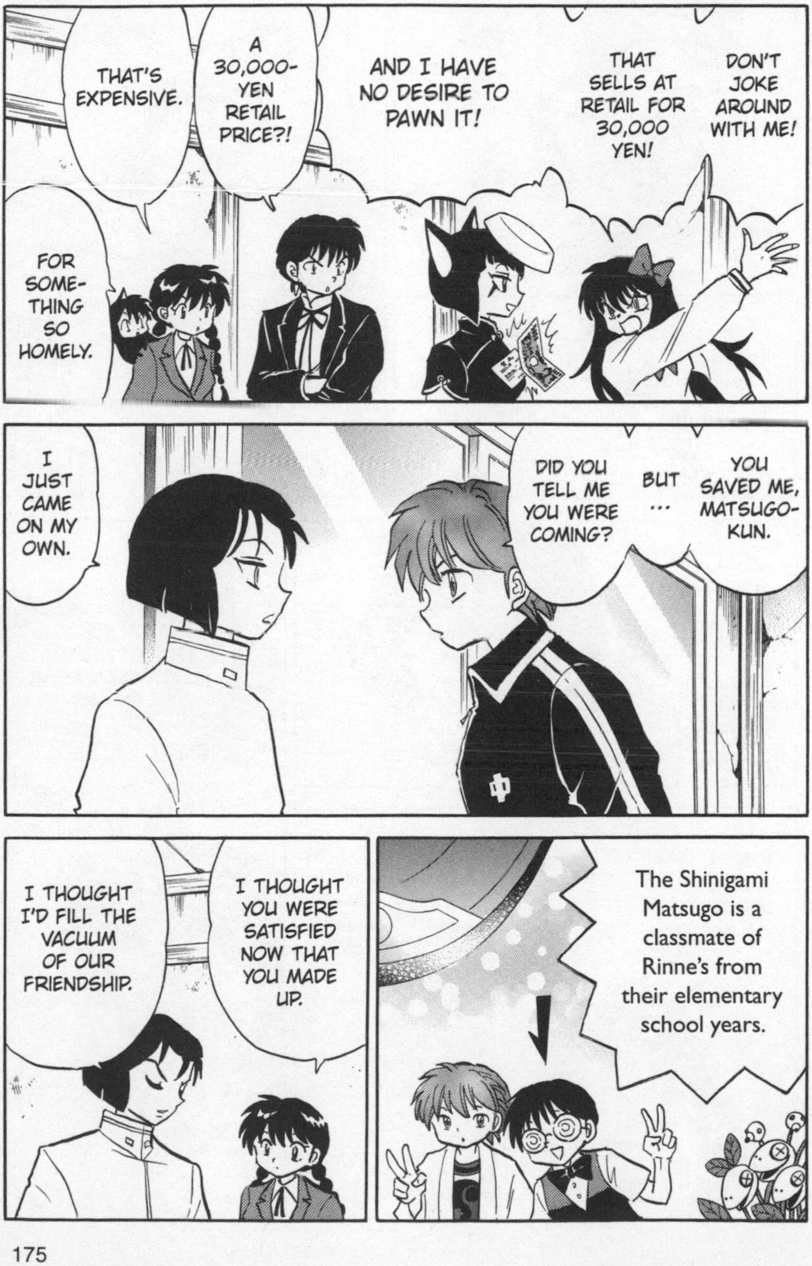

DON'T JOKE AROUND WITH ME!
THAT SELLS AT RETAIL FOR 30,000 YEN!
AND I HAVE NO DESIRE TO PAWN IT!
A 30,000-YEN RETAIL PRICE?!
THAT'S EXPENSIVE.
FOR SOMETHING SO HOMELY.
YOU SAVED ME, MATSUGO-KUN.
BUT ...
DID YOU TELL ME YOU WERE COMING?
I JUST CAME ON MY OWN.
The Shinigami Matsugo is a classmate of Rinne's from their elementary school years.
I THOUGHT YOU WERE SATISFIED NOW THAT YOU MADE UP.
I THOUGHT I'D FILL THE VACUUM OF OUR FRIENDSHIP.

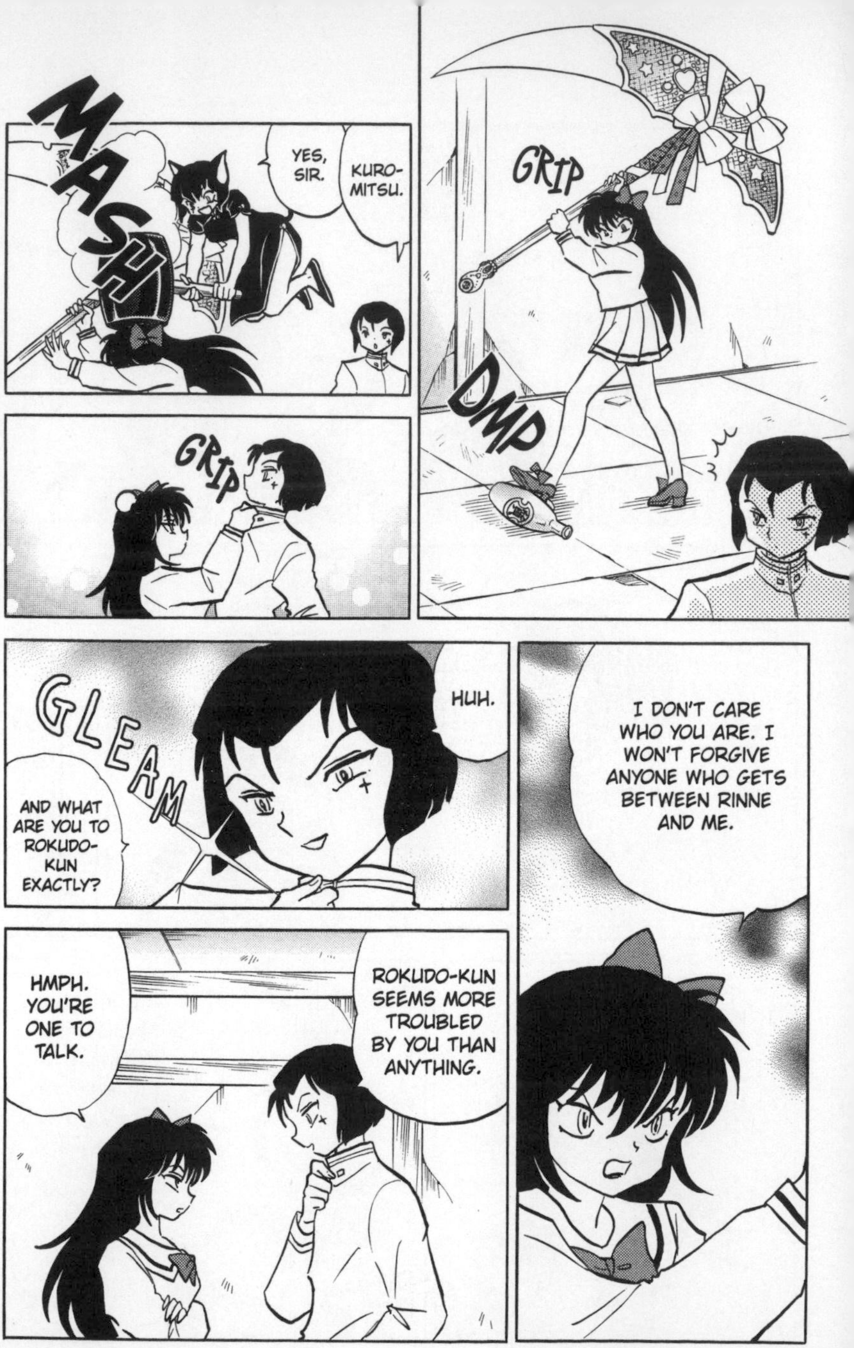
GRIP
DMP
KURO-MITSU.
YES, SIR.
MASH
GRIP
I DON'T CARE WHO YOU ARE. I WON'T FORGIVE ANYONE WHO GETS BETWEEN RINNE AND ME.
HUH.
AND WHAT ARE YOU TO ROKUDO-KUN EXACTLY?
GLEAM
ROKUDO-KUN SEEMS MORE TROUBLED BY YOU THAN ANYTHING.
HMPH. YOU'RE ONE TO TALK.

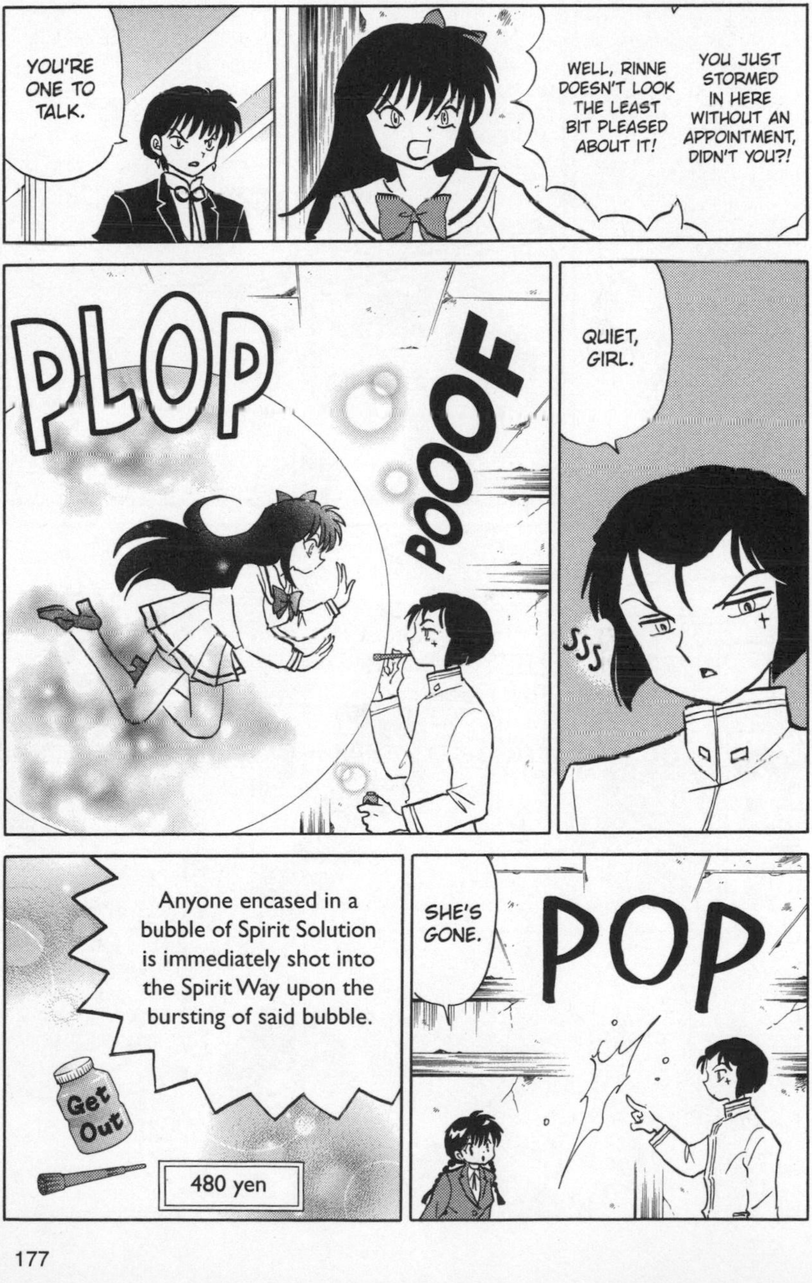
YOU JUST STORMED IN HERE WITHOUT AN APPOINTMENT, DIDN'T YOU?!
WELL, RINNE DOESN'T LOOK THE LEAST BIT PLEASED ABOUT IT!
YOU'RE ONE TO TALK.
QUIET, GIRL.
SSS
POOOF
PLOP
POP
SHE'S GONE.
Anyone encased in a bubble of Spirit Solution is immediately shot into the Spirit Way upon the bursting of said bubble.
Get Out
480 yen

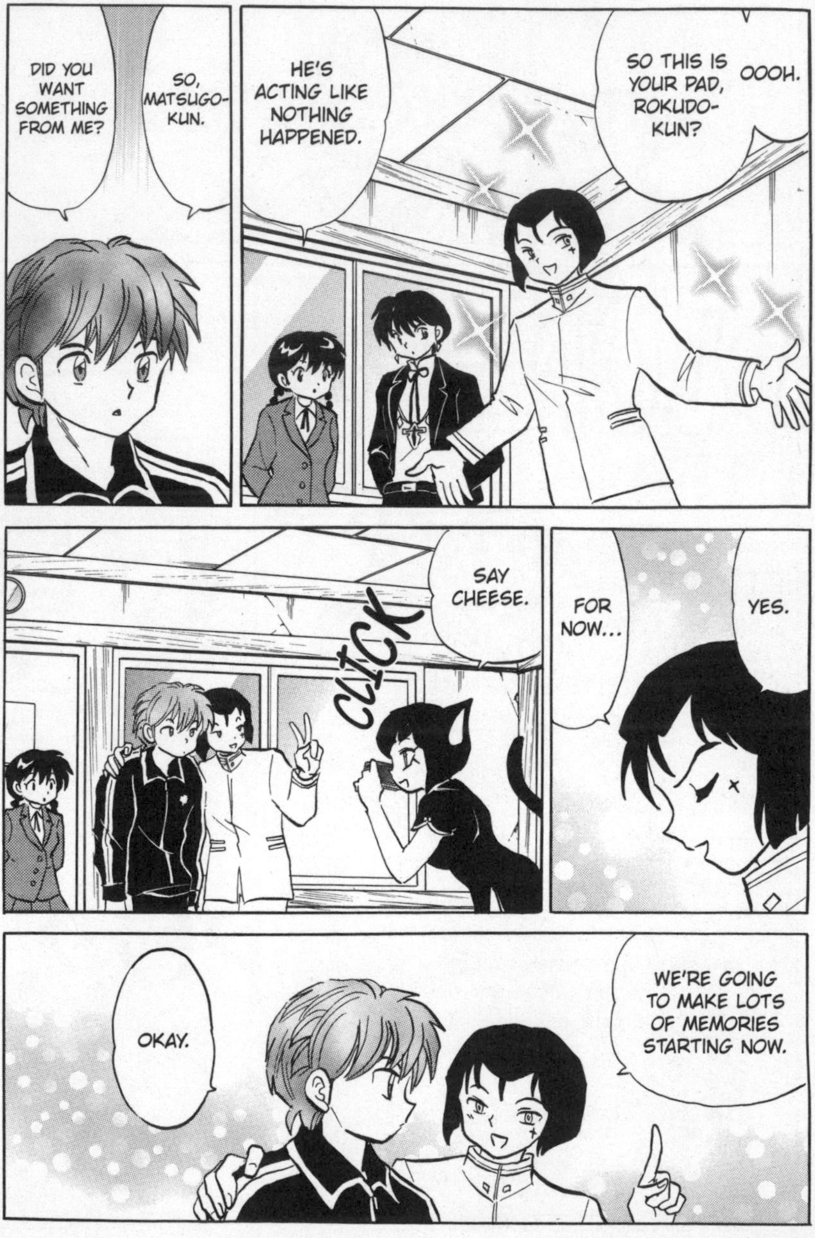
OOOH.
SO THIS IS YOUR PAD, ROKUDO-KUN?
HE'S ACTING LIKE NOTHING HAPPENED.
SO, MATSUGO-KUN.
DID YOU WANT SOMETHING FROM ME?
YES.
FOR NOW...
SAY CHEESE.
CLICK
WE'RE GOING TO MAKE LOTS OF MEMORIES STARTING NOW.
OKAY.

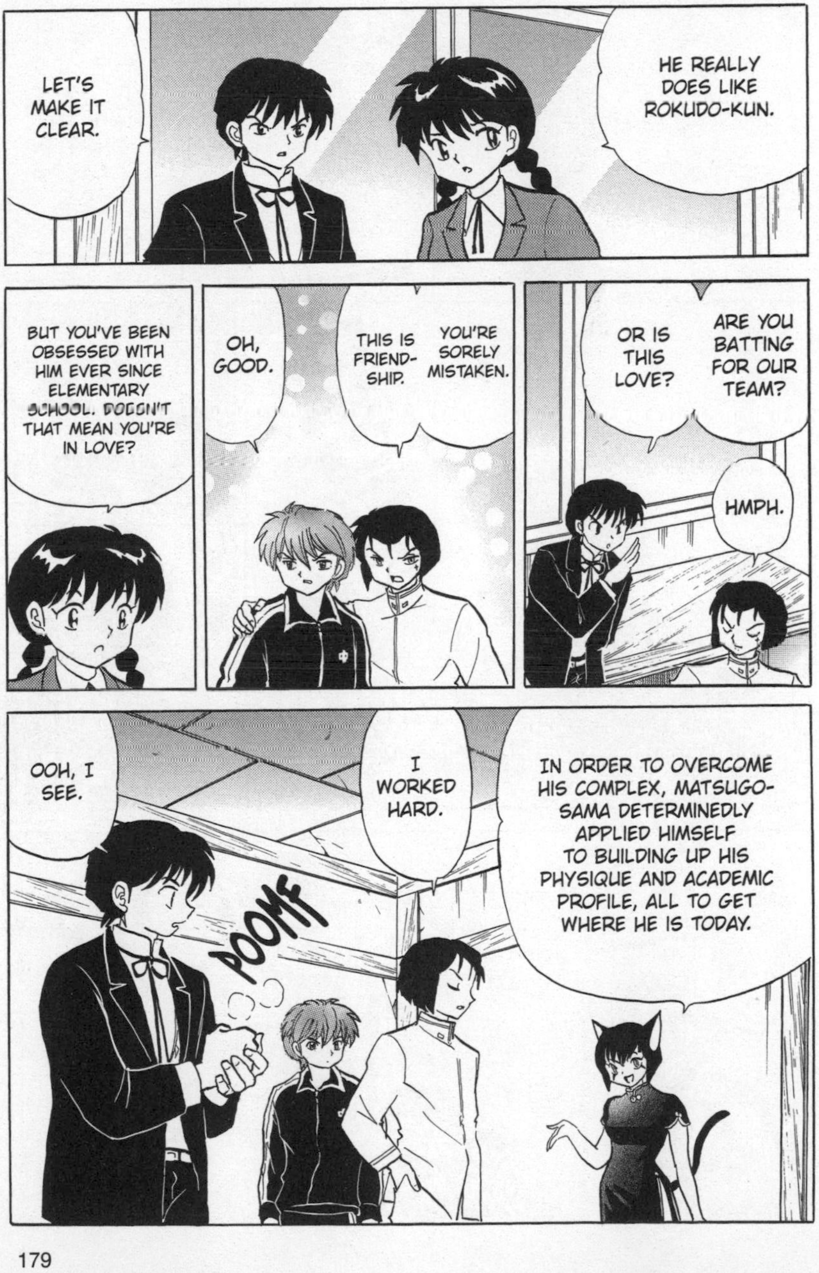
HE REALLY DOES LIKE ROKUDO-KUN.
LET'S MAKE IT CLEAR.
ARE YOU BATTING FOR OUR TEAM?
OR IS THIS LOVE?
HMPH.
YOU'RE SORELY MISTAKEN.
THIS IS FRIEND-SHIP.
OH, GOOD.
BUT YOU'VE BEEN OBSESSED WITH HIM EVER SINCE ELEMENTARY SCHOOL. DOESN'T THAT MEAN YOU'RE IN LOVE?
IN ORDER TO OVERCOME HIS COMPLEX, MATSUGO-SAMA DETERMINEDLY APPLIED HIMSELF TO BUILDING UP HIS PHYSIQUE AND ACADEMIC PROFILE, ALL TO GET WHERE HE IS TODAY.
I WORKED HARD.
POOMF
OOH, I SEE.

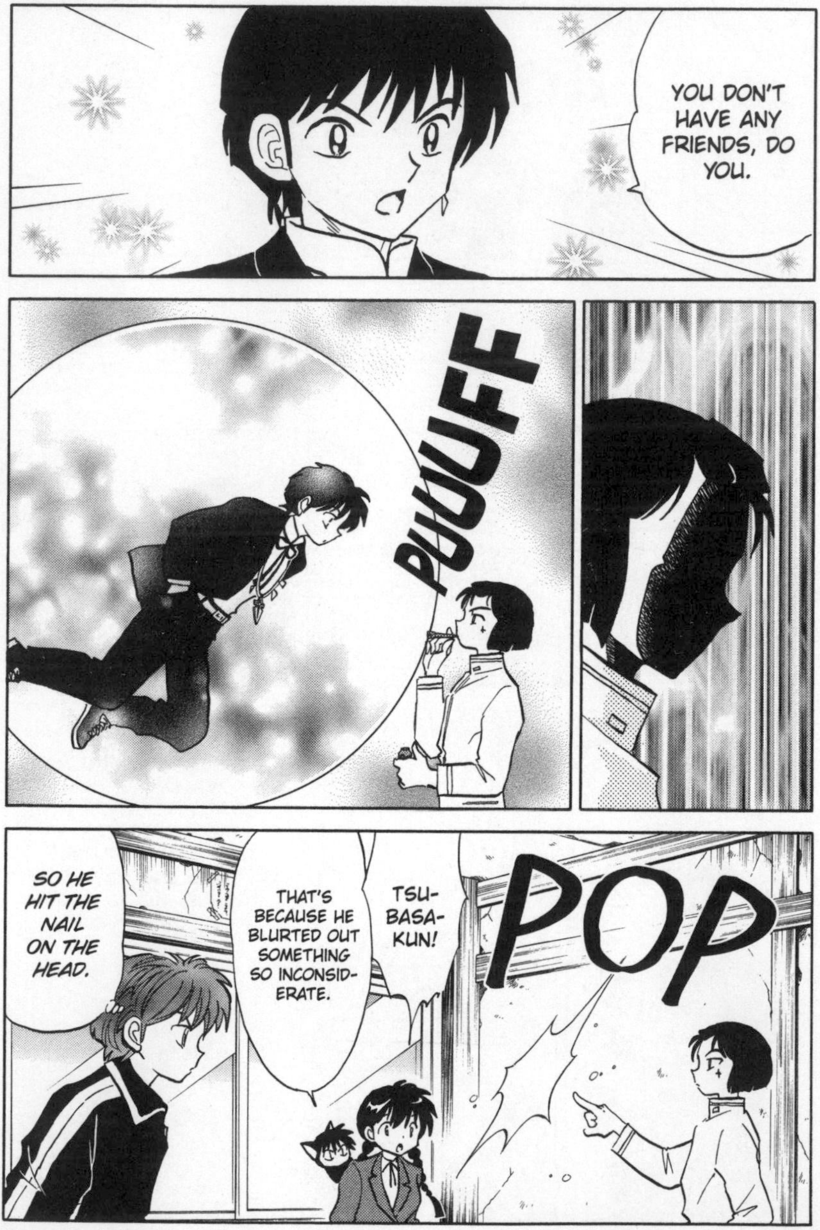
YOU DON'T HAVE ANY FRIENDS, DO YOU.
PUUUFF
POP
TSU-BASA-KUN!
THAT'S BECAUSE HE BLURTED OUT SOMETHING SO INCONSIDER-ERATE.
SO HE HIT THE NAIL ON THE HEAD.

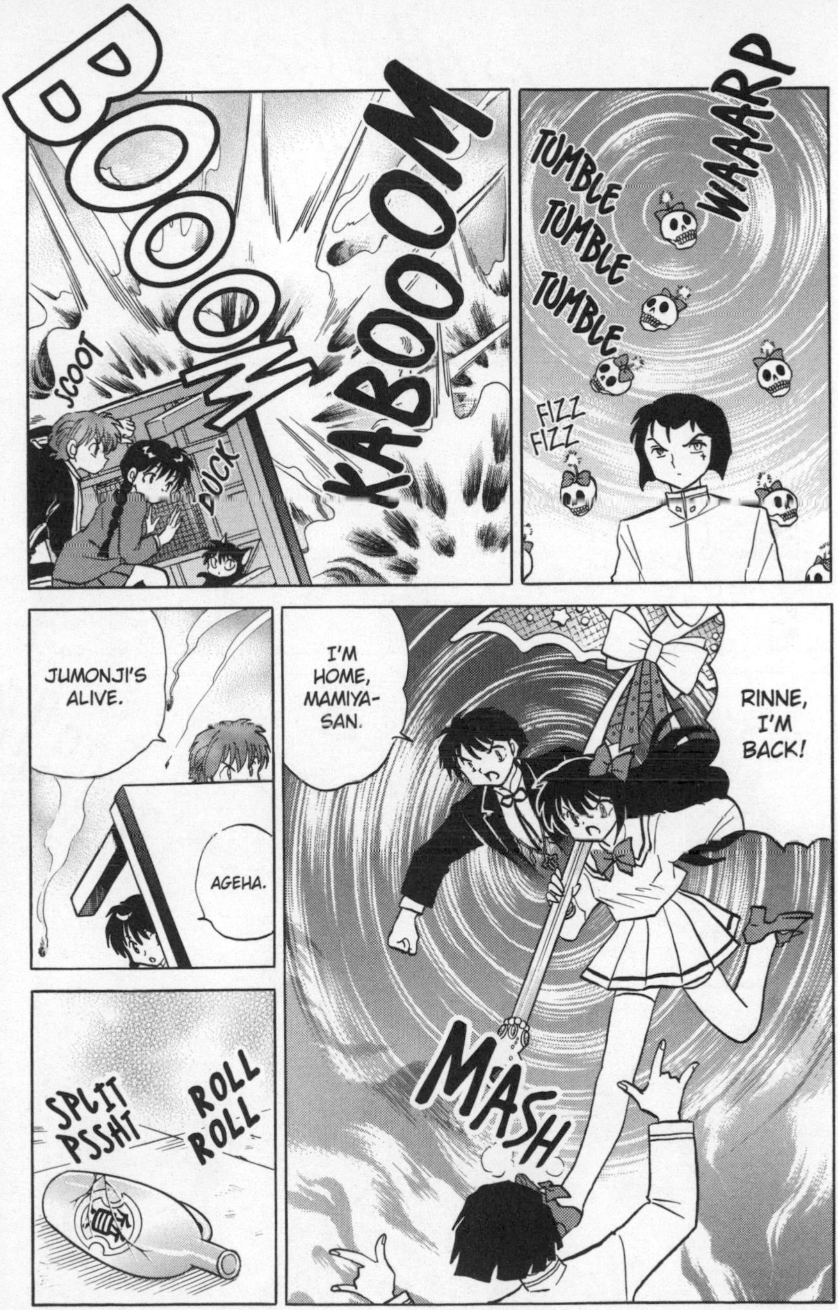
WAAARP
TUMBLE TUMBLE TUMBLE TUMBLE
FIZZ FIZZ
BOOOOOM
KABOOOM
SCOOT
DUCK
RINNE, I'M BACK!
I'M HOME, MAMIYA-SAN.
MASH
JUMONJI'S ALIVE.
AGEHA.
ROLL ROLL
SPLIT PSSHT

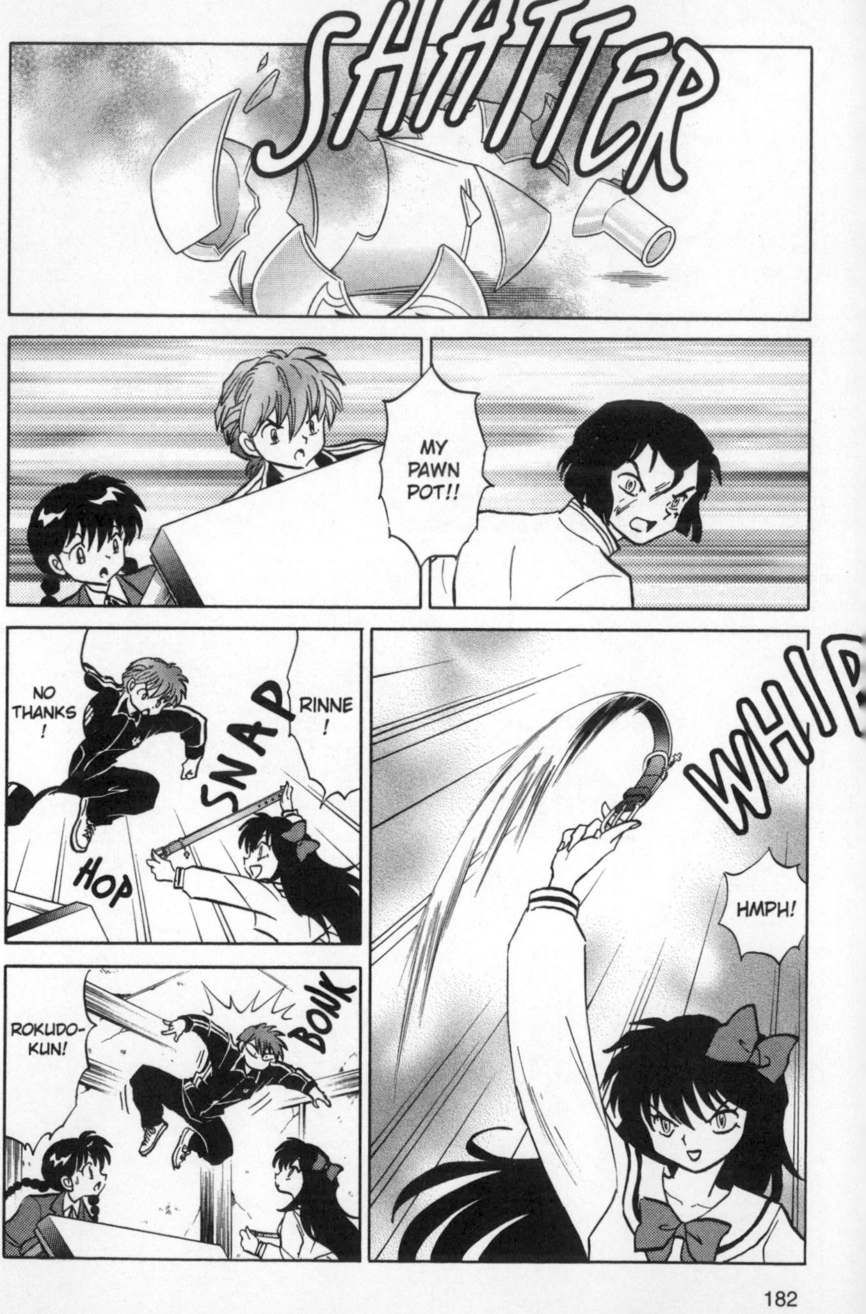
SHATTER
MY PAWN POT!!
WHIP
HMPH!
RINNE!
SNAP
NO THANKS!
HOP
BONK
ROKUDO-KUN!

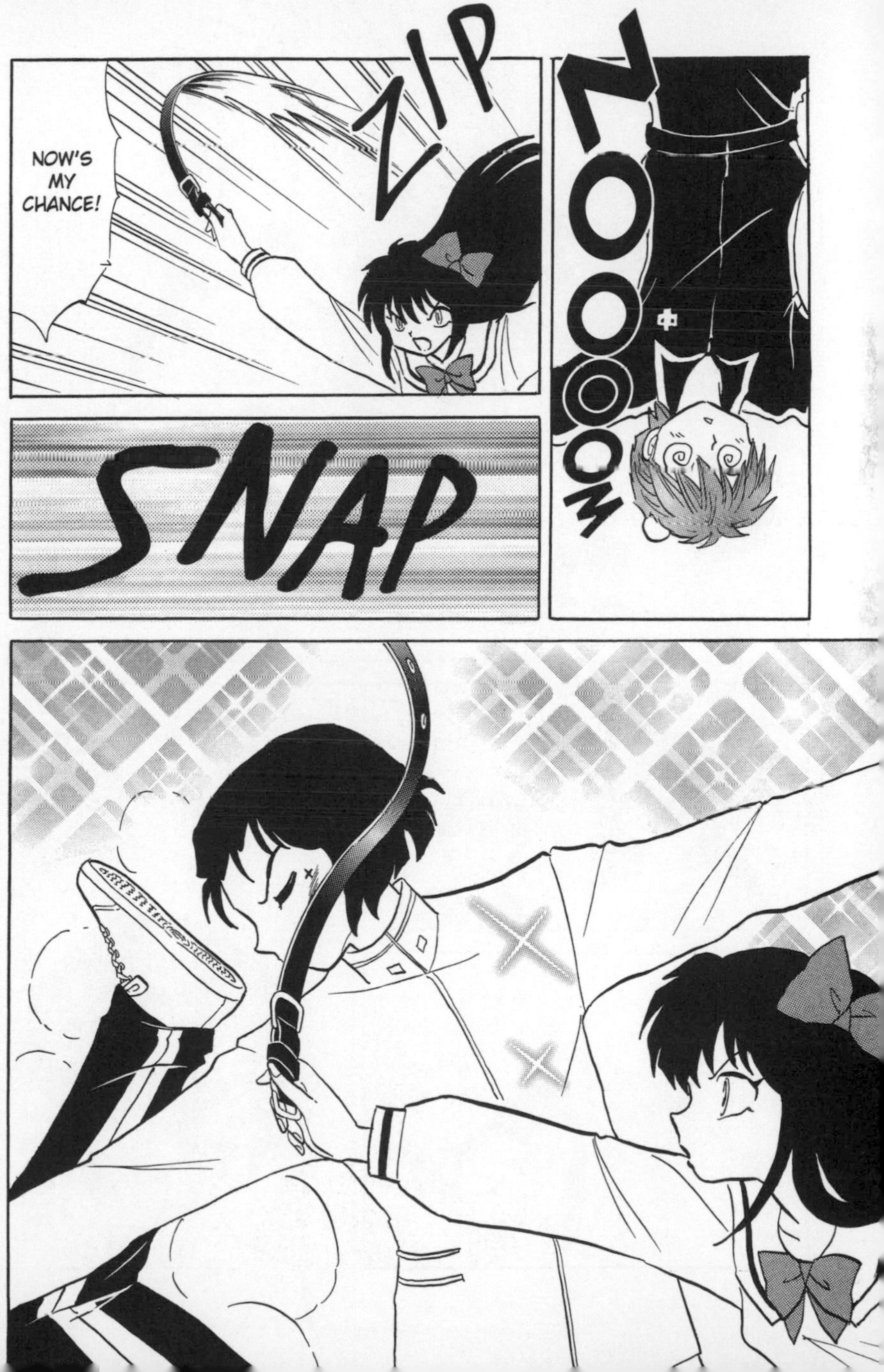
ZOOOOM
ZIP
NOW'S MY CHANCE!
SNAP

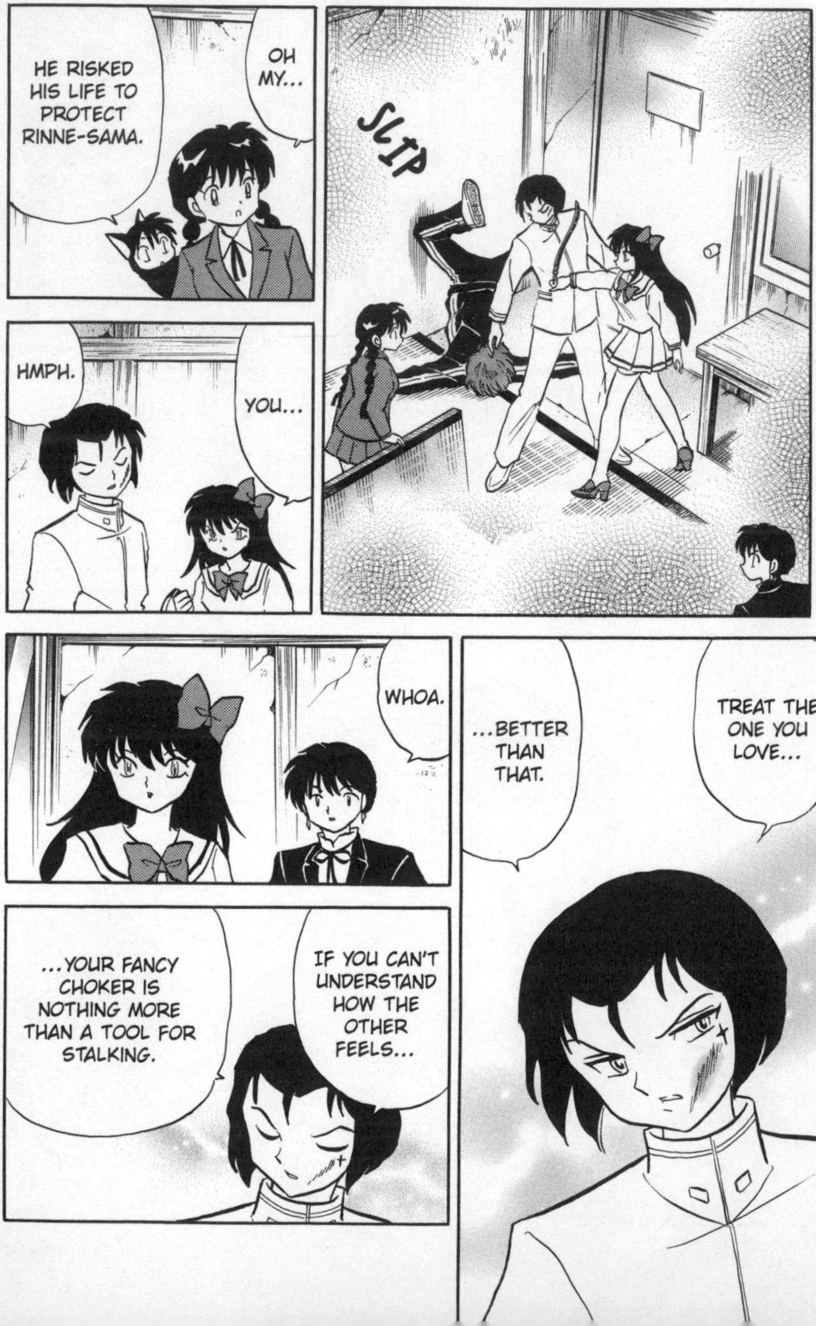
SLIP
OH MY...
HE RISKED HIS LIFE TO PROTECT RINNE-SAMA.
YOU...
HMPH.
TREAT THE ONE YOU LOVE...
...BETTER THAN THAT.
WHOA.
IF YOU CAN'T UNDERSTAND HOW THE OTHER FEELS...
...YOUR FANCY CHOKER IS NOTHING MORE THAN A TOOL FOR STALKING.

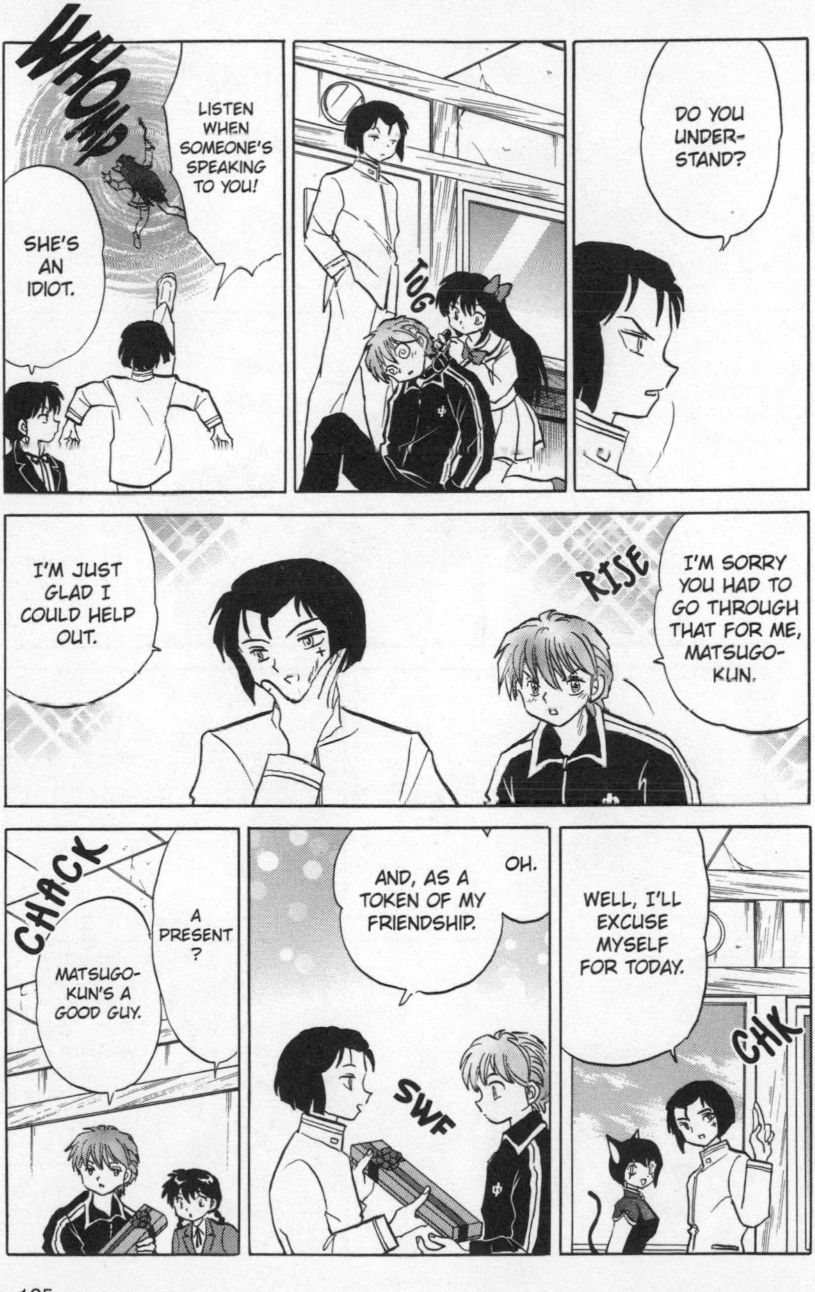
DO YOU UNDER-STAND?
TUG
LISTEN WHEN SOMEONE'S SPEAKING TO YOU!
WHOMP
SHE'S AN IDIOT.
I'M SORRY YOU HAD TO GO THROUGH THAT FOR ME, MATSUGO-KUN.
RISE
I'M JUST GLAD I COULD HELP OUT.
WELL, I'LL EXCUSE MYSELF FOR TODAY.
CHK
OH.
AND, AS A TOKEN OF MY FRIENDSHIP.
SWF
A PRESENT?
CHACK
MATSUGO-KUN'S A GOOD GUY.

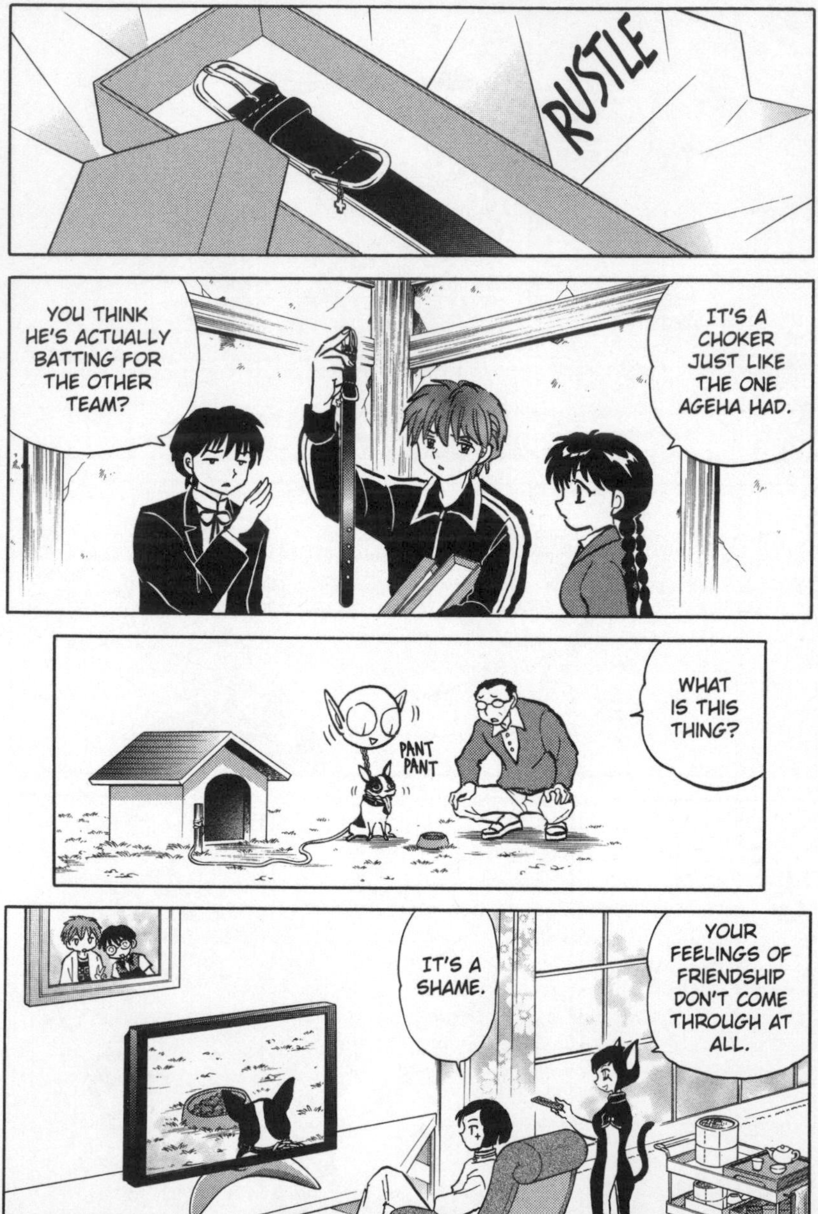
RUSTLE
IT'S A CHOKER JUST LIKE THE ONE AGEHA HAD.
YOU THINK HE'S ACTUALLY BATTING FOR THE OTHER TEAM?
WHAT IS THIS THING?
PANT PANT
YOUR FEELINGS OF FRIENDSHIP DON'T COME THROUGH AT ALL.
IT'S A SHAME.

RIN-NE VOLUME 19 - END -

Rumiko Takahashi

The spotlight on Rumiko Takahashi's career began in 1978 when she won an honorable mention in Shogakukan's annual New Comic Artist Contest for *Those Selfish Aliens*. Later that same year, her boy-meets-alien comedy series, *Urusei Yatsura*, was serialized in *Weekly Shonen Sunday*. This phenomenally successful manga series was adapted into anime format and spawned a TV series and half a dozen theatrical-release movies, all incredibly popular in their own right. Takahashi followed up the success of her debut series with one blockbuster hit after another—*Maison Ikkoku* ran from 1980 to 1987, *Ranma ½* from 1987 to 1996, and *Inuyasha* from 1996 to 2008. Other notable works include *Mermaid Saga*, *Rumic Theater*, and *One-Pound Gospel*.

Takahashi won the prestigious Shogakukan Manga Award twice in her career, once for *Urusei Yatsura* in 1981 and the second time for *Inuyasha* in 2002. A majority of the Takahashi canon has been adapted into other media such as anime, live-action TV series, and film. Takahashi's manga, as well as the other formats her work has been adapted into, have continued to delight generations of fans around the world. Distinguished by her wonderfully endearing characters, Takahashi's work adeptly incorporates a wide variety of elements such as comedy, romance, fantasy, and martial arts. While her series are difficult to pin down into one simple genre, the signature style she has created has come to be known as the "Rumic World." Rumiko Takahashi is an artist who truly represents the very best from the world of manga.

RIN-NE
VOLUME 19
Shonen Sunday Edition

STORY AND ART BY
RUMIKO TAKAHASHI

KYOKAI NO RINNE Vol. 19
by Rumiko TAKAHASHI
© 2009 Rumiko TAKAHASHI
All rights reserved.
Original Japanese edition published by SHOGAKUKAN.
English translation rights in the United States of America,
Canada, the United Kingdom and Ireland arranged with
SHOGAKUKAN.

Translation/Christine Dashiell
Touch-up Art & Lettering/Evan Waldinger
Design/Yukiko Whitley
Editor/Megan Bates

The stories, characters and incidents mentioned in
this publication are entirely fictional.

Printed in the U.S.A.

Published by VIZ Media, LLC
P.O. Box 77010
San Francisco, CA 94107

10 9 8 7 6 5 4 3 2 1
First printing, November 2015

www.viz.com   WWW.SHONENSUNDAY.COM

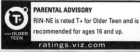

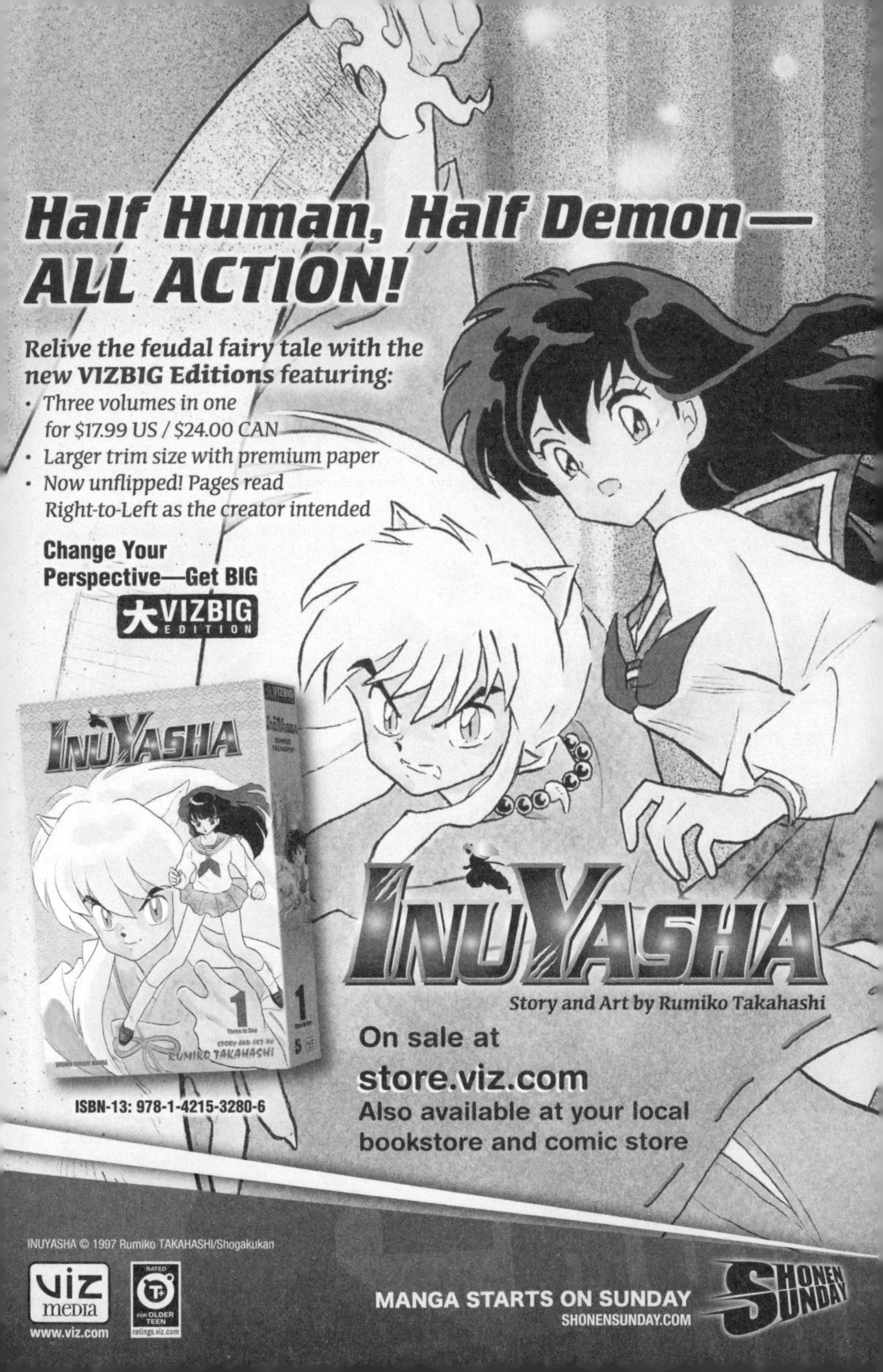
Half Human, Half Demon—
ALL ACTION!
Relive the feudal fairy tale with the new VIZBIG Editions featuring:
• Three volumes in one for $17.99 US / $24.00 CAN
• Larger trim size with premium paper
• Now unflipped! Pages read Right-to-Left as the creator intended
Change Your Perspective—Get BIG
大 VIZBIG EDITION
INUYASHA
1
STORY AND ART BY RUMIKO TAKAHASHI
ISBN-13: 978-1-4215-3280-6
INUYASHA
Story and Art by Rumiko Takahashi
On sale at
store.viz.com
Also available at your local bookstore and comic store
INUYASHA © 1997 Rumiko TAKAHASHI/Shogakukan
viz media
www.viz.com
RATED T+ FOR OLDER TEEN
ratings.viz.com
MANGA STARTS ON SUNDAY
SHONENSUNDAY.COM
SHONEN SUNDAY

Hey! You're Reading in the Wrong Direction!

This is the end of this graphic novel!

To properly enjoy this VIZ graphic novel, please turn it around and begin reading from right to left. Unlike English, Japanese is read right to left, so Japanese comics are read in reverse order from the way English comics are typically read.

This book has been printed in the original Japanese format in order to preserve the orientation of the original artwork. Have fun with it!

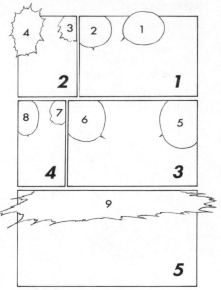

Follow the action this way